Land Governance and Gender: The Tenure–Gender Nexus in Land Management and Land Policy

Land Governance and Gender: The Tenure–Gender Nexus in Land Management and Land Policy

Edited by

Uchendu Eugene Chigbu

Namibia University of Science and Technology, Namibia

CABI

CABI is a trading name of CAB International

CABI
Nosworthy Way
Wallingford
Oxfordshire OX10 8DE
UK

Tel: +44 (0)1491 832111
Fax: +44 (0)1491 833508
E-mail: info@cabi.org
Website: www.cabi.org

CABI
WeWork
One Lincoln Street
24th Floor
Boston, MA 02111
USA

Tel: +1 (617)682-9015
E-mail: cabi-nao@cabi.org

A catalogue record for this book is available from the British Library, London, UK.

Library of Congress Cataloging-in-Publication Data

Names: Chigbu, Uchendu Eugene, editor.
Title: Land governance and gender : the tenure-gender nexus in land management and land policy / edited by Uchendu Eugene Chigbu, Namibia University of Science and Technology, Namibia.
Description: Oxfordshire, UK ; Boston, MA : CABI, [2022] | Includes bibliographical references and index. | Summary: "This book offers conceptual and empirical studies of land governance, focusing on land management approaches, land policy issues, advances in pro-poor land tenure, and land-based gender concerns. Topics include "Creating new understandings," "Exploring alternative approaches for land management and land tenure," "Viewing vistas of tenure experiences across the globe," and "Stretching the gender perspectives""-- Provided by publisher.
Identifiers: LCCN 2021031946 (print) | LCCN 2021031947 (ebook) | ISBN 9781789247664 (hardback) | ISBN 9781789247671 (ebook) | ISBN 9781789247688 (epub)
Subjects: LCSH: Land tenure. | Agriculture and state. | Land use--Planning. | Women in agriculture.
Classification: LCC HD1251 .L34 2022 (print) | LCC HD1251 (ebook) | DDC 333.3--dc23
LC record available at https://lccn.loc.gov/2021031946
LC ebook record available at https://lccn.loc.gov/2021031947

References to Internet websites (URLs) were accurate at the time of writing.

ISBN-13: 9781789247664 (hardback)
9781789247671 (OA ePDF)
9781789247688 (OA ePub)

DOI: 10.1079/9781789247664.0000

Commissioning Editor: David Hemming
Editorial Assistant: Emma McCann
Production Editor: Marta Patiño

Typeset by SPi, Pondicherry, India
Printed and bound in the USA by Integrated Books International, Dulles, Virginia

Contents

List of Contributors

Liz Alden Wily, Van Vollenhoven Institute for Law, Governance and Society, Leiden Law School, Leiden, The Netherlands; lizaldenwily@gmail.com / e.alden.wily@law.leidenuniv.nl

Sara Berry, Department of History, Johns Hopkins University, Baltimore, MD, USA; sberry1@jhu.edu

Cynthia M. Caron, International Development, Community and Environment, Clark University, Worcester, MA, USA; ccaron@clarku.edu

Uchendu Eugene Chigbu, Department of Land and Property Sciences, Namibia University of Science and Technology, Windhoek, Namibia; echigbu@nust.na

Walter Dachaga, Chair of Land Management, Technical University of Munich, Munich, Germany; wdachaga@gmail.com

Pamela Durán-Díaz, Chair of Land Management, Technical University of Munich, Munich, Germany; pamela.duran@tum.de

Stig Enemark, Department of Planning, Aalborg University, Aalborg, Denmark; enemark@plan.aau.dk

Ikechukwu O. Ezeuduji, University of Zululand, KwaDlangezwa, South Africa; EzeudujiI@unizulu.ac.za

Charles Fogelman, University of Illinois at Urbana-Champaign, Champaign, IL, USA; Fogelma2@illinois.edu

Lora Forsythe, Natural Resources Institute, University of Greenwich, London, UK; L.Forsythe@greenwich.ac.uk

Stein T. Holden, School of Economics and Business / Centre for Land Tenure Studies, Norwegian University of Life Sciences, Ås, Norway; stein.holden@nmbu.no

Nancy Kankam Kusi, West Africa Civil Society Institute, Accra, Ghana; nancykankam@gmail.com

Michael Klaus, Hanns-Seidel-Stiftung (Hanns-Seidel Foundation), Shandong, China; klaus@hss.de

Cheonjae Lee, Global Development Partnership Center, Korea Research Institute for Human Settlements (KRIHS); cheonjae.lee@krihs.re.kr

Menare Royal Mabakeng, Department of Land and Property Sciences, Namibia University of Science and Technology, Windhoek, Namibia; rmabakeng@nust.na

Holger Magel, Technical University of Munich/International Federation of Surveyors, Munich, Germany; Magel@landentwicklung-muenchen.de

Katriel Marks, Purdue University, West Lafayette, IN, USA; katriel.marks@gmail.com

Nontuthuzelo N. Mbane, Cape Peninsula University of Technology, South Africa; 202087336@mycput.ac.za

Frank Mintah, Department of Planning, Kwame Nkrumah University of Science and Technology, Kumasi, Ashanti, Ghana; frankmintah15@gmail.com

Emma R. Morales, Department of Art, Design and Architecture, Universidad Iberoamericana Puebla, Cholula, Puebla, Mexico; emma.morales@iberopuebla.edu.mx

Colleen Murphy, University of Illinois at Urbana-Champaign, Champaign, IL, USA.; colleenm@illinois.edu

Valentina Nyame, Youth Advocates Ghana, Nsawam, Ghana; valentinanyame@yahoo.com

Marie Jeanne Nyiransabimana, School of Engineering, University of Rwanda, Kigali, Rwanda; nyiransamj@gmail.com

Antonia T. Nzama, University of Zululand, KwaDlangezwa, South Africa; NzamaA@unizulu.ac.za

Nompumelelo Nzama, University of Zululand, KwaDlangezwa, South Africa; nzamaphiwekonke@gmail.com

Barikisa Owusu Ansah, Leibniz University of Hannover, Hannover, Germany; barikisa21@gmail.com

Gaynor Gamuchirai Paradza, Public Affairs Research Institute, University of the Witwatersrand, Johannesburg, South Africa; gaynorp@pari.org.za

Rhonda Phillips, Purdue University, West Lafayette, IN, USA; rphillips@purdue.edu

June Y.T. Po, Natural Resources Institute, University of Greenwich, London, UK; J.Y.T.Po@greenwich.ac.uk

Julian Quan, Natural Resources Institute, University of Greenwich, London, UK; j.f.quan@gre.ac.uk

M. Adil Sait, Department of Geography and Environment, London School of Economics and Political Science, London, UK; saitadil@hotmail.com

M. Siraj Sait, Royal Docks School of Business and Law, University of East London, London, UK; S.Sait@uel.ac.uk

Melissa Schumacher, Department of Architecture, Universidad de las Américas Puebla, Cholula, Puebla, Mexico; Melissa.schumacher@udlap.mx

Ernest Uwayezu, Centre for Geographic Information Systems and Remote Sensing, University of Rwanda, Kigali, Rwanda; wayezuernest@gmail.com

Yanmei Ye, Zhejiang University, Hangzhou, China; yeyanmei@zju.edu.cn

Xiaobin Zhang, Lanzhou University, Lanzhou, China; zhangxiaobin@zju.edu.cn

Foreword

It is a reasonable assumption that if the outcomes of a policy cannot be anticipated with reasonable confidence that they will be different from those expected. This is why it is so important for policies, especially those on sensitive issues like land governance, to be based on sound and comprehensive evidence. This requires digging below stereotypes of binary definitions and adopting a multifaceted and multidisciplinary approach when relating land and social aspects such as gender.

In preparing and editing this volume on land governance and gender, Professor Chigbu has brought together leading analysts and practitioners on both land and gender issues to provide the evidential basis so vital in developing policies appropriate to a wide range of regional, political and cultural contexts. In doing so, he has provided a great service to both academics, practitioners and particularly policy makers.

While it is now accepted that understanding on land tenure has moved on from the earlier binary stereotypes of legal–illegal and formal–informal, the book applies a carefully nuanced analysis of the range of tenure forms and their relationships. It applies an equally nuanced approach to definitions of gender and the implications this has for different social groups to ensure a more equitable future.

The book is the outcome of an invitation by CABI and a series of creative discussions to achieve the right mix of contributors. This included well-known experts including Holger Magel, Stig Enemark, Liz Alden Wily, Julian Quan, Sara Berry, Stein Holden, Rhonda Phillips and Siraj Sait, as well as several other specialists from the fields of geography, land governance and gender studies.

After the introductory chapter by Professor Chigbu, the book is organized into four parts. Part 1 addresses concepts, debates and understanding on the governance and gender aspects of land, with chapters on structural inequality, tenure in sub-Saharan Africa and the need to consider the Global Agenda 2030. Part 2 comprises chapters addressing ways of advancing women's position within customary land systems and their bargaining power, a case study of South Korea, and a global analysis of non-legal barriers to land ownership by women. Part 3 focuses on experiences in applying different techniques, strategies and methods with case studies of rural China, Ghana, Ethiopia and Islamic contexts. Finally, Part 4 provides a range of conclusions and recommendations for transforming the role of gender within land governance, including customary and statutory tenure systems, rural, urban and peri-urban contexts and tools for measuring progress.

As indigenous forms of land tenure, of which customary systems are the most long-standing and widespread, come under increasing pressure from urbanization and globalization, so the means by which people can access land also change. Deeply embedded patrilineal systems are also being challenged by a range of human rights groups and some countries are making progress in ensuring that rights to land recognize the need for gender equity, though there is still a long way to go before the full range of gender groups receive justice.

Therefore, the book could not have come at a better time. The role of land in facilitating or constraining the development of societies to meet the needs of diverse social groups has never been more important. As demand increases for what is a finite resource, land is subject to increasing competition for access and development rights, while the globalization of market-based economic policies means that access is determined more and more by those with the greatest financial resources or influence. Social needs, including those of vulnerable groups, are invariably of secondary, or even tertiary priority, creating social tension that inhibits personal well-being. Gender considerations are now attracting the degree of attention and urgency that is needed and the book recognizes that gender includes not only the needs of women, an issue that has been overlooked for far too long, but a continuum including males who identify as female, non-binary, transgender and other groups. By demonstrating that both land tenure and gender exist within a continuum, the need for sensitivity in understanding how land governance can meet the needs of these different groups within cultural norms that are changing at globally very different rates, poses a major challenge. By providing a series of well-researched and well-presented research articles on these important issues, the book helps to fill a yawning gap in a highly readable form. I recommend it as essential reading in educating all those seeking to understand how land governance can contribute to improving social justice and gender equality in its broadest sense.

Geoffrey Payne
Geoffrey Payne and Associates, London

Geoffrey Payne is a housing and urban development consultant with five decades of experience throughout the world. He has taught in leading universities and undertaken consultancy, research and training assignments for a wide range of development agencies, particularly the World Bank and UN-Habitat. He founded Geoffrey Payne and Associates (www.gpa.org.uk) in 1995 and focuses on affordable housing, land policy, property rights, regulatory frameworks and public–private partnerships. A key focus of his work is building local capacity.

Acknowledgement

The editing of *Land Governance and Gender: The Tenure–Gender Nexus in Land Management and Land Policy* is my attempt to build a vast knowledge base on land-related issues that would be useful for students, policy makers and land professionals. That is why many contributors to this volume come from different arms of land-related professions: lawyers, geodesists, anthropologists, sociologists, geographers, historians, planners, architects, community organizers, public administrators, economists and development experts. It would not have been possible to engage these contributors, most of whom are affiliated with some of the best universities and professional organizations in the world, to make contributions to this volume without a great deal of effort.

My most sincere thanks go to Professors Holger Magel and Stig Enemark. These two Honorary Presidents of the International Federation of Surveyors (FIG) deserve many thanks for taking time off their hectic schedules to contribute to this volume. Other contributors deserving special mention include Sara Berry (Johns Hopkins University), Liz Alden Wily (Independent Consultant / University of Leiden), Rhonda Philips (Purdue University), Julian Quan (University of Greenwich), Stein T. Holden (Norwegian University of Life Sciences), Cynthia Caron (Clark University), Colleen Murphy (University of Illinois at Urbana-Champaign), and Michael Klaus (Hanns Seidel Foundation). I would also like to thank Karol Boudreaux for evaluating some of the manuscripts. Thanks to Geoffrey Payne (of Geoffrey Payne and Associates) for writing the foreword and advising. Thanks to Pauline Peters (Harvard University) for advising. All these people not only contributed, but they inspired me in one way or another. By being part of this project, they offered me an opportunity to work with them and gain their trust that I could deliver a volume worthy of publication.

To all the authors, many of whom come from various disciplines. I thank you for the inspiring contributions. My thanks to those who generously reviewed the chapters. Special thanks to CABI: to Dave Hemming, Ali Thompson and Sarah M. Hall for the production of this volume. Special thanks to Professors Rolf Becker and Mutjinde Katjiua; and Laina Alexander, Ntwala Vanessa Simataa and Mario Siukuta.

I want to thank all my colleagues at the Namibia University of Science and Technology (NUST).

And finally, to my family here and there. I would like to thank my mama, brother and sisters, and friends who always channelled (and continue to channel) their positive energies to me to motivate me in all my undertakings. To Alpha and Omega (my beginning and end) and Kris, thank you for your support.

Uchendu Eugene Chigbu

1 Introducing Land Governance and Gender in the Context of Land Tenure

Uchendu Eugene Chigbu*
Department of Land and Property Sciences, Namibia University of Science and Technology, Windhoek, Namibia

1.1 Background

The collection of chapters in this book comprises different studies related to land governance, gender, land tenure, land management and land policy. The volume brings together scholarship from various disciplines in the legal, humanities, geographical, physical, spatial, and social sciences. It explores the socioeconomic, environmental, political, and socio-spatial contexts of the tenure–gender nexus to offer readers a multidimensional lens on land governance (including land management and land policy issues). To achieve this aim and provide a multidisciplinary perspective, the volume includes contributors from various disciplines and geographical contexts. The contributors' differing cultural and socio-spatial contexts lead to a first-hand knowledge on land governance and tenure–gender nexus realities. The contributors approach their chapters from a wide diversity of tools that facilitates a unique understanding of the interlinkages between land tenure, land governance and gender. In this way, the book provides a variety of disciplinary perspectives. Some chapters include a policy dimension that links land governance principles and practice and its tenure–gender dimensions.

1.2 Why Land Governance, Land Tenure and Gender Matter

There are several arrays of the concepts of land. They include the concepts of land as *terra firma* (the ground upon which people stand), commodity, natural resource, factor of production, physical space, the environment, consumption good, human right, property institution, capital, spirit or deity, community, and nature (Williamson *et al.*, 2010). These myriads of the concepts of land (and there are still many others unmentioned) rightly reflect all aspects of human needs (including wants and desires) that are hinged on land. Putting it very succinctly and simply (and considering the current wave of globalization), land is an invaluable, but immovable factor of development. Therefore, land is intricately tied to development initiatives all over the world.

The primary source of development challenges around the world is the failure of institutions and weak policy performances concerning how land (and related natural) resources are managed. This implies that interventions geared towards improving the current state of development affairs globally, especially in economically developing countries, should put land-related goals at the forefront of policymaking and

*Corresponding author: echigbu@nust.na

DOI: 10.1079/9781789247664.0001

programme implementations. The need for establishing an enabling environment for development to thrive is one of the reasons the governance of land and natural resources have become a big concern. That is also why there is an urgent concern to understand and monitor land governance to enable the creation of sustainable societies (Azadi, 2020). Nevertheless, the chances of achieving development objectives (whether global, national or local) are minimized when the land-and-human (land tenure) and gender relations are adequately reconciled.

The urgency for creating sustainable societies (i.e. development) has stretched the debates on the practical concepts, principles, instruments, and practices to support human and environmental developments. These principles, instruments and practices keep evolving. This has been the case in many parts of the world during a pandemic (e.g. during the COVID-19 or coronavirus pandemic situation) or in a post-pandemic period. The implication is that at the centre of the urgency to develop sustainably lies the concern about people's welfare. People are a concrete factor in development because everything that is done in development practices is centred on ensuring that the living conditions of people rise above primary liveable conditions. Whether it is the improvement of landscapes, institutions, socioeconomic situations, politics, climate change, sociospatial issues, forestry, wildlife protection or any other environmental concerns, the underlying factor is always a concern for humans (or people). How these issues affect people is the foremost reason why scholars, activists and practitioners worry about them. However, improving the living conditions of people in societies (or aspects of their lives in their societies) always depends on the nature of decisions and actions applied in the management, policy making, and implementation of processes connected to natural resources or land. This makes land governance a unique subject. It also makes land tenure, and its associated gender equality concerns crucial aspects in the governance of land.

1.3 Grasping Land Governance as an All-Disciplinary Concern

The notions concerning land governance and its role in the development process are fluid. This is not only because it involves the exercise of legal or normative frameworks over land-based decisions and activities. It encompasses a domain of knowledge that crosses traditional academic disciplines, boundaries of professions, lines of geographies, and schools of thoughts. Land governance embraces any academic or professional field where the concern is on decisions and activities related to the land or natural resources – be it the social sciences, arts and humanities, legal studies, natural sciences, medical and health sciences, engineering and technological or applied sciences and beyond. Being an all-discipline subject (i.e, a subject that cuts across all disciplines and sectors of development practices), it is difficult to understand land governance without embedding it within specific contexts or perspectives.

This chapter is an attempt to unpack the land governance discourse in the context of tenure and gender in a manner that allows emerging scholars and practitioners in the land-related disciplines and professions to grasp it simply. Creating such an understanding of land governance is necessary to build and disseminate knowledge on the crucial aspects of land and natural resources studies in a detailed manner.

1.4 Unpacking Land Governance

Land governance has been described in various ways. Palmer *et al.* (2009) consider the way land access is defined and managed land governance. This definition alludes to the need for setting up of rules, norms, and procedures to be followed by people to gain access to land. From another perspective, Enemark *et al.* (2010) described land governance as a process that entails the assessment and implementation of sustainable land policies based on the enablement of strong relationships between people and land. Putting it very directly, Ayelazuno (2019, p. 844) referred to land governance as 'a range of laws, regulations, norms, procedures, and policies which constitute the regime governing land ownership, rights, distribution, access, and use in a particular society'. All these definitions provide an understanding of land governance. However, they evoke (and embody) more land-related concepts, that if left unboxed, hides the broad meaning of land governance in its barest definition, especially as it relates to land tenure, gender and other land issues.

The clearest graphical description of land governance is one provided by the Department of Land and Property Sciences of Namibia University of Science and Technology (DLPS-NUST, 2018), which was an adaptation of another provided by Williamson *et al.* (2010). However, the unpacking of land governance and its associated concepts did not boldly depict the place of land policy in a land governance system.

To advance the works of Williamson *et al.* (2010) and DLPS-NUST (2018), it is crucial that a clearer understanding of land governance and its relationship with associated concepts be further delineated to ensure a better grasp of tenure and gender issues.

Figure 1.1 is relevant because it allows for a more straightforward illustration of what land governance entails when viewed in the context of other land-related concepts – e.g. land management, land policy, land administration, among many other concepts. Any framework for land

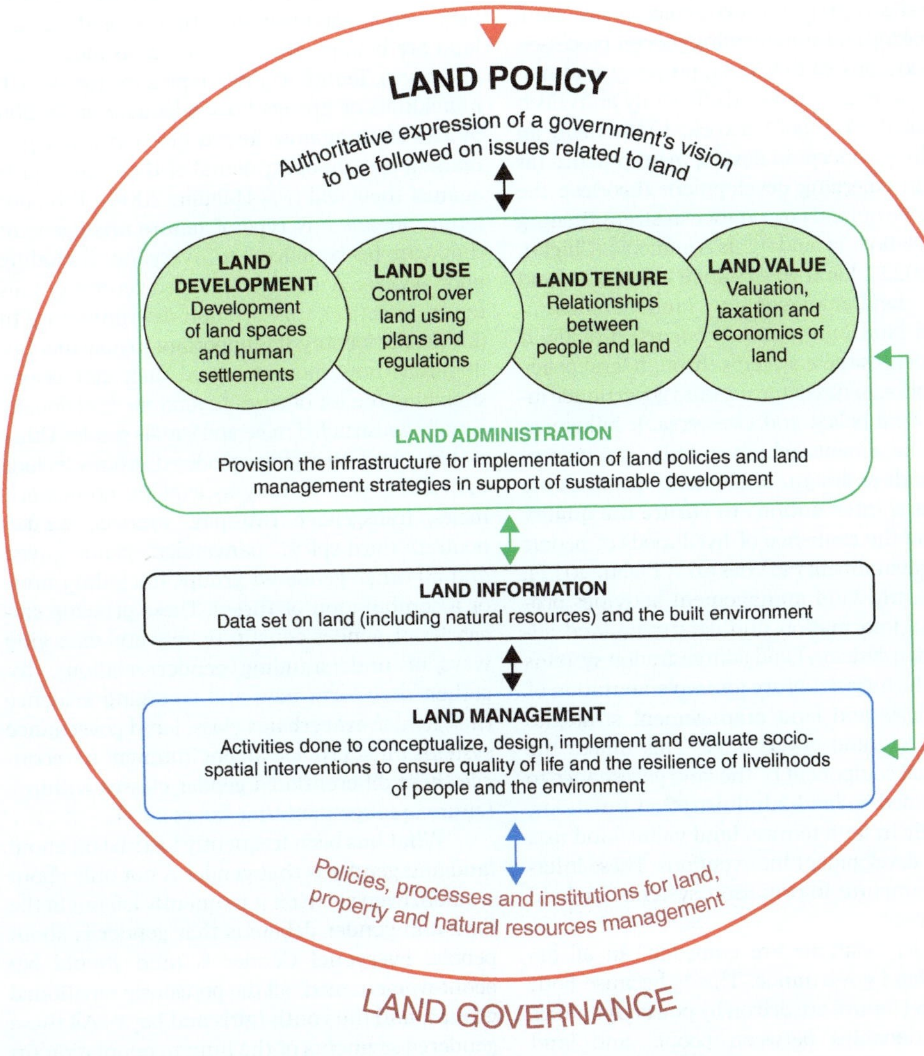

Fig. 1.1. A framework for understanding land governance and its associated concepts (Editor's illustration).

governance will differ widely between countries because they are influenced by the legal jurisdictions, legislations, policies and land-sector cultures in different countries. In a general sense, land governance entails decision-making and activity-inducing interventions which are used to address land and natural resource use and implement policy options. Land policy is a critical element of land governance that includes the framing and enforcement of relevant plans, visions, rules, norms and regulations; and strategies of coordinating them with stakeholders (including individuals and organizations) across different spatial and administrative levels.

Land governance entails an acceptable manner of making and implementing policies, processes, and institutions so that land, property, and natural resources are managed efficiently and effectively (Global Land Tool Network, 2018). Being an overarching concept in development practice (as well as in emerging development theories), the importance of land governance in strengthening gender relations in land rights is immense (Chigbu, 2020, 2021). Land governance influences land systems (land management, land administration and land information systems) directly. It also influences these systems through land policy frameworks. In direct terms, land governance influences land policy, and vice versa. It influences land management, which entails activities to conceptualize, design, implement and evaluate sociospatial interventions to ensure the quality of life and the resilience of livelihoods of people and the environment (de Vries and Chigbu, 2017). Consequently, land management activities produce land information and determine land administration systems. Land administration systems provide the infrastructure for implementation of land policies and land management strategies informed by land governance. This makes the operational component of the land governance to be embedded in land administration functions, specifically in land tenure, land value, land use, and land development interventions. These interventions nurture information systems for land management.

Gender relations are embedded in all aspects of land governance. This is because both gender and tenure are driven by power dynamics and relationships between people and land (through prevailing land-based activities, behaviours, cultures and decision making). The challenges posed by the intertwined relationships between tenure and gender – in ensuring that institutions work in ways that improve people's living conditions and the state of the environment – is the role that land governance is meant to play.

1.5 Unfolding New and Emerging Tenure–Gender Nexus of Land Governance

Land tenure is how the rights, restrictions, privileges and responsibilities that subsist on the land are held by people (whether as individuals or groups). Tenure security implies the rights such individuals or groups have adequate protection by the state against forced eviction avoid permanent or temporary denial of their land rights against their will (UN-Habitat, 2008). Pro-poor tenure means any type of tenure arrangement that can be beneficial to everyone, including poor people. A gender-balanced tenure entails tenure practices that are non-discriminatory to any gender identity. It is important to note that humanity is now more gendered than ever before, stretching the list of sexes beyond the traditionally socially constructed male and female gender. Other existing (and emerging) gendered groups include individuals who identify as females, non-binary, males, transgender, two-spirit, agender, gender-neutral, third-spirit, pangender, genderqueer, and all other gendered groups (including none or a combination of these). These growing categories of gender constitute new and emerging ways of understanding gender relations. Together, they form new and emerging evidence that gender exacerbates class. Land governance systems must provide an environment to reconcile these differentiated gender classes within a tenure arrangement that caters for all.

What has been frequently focused on about land and gender is that gender is not only about women. Even so, what is frequently left out in the land and gender debate is that gender is about people. Everyone! Gender is (and should be) about women, men, all the previously mentioned groups, and the youth (girls and boys). All these gendered segments of the human population (in addition to the youth) have differentiated needs and face variable vulnerabilities in land and natural resource access, tenure security and use. Access to land (and its security of tenure) elude vulnerable men, women, and youth because their land rights are frequently hindered by patriarchal orientations and paucity of pro-poor practices that are embedded in land governance systems through culture, unjust laws, and counter-developmental tenure practices.

Land governance is an embodiment of the institutions (laws, regulations and organizations) which can decide on and who administers land use, land ownership, land tenure, land value and land development, among many others. Land governance is instituted to *govern* land and its relationship to people. Therefore, the people element is as important as the land element in land governance. That is why land governance can determine the mechanisms of people's access to land, the nature of people's rights on land, the security of tenure people enjoy or have in their use of the land. Hence, people matter because gender issues are a real aspect of land governance. By determining the nature of rights exercised on land, it influences the role citizens can play in land management, land administration and land information systems' decisions. It also dictates how governments can be held accountable for land-related actions, decisions, and related matters. Through its influence on land policies, it can also dictate the administrative and management approaches that determine project and programme delivery within the general domain of development at national, regional, and local levels.

Every country or community has some sort of prevailing land governance system. Whether these systems provide appropriate governance of tenure depends on whether the prevailing governance system, in normative terms, is effective, weak, efficient, good, developmental, or bad to the tenure and gender needs of the people. Generally, land governance systems cannot enable gender-balanced and pro-poor land tenure if they are weak. Considerable literature (see Chigbu *et al.*, 2019a,b; Paradza *et al.* 2020; Doss and Meinzen-Dick, 2020; Chigbu, 2020) show that implementing gender and tenure responsive land governance systems in many countries have met severe challenges. This is due to the embeddedness of patriarchy in the body of many land governance systems, especially in the economically less developed countries around the world. Patriarchy is one of the dominant institutions governing resource access along with governance structures and institutions that draw power from a variety of sources, including the government, the dominant political party, traditional authorities, and formal legislation. Even in jurisdictions where the laws have been strengthened to become gender-responsive, 'equality between the sexes is about equal rights, equal opportunities and equal recognition before the law and society' remains a problem due to a lack of the political and social will to implement the applicable laws (Chigbu, 2016, p. 37). Whether a governance system can deliver pro-poor and gender-balanced outcomes depends on its structure. It also depends on whether all the stakeholders involved in the gender continuum play their respective roles in land governance.

1.6 Deconstructing Gender as a Continuum: From Bilinear to Multilinear Concepts and Applications

Future societal requirements in land governance would vary between the global poles (north and south) and between countries and regions within countries. This is not surprising because national, regional and local needs are different everywhere. Hence, each land governance jurisdiction would have its own sets of problems to address and would operate within its own locally unique ecosystem. However, common land governance concerns – such as the search for strategies to improve tenure security and gender-balance in land matter, and how to apply solutions in transparency and efficient ways – would persist. Research in land governance is expected to stand at the centre of land governance decisions and activities. This is because research, more than ever before, would be needed to produce land data and evidence for decision making.

Prevailing thoughts on gender and tenure would need to be expanded to accommodate the scope of challenges to be tackled through land governance. Understanding gender as a continuum in land governance is crucial. For instance, contemporary land governance systems embrace gender issues in bilinear lines – that is women and men. This bilinear lens of gender excludes the youth, and the several other gendered groups (e.g. non-binary, intersex, transgender, two-spirit, agender, gender neutral, third-spirit, pangender, genderqueer, among others) who may have different tenure needs in land matters within their societies. These existing and emerging gender groupings are explained below.

- Intersex: Those who consider their gender to be ambiguous. They are people who could be born with genitals that appear male on the outside but have female-typical anatomy internally.
- Transgender: Those whose gender does not align with the congenital (anatomical) gender they were assigned at birth. They can be trans-male or trans-female.
- Two-spirit or third spirit: Those who are biological males or female but culturally identify as belonging to a gender that is separate from male and female, and culturally distinct such that they fulfil one of the mixed gendered roles within their traditional environment (Wilson, 2011). These can be found among the indigenous peoples (including Native Americans and Canadian First Nations indigenous groups) (Hollimon, 2015).
- Gender fluid and pangender: Those whose gender can change and vary over time. Some people can be born males but feel more comfortable to identify as females (and vice versa) at different periods of their lives.
- Gender neutral: Those who do not identify with any sort of gender identity at all.
- Genderqueer and agender: Those who identify as neither man nor woman nor a combination of both. They can feel like a woman one moment and feel like a man in another moment.
- Youth: These are intermediary mix of all the above-mentioned gender groups whose lifecycle is between childhood and adulthood (depending on what adulthood and childhood mean within any land governance jurisdiction).

There are many non-binary gender classifications (Sharp, 2019; Johnson *et al.*, 2020). The outline of different gender emerging from the men-and-women traditional group is indicative that gender, as a concept, is in a state of flux (Chigbu, 2015). It is also a continuum which would continue to grow or shrink according to the constructs of specific social groups or societies. Therefore, any gendered objective of future land governance must be framed to cater for the needs of all these gender groups (multilinear), rather than the current focus on men and women (bilinear). Such reframing of gender relations must also incorporate the youth as an all-encompassing gender group because every other gender (whether emerging or existing) is embodied in the future (Fig. 1.2).

Gender as is more of a social construct than the anatomical constructs upon which humanity have come to base the identities of women and men or boys and girls or female and male. All gendered groups have different needs in relation to land and property rights. The housing rights (including private and public housing needs) of women and men would most likely vary from those of trans-women and trans-men. Same applies to other gender groups such as the gender fluid, gender neutral, agender, pangender, gender queer, and the others. The type of descent-based land ownership and transfers may have social and legal implications that vary among these groups. The same applies to issues land rights, and how land rights are conceived as a form of human rights by the different genders. An example of gendered problems is that landlessness is associated with women and the female gender in the Global South (Chigbu, 2019). However, in the Global North, non-binary genders (such as transgender men and women, and other groups) are associated with *propertylessness* in the Global North (Corrigan, 2019). Non-binary genders (especially trans-genders) complain about having limited access to public bathrooms. Critical gendered questions that future land governance systems must answer would hinge on how to ensure gender equity and gender parity in access to land and natural resources, as well as the use and exercise of other forms of usufruct and hereditary land rights. For instance (in the Global South), traditional gendered families – consisting of man and women – may deny their non-binary children of the right to inherit property. Likewise, in customary tenure societies, kinsmen may deny non-binary members of the kinship their rights to inherit, use and derive benefits from communal lands. These are critical governance issues that must be tackled to ensure that issue of equality in the distribution of land resources are

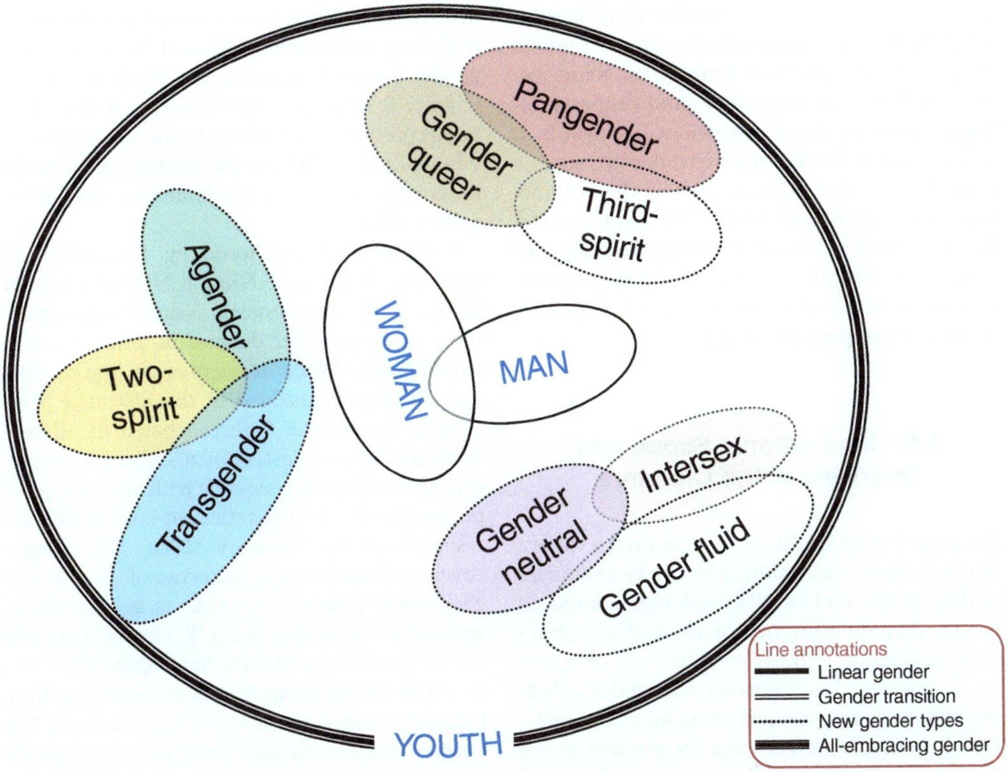

Fig. 1.2. A shift to continuum of gender from bilinear to multilinear gender concept and applications in land governance (Editor's illustration).

achieved. Removing gender barriers through land governance is the way to institute equity, equality and inclusion in land resource use, distribution, and ownership. Other impediments grasping the continuum that exist in descent-based tenure structures in land governance systems.

1.7 Multiplicity of Descent-Based Tenure Structures in Land Governance Systems

In the same vein, current gender based land governance problems have widely been emphasized along two descent-based tenure structures – the patrilineal (paternal) and matrilineal (maternal) lines of tenure. Less emphasis has been put on understanding other tenurial descents such as matrilocal or matrilocality (also referred to uxorilocal or uxorilocality), matrifocal or matrifocality, patrilocal or patrilocality, patrifocal or patrifocality, and other categories of group-based descent lines such as community-centred descents, among others. Future tools or instruments for ensuring gender-balanced tenure must tap into the tenure knowledge derivable from existing structures to devise means for improvement. A study of these descent-based tenure could lead to identitying different perspectives for 'gendered allocation of assets' that are capable of securing tenure in more traditional or indigenous societies in Africa, Asia, and Latin American continents (Peters, 2019, p. 46). The question that arises is: How can this multiplicity of gendered identities be satisfied in a highly emerging descent-based tenure structure? In freer societies where legal and social provisions allow for the willing of properties, it is possible to encounter minimal difficulties in the descent of properties. However, the challenge is dealing with situations where the descent of properties is lightly or strictly guided by the binary notions of gender. Any effective framework going forward will rely on projecting land/property related decisions (land governance) towards a multi-scale gender and tenure responsive actions in the future. Several key ideas from this volume, *Land Governance and Gender: The Tenure–Gender Nexus in Land Management and Land Policy*, can be incorporated to ensure that land governance at various levels contribute towards a gender and tenure-responsive future.

1.8 Innovations, Scope and Overview of the Chapters

The contributors for this book come from a variety of career levels – including scholars/practitioners in their early-, mid-, established- and late-career stages. Tapping from the mix of academic/practical wisdom from these scholars, the chapters (excluding the editor's introductory and concluding chapters) are grouped into four main parts: Part 1 (Concepts, Debates and Perspectives on the Governance and Gender Aspects of Land), Part 2 (Tenure–Gender Dimensions in Land Management, Land Administration and Land Policy), Part 3 (Applications and Experiences: Techniques, Strategies, Tools, Methods and Case Studies), and Part 4 (Land Governance, Gender and Tenure Innovations). Below is a discussion and overview of the chapters within each part.

Part 1 – Concepts, Debates and Perspectives on the Governance and Gender Aspects of Land: This part of the book comprises Chapters 2, 3, 4 and 5. Chapter 2, written by Colleen Murphy and Charles Fogelman, conceptually investigates how gendered structural inequality inhibits the just governance of land. First, the chapter focuses on structural inequality as it exists for women and how gender inequality impedes just governance of land. This chapter, which is entitled 'Gender, Structural Inequality and Just Governance', argues (in the words of the authors) that 'tackling inequitable governance along gender lines will require tackling informal social norms that reflect and justify existing laws and practices'. Next, the chapter discusses the most successful reforms and the areas in which they fall short. Further, it then details that land interventions should be subjected to gender justice to succeed effectively. Lastly, the chapter is conceptually connected to the arguments presented by Cynthia Caron (in Chapter 7), who calls for widening the horizon of women's bargaining power in the land and natural resource affairs.

Chapter 3 (authored by Ikechukwu O. Ezeuduji, Antonia T. Nzama, Nontuthuzelo N. Mbane and Nompumelelo Nzama) investigates the nuanced gender debates in land tenure in sub-Saharan Africa and teases out the realities and illusions embedded in the discourse. This chapter covers the tenure debated in all sub-Saharan Africa – East, Central, West and Southern Africa. The chapter ends with an eight-point proposition for best practices in land policy and research in sub-Saharan Africa. The chapter covers a broad scope in terms of theme and geography. Hence, it provides a general background for grasping Stein T. Holden's specific tenure treatise on Ethiopia in Chapter 12.

The fourth chapter is a contribution from Uchendu Eugene Chigbu and Stig Enemark. The chapter frames how land governance and gender can support the achievement of the Global Agenda 2030. This chapter begins by conceptually deconstructing the relationship between land governance, gender and the Global Agenda 2030. Then, it presents graphical representations of these relationships. It also identifies the elements of land governance and gender within the SDGs, the key challenges ahead, and the suggestions for dealing with the identified challenges.

In Chapter 5, Sara Berry examines the concerns of governing African land in an era of instability. The chapter looks at the 'many-faceted process' involved in the governance of a valuable resource, such as land in Africa. Next, the chapter delves into the multiple rules, competition between authorities and the lines of conflicts encountered in governance practices.

Part 2 – Tenure–Gender Dimensions in Land Management, Land Administration and Land Policy: This part of the book comprises Chapters 6, 7, 8 and 9. Chapter 6 is about 'Advancing Women's Position by Recognizing and Strengthening Customary Land Rights: Lessons from Community-Based Land Interventions in Mozambique'. This chapter (by Julian

Quan, Lora Forsythe and June Y.T. Po) investigates the transformative outcomes in land-based development programmes. The chapter presents gender-sensitive lessons from recent land projects. It demonstrates why gender is essential in the planning, design and modification of future land programmes. The chapter presents three crucial lessons within the sphere of 'gendered land tenure and livelihood systems', 'private sector agricultural investments', and the 'methods involved in delivering land and development programmes to rural communities.'

Cynthia Caron, in Chapter 7, probes women's access to land and bargaining power. The chapter provides insights into the bargaining strategies associated with customary tenure systems and land access as an individual and collective concern. The author uses the voices of women (through interviews) to reflect on real-life experiences of women bargaining with traditional authorities, widows bargaining with in-laws, and married women bargaining with a husband. Using these various scenarios of women in land bargaining (at both individual and collective levels), the author successfully reveals the individual and collective structural problem women encounter in land access.

Chapter 8, entitled 'Gender-Sensitivity in Land Management: Trajectory of Housing, Agriculture and Land Ownership in South Korea', presents the gender perspective of land management and related practices in South Korea. In this chapter, Cheonjae Lee provides a developed country perspective of gender inequality based on land/housing and women's issues. This chapter is both significant and provocative. Very little is available in the literature about how gender is implemented in land management in the developed countries of Asia, where less attention has been paid to understand the men-and-women situation in property and land-based empowerment. This is one of the few studies that has presented evidence on East Asia's land-gender perspective of development. In addition, it highlights gender-related land policy issues in South Korea.

Katriel Marks and Rhonda Phillips, in the ninth chapter, explore a global analysis of non-legal barriers to land ownership by women. The chapter probes 'the potential factors behind why women's rights to own land are often ignored despite laws permitting women to own and inherit land.' The analysis is based on data on measures of gender equality from the Global Gender Gap Index 2020 and data for the percentage of land owned by women by the FAO. By correlating data from the Global Gender Gap Index 2020 with the FAO data on the percentage of total landowners who are female, the authors provided insight into specific factors affecting land ownership by women. The authors conclude that, among many other issues, 'a lack of education, access to information, and credit stem from economic institutions which do not place women on an equal playing field as men'. The chapter recommended broad cultural changes for bringing equality into women's land ownership structures.

Part 3 – Applications and Experiences: Techniques, Strategies, Tools, Methods and Case Studies: This part of the book comprises Chapters 10, 11, 12 and 13. Chapter 10, by Xiaobin Zhang and Yanmei Ye, brings to the fore the perspective of governing tension between construction land expansion and farmland protection in rural China, focusing on land consolidation. The chapter reveals the evolution of land consolidation. In addition, it provides narratives on the process of changing rural land to urban construction land. In general, the chapter delves into a critical perspective of land consolidation processes in China, supporting mechanism for land consolidation implementation.

The eleventh chapter is another provocative piece. It questions the existence of matrilineal land tenure systems that do little to empower women and lift them out of land-related poverty. The 'Discourse on Women and Land Tenure in Ghana: Does a Matrilineal Land Tenure System Make a Difference for Women?' is written by Nancy Kankam Kusi, Frank Mintah, Valentina Nyame, Uchendu Eugene Chigbu, Menare Royal Mabakeng, Barikisa Owusu Ansah, and Walter Dachaga. The study presented in the chapter focuses on women's land rights in the Asante ethnic group of Ghana, where matriarchy is part and parcel of the culture. The authors used local narratives of the Asante to show how 'verbal abuse' (through oral traditions) promotes social stereotypes of women that are disempowering in land ownership. Tracing the history and structure of matriarchy in the Asante society, they conclude that there is either the existence of 'false matriarchy' or a 'matriarchy crisis' that has left women land-poor within the Asante. In search of an appropriate concept to describe the nature of 'matriarchy' in Asante, they called this scenario 'male matriarchy'.

Stein T. Holden, in Chapter 12, gives a historical account of the gender dimensions of land tenure reforms in Ethiopia 1995–2020. The chapter takes readers through the historical context of land tenure in Ethiopia from feudal times to 1974 to identify women's traditional positions in land issues. Overall, the chapter answers three critical questions: (i) whether the land laws ensure gender equity; (ii) whether knowledge and practice of the law grant gender equity; and (iii) whether there is productivity and welfare outcome from strengthening women's land rights.

Chapter 13, by M. Siraj Sait and M. Adil Sait, focuses on the 'The Paradox of Islamic Land Governance and Gender Equality'. This chapter places the Islamic land perspectives into historical context and then unties the knotty issues concerning Islamic land governance and gender equality. It also provides practical ideas on improving women's access to land as an essential element to socioeconomic development in the context of the Muslim world.

Part 4 – Land Governance, Gender and Tenure Innovations: This is the last part of the book. It comprises chapters 14, 15, 16, 17 and 18. Liz Alden Wily, in Chapter 14, details what transforming the legal status of customary land rights would mean for women and men in rural Africa. The chapter theoretically argues that land tenure reform is a 'potent trigger towards equitable land relations between men and women in the customary land sector'. It provides a critical perspective of the modern-day customary tenure and contemporary land reform and explores the gender provisions in modern land laws. This chapter provides a clearer and insightful grasp of why land tenure regimes can best be described as continually in a state of flux in Africa. Lastly, the chapter provides an orientation to the tenure–gender nexus concerns dealt with in Chapters 11 (by Nancy Kankam Kusi *et al.*) and 15 (by Gaynor Gamuchirai Paradza) on Africa and beyond.

Chapter 15, by Gaynor Gamuchirai Paradza, addresses 'Women and Land Inheritance under Legal Pluralism in Lesotho'. The chapter provides an overview of women's land inheritance rights under legal pluralism in sub-Saharan Africa and justifies why land inheritance matters for women across Africa. It mainly explores the land tenure architecture of Lesotho as it affects women's rights to inherit land. Key aspects addressed include the succession planning under custom and statute in Lesotho, how women experience land and inheritance under legal pluralism, and how marriage informs land inheritance dynamics for Basotho widows in Lesotho.

Ernest Uwayezu and Marie Jeanne Nyiransabimana, in Chapter 16, presents the 'Tenure-Responsive Zoning Regulations for Better Gender Equality in Land Management in Kigali City, Rwanda'. The authors approach their arguments from the perspective of planning, focusing on the land use rights concerns from the lens of spatial planning in Rwanda. This chapter (though focused on Rwanda) is linked to the African perspectives of gender and land rights as presented in other chapters. In addition, it is linked to the themes presented in Chapters 3, 7, 11, 14 and 15. The authors provide an in-depth insight into the 'Trajectory of gender equality in land ownership from the lens of the African land reform' as a preamble to their work in Rwanda. An essential contribution of this chapter is that it presents various tenure options for integration into sociospatial planning for achieving better gender equality in land management in Kigali City in Rwanda.

Chapter 17 (written by Uchendu Eugene Chigbu, Michael Klaus and Holger Magel) presents the best way to create balanced development conditions between rural and urban areas. First, it denotes how rural–urban migration issues often reinforce the concentration of economic activities, accelerated growth and dominance of cities over rural areas. Then it argues for a renewed way for tackling rural development challenges by engaging in visions and practices of sustainable development that cater to concerns about rural exodus and a stronger focus on urban-to-rural migration. A global outlook of the reverse migration occurring in various countries worldwide is used as the basis for this argument. Theoretically, the chapter frames its discussions around the concepts of pandemic liveability, rural development and reverse migration.

Then these concepts are used to evoke rural concerns and raise the issue of rural populations during the global pandemic. Next, it outlines how to tap into the pandemic crisis as an opportunity for a renewed rural development approach instead of focusing only on its challenges. Then, the chapter concisely addresses the future of rural areas under COVID-19, answering the question of what sort of future rural areas should have considering the COVID-19 pandemic.

Chapter 18 (by Pamela Durán-Díaz, Emma R. Morales and Melissa Schumacher) provides an urban cum peri-urban land governance perspective from Latin America. The chapter presents a case study of how urban literacy was used to strengthen land governance and women's empowerment in the peri-urban communities of San Andrés Cholula in Mexico. The emerging discourse in this chapter hinges on the application of land governance principles in traditional peri-urban communities in Mexico and the challenge it brings to urban development.

Concluding the book with Chapter 19, 'Land Governance and Gender for a Tenure-Responsive Future', the volume editor, Uchendu Eugene Chigbu, reviews ways to restructure land governance for knowledge and practice. This chapter also discusses why it is important to consider gender in land governance and how to diagnose land governance and gender concerns using some essential land methods and tools. Finally, the editor ends the book by discussing how to take the tenure–gender nexus in land governance forward to better the world.

Through the content of this book and its 19 chapters, the editor is hopeful that it will generate more research and discussion on land governance and gender and its associated tenure–gender nexus in land management and land policy. Further, it is predictable that as more land governance and gender challenges continue to emerge, it will motivate more interest in exploring the approaches presented in the book and fostering a deeper understanding of what can work in communities and regions around the world. Therefore, the editor encourages readers to continue to explore these land-related issues to make more significant impacts in theory and practice.

References

Ayelazuno, J.A. (2019) Land governance for extractivism and capitalist farming in Africa: An overview. *Land Use Policy*, 81, 843–851. DOI: 10.1016/j.landusepol.2018.06.037.

Azadi, H. (2020) Monitoring land governance: Understanding roots and shoots. *Land Use Policy*, 94, 104530. DOI: 10.1016/j.landusepol.2020.104530.

Chigbu, U.E. (2015) Repositioning culture for development: Women and development in a Nigerian rural community. *Community, Work & Family*, 18(3), 336–352. DOI: 10.1080/13668803.2014.981506.

Chigbu, U.E. (2016). A cursory glance at gender equality in Africa. *Sonne Magazine*, July–August.

Chigbu, U.E. (2019) Anatomy of women's landlessness in the patrilineal customary land tenure systems of sub-Saharan Africa and a policy pathway. *Land Use Policy*, 86, 126–135.

Chigbu, U.E. (2021) The quest for 'good governance' of urban land in sub-Saharan Africa. In: Home, R. (Ed.) *Urban Governance in Sub-Saharan Africa*. Springer, Cham, Switzerland, pp. 17–34.

Chigbu, U.E. (2020) Negotiating land rights to redress land wrongs: Women in Africa's land reforms. In: Ochieng, C.M.O. (Ed.), *Rethinking Land Reform in Africa: New Ideas, Opportunities and Challenges*. African Development Bank, Abidjan, Ivory Coast, pp. 156–167.

Chigbu, U.E. Alemayehu, Z. and Dachaga, W. (2019a) Uncovering land tenure insecurities: Tips for tenure responsive land-use planning in Ethiopia. *Development in Practice*, 29(3), 371–383. DOI: 10.1080/09614524.2019.1567688.

Chigbu, U.E. Paradza, G. and Dachaga, W. (2019b) Differentiations in women's land tenure experiences: Implications for women's land access and tenure security in sub-Saharan Africa. *Land*, 8, 22. DOI: 10.3390/land8020022.

Corrigan, L.M. (2019) The #MeToo moment: A rhetorical zeitgeist. *Women's Studies in Communication*, 42(3), 264–268. DOI: 10.1080/07491409.2019.1652528.

de Vries W. and Chigbu U.E. (2017) Responsible land management – Concept and application in a territorial rural context. *Fub – Flächenmanagement und Bodenordnung* [Spatial Planning and Land Management], 79(2), 65–73.

Department of Land and Property Sciences of Namibia University of Science and Technology, DLPS-NUST. (2018) *Research Strategy: Land Governance*. DLPS-NUST, Windhoek, Namibia.
Doss, C. and Meinzen-Dick, R. (2020) Land tenure security for women: A conceptual framework. *Land Use Policy*, 99, 105080. DOI: 10.1016/j.landusepol.2020.105080.
Enemark, S., McLaren, R. and Van der Molen, P. (2010) *Land Governance in Support of the Millennium Development Goals.* International Federation of Surveyors, Copenhagen, Denmark.
Global Land Tool Network. (2018). *Fit-for-Purpose Land Administration: A Country Level Implementation Strategy for Nepal*. UN-Habitat / Global Land Tool Network, Nairobi, Kenya.
Hollimon, S.E. (2015) Third gender. In: Bolin, A. and Whelehan, P. (Eds), *The International Encyclopedia of Human Sexuality.* DOI: 10.1002/9781118896877.wbiehs509.
Johnson, K.C., LeBlanc, A.J., Deardorff, J. and Bockting, W.O. (2020) Invalidation experiences among non-binary adolescents. *Journal of Sex Research*, 57(2), 222–233. DOI: 10.1080/00224499.2019.1608422.
Palmer, D., Fricska, S. and Wehrmann, B. (2009) *Towards Improved Land Governance.* Food and Agriculture Organization, Rome, Italy.
Paradza, G., Mokwena, L. and Musakwa, W. (2020) Could mapping initiatives catalyze the interpretation of customary land rights in ways that secure women's land rights? *Land*, 9(10), 344. DOI: 10.3390/land9100344.
Peters, E.P. (2019) Revisiting the social bedrock of kingships and descent in the anthropology of Africa. In: *Grinker. R.R.*, Lubkemann, S.C., Steiner, C.B. and Gonçalves, B. (Eds.), *A Companion to the Anthropology of Africa.* John Wiley & Sons, Inc., Hoboken, NJ, USA, pp. 33–62.
Sharp, M. (2019) Hypervisibility in Australian punk scenes: Queer experiences of spatial logics of gender and sexuality. *Punk & Post Punk*, 8(3), 363–378. DOI: 10.1386/punk_00004_1.
UN-Habitat. (2008) *Secure Land Rights for All*. Global Land Tool Network / UN-Habitat, Nairobi, Kenya.
Williamson, I., Enemark, S., Wallace, J. and Rajabifard, A., (2010) *Land Administration for Sustainable Development*. ESRI Press Academic, Redlands, CA, USA.
Wilson, T. (2011) Changed embraces, changes embraced? Renouncing the heterosexist majority in favor of a return to traditional two-spirit culture. *American Indian Law Review*, 36(1), 161–188. Available at: https://digitalcommons.law.ou.edu/ailr/vol36/iss1/3.

Part 1

Concepts, Debates and Perspectives on the Governance and Gender Aspects of Land

2 Gender, Structural Inequality and Just Governance

Colleen Murphy* and Charles Fogelman
University of Illinois at Urbana-Champaign, Champaign, IL, USA

2.1 Introduction

This chapter examines the ways in which gendered structural inequality inhibits the just governance of land. Institutions of various kinds (legal, governmental, economic, social, and cultural) specify rules and norms for interaction. Rules and norms outline what types of action are permitted, required, or prohibited by certain groups of actors, as well as the formal and informal penalties for violating such rules and norms. Structural inequality exists when institutional rules and norms differentially restrict opportunities for certain groups to do and become things of value (e.g. being healthy, being employed, being educated) and differentially restrict the ability of certain groups to shape and define institutional rules and norms.

Our interest in this chapter is on structural inequality as it exists for women, and the ways in which gender inequality impedes just governance of land. Our first section examines the distinctive importance of land. Land is not only a commodity, but also plays a key role in social relationships. The second section turns then to the governance of land, and outlines some of the ways in which gendered inequalities in land tenure exist. The third section is normative and prescriptive, arguing that to establish just, gender-equitable governance of land it is necessary to prioritize gender justice and poverty reduction in land governance policies and institutions.

2.2 Land

The importance of land is often reduced to two interrelated uses: land as a commodity and land as a place of agriculture. These simplifications reflect important truths. The ability to exchange or collateralize one's land, and the ability to engage in agriculture (and to benefit from agricultural surpluses) are among the most important functions of relationships between people and land. These are not, however, the only relationships that exist between people and land. In this section, we will discuss those two vital relationships, but also explore some of the myriad other things that connect people and land. Last, we will consider the ways that those many connections are becoming more limited in the capitalist expansion engendered by the 'global land grab' (or, as some call it, the 'global land rush').

Most policy- and development-driven discussions of land tenure focus on profit maximization, either through reforms that allow land to be controlled by those who will use it most efficiently (Binswanger and Deininger, 1999;

*Corresponding author: colleenm@illinois.edu

 Land Governance and Gender: The Tenure-Gender Nexus in Land Management and Land Policy (ed. U.E. Chigbu)
DOI: 10.1079/9781789247664.0002

Place, 2009; Chimhowu, 2019) or those who will be able to unlock potential from the land by mortgaging a parcel to release the land's dormant capital (de Soto, 2000). Such landholders will take the money they borrow and, in de Soto's framing, 'vivify' it and mix it with labour to produce greater economic surplus. Another thread of study around land tenure is more explicitly concerned with enhancing equity and poverty reduction than the theorists above, but these development-minded theorists tend to focus on questions of yield and efficiency as well. These foci provide a valuable, but a limited, view of what land is and how land should be used (Li, 2014).

Ontologies and Affordances

Especially for poor and otherwise vulnerable people, land's ontologies – what land *is* – are far more than a place of agriculture or collateral. Many matters, among them kinship, political alliances, health and illness, burial, belonging, and identity, are all deeply embedded in land (Ferguson, 2013). Land rights are deeply embedded in the fabric of social relations; it is a dramatic disservice to reduce them to their agricultural or mortgage value. The ways that the rights and uses of land are determined is related to profit maximization. Agriculture and collateral are integral uses of land, but they are hardly the only ones. What they do reflect, however, is the reality that in the contemporary moment, land is generally seen as a commodity before anything else, especially by the wealthy and powerful. The process by which land becomes commodified is a complex one, involving interpretation of land's affordances – what land *does*.

Land is not inherently fit for investment – it must be made into a vehicle fit for exchange. To use Tania Murray Li's term, it must be 'rendered investable' (Li, 2014). The process by which land is rendered investable requires a litany of actors, all of whom work, wittingly or not, toward a common goal of turning land into an exchangeable good. These actors – among them people, spreadsheets, maps, axes, practices, and discourses – work together to simplify land's meaning to measurable and seemingly-objective components, despite the complex social relations that give land its meanings (Scott, 1998; Li, 2014; Fogelman and Bassett, 2017). Removing these nuanced social forces from understandings of land empowers some actors and components at the expense of others.

Power over land rights and land use are also power over labour and capital. The way that this power relates to the production and reproduction of inequalities is not simply a matter of agricultural productivity and mortgages, but also a full consideration of the many uses, actors, and forces that imbue it with power. The tendency to reduce land to its 'yield gap', or the difference between its current economic productivity and its ideal productive potential (Deininger *et al.*, 2011), privileges certain actors and forces at the expense of others. When land is 'rendered investable', it is no longer a place of kinship, health, or identity. Instead, it is merely a commodity to be used as economically efficiently as possible. Rendering land investable is effectively an act of enclosure that permits land rights only for certain people or groups. Because the constellation of social forces that enclose the land are inevitably shaped by power relations, rendering land investable tends to duplicate and deepen existing inequalities (Peters, 2004).

Who Has Land Access?

The term 'land grab' is nothing new, nor is the phenomenon of more powerful actors dispossessing others from their land. What is new in the contemporary moment is that the global meaning of land is defined more narrowly than ever before.

We live amid a 'global land grab'. Well-capitalized private equity firms, transnational corporations, university endowments, and many others in the Global North have invested in the land markets of the developing world with the intent of gaining long-term profit streams from agricultural production in the Global South (Bergdolt and Mittal, 2012). On the surface, it seems that there is little substantive difference between local and global land grabs. Dispossession is dispossession, whether it is done by neighbours or by multinational corporations; the outcomes for the dispossessed are similar regardless of where the capital originates (Fogelman,

2018). However, the fact that the 'global land grab' is novel, foreign, and large scale (Verma, 2014) does markedly limit the ontologies and affordances of land.

North American pension funds and European multinationals are not interested in a hypothetical Ethiopian field's relationship to identity, health or burial. They are interested in maximizing yields, productivity and profit. They are not interested in neighbours as political allies or kin. They are interested in those neighbours as a labour force to work the land that is now theirs. In no small part through the spreadsheets, maps, and 'yield gaps' that they have imposed on the land, its meaning has been foreclosed (Demeritt, 2001; Li, 2014; Fogelman and Bassett, 2017). The imagined Ethiopian field no longer reflects the many meanings outlined by Ferguson; it is now defined strictly a place of productivity. The many other ways that land can shape, produce, or mitigate inequalities have also been removed; all actors are now subject to market forces and the inequalities produced and reproduced by those market forces.

2.3 Gender and Governance

Land tenure refers to the relationship(s) of individuals and groups to land and land-based resources. Land tenure rules define the ways in which property rights to land are allocated, transferred, used or managed in a particular society. Governance refers to the process of defining and regulating individuals' actions and interactions over a specified domain. Governance is critical to land tenure by defining the contours of the relationships that individuals and communities can have. Land governance specifically involves defining who does or can own land, where ownership confers a bundle of rights including the right to exclude others from access to land one owns.

Governance at the national level includes specifying and enforcing the legal rights, duties, privileges, and powers enjoyed by individuals and groups within a given jurisdiction (Hohfeld, 1919). Rights confer certain claims on individuals that generate corresponding duties on others who must act or refrain from acting in specified ways. In addition, governance helps define what powers individuals enjoy changing, their rights or their legal status, and who is liable to be affected by such changes. Finally, immunities define who is protected from specified forms of changes in legal status. Rights conferred can be limited in the powers they grant; certain uses of land may be precluded for example. Ownership furthermore carries the power to create rights in others through transferring some or all property.

Governments at the local and national levels characteristically govern through the law. In systems of federalism state level and national level governments coexist. Legal systems are used to govern conduct based on declared rules. Such rules specify what land governance looks like in a particular context, and such rules are enforced (to varying degrees) by government officials. Globally, various forms of legal systems exist, including civil legal orders, common law legal orders and various forms of customary legal orders.

Gender has long been a clear determinant of land rights and land access. Legal reforms, commercialization of land, and changes to land tenure systems around the world have promised to be a necessary element of gender equality, but few, if any, have delivered on those promises. An important cause for this shortcoming is that other institutions, including marriage (Fogelman, 2016), inheritance (Peters, 2010; Scott *et al.*, 2010), credit (Awumbila and Tsikata, 2010), and others maintain systematic gender biases that cannot be overcome by land tenure reforms, no matter how sensitive to gender those reforms are (Tsikata and Golah, 2010; Whitehead, 2010). In short, efforts to create gender equality in terms of land through land reforms alone have fallen short because of the myriad other legal and social factors that preclude women from substantively benefitting from those reforms.

Criticisms of governance as it occurs in a particular context can be of two kinds. The first is a criticism of the absence or failure of governance. This can be a function of either an absence of rules, a failure to enforce rules that exist, or both. The second is a criticism of the justice or fairness of the form of governance that does exist. In the remainder of this section, we examine the places of gender in both kinds of criticisms.

Failures of Governance

Failures of governance or imperfect forms of governance fall into two general categories. We illustrate these general types of imperfection or failure using examples that underscore the role of gender. The first form of failure or imperfect is *formal and/or procedural.* This set of failures stems from the ways in which attempts to govern by law can fail to govern the conduct of legal subjects and/or officials. Seven conditions laid out by legal scholar, Lon Fuller (1969), identify what is necessary for legal rules to be able to figure in the deliberation of legal subjects. Laws must be *general,* identifying rules or general baselines for conduct. They must be *promulgated,* or publicly accessible. Laws must be *non-contradictory;* citizens cannot govern their conduct by law if the law is asking them to do contradictory things. To see whether this is satisfied it is necessary to see how a given rule, for example concerning land rights or land inheritance, fits into the other rules governing conduct in a legal system. Laws must be *clear,* so legal subjects know what is being asked, and *not ask the impossible,* so legal subjects are practically able to do what is required or refrain from doing what is forbidden by law. Laws must be *prospective,* so individuals can govern their conduct according to rules that are effective at the time of action.

What it means for rules to satisfy these various conditions, such as being publicly accessible, will vary across social contexts. Since the point of law is to govern conduct and be such that it can figure in the practical deliberation of legal subjects, it is important to know when the law is able of doing that in a given context.

The eighth condition that Fuller discusses – *congruence* – specifies what must be the case for there to be a relationship between what legal rules say and what happens in fact or practice. Only when there is congruence between declared rules and the actions of legal subjects and officials does law (as opposed to the whim of officials or subjects) govern.

Lack of congruence can arise in cases where land rights of women are recognized on paper but are not enforced in practice. Lack of enforcement can come in many forms. The right to exclude that a property right entails may not be effectively exercised in practice. Women may lack effective decision-making power with respect to the uses to which property is put or whether land is sold or leased. Those who have the ability, and not merely the right, to benefit from a piece of land are those with true access to land (Ribot and Peluso, 2003). There is a long history of 'exclusion, deepening social divisions and class formation' (Peters, 2004, p. 269) that limits the rights and negotiating power of some groups, regardless of their formal rights. These power imbalances are routinely exploited by those who desire the land – opportunistic in-laws of a recently widowed woman are a common example of those who attempt to dispossess others of their land outside of formally sanctioned channels. Conflicts between what legal frameworks demand, on the one hand, and the norms of social and cultural practices, on the other, can result in legal frameworks that are equitable failing to be effective in regulating behaviour in practice. This leads to discriminatory practices continuing, despite the development of equitable laws.

Many accounts of the rule of law go beyond the formal conditions laid out above to look at procedural protections which must exist. Behind the ideal of governing by law is a reciprocal commitment between official and legal subject. Fuller articulates that commitment with these words: 'These are the rules we expect you to follow. If you follow them, you have our assurance that they are the rules that will be applied to your conduct' (1969, p. 40). The basic thought is that if we are to treat individuals as agents, and so respond to them based on the choices they have made (including whether to conform to legal requirements or not), then it is important that we have a sufficient basis for determining an infraction of a legal rule has occurred before inflicting penalty or punishment. This requires a hearing for the accused, where the accused enjoys procedural protections, to determine whether they are in fact guilty. Conversely, there must be effective recourse or remedy available for those whose rights are violated. An inability for women to access courts, or have testimony taken seriously, or call rights violators to account undermines the effectiveness of the land claims women enjoy nominally.

Unjust Governance

A second kind of failure in governance is not formal but *substantive.* Substantive failures in governance by law are measured against specific goals or objectives. Consider gender equity. Insofar as law has a fundamentally masculine orientation, as West (1988) has argued, there will be systematic limits in the ability of the law to recognize women as landowners and to devise adequate remedies for risks to land ownership and control that women face. To illustrate the masculine orientation of law, West (1988) focuses on accounts in jurisprudence of the origins of law as a method of social control and organization. In a standard story, in a context where government and law do not exist, individuals live a 'nasty, brutish and short' existence (as Thomas Hobbes put it). Roughly equal (in terms of physical ability and strength), no one individual can dominate. Even when conflict is motivated by self-defence, in some instances, aggression ensues. A state governing by law establishes conditions that protect individuals from annihilation thereby improving the situation of men.

But, West notes, the gains law created for men came with costs for women. Legal rules in their substance remain disproportionately responsive to the priorities of men and the risks to which men are subject from others. Because of how the primary threat to our safety is conceptualized, law has been late and remains inadequate in addressing intimate, sexual assault and invasion to which women are especially vulnerable. Rape remains most easily recognized as rape if it occurs in a form more readily comprehensible by men, that is, accompanied by violence or explicit threat of annihilation (West, 1988). Law has struggled to see pregnancy as a threat from which legal protection is warranted, through safe access to abortion. The values that are associated as female the law often fails to recognize or sufficiently protect. Intimacy and the nurturing of labour are adequately compensated in the workplace or treated as labour (West, 1988).

West's feminist analysis of the limits of law's responsiveness to women because of its fundamentally masculine orientation have specific implications for land governance. It suggests we should expect the threats to governance and the ability to exercise one's property rights that law does recognize and protect will be characteristically threats that men face. External threats, rather than threats from within one's own family, will be one's men face given the ways in which men are able to exercise control within familial contexts in patriarchal contexts. Tenure security, which disproportionately is either held by men or else derived by women from men (Chigbu, 2019), is both constitutive and reflective of class, gender and other unequal power relations. Valuation of land that invokes uses and values associated with community and nurturing relationships will be valuation that a commodity-oriented framework will struggle to recognize.

2.4 Prescriptions

The presence or absence of certain social conditions shapes the prospect of governance by law. Governance by law requires constraint on the part both of government officials and of legal subjects. The willingness to show such constraint can be affected by several social conditions. One important condition Fuller discusses is systematic congruence between informal practices and the law (Fuller, 1977, p. 58). Legal rules are general and require judgement by individuals to determine what general rules require in their situation. To the extent that individuals can draw on existing, informal social understandings of acceptable or unacceptable action, this can increase their ability to successfully interpret legal rules in a manner that will be consistent with the interpretation of government officials. This requirement, however, underscores an important challenge to land governance rules that aim to promote gender equity but are enacted in a context where gender relations are deeply and systematically unequal. Laws and legal interpretations disconnected from the broader social context, may seem arbitrary from the perspective of legal subjects if the overall context is one of inequality. Such arbitrariness can in turn encourage evasion or outright violation of legal requirements. Thus, tackling inequitable governance along gender lines will require tackling informal social norms that reflect and justify existing laws and practices.

Many land reforms have proven successful in achieving some of the World Bank's stated goals of economic growth (often in the form of increased entrepreneurship), enhanced gender justice, and equitable poverty reduction (Varga, 2020). However, no notable reforms have proven successful at realizing all three goals. In this section, we discuss the most successful reforms and the areas in which they fell short. We finish by making the argument that no reform is likely to be successful on all three counts, and that decommodification of land is necessary to create truly successful and equitable land reform. In short, the objectives of economic growth and entrepreneurship must be subordinated to those of gender justice and poverty reduction to successfully realize those aims.

Tenure reform tends to increase land productivity and farmer income, according to a systematic review of 20 studies, but that same review found that 'reform may also have negative social effects, including on women's access to land and on displacement of the poor or others facing social and financial barriers to participating in the reformed regime' (Lawry *et al.*, 2017, p. 76). In effect, the economic growth objective succeeds at the expense of the gender justice and poverty reduction goals. Their review is consistent with findings from a growth-focused reform in Lesotho, where a reform that was targeted at the three World Bank goals appeared to increase participation in the formal economy but seems have done harm to the aims of gender justice and poverty reduction (Fogelman, 2018). A similar outcome is warned about in the case of Ghana, where an ongoing land reform project threatens to deepen gender inequalities because of the spectre of dispossession. In Ghana, 'despite a progressive legal framework in relation to inheritance, customary and cultural practices which are discriminatory remain the norm' (Spichiger and Stacey, 2014, p. 29). Phase II of the project included an explicit gender strategy (World Bank, 2011), but research since then indicates that women's vulnerability to dispossession has continued (Schoneveld and German, 2014; Tsikata and Yaro, 2014). Without a broader set of rights, enforcement, and abilities to benefit from those rights, progressive-sounding laws do little to help vulnerable people.

Three cases, however, provide a compelling counterexample to the World Bank-friendly reforms that may tend to exacerbate existing social inequalities. In Vietnam, where gender justice and poverty reduction were the main foci of their 1993 reform, women who received land title saw substantive increases in bargaining power and social status, and their households were less vulnerable to poverty than before the reform (Menon *et al.*, 2016). Similarly, in Zimbabwe's land reform, there is compelling evidence that land redistribution policies – or the 'seizure of white farms', depending on the nomenclature one prefers – led to dramatic reductions in socio-economic vulnerability and food insecurity (Moyo, 2011; Scoones *et al.*, 2011; Tekwa and Adesina, 2018). Women have disproportionately benefited from what has been termed a 're-peasantization' of Zimbabwe (Mutopo *et al.*, 2014), where a growing proportion of the population lives in rural areas – nearly 70%, according to the World Bank's most recent data. In cases with such high rural populations, land tenure is far more central to livelihoods than in more urbanized countries. Zimbabwe's case is particularly instructive for poor countries, whose people tend to live far more rurally than those in wealthier countries.

A final example is that of Kerala State in India's southwest. Long an example of successful participatory democracy, Kerala has demonstrated equitable and admirable development outcomes for men and women, for low and high castes, and for rural and urban people in terms of health, wealth and education. According to the Human Development Index, Kerala has the highest level of development of any of India's 28 states, despite ranking tenth in GDP per capita (Franke and Chasin, 1992; Dreze and Sen, 1999). This mismatch illustrates two things: Kerala's focus on well-being is more broadly defined than wealth or income; and our own argument in this section, namely that the decommodification of land is central to its ability to serve as a pathway to broader human development. In Kerala, the land reforms of 1957, 1969 and 1977 subordinated economic growth to gender equity and poverty reduction, and the state has shown massive improvements in human development since then. The reforms did not focus in any meaningful way on economic growth, instead working to return 'land to the tiller' and vest tenure rights in those who worked the land (Herring, 1983).

This is not to make the claim that Kerala's pro-poor land reforms have been perfect. Herring made clear that some of the 'tillers' in Kerala were effectively a *petit bourgeoisie* who simply became a new landlord class. What Herring also demonstrated is that the outcomes of Kerala's land reforms were the product of a whole constellation of social, political, and economic forces. It is impossible to make an argument that land reforms, however pro-poor and equitable, are entirely responsible for Kerala's broader development success. Those reforms may not be a sufficient cause of positive development outcomes, but they are a necessary one.

Even in his own ambivalent conclusions about Kerala's reforms, Herring argued that 'if pressure for radical reform does not succeed, the social process set in motion is nevertheless important' (Herring, 1983, p. 287). These social processes are the forces that have created gender equity and poverty reduction in Kerala. In terms of land, one element appears to be necessary to these successes and that unites the cases of Vietnam, Zimbabwe, and Kerala. That element is decommodification. In all three cases, land was returned to small-scale farmers whose livelihoods were considered ahead of the economic potential of the land. When land is decommodified, it can then be viewed as something other than a place of yields and mortgages, the diversity of its affordances becomes much clearer, and its role in development outcomes – like health, wealth and equity – is no longer subjugated to that of economic growth.

References

Awumbila, M. and Tsikata, D. (2010) Economic liberalisation, changing resource tenures and gendered livelihoods. In: Tsikata, D. and Golah, P. (Eds), *Land Tenure, Gender, and Globalization: Research and Analysis from Africa, Asia, and Latin America.* Zubaan and International Development Research Centre, New Dehli, India, and Ottawa, Canada, pp. 98–144.

Bergdolt, C. and Mittal, A. (2012) *Betting on world agriculture: US private equity managers eye agricultural returns.* The Oakland Institute, Oakland, CA, USA.

Binswanger, H.P. and Deininger, K. (1999) *Explaining Agricultural and Agrarian Policies in Developing Countries*. The World Bank, Washington, DC, USA.

Chigbu, U.E. (2019) Anatomy of women's landlessness in the patrilineal customary land tenure systems of sub-Saharan Africa and a policy pathway. *Land Use Policy*, 86, 126–135.

Chimhowu, A. (2019) The 'new' African customary land tenure. Characteristic features and policy implications of a new paradigm. *Land Use Policy*, 81, 897–903.

Deininger, K., Byerlee, D., Lindsay, J., Norton, A., Selod, H. and Stickler, M. (2011) *Rising Global Interest in Farmland: Can It Yield Sustainable and Equitable Benefits?* The World Bank, Washington, DC.

Demeritt, D. (2001) The construction of global warming and the politics of science. *Annals of the Association of American Geographers*, 91(2), 307–337.

de Soto, H. (2000) *The Mystery of Capital: Why Capitalism Triumphs in the West and Fails Everywhere Else*. Basic Books, New York, NY, USA.

Dreze, J. and Sen, A. (1999) *India: Economic Development and Social Opportunity*. Oxford University Press, New York, NY, USA.

Ferguson, S.J. (2013) *Race, Gender, Sexuality, and Social Class: Dimensions of Inequality*. Sage, Thousand Oaks, CA, USA.

Fogelman, C. (2016) Measuring gender, development, and land: Data-driven analysis and land reform in Lesotho. *World Development Perspectives*, 1, 36–42.

Fogelman, C. (2018) Development by dispossession: The post-2000 development agenda and land rights in Lesotho. *African Geographical Review*, 37(3), 257–272.

Fogelman, C. and Bassett, T.J. (2017) Mapping for investability: Remaking land and maps in Lesotho. *Geoforum*, 82, 252–258.

Franke, R.W. and Chasin, B.H. (1992) Kerala State, India: Radical reform as development. *International Journal of Health Services*, 22(1), 139–156.

Fuller, L. (1969) *The Morality of Law*, rev. ed. Yale University Press, New Haven, CT, USA.

Fuller, L. (1977) *Anatomy of the Law.* Praeger, Westport, CT, USA.

Herring, R.J. (1983) *Land to the Tiller: The Political Economy of Agrarian Reform in South Asia*. Yale University Press, New Haven, CT, USA.

Hohfeld, W. (1919) *Fundamental Legal Conceptions*. Yale University Press, New Haven, CT, USA.

Lawry, S., Samii, C., Hall, R., Leopold, A., Hornby, D. and Mtero, F. (2017) The impact of land property rights interventions on investment and agricultural productivity in developing countries: A systematic review. *Journal of Development Effectiveness*, 9(1), 61–81.

Li, T.M. (2014) What is land? Assembling a resource for global investment. *Transactions of the Institute of British Geographers*, 39(4), 589–602.
Menon, N., Van der Meulen Rodgers, Y. and Kennedy, A.R. (2016) Land reform and welfare in Vietnam: Why gender of the land-rights holder matters. *Journal of International Development*, 29(4), 454–472.
Moyo, S. (2011) Three decades of agrarian reform in Zimbabwe. *Journal of Peasant Studies*, 38(3), 493–531.
Mutopo, P., Manjengwa, J. and Chiweshe, M. (2014) Shifting gender dimensions and rural livelihoods after Zimbabwe's fast-track land reform programme. *Agrarian South: Journal of Political Economy*, 3(1), 45–61.
Peters, P.E. (2004) Inequality and social conflict over land in Africa. *Journal of Agrarian Change*, 4(3), 269–314.
Peters, P.E. (2010) 'Our daughters inherit our land, but our sons use their wives' fields': Matrilineal–matrilocal land tenure and the New Land Policy in Malawi. *Journal of Eastern African Studies*, 4(1), 179–199.
Place, F. (2009) Land tenure and agricultural productivity in Africa: A comparative analysis of the economics literature and recent policy strategies and reforms. *World Development*, 37(8), 1326–1336.
Ribot, J.C. and Peluso, N.L. (2003) A theory of access. *Rural Sociology*, 68(2), 153–181.
Schoneveld, G.C. and German, L. (2014) Translating legal rights into tenure security: Lessons from the new commercial pressures on land in Ghana. *The Journal of Development Studies*, 50(2), 187–203.
Scoones, I., Marongwe, N., Mavedzenge, B., Murimbarimba, F., Mahenehene, J. and Sukume, C. (2011) Zimbabwe's land reform: Challenging the myths. *Journal of Peasant Studies*, 38(5), 967–993.
Scott, J.C. (1998) *Seeing Like a State: How Certain Schemes to Improve the Human Condition Have Failed*. Yale University Press, New Haven, CT, USA.
Scott, S., Bélanger, D., Van Anh, N.T. and Hong, K.T. (2010) Gender, kinship and agrarian transitions in Vietnam. In: *Land Tenure, Gender, and Globalization: Research and Analysis from Africa, Asia, and Latin America.* Zubaan and International Development Research Centre, New Dehli, India, and Ottawa, Canada, pp. 228–270.
Spichiger, R. and Stacey, P. (2014) *Ghana's Land Reform and Gender Equality*. DIIS Working Paper. Danish Institute for International Studies, Copenhagen, Denmark.
Tekwa, N. and Adesina, J. (2018) Gender, poverty and inequality in the aftermath of Zimbabwe's land reform: A transformative social policy perspective. *Journal of International Women's Studies*, 19(5), 45–46.
Tsikata, D. and Golah, P. (Eds) (2010) *Land Tenure, Gender and Globalisation: Research and Analysis from Africa, Asia and Latin America*. Zubaan and International Development Research Centre, New Dehli, India, and Ottawa, Canada.
Tsikata, D. and Yaro, J.A. (2014) When a good business model is not enough: Land transactions and gendered livelihood prospects in rural Ghana. *Feminist Economics*, 20(1), 202–226.
Varga, M. (2020) Poverty reduction through land transfers? The World Bank's titling reforms and the making of 'subsistence' agriculture. *World Development*, 135, 1050–1058.
Verma, R. (2014) Land grabs, power, and gender in East and Southern Africa: So, what's new? *Feminist Economics*, 20, 52–75.
West, R. (1988) Jurisprudence and gender. *The University of Chicago Law Review*, 55, 1–72.
Whitehead, A. (2010) Foreword. In: Tsikata, D. and Golah, P. (Eds), *Land Tenure, Gender, and Globalization: Research and Analysis from Africa, Asia, and Latin America.* Zubaan and International Development Research Centre, New Dehli, India, and Ottawa, Canada, pp. vii–xii.
World Bank. (2011) *Implementation completion and results report* (Report No: ICR00002083). World Bank, Washington, DC, USA.

3 Land Tenure and the Nuanced Gender Debates in Sub-Saharan Africa: Realities and Illusions

Ikechukwu O. Ezeuduji,*[1] Antonia T. Nzama,[1] Nontuthuzelo N. Mbane[2] and Nompumelelo Nzama[1]

[1]University of Zululand, KwaDlangezwa, South Africa; [2]Cape Peninsula University of Technology, Cape Town, South Africa

3.1 Introduction

Women's land rights have been affirmed unequivocally in constitutions and international human rights in many sub-Saharan African (SSA) countries; however, customary practices predominate on the ground and most often marginalize women's land rights (Evans, 2016). A study conducted by Izumi (1999) on liberalization, gender, and the land question in sub-Saharan Africa, found that the formal policies and laws relating to gender equality are failing to enforce women's formal rights in practice. This is because 'formal and legal rights to land do not necessarily provide women secure rights in reality, if such rights are not made socially legitimate and enforceable' (Izumi, 1999, p. 16). Consequently, analysis of land tenure and nuanced gender debates in SSA is needed, to unearth gender-based realities of land tenure (actual practice) in these SSA countries, compared with formal policies on land rights, to check for alignments or illusions thereof. Ezeuduji (2015, p. 213) puts forward the United Nations' designation – sub-Saharan Africa, to indicate 'all African countries, except northern Africa, fully or partially situated south of the Sahara, with Sudan and South Sudan included' (see United Nations Statistics Division, 2011).

Some authors on land tenure systems in SSA have argued that, formal land policies notwithstanding, structural inequalities exist in relation to gender dimensions of tenure rights. Chigbu (2019, p. 129), in his attempt to define a policy pathway and discussion towards addressing women's landlessness in SSA, identified three pillars of women's marginalization regarding land, namely: 'structure of male power'; 'gender insensitive worldviews in everyday communication'; and 'restrictions outside ownership borders in customary land tenure spaces'. He went further to argue that much of the women's land issues which Doss *et al.* (2018, p. 69) termed the 'four myths' of gender in the world cannot be referred to as myths in SSA. The situation in SSA societies is portrayed by several authors as a mix of community interest in land, family (household) interest and individual (male) interest to exclude women from direct ownership (such as Asiama, 1997; Chigbu, 2015). Chigbu (2019) states that this is evident in the prevalent social set-ups in SSA which have been woven in customary societies to favour males in land matters, especially regarding

*Corresponding author: Ezeudujil@unizulu.ac.za

 Land Governance and Gender: The Tenure-Gender Nexus in Land Management and Land Policy (ed. U.E. Chigbu)
DOI: 10.1079/9781789247664.0003

marriage, governance (chieftaincy), customary land acquisition and inheritance rites. A discord can be highlighted between statistics from Mathaai (2003); Food and Agriculture Organization (2011); and Doss *et al.* (2015) which show that in SSA, women own only about 3% of its arable land; and that women are better stewards of SSA home environment, on the one hand; compared with their statistics that more than 70% of SSA's poor population are women; and that women deliver 60–80% of its food production, on the other hand.

This chapter sets to analyse nuanced gender debates in SSA, explore realities and illusions of land tenure between women and men in this region; and gendered-land outcomes in relation to land access, ownership, and control by gender. Land tenure relates to how access to land is granted, the rights to use, control, and transfer land, including the associated responsibilities and restraints. Recent empirical studies from different SSA nations on gender and land will reveal nuanced opinions on land indicators for gendered development in this region and will support stakeholder discussions of gender-land equalities or inequalities. Doss *et al.* (2015) posit that the claim that women own approximately 15% of land in SSA has been mostly used by authors who seek to promote women's land rights and agricultural development. The authors state that such claims do not provide citations, or they reproduce previous citations without a clear source of data. Authors (such as Peterman, 2011; Kumar and Quisumbing, 2013) state that the knowledge of the extent of women's land rights is important due to the growing empirical evidence that fostering women's property rights will contribute to less poverty and community vulnerability, environmental sustainability and general investments for future generations. The possession of secure rights to land enables women's incentives to manage that land in a more sustainable way, by planting trees and adopting sustainable farming techniques. Quisumbing *et al.* (2001) supplied such evidence in Ghana, where women were more prone to plant cocoa trees on land which they have secure private property rights. In a shifting cultivation system, land with less secure property rights is less often left fallow, allowing the land less time to regain its fertility (Otsuka *et al.*, 2003). It is also found in Ghana (Goldstein and Udry, 2008) that the perceived productivity difference between male and female farmers arose because female farmers had more insecure land rights and are less likely to leave their land fallow, as they risk losing the land without actively farming it. Quisumbing (2003) posits that having secure rights to land and other assets enables women's bargaining power associated with greater investments in children's nutrition and education within the households. Ethiopia's family law gave women stronger rights to own property after divorce, and Kumar and Quisumbing (2012) found that children in households where women fear they will get less in divorce settlement perform less well in school compared to children of the same age; and girls perform even worse than boys in such households. These and other nuanced gender debates around land tenure in SSA will be theoretically explored in this chapter, highlighting realities and illusions, to reach more objective conclusions and recommendations. The next section of this chapter will explore gendered land tenure debates across SSA.

3.2 Overview of Gendered Land Tenure Debates across Sub-Saharan Africa

According to Naybor (2015), in SSA, the influences of colonialism have changed traditional practices to manage land, labour, and money. Land has become highly marketable and an intrinsic part of the global economy. Previous authors (such as Yngstrom, 2002; Whitehead and Tsikata, 2003; Tripp, 2004; Kevane and Gray, 2008; Ahawo, 2011; Ali *et al.*, 2011; Daley and Pallas, 2014; Ossome, 2014; Antwi-Agyei *et al.*, 2015; Njoh and Ananga, 2016; Ndi, 2017; Ayano, 2018; Njoh *et al.*, 2018; Brottem and Ba, 2019; Chigbu, 2019; Doghle *et al.*, 2019; Essougong and Teguia, 2019) submit that women are implicitly or explicitly marginalized when it comes to land tenure or property systems in SSA. A recent study by Chigbu (2019) highlights social, political, cultural and legal barriers impeding women's land rights and explained the different types of powers with which male members of the SSA societies dominate women regarding customary land tenure and property rights, systematically disempowering them sociopolitically and economically. These include 'linguistic power, son power, husband power, and father power' (Chigbu 2019, p. 126), that introduce principles of gender compensation as against gender competition in the design and implementation of land policy. Chigbu posits that ways of operationalizing equal and equitable access to land, prioritizing women's land access and securing land tenure should be a core development goal in SSA countries. Women are agents of community development, hence having equal and equitable rights to land will support their efforts in boosting community livelihood and productivity.

Daley and Pallas (2014) state that African women are more likely to be negatively affected by land deals than men. They elucidated practical measures to help change the land deals game for women. First, they cited a programme used in Liberia, Uganda, and Mozambique to protect rural communities against encroachments on land deals through community land titling and establishment of a legal and coherent community that can negotiate with outsiders. These communities can be supported (for example, by non-governmental organizations working with customary leaders and other relevant institutions) to establish internal land governance that protects the rights of vulnerable members of the community, such as women. If women's land tenure is secured, such as through land registration and titling, women's interests will be supported, mitigating the potential negative effects for them from land deals; and empowering women to participate more vocally in their communities' decision making. Second, companies can also be encouraged to make it easier for women to obtain employment and recognize their specific concerns. More family-friendly working practices that take care of women-specific concerns, such as allowing pregnant women to do non-physical work that does not require overtime, assisting them with school fees, and granting them leave of absence without pay to handle family emergencies and harvesting, can support and alleviate the relative income poverty of women. Third, during negotiations on proposed land deals, certain measures to support women's participation in decision making will boost the overall level of community engagement and challenge practices of women' seclusion from the public sphere (such as having women-only forums, whether customary or government sponsored). Daley and Pallas (2014) mention that these few examples of practical measures of implementing gender equality and responsible governance (access to productive resources, relative income poverty, and participation in decision making) can help change the land deals game for women. Doss *et al.* (2014b) maintain that some of the land deal issues transcend gender-equity concerns and do relate to broader problems of dispossession and loss of livelihoods. They state that huge gaps remain in our knowledge of gender and land rights, requiring urgent attention and systematic integration of gender analysis into mainstream research.

Djurfeldt (2020) suggests that the literature exposes a mismatch between laudable ambitions for gender equality detailed in formal legal code and the actual gender discriminatory customary practices and norms in different SSA countries, bringing to the fore the realities and illusions of gendered land tenure.

> Legal pluralism, poor legal infrastructure, low awareness and limited administrative and technical capacity pose challenges to implementing statutory law which in some cases (such as Rwanda), despite strong male resistance, has a strong gender-equalizing intention. In Uganda and Kenya patriarchal customary law prevails in practice, with consequences for tenure rights and access to land more generally, property rights within and upon dissolution of marriage and laws of succession.
>
> (Djurfeldt, 2020, p. 8)

For the latter, the praxis of the customary is driven by the lack of legal enforcement (caused by corruption and lack of political will at the central level). The magnitude of male resistance in the case of Rwanda becomes a formidable obstacle to genuinely enacting equal rights to land. Djurfeldt found much social and economic pressure on women to forfeit their land under conditions of growing population pressure, especially in many national contexts where law makers do not in earnest strive to protect women's property rights. Hence there are limited effects of land tenure reforms in SSA to redress gender inequality, and the poor possibilities for exploiting welfare effects from such reforms. Djurfeldt (2020) argues that this can be amended through a redress of broader structural and normative constraints to women's property rights. The author also unearths a fundamental tension between rural communities and land allocation processes built on lineage and efforts from the political centre and some women's groups to support the land rights of wives and widows.

Kevane and Gray (2008) studied the diminished access and diverted exclusion of women in SSA land tenure. While the situation is grim, they submitted that women have responded to reductions in access to land. These actions have enabled women to create new routes of access to land and in certain cases new rights. Women have mounted both legal and customary challenges to discriminatory inheritance laws, made use of anonymous land markets, organized formal cooperative groups to improve tenure rights, and manipulated customary rules using woman-to-woman marriages and mother–son partnerships. Njoh and Ananga (2016) argue that improving the education of women and having them participate actively in decent employment in SSA will help close the gender gap in access to land and other resources. Whitehead and Tsikata (2003) posit that some African women lawyers, a minority dissenting voice, are very equivocal about trusting the customary systems of land tenure and administration, preferring instead to look to the State for laws to protect women's interests and achieve gender justice regarding land claims. The authors, however, warned that much attention should also be paid to the actual power relations in the SSA rural areas and the implications for social groups (such as women) who may not be properly positioned and well represented in local-level power structures. In search of more robust knowledge, it is pertinent to zoom into gendered land tenure situations from various countries across SSA, to check for commonalities and differences. This has been done in the following section.

3.3 Gendered Land Tenure – Highlights of some Sub-Saharan Africa Country-Specific Cases

Uganda (East Africa)

Uganda's land rights have evolved from communal rights to that of individual ownership, and male-dominated practices that have excluded women. Constitutional provisions confer title of both a deceased husband's property rights and equal rights to property within a marriage to a wife; however, postcolonial patriarchal tradition prevails (Naybor, 2015). The Ugandan women's movement's opposition to policies and implementation of laws that exclude women has failed to effectively facilitate the required changes in unbiased access to land rights, though apparent victories in revisions to the letter of the law have been won. Naybor (2015) posits that women's access to land ownership and use are limited by misinterpretation of traditional law and a lack of enforcement of contemporary legal rights. The author conducted an empirical case study of widowed subsistence farmers in southern Uganda and unearthed the fact that women in Uganda continue to lose land, decreasing the possibility of gender equity in terms of land. One of the widows interviewed related that the land she uses does not belong to her but was lent to her by friends. The land is not fertile enough to support crop growth, hence she depends on her neighbour's food, making her see herself as a commoner and 'lost sheep' in her own country. Although Ugandan precolonial patterns of tribal land ownership were often patriarchal, this communal structure enabled protection of women's land use. The new global shift to cash-driven economies encouraged individual land ownership in Uganda and deconstructed protectionist tribal values that had threatened colonial export expansion. The reproductive work, performed almost exclusively by women, has decreased in value as the new currency-based economy weakened the need for subsistence living. The growth of a free market system of land title in Uganda has obviously created high land transaction costs and made it more difficult for smallholder farmers, many of whom are women, to acquire land (Baland *et al.*, 2007). The destabilization of subsistence farming by the introduction of the fictitious commodities of land, labour and money, has failed to yield economic stability, especially in rural areas where 'rural poverty is strongly associated with lack of land and livestock, as well as inability to secure nonfarm alternatives to diminishing farm opportunities' (Ellis and Bahiigwa, 2003, p. 997). There has been much advocacy for women's land rights in Uganda, but little progress has been made. Customary law continues to suppress the rule of law within the constitution and the contested Land Act of 1998. But for privatized title rights or customary rights, the key to protection of women's rights of inheritance, ownership, and use of land is enforcement. Doss *et al.* (2012) argue that there is a need for policies to protect land farmed by rural women to sustain income generation, especially in the case of marriage dissolution. The authors argue that this development may or may not require granting married women independent land rights; however, it will ensure that women have claims to land in the event of divorce or the death of their husbands. To correct gender imbalances in control of land use and ownership rights in Uganda, it is necessary to reconstruct both customary and statutory law to recognize women's value as related to land and to empower institutions to carry out the enactment of women's rights to land (Naybor, 2015).

Cameroon (Central Africa)

Equal rights and opportunities to resources are advocated in the legal framework in Cameroon; however, the majority of rural women in the country, who are mostly peasant farmers, can neither inherit nor own land due to gender discriminatory customary practices. A study of implications of gender discriminatory customary practices regarding land ownership in Anglophone Cameroon (Fonjong *et al.*, 2012; Fonjong *et al.*, 2013) shows that customs have a strong influence and impact on land tenure systems, and these have global implications on women's land rights, food security and sustainable development. Hence, gender equality in land matters can be made possible only if the critical role of ethics is recognized in pursuit of the economic motive of land rights. The authors criticized the unequal power relations in customary practices as unethical, devoid of any natural basis. These unwritten practices are more powerful than written laws, been the norm over a long period of time, and serve male economic and political agendas and privileges. They exploit the weaknesses of statutory laws, which, though gender neutral and non-discriminatory, cannot readily protect the interests of women and other vulnerable groups in practical terms. Fonjong *et al.* (2012) argue that we now live in a different society compared with the past. Men are no longer the sole breadwinners in respective families, single mothers are growing in number; hence the contribution of women to societal development has become enormous. It becomes clear that customary practices which are both discriminatory and static become barriers to evolving societies and should no longer be given prominence in this very dynamic and globalized era. This calls for broad-based consultations that will lead to gender-based land reforms, as improved women's ownership, control and access to land and other natural resources are key factors in fighting hunger and rural poverty. This notwithstanding, some authors offer a positive prospect in SSA, as women are gradually making claims over customary land; for example, among female rice producers in Ndop palin, Cameroon (Fonjong and Mbah, 2007); low-lying rice swamps in The Gambia; and Goin in south-western Burkina Faso (Fonjong *et al.*, 2012). Fonjong *et al.* (2013), in their empirical study, state that in Anglophone Cameroon, although women are taking increasing responsibilities in the education of the children, provision of food and bearing medical expenses in their households, there are still some traditional belief systems that impede their rights to land. The authors posit that these belief systems have a strong grip on the attitudes and mental perception of both genders on women's rights to land. Even though men and women agree on the need for women to own land, they disagree on how they should own the land. The logical outcome of this dilemma, according to the study, is that men own the land while women work on it. Women therefore have very few possibilities to carry out any long-term investment on land without the blessing of the men. The authors thus, advocate for gender mainstreaming in land reforms and creating gender consciousness among local community members (traditional authorities, men and women) as some of the ways of redressing gender discrimination in land ownership rights and fight against poverty, particularly in rural areas.

Ndi (2017), who conducted a study on the political economic processes and gendered consequences involved in large-scale land acquisition (LSLA) in rural Southwest Cameroon, explained how traditional cultural prescriptions in these regions have worked with contemporary land laws to masculinize power over land to the detriment of women. The author argues that amid societal discrimination over landownership rights, perceived gender differences between men and women appear 'rational' in the case of LSLA. Men follow their ascribed role in overt reactions, and women are more covert and much less vocal in land-related contests. Ndi (2017) therefore submits that new policies that promote rural women's land rights will not only empower them during land struggles, but they will also provide the communities with greater security to sustain ecologically viable livelihoods.

Njoh *et al.* (2018) also identified and analysed factors causing women to procure fewer land titles than men in Cameroon. The identified factors are grouped under five broad categories: institutional impediments; indigenous culture; received culture; productive and reproductive roles of women; and economic constraints. The authors therefore suggested a number of policy recommendations prominent among which are: to significantly reduce the cost and number of agencies and steps involved in the land title application process; to employ informal channels of communication regarding the dissemination of information on land; and to maintain office hours that recognize the tight schedules of women.

Ghana (West Africa)

Akaateba (2019) studied the politics of customary land rights transformation in peri-urban Ghana (Tamale and Techiman) and reported that state and market powers are mutually reinforcing regarding the politics of exclusion and the transformation of customary land rights in peri-urban Ghana. The author posits that despite international land policy trends that praise the adaptability and negotiability of customary tenure, customary tenure regimes can be manipulated, in synergy with market forces, to produce exclusionary outcomes. Power asymmetries and social inequalities which are common among the various actors in peri-urban land delivery have led to the reinterpretation and transformation of customary land tenure system. Hence, indigenes of peri-urban areas who hitherto had usufructuary interests in land are displaced of such land rights as well as their agrarian livelihoods. Akaateba (2019) states that powerful chiefs and public bureaucrats who can draw upon both *de facto* and *de jure* systems, as well as prospective developers with capital, hijack and benefit from the proceeds of peri-urban land conversions. The author therefore calls for a cautious stance on strengthening customary tenure systems in Ghana's current land policy reform approaches to guarantee that usufructuary right holders are protected. It is important that closer attention in both policy and research needs be paid to who benefits and who loses from strengthening customary tenure systems and integrating them with state land administration systems.

Antwi-Agyei *et al.* (2015), who studied impacts of land tenure arrangements on the adaptive capacity of marginalized groups in Ghana's Ejura Sekyedumase and Bongo districts, suggested that women's rights with regards to land ownership should be formalized in land policy to reduce cultural discriminations against them. This will aid women to secure property rights over land and land use through mechanisms such as collateral to access credit, which could be used to implement climate adaptation practices. They also add that the rights of migrant workers should also be recognized in Ghana's land policy to provide them with opportunities for adaptation in a similar manner to non-migrants.

Doghle *et al.* (2019) posit that customary practices deprive women of land ownership and limit their access rights. Their study results in Nandom District, Ghana, show that female-headed households experienced much more severe food security conditions than male-headed and co-headed households. This is due to the differences in land ownership and access rights; and they called for the promotion of equal ownership and access rights for all gender groups, to fight problems of food insecurity and poverty in Africa.

Zambia (Southern Africa)

Dillon and Voena (2018) studied the relationship between the widow's land inheritance rights and land investments in Zambia. They explored whether the threat of land expropriation upon widowhood prevents households from fallowing, applying fertilizer, and using labour-intensive techniques; and found lower levels of land investments in land quality by married couples in villages where widows are not allowed to inherit. This is because of concern over prospective loss of land by the wives, and this happens even while the husband is alive. Dillon and Voena (2018), in Zambia, demonstrated a strong causal connection between the security of widow's land inheritance rights and investments in land productivity.

To reach conclusions and policy recommendations from gendered land tenure debates which have shown marked similarities (those of implicit and explicit marginalization of women) across SSA countries; the next section of this chapter sought further objective statistics drawn from previous empirical studies regarding gendered land tenure debates in SSA.

3.4 Gendered Land Indicators and Statistics across Sub-Saharan Africa

Doss *et al.* (2015) criticized the data collection methods and statistics used by many authors to reach conclusions regarding gendered land tenure in Africa, in terms of their empirical evidence and reliability. They, after exploring existing estimates and created indicators using FAO's Gender and Land Rights Database, DHS, and the LSMS-ISA database, acknowledge that many gaps remain, in terms of country coverage and quality of data available. They posit that large geographical areas in northern and central Africa have virtually no estimates. Out of the 20 countries represented, only nine can be triangulated having two or more data points. Hence the authors posit that many often cited references regarding women's land ownership are not very reliable. Their study, however, found that this situation notwithstanding, the pattern of women possessing less land than men, regardless of ownership conceptualization, is very consistent; and in many cases, there are large gender gaps. A nine-country analysis from the FAO's Gender and Land Rights Database shows that women account for an average of 22% of agricultural landholders (ranging from 3.1% in Mali to 50.5% in Cape Verde). Results from surveys conducted by DHS in ten countries show that as a country-level average, 39% of women own land either solely or jointly, and 12% of women own land solely, which contrasts to 48% and 31% of men, respectively. Results from LSMS-ISA's database derived from six countries show that of the total land area owned or accessed by households, women collectively own (documented and undocumented) 31% in Malawi, followed by Uganda (16%), Tanzania (15%), Niger (8%), and Nigeria (3%). Comparatively, men solely own, on average, 21.8 times as much land area as women in Nigeria, and between 1.1 and 6.9 times as much land area as land solely owned by women in the other countries. Doss *et al.* (2015), towards their contribution to improving research and policy on women's land ownership in Africa, therefore conclude that better clarification of 'ownership' and its indicators is needed regarding gendered patterns of land ownership. This will enable comparisons between countries or studies to discern overall patterns. Standardized definitions and methodology, and differences in methodology need to be made explicit when replicating or comparing studies. Comparing the proportion of women who own land and the proportion of men who own land will make this comparison more meaningful. How jointly owned land is treated will also unearth inequality in land ownership. For example, in Uganda, women own only 18% of land individually, but own another 48% jointly with men. Doss *et al.* (2015) also posit that the definitions and data that most closely resemble the country context should be used as far as possible. For example, in the African context, many countries have community- or clan-owned land. How this ownership relates to individual ownership should be assessed qualitatively before questionnaire development, enabling such categories and relationships to be properly captured. Methods of collecting individual-level land data need to be standardized, and surveys should be asking who within the household owns the land and should allow for the inclusion of multiple names to facilitate analysis of both individual and joint ownership.

Researchers should also systematically test whether the identity of the respondent in these surveys significantly affects the validity and consistency of individual responses within the household (Fisher *et al.*, 2010). Rigorous, well-defined, and contextually relevant measurements of gender differences in land ownership and control, implemented in population-representative surveys that use countries' statistical systems, will be relevant to future efforts to reduce gender gaps in bundles of land ownership rights (Doss *et al.*, 2015).

Yngstrom (2002) posits that land reform in SSA is situated in evolutionary models, assuming that landholding systems are evolving into individualized ownership systems with greater market integration. However, gender as an analytical category has been excluded in evolutionary models. Women are still seen to be dependent on men as wives of landholders in ideal households. The study by Gaddis *et al.* (2018), using the Demographic and Health Surveys' (DHS) data from 28 countries, explored gender gaps in property (land and housing) ownership in SSA, and came up with the results that: men are about three times as likely as women to have sole ownership over property; gender gaps are minimized if joint ownership is taken into consideration, but still materially disadvantage women; and men are significantly more likely to own property than women even after controlling for a host of other factors.

The questions around access to land, land ownership, formalization, and documentation, and right to sell the land were explored by Doss *et al.* (2015). It is to be noted that regarding formal land documentation in sub-Saharan Africa, individual arrangements will vary in the case of communally or clan-owned land, depending on the rules governing the clan, and land may or may not be formally documented. Individual and joint ownership of land, for example having land titled solely to women or jointly with their husband (or another household member) are also being discussed and it has been found that the patterns of such ownerships are often complex and differ markedly across contexts, as joint ownership does not directly imply equal ownership (Doss *et al.*, 2014a).

From the analyses and discussions presented in the previous sections, it is necessary to synthesize this chapter and propose policy recommendations based on qualitative and quantitative data generated from this discussion.

3.5 Synthesis and Policy Recommendations

The issues of empirical research evidence and reliability regarding gendered land tenure in SSA notwithstanding, Verma (2014), focusing on policy implementation, alludes to the huge gap between policy and law, and their just (fair and effective) implementation. Though agents of the state want to enforce laws requiring more gender-empowering practice, many states in SSA do not have the capacity to do so. This unfair and ineffective implementation is partially therefore, a result of the weakness of so many SSA states (De Schutter, 2011). In many of these countries, the institutions of the state play only a marginal role, and this is specifically true in the isolated rural areas where many large land acquisitions and redistribution are occurring. It is likely to be for this reason that many academics turn to the international legal mechanisms of justice and human rights (Millar, 2015). Verma (2014, p. 69), for example, calls for 'a set of enforceable and binding international regulations and legal mechanisms'; Claeys and Vanlogqueren (2013) ascribe great emphasis on the developing 'right to food'; and Wisborg (2014, p. 35) mentions the various treaties and agreements that apparently protect human rights to 'food, home, paid work, property, political participation, gender equality, and racial equality'. Nonetheless, the problem again lies with fair and effective implementation. Wisborg himself posits that 'those who are most directly affected by global processes of dispossession have the least power to defend ethical principles and human rights' (2014, p. 42), while Edelman *et al.* (2013) state that international legal instruments believed to protect such rights compete for primacy with those that protect free trade and agro-business interests. It must be noted that the key problem is that international laws rely on the state for their enforcement. Most SSA countries are signatories to many international legal mechanisms but simply do not have the capacity, or the willpower to enforce them on the ground.

In the same vein, Polavarapu (2013) posits that customary law is defined by a single or few leaders. Subjecting norms to much negotiation, by both men and women, with an honest objective to revisit each of the norms when concerns are raised, would be more in line with the oft-discussed original driving force of customary law: to take care of the needs of the community. In practical terms, increasing the number of women within decision-making bodies is more likely to ensure that the results of any consultations are reflective of women's needs. More so, establishing a firm system of accountability is necessary to prevent customary institutions from operating outside the lines of constitutional and international rights requirements. If these fundamental changes are not made, women will be unable to achieve substantive equality under the customary system. This is also in line with Whitehead and Tsikata (2003) who argue that significant changes need to be made in relation to political and legal practices and cultures, before SSA states can begin to deliver gender justice with respect to land.

Formal and legal rights to land do not necessarily provide women secure rights, if such rights are not made socially legitimate and enforceable. Enforcing the formal policy on land rights can be supported by Kevane and Gray's (2008) findings on successful actions that have enabled women to create new routes of access to land and in certain cases new rights. Women should continue to mount both legal and customary challenges to discriminatory inheritance laws, make use of anonymous land markets, organized formal cooperative groups to improve tenure rights, and manipulate customary rules depending on their national or local contexts (for example, using woman-to-woman marriages and mother–son partnerships). In many SSA countries, a childless widow or a widow without sons is permitted to take a wife and give her a part of her land as bride wealth to protect her access to her deceased husband's land. The resulting woman-to-woman marriage will give the older 'female husband' an heir; the child of the young women (fathered perhaps by an agnate of the older woman) would be a customary legitimate heir to the late husband.

This chapter has more implications for development policy making in general and land policy in SSA. These countries should redirect their efforts to improve the education and increasing the formal labour participation of women. This can constitute a viable means of closing the gender gap in access to land and other resources (see Njoh and Ananga, 2016). Chigbu *et al.* (2019) warned that women are heterogeneous in their land tenure experiences and a highly differentiated gender group. The authors, for example, posit that high-income and middle-income women tend to benefit more from efforts towards improving land access and tenure security challenges, compared with the poor, vulnerable and disempowered women. Hence, they suggest that researchers and policy makers should beware of over-generalizations in land policy and programmes.

The major challenge of SSA countries in this century regarding gender-neutral land tenure is to ensure that the expected outcome, in the near future, become a celebrated reality rather than a lasting illusion. The civil society, researchers, traditional leaders, and government bodies all have roles to play. From the literature analysis, it seems that there is more gender gap, regarding land tenure, in rural than urban societies in SSA. Urban areas are more guided by formal policy and legal rights, while rural areas are guided predominantly by customary norms and practices. We end this chapter by proposing research and policy recommendations to this effect, in SSA, based on literature analysis.

- Researchers should use more in-depth, objective, and contextually relevant measurements to explore and assess gender differences in land ownership and control; such studies should be conducted using SSA countries' statistical systems and population-representative surveys to reduce gender gaps in bundles of land ownership rights.
- It is imperative to reconstruct both customary and statutory laws to recognize women's value in relation to land and to build institutional capabilities to carry out the enactment of women's rights to land.
- It is necessary to adapt customary land inheritance practices to move closer to a rights-based approach to gender equality. This calls for broad-based consultations that will ultimately give rise to gender-based land reforms, as improved women's ownership, control and access to land and other natural resources are enabling factors in fighting hunger and rural poverty.
- In the customary system, ensuring that women are quantitatively and qualitatively represented within decision-making bodies are most likely to ensure that the results of any consultations are more reflective of women's needs. More so, having a firm system of accountability is expedient to prevent customary institutions from deviating from

constitutional and international rights requirements.

- Advocating for gender mainstreaming in land reforms and creating gender consciousness among local community members (traditional authorities, men and women) is one of the viable ways of redressing gender discrimination in land ownership rights and fighting against poverty, particularly in rural areas.
- Formal and legal rights to land should be made socially legitimate and enforceable. Women should continue to make use of organized formal cooperative groups to improve tenure rights, and manipulate customary rules depending on their national or local contexts. Women who mount legal and customary challenges to discriminatory inheritance laws should be consulted and their concerns addressed.
- Women education should be taken more seriously in SSA. Improving women's education and increasing their formal labour participation is more likely to empower women and add impetus to their land struggle.
- In view of the key role of women in the society and their economic standing in SSA, it is practicable to significantly reduce the costs, number of agencies and steps involved in the land title application process. It will also be beneficial to make use of informal channels of communication regarding the dissemination of information on land; and to maintain office hours that recognize the tight schedules of women.

References

Ahawo, O. (2011) Policy for land and gender in Kenya: Reality or illusion? *Journal of Poverty Alleviation and International Development*, 2(2), 1–16.

Akaateba, M.A. (2019) The politics of customary land rights transformation in peri-urban Ghana: Powers of exclusion in the era of land commodification. *Land Use Policy*, 88. DOI: 10.1016/j.landusepol.2019.104197.

Ali, D.A., Deininger, K. and Goldstein, M. (2011) *Environmental and Gender Impacts of Land Tenure Regularization in Africa: Pilot evidence from Rwanda.* Policy Research Working Paper 5765. The World Bank Development Research Group: Agriculture and Rural Development Team & Africa Region Gender Team.

Antwi-Agyei, P., Dougill, A.J. and Stringer, L.C. (2015) Impacts of land tenure arrangements on the adaptive capacity ofmarginalized groups: The case of Ghana's Ejura Sekyedumase and Bongo districts. *Land Use Policy*, 49, 203–212.

Asiama, S.O. (1997) Crossing the barrier of time: The Asanteh woman in urban development. *Africa*, 52(2), 212–236.

Ayano, M.F. (2018) Rural land registration in Ethiopia: Myths and realities. *Law & Society Review*, 52(4), 1060–1097.

Baland, J., Gaspart, F., Platteau, J. and Place, F. (2007) The Distributive Impact of Land Markets in Uganda. *Economic Development and Cultural Change*, 55(2), 283–311.

Brottem, L.V. and Ba, L. (2019) Gendered livelihoods and land tenure: The case of artisanal gold miners in Mali, West Africa. *Geoforum*, 105, 54–62.

Chigbu, U.E. (2015) Repositioning culture for development: Women and development in a Nigerian rural community. *Community, Work & Family*, 18(3), 334–350.

Chigbu, U.E. (2019) Anatomy of women's landlessness in the patrilineal customary land tenure systems of sub-Saharan Africa and a policy pathway. *Land Use Policy*, 86, 126–135.

Chigbu, U.E., Paradza, G. and Dachaga, W. (2019) Differentiations in women's land tenure experiences: Implications for women's land access and tenure security in sub-Saharan Africa. *Land*, 8, 1–21.

Claeys, P. and Vanlogqueren, G. (2013) The minimum human rights principles applicable to large-scale land acquisitions or lease. *Globalizations*, 10(1), 193–198.

Daley, E. and Pallas, S. (2014) Women and land deals in Africa and Asia: Weighing the implications and changing the game. *Feminist Economics*, 20(1), 178–201.

De Schutter, O. (2011) How not to think of land-grabbing: Three critiques of large-scale investments in farmland. *The Journal of Peasant Studies*, 38(2), 249–279.

Dillon, B. and Voena, A. (2018) Widows' land rights and agricultural investment. *Journal of Development Economics*, 135, 449–460.

Djurfeldt, A.A. (2020) Gendered land rights, legal reform and social norms in the context of land fragmentation – A review of the literature for Kenya, Rwanda and Uganda. *Land Use Policy*, 90. DOI: 10.1016/j.landusepol.2019.104305.

Doghle, K., Owusu-Ansah, J. and Akaabre, P.B. (2019) The influences of gendered customary land tenure system on food security in Nandom District, Ghana. *African Journal of Land Policy and Geospatial Sciences, Special Issue* 2, 71–92.

Doss, C., Truong, M., Nabanoga, G. and Namaalwa, J. (2012). Women, Marriage and Asset Inheritance in Uganda. *Development Policy Review*, 35(5), 597–616.

Doss, C., Meinzen-Dick, R. and Bomuhangi, A. (2014a) Who owns the land? Perspectives from rural Ugandans and implications for large-scale land acquisitions. *Feminist Economics*, 20(1), 76–100.

Doss, C., Summerfield, G. and Tsikata, D. (2014b) Land, gender, and food security. *Feminist Economics*, 20(1), 1–23.Doss, C., Kovarik, C., Peterman, A., Quisumbing, A. and van den Bold, M. (2015). Gender inequalities in ownership and control of land in Africa: Myth and reality. *Agricultural Economics*, 46, 403–434.

Doss, C., Meinzen-Dick, R., Quisumbing, A. and Theis, S. (2018). Women in agriculture: Four myths. *Global Food Security*, 16, 69–74.

Edelman, M., Oya, C. and Borras, S.M. (2013) Global land grabs: Historical processes, theoretical and methodological implications and current trajectories. *Third World Quarterly*, 34(9), 1517–1531.

Ellis, F. and Bahiigwa, G. (2003) Livelihoods and rural poverty reduction in Uganda. *World Development*, 31(6), 997–1013.

Essougong, U.P.K. and Teguia, S.J.M. (2019) How secure are land rights in Cameroon? A review of the evolution of land tenure system and its implications on tenure security and rural livelihoods. *GeoJournal*, 84, 1645–1656.

Evans, R. (2016) Gendered struggles over land: Shifting inheritance practices among the Serer in rural Senegal. *Gender, Place & Culture*, 23(9), 1360–1375.

Ezeuduji, I.O. (2015) Strategic event-based rural tourism development for sub-Saharan Africa. *Current Issues in Tourism*, 18(3), 212–228.

Fisher, M., Reimer, J.J. and Carr, E.R. (2010) Who should be interviewed in surveys of household income? *World Development*, 38(7), 966–973.

Fonjong, L. and Mbah, F. (2007) The fortunes and misfortunes of women rice producers in Ndop, Cameroon and the implications for gender roles. *Journal of International Women's Studies*, 8(4), 133–147.

Fonjong, L., Sama-Lang, I.F. and Fombe, L.F. (2012) Implications of customary practices on gender discrimination in land ownership in Cameroon. *Ethics and Social Welfare*, 6(3), 260–274.

Fonjong, L., Fombe, L. and Sama-Lang, I. (2013) The paradox of gender discrimination in land ownership and women's contribution to poverty reduction in Anglophone Cameroon. *GeoJournal*, 78, 575–589.

Food and Agriculture Organization (FAO) (2011) *State of Food and Agriculture 2010–2011: Women and Agriculture Closing the Gender Gap for Development*. Food and Agriculture Organization, Rome. Available at: http://www.fao.org/publications/sofa/2010-11/en/ (accessed 15 June 2020).

Gaddis, I., Lahoti, R. and Li, W. (2018) *Gender Gaps in Property Ownership in Sub-Saharan Africa*. Policy Research Working Paper 8573, World Bank Group, Research Support Team.

Goldstein, M. and Udry, C. (2008) The profits of power: Land rights and agricultural investment in Ghana. *Journal of Political Economy*, 116(6), 981–1022.

Izumi, K. (1999) Liberalisation, gender, and the land question in sub-Saharan Africa. *Gender and Development*, 7(3), 9–18.

Kevane, M. and Gray, L. (2008) Diminished access, diverted exclusion: Women and land tenure in sub-Saharan Africa. DOI: 10.2139/ssrn.1096247.

Kumar, N. and Quisumbing, A.R. (2012) Beyond 'death do us part': The long-term implications of divorce perceptions on women's well-being and child schooling in rural Ethiopia. *World Development*, 40(12), 2478–2489.

Kumar, N., and Quisumbing, A.R. (2013) Gendered impacts of the 2007–2008 food price crisis: Evidence using panel data. *Food Policy*, 38, 11–22.

Mathaai, W. (2003) *The Green Belt Movement: Sharing the Approach and Experience*. Lantern Books, New York.

Millar, G. (2015) 'We have no voice for that': Land rights, power, and gender in rural Sierra Leone. *Journal of Human Rights*, 14, 445–462.

Naybor, D. (2015) Land as fictitious commodity: The continuing evolution of women's land rights in Uganda. *Gender, Place and Culture*, 22(6), 884–900.

Ndi, F.A. (2017) Land grabbing: A gendered understanding of perceptions and reactions from affected communities in Nguti Subdivision of South West Cameroon. *Development Policy Review*, 2017, 37, 348–366.

Njoh, A.J. and Ananga, E. (2016) The development hypothesis of women empowerment in the Millennium Development Goals tested in the context women's access to land in Africa. *Social Indicators Research*, 128, 89–104.

Njoh, A.J., Bigon, L., Ananga, E.O. and Ayuk-Etang, R.A. (2018) Institutional, economic and socio-cultural factors accounting for gender-based inequalities in land title procurement in Cameroon. *Land Use Policy*, 78, 116–125.

Ossome, L. (2014) Can the law secure women's rights to land in Africa? Revisiting tensions between culture and land commercialization. *Feminist Economics*, 20(1), 155–177.

Otsuka, K., Quisumbing, A.R., Payongayong, E. and Aidoo, J.B. (2003) Land tenure and the management of land and trees: The case of customary land areas of Ghana. *Environment and Development Economics*, 8(1), 77–104.

Peterman, A. (2011) Women's property rights and gendered policies: Implications for women's long-term welfare in rural Tanzania. *Journal of Development Studies*, 47(1), 1–30.

Polavarapu, A. (2013) Reconciling indigenous and women's rights to land in Sub-Saharan Africa. *Georgia Journal of International and Comparative Law*, 42, 93–131.

Quisumbing, A.R. (Ed.). (2003) *Household Decisions, Gender and Development: A Synthesis of Recent Research*. International Food Policy Research Institute, Washington, DC, USA.

Quisumbing, A.R., Payongayong, E., Aidoo, J.B. and Otsuka, K. (2001) Women's land rights in the transition to individualized ownership: Implications for the management of tree resources in western Ghana. *Economic Development and Cultural Change*, 50(1), 157–182.

Tripp, A.M. (2004) Women's movements, customary law, and land rights in Africa: The case of Uganda. *African Studies Quarterly*, 7(4), 1–19.

United Nations Statistics Division. (2011) *Standard Country and Area Codes Classifications (M49)*. Available at: http://unstats.un.org/unsd/methods/m49/m49regin.htm (accessed 3 June 2014).

Verma, R. (2014) Land grabs, power, and gender in East and Southern Africa: So, what's new? *Feminist Economics*, 20(1), 52–75.

Whitehead, A. and Tsikata, D. (2003) Policy discourses on women's land rights in sub-Saharan Africa: The implications of the re-turn to the customary. *Journal of Agrarian Change*, 3(1/2), 67–112.

Wisborg, P. (2014) Transnational land deals and gender equality: Utilitarian and human rights approaches. *Feminist Economics*, 20(1), 24–51.

Yngstrom, I. (2002) Women, wives and land rights in Africa: Situating gender beyond the household in the debate over land policy and changing tenure systems. *Oxford Development Studies*, 30(1), 21–40.

4 Land Governance and Gender in Support of the Global Agenda 2030

Uchendu Eugene Chigbu*[1] and Stig Enemark[2]
[1]*Department of Land and Property Sciences, Namibia University of Science and Technology, Windhoek, Namibia;* [2]*Department of Planning, Aalborg University, Aalborg, Denmark*

4.1 Introduction

The meanings behind the concepts of *governance* and *gender* are diverse. Generally, the meaning of governance can be summarized to imply all 'the procedures involved in making or not making decisions and the process involved in implementing or not implementing made decisions (Chigbu, 2021a, p. 18). It is this broad meaning of governance that makes its derivative, *land governance*, also diverse. Land governance covers all activities associated with the management and administration of land and natural resources that are required to fulfil political and social objectives and achieve sustainable development. This relates to policy making and, more specifically, to the design of the legal and institutional frameworks for the land sector. The operational component of the land management concept is the range of land administration functions that include the areas of land tenure, land value, land use and land development (Williamson *et al.*, 2010). All these functions are essential to ensure the control and management of the people-to-land relationship and the environmental, economic, and social outcomes emerging from it.

The concept of *gender* refers to the cultural and socioeconomic attributes associated with being male or female in societies. It is a construct that is important in the development of societies because being a man or a woman is more than simply a matter of mere biological and physical characteristics of people. Gender, despite its highly contentious meaning, is a universal issue. It is an essential aspect of land governance because legal and policy framework (and their associated land tenure types) are gender sensitive. Derived from the concept of gender are *gender equality* and *gender equity*, both of which represent critical aspects of human rights.

> Gender equity is the process of being fair to women and men. To ensure fairness, strategies and measures must often be available to compensate for the historical and social disadvantages that prevent women and men from operating on a level playing field.
>
> (UNFPA, 2005)

It is gender equity that leads to gender equality (i.e. the equal enjoyment by women and men of socially valued goods, opportunities, resources and rewards). In the context of socioeconomic development, land governance promotes gender through its empowerment of people (men and women) with a focus on identifying and redressing power imbalances in the ownership and use of land and other natural resources.

Both land governance and gender are crucial aspects of the global development agenda

*Corresponding author: echigbu@nust.na

 Land Governance and Gender: The Tenure-Gender Nexus in Land Management and Land Policy (ed. U.E. Chigbu)
DOI: 10.1079/9781789247664.0004

which must be achieved to ensure sustainable development in the world. The global agenda landscape has changed over the recent decades. In the 1990s the focus was on sustainable development. In the 2000s the Millennium Development Goals (MDGs) were adopted as the overarching agenda worldwide. Starting in the early 2010s, there was increasingly a focus on climate change and environment-related challenges such as natural disasters, food shortage and environmental degradation. In 2015 the MDGs were replaced by the Sustainable Development Goals or SDGs (UN, 2015a) which was adopted by all the world´s leaders and set the scene towards 2030 target. This 2030 global agenda is ambitious and calls for interventions at all levels of government, the private sector and civil society. Land governance plays a key role in this regard in terms of setting the policies and the legal and institutional framework for managing the rights, restrictions and responsibilities in land facing the challenges of sustainable use of land and other natural resources. Gender issues are at the core of some of those policies (including legal principles and institutional frameworks) which are regulated under land governance. For instance, ensuring gender equity for land and property rights is a key principle in the governance of land (Enemark *et al.*, 2016).

This chapter looks at the role land governance and gender play in support of the Global Agenda 2030. The chapter begins by introducing land governance and gender. This is followed by their relationships and connections with the SDGs. Then their roles and challenges encountered in their roles.

4.2 Land Governance, Gender and Global Agenda 2030: Tripartite Relationship

Land governance is about the policies, processes and institutions by which land, property and natural resources are managed (Enemark, 2012). All countries deal with the management of land. In the more developed (Western) world, the systems for governing and administering land issues have evolved to an advanced level for coping with cultural and economic development. Looking at the less developed world, and especially sub-Saharan Africa, the basic systems of land registration are still not fully in place. Even where they are in place, they tend to serve only the elites and the perspectives of human rights and sustainability are largely ignored. In such regions, there is a need to improve the land governance systems more generally to cope with current and future challenges.

The organizational structures for land governance and administration differ widely between countries and regions throughout the world and reflect the cultural and judicial setting of the country and jurisdiction. Furthermore, the judicial and institutional arrangements may change over time to better support implementation of land policies and good land governance. A simple entry point for understanding the land governance issues is a reflection on the hierarchy of land issues from the land governance level to the land parcel (Williamson *et al.*, 2010), where:

- **Land governance** is about the policies, processes and institutions by which land, property and natural resources are managed.
- **Land policy** determines values, objectives and the legal framework for management of a society's major asset, its land.
- **Land management** includes the management of land and natural resources for achieving sustainable development.
- **Land administration system** includes the core functions of land tenure, land value, land use and land development in support of efficient land markets and effective land use management.
- **Spatial data infrastructure** provides access to and interoperability of cadastral and other land-related information.
- **Cadastre** provides the spatial integrity of every land parcel. This parcel identification provides the link for securing land rights and planning and control of the use of land.
- **Land parcel** is the key object for identification of land rights and administration of restrictions

The hierarchical evolution of land issues and their relationships illustrates the complexity of organizing policies, institutions, processes and information for dealing with land in any society. However, it provides a conceptual understanding of land governance which also provides the overall guidance for dealing with land governance in any society, no matter their level of development.

Gender relates to the characteristics and power dynamics that exist between men (and boys) and women (and girls) concerning their role in their communities. Women's rights to control and access land are often less secure than men's in many countries of the Global South (Landesa, 2013). Women are less likely to own or control land, even in situations where they perform more than half of the agricultural labour globally. This imbalance in men's and women's access to and control of land resources produces an imbalance in general development activities within countries, regions and local communities. Hence, there is a need for closing the gender gap in land rights where, for example, a customary land tenure system treats men more favourably than women. These sorts of land tenure regimes that assign primary rights to men and secondary rights to women leads to women's exclusion from structures of wealth and power. Land governance and gender characteristics and practices have the potential to address these structural challenges embedded in land tenure systems. This is because land governance and gender have both symmetrical relationship and complementary relationships (Fig. 4.1).

A symmetrical relationship exists because land governance and gender separately emphasize fairness in land distribution (and exercise of land rights) and equal human rights in the use of natural resources, respectively. Land governance uses tools (such as land policies and regulatory frameworks to decide on land use opportunities and the allocation of land rights. Gender uses power relations among men and women to allocate human activities (i.e. development activities in the context of SDGs) activities within communities that can create good or bad societal changes. A complementary relationship exists between land governance and gender because land governance provides the platform (e.g. through land-based interventions) which enables implementation of gender practices to achieve gender-related goals. Gender also enables men-and-women-related rules, values and principles that enable land governance to be gender responsive through policies, processes and decision making. Therefore, when gender is unequal in land matters, land governance has the potential to create an inclusive system. Where land governance is gender blind, the principles of gender can make it to become gender responsive.

The SDGs is a set of globally agreed goals that put focus on the humanity (people) and the earth (including land). The SDGs then provides a platform for operationalizing both gender and land governance in interlinked ways (Fig. 4.2).

Evidence from experiences and cases studies from around the world confirm that secure land (and natural resource) rights are a cornerstone

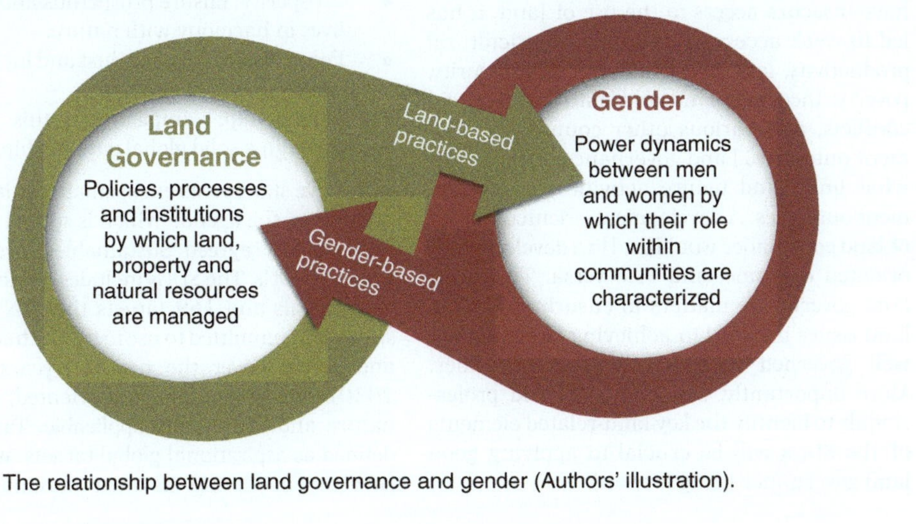

Fig. 4.1. The relationship between land governance and gender (Authors' illustration).

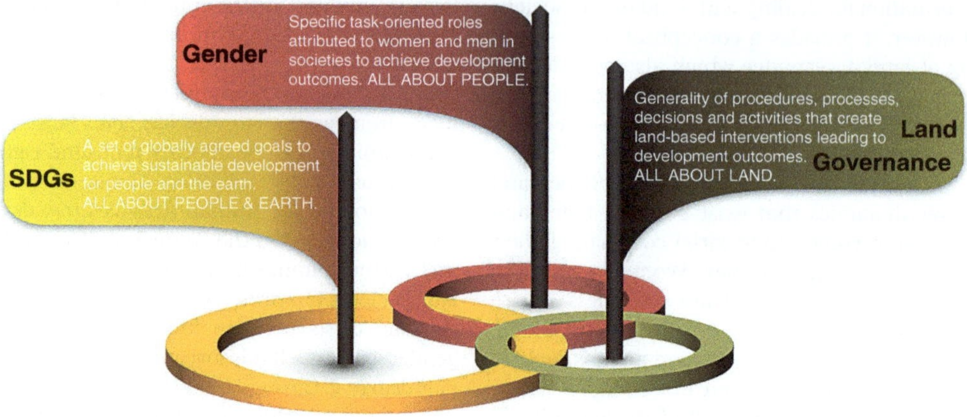

Fig. 4.2. Relationship between land governance, gender and Global Agenda 2030 (SDGs) (Authors' illustration).

of socioeconomic development. Particularly, land access and secure tenure on land are the key factors for poverty alleviation and reduction in the economically less developed countries of the world. How people use and own land (or exercise the rights they have on land) is linked to their well-being, as well as the well-being of their immediate community or society (Chigbu, 2021b). Where people have secure tenure in their holding and use of land it has resulted in improved land and resource governance that led to local economic growth, improved afforestation or reduced deforestation, food security, increased on-farm investment, women and youth empowerment, and a range of other pro-development benefits. However, where people have insecure access to the use of land, it has led to weak access to credit, poor agricultural productivity, land degradation, food insecurity, poverty, incessant land and natural resources conflicts, and various other counter-development outcomes. Land governance, therefore, is what links land tenure activities to development outcomes. A development-oriented system of land governance would lead to a development-oriented outcome, and vice versa. Therefore, land governance matters in ensuring that the land issues involved in achieving the SDGs are well governed to secure reliable outcomes. More importantly, the ability of land professionals to identify the key land-related elements of the SDGs will be crucial to applying good land governance going forward.

4.3. The Elements of Land Governance and Gender within the SDGs

The **Global Agenda 2030** was presented in the UN declaration on 'Transforming our world: the 2030 Agenda for Sustainable Development' (UN, 2015a) as adopted by all the world´s leaders are based on five key P-statements and ending up by stating 'As we embark in the collective journey, we pledge that no one will be left behind'. The five P-statements are as follows.

- People: End poverty and hunger in all forms and ensure dignity and equality.
- Planet: Protect our planet´s natural resources and climate for future generations.
- Prosperity: Ensure prosperous and fulfilling lives in harmony with nature.
- Peace: Foster peaceful, just and inclusive societies.
- Partnership: Implement this agenda through a solid global partnership.

These five statements encapsulate the land components of the agenda which is spread over several globally agreed Sustainable Development Goals or SDGs. The SDGs includes a universal set of 17 goals and 169 targets that UN member states are committed to use to frame their agenda and policies over the next 15 years (2016–2030). The goals are action-oriented, global in nature and universally applicable. Targets are defined as aspirational global targets, with each government setting its own national targets guided by the global level of ambition but considering national circumstances. The goals and targets integrate economic, social and environmental aspects and recognize their interlinkages in achieving sustainable development in all its dimensions.

The SDGs, thereby, provide a framework around which governments, especially in developing countries, can develop policies and overseas aid programmes designed to alleviate poverty and improve the lives of the poor, as well as a rallying point for NGOs to hold them to account. In other words, the SDGs are key drivers for countries throughout the world – and especially developing countries – to develop adequate and accountable land policies and regulatory frameworks for meeting the goals.

While the MDGs in theory applied to all countries, they were considered targets for poor countries to achieve with support from the wealthier countries. In contrast, every country throughout the world will be expected to work towards achieving the SDGs. This relates to, for example, Goal 10 aiming to 'Reduce inequality within and among countries'. This challenge of reducing inequity has appeared in most developed countries over recent decades. The SDGs, this way, seek to build on the Millennium Development Goals and complete what they did not achieve. The SDGs also seek to realize the human rights of all and to achieve gender-related outcomes (such as the empowerment of all women and girls). They are integrated and indivisible and balance the three dimensions of sustainable development: the economic, social, and environmental (UN, 2015a). The SDGs include seven goals with a significant land or land governance focus and five goals related to gender component (see Table 4.1).

Table 4.1 shows the SDGs and identifies their land governance and gender elements (shaded). With regards to land governance, Goal 1 calls for ending poverty in all its forms everywhere, and target 1.4 states that by 2030 all men and women will have equal rights to ownership and control over land and other forms of property. Similarly, the land component is referred to in targets of Goal 2 on ending hunger and Goal 5 on gender equity. Land and land use planning are key components in the targets of Goal 11 on achieving sustainable urbanization. Land governance and management are included in targets of Goal 13 on climate action and Goal 15 on promoting sustainable use of land. Finally, (land) governance is a key component in most of the targets for achieving Goal 16 on promoting peace, justice and strong institutions.

Concerning gender, goals 1 and 2 call for ending poverty and hunger, respectively. These goals cannot be achieved without ensuring that men and women have equal access to land resources. Goals 4 and 5 require that women be given equal opportunities in education, and for gender (in the context of equality) to be treated as a principle for delivering development in any form, respectively. Goal 5 is gender specific. It is a definite statement on gender equality as a principle and practice in all aspects of human activities, while Goal 8 calls for inclusiveness in employment.

In general, these SDGs are a call for action by all countries to promote prosperity while protecting the planet. They recognize that ending poverty must go together with strategies for economic growth, and also address societal needs including education, health, social protection and job creation, all within the frame of tackling climate change issues, biodiversity loss and environmental protection. People-to-land relationships directly and indirectly influence all SDGs (UN-GGIM, 2020).

4.4 The Monitoring and Assessment of Land Governance and Gender

The targets developed for the SDGs serve as guidelines to help governments at all levels to develop implementation strategies and allocate resources accordingly (ICLEI, 2015). Data and indicators play critical parts in ensuring transparency and accountability in the 2030 Agenda. They also help in monitoring the progress towards the SDG targets at the local.

The goals and targets of the SDGs are followed up and reviewed based on a global framework of about 240 indicators. An annual progress report on achieving the SDGs is prepared by the UN, based on data produced by national statistical systems and information collected at the regional level (UN, 2016). The targets and indicators of the 17 SDGs and the

Table 4.1. SDGs with land governance (LG) and gender (GE) elements identified (based on Authors' analysis).

SDGs	Focal issues	LG	GE
Goal 1	End poverty: End poverty in all its forms everywhere.	■	■
Goal 2	Zero hunger: End hunger and achieve food security and improved nutrition and promote sustainable agriculture.	■	■
Goal 3	Good health and well-being: Ensure healthy lives and promote well-being for all at all ages.	■	
Goal 4	Quality education: Ensure inclusive and equitable quality education and promote lifelong learning opportunities for all.		■
Goal 5	Gender equality: Ensure gender equality and empower all women and girls.	■	■
Goal 6	Clean water and sanitation: Ensure availability and sustainable management of water and sanitation for all.		
Goal 7	Affordable and clean energy: Ensure access to affordable, reliable, sustainable and modern energy for all.		
Goal 8	Decent work and economic growth: Promote sustained, inclusive economic growth, full and productive employment, and decent work for all.		■
Goal 9	Industry, innovation, and infrastructure: Build resilient infrastructure, promote inclusive and sustainable industrialization and foster innovation.		
Goal 10	Reduced inequality: Reduce inequality within and among countries.		
Goal 11	Sustainable cities and communities: Make cities and human settlements inclusive, safe, resilient and sustainable.	■	
Goal 12	Responsible consumption and production: Ensure sustainable consumption and production patterns.		
Goal 13	Climate action: Take urgent action to combat climate change and its impacts.	■	
Goal 14	Life below water: Conserved and sustainably use the oceans, seas and marine resources for sustainable development.		
Goal 15	Life on land: Protect, restore and promote sustainable use of terrestrial ecosystems, sustainably manage forests, combat desertification, and halt and reverse land degradation and halt biodiversity loss.	■	
Goal 16	Peace, justice and strong institutions: Promote peaceful and inclusive societies for sustainable development, provide access to justice for all, and build effective, accountable and inclusive institutions at all levels.	■	
Goal 17	Partnerships for the goals: Strengthen the means of implementation and revitalize the Global partnership Sustainable Development.		

connected metadata framework are explained in more details by the UN (2017).

The targets and indicators (as illustrated in Table 4.2) for the SDGs 1, 5 and 16 relate to global land and gender concerns. The principle behind the adoption of the target and indicator framework is underlined by the phrase: 'If we can measure it – we can better it' (Gates, 2013). Experience shows that by monitoring and documenting the on-going progress governments can justify activities and costs – and attract donor funding toward meeting country specific targets. The success of the new SDGs will depend on the ability of governments, businesses, and civil society to collect and manage data for decision making. In this regard the SDGs are ambitious and there is an urgent need to mobilize data collection to monitor progress, hold governments accountable and foster sustainable development. This calls for a 'data revolution' for sustainable development to empower people with information on the progress towards meeting the SDG targets (UN, 2014).

For example, in relation to the monitoring the achievement of the MDG, Goal 1 recorded worldwide success, but the success did not translate to regional impacts in certain continents. According to the 2014 progress report of the MDGs (UN, 2014), the extreme poverty rate was halved and MDGs Goal 1 was thereby met at a global scale – but with huge regional deviations. Goal 1 (of the MDGs) was achieved mainly due to the contribution from

Table 4.2. Examples of goals, targets and indicators related to land and gender (based on Authors' analyses of United Nations' SDGs indicators).

Target	Indicator
Goal 1 End poverty and all its forms everywhere	
Target 1.4 By 2030, ensure that all men and women, the poor and vulnerable, have equal rights to economic resources, as well as access to basic services, ownership and control over land and forms of property, inheritance, natural resources, appropriate new technology and financial services, including microfinance.	**Indicator 1.4.2** Proportion of total population with secure tenure rights to land, legally recognized documentation, and who perceive their rights to land as secure, by sex and type of tenure.
Goal 5 Achieve gender equity and empower all women and girls	
Target 5.a Undertake reforms to give women equal rights to economic resources, as well as access to ownership and control over land and other forms of property, financial services, inheritance, and natural resources, in accordance with national laws.	**Indicator 5.a.1** Proportion of total agricultural population with ownership or secure rights over agricultural land and sex; and share of women among owners or rights-bearers of agricultural land, by type of tenure. **Indicator 5.a.2** Proportion of countries where the legal framework (including customary law) guarantees women's equal rights to land ownership and/or control.
Goal 16 Make cities and human settlements inclusive, safe, resilient and sustainable	
Target 16.3 By 2030, enhance inclusive and sustainable urbanization and capacity for participatory, integrated and sustainable human settlement planning and management in all countries	**Indicator 11.3.1** Ratio of land consumption rate to population growth rate. **Indicator 11.3.2** Proportion of cities with a direct participation structure of civil society in urban planning and management that operate regularly and democratically

China where, in 1978, the collective farms were dismantled and replaced by long-term leases to allocate land rights to farming households. This policy enforced an era of agricultural growth that trans-formed rural China and led to the largest reduction of poverty in history. The percentage of people living in extreme poverty declined from about 80% of the population in 1981 (the highest in the world at that time) to only 13% in 2008. In contrast, sub-Saharan Africa has seen a considerable annual growth rate of above 5% over recent years, but the region has been unable to translate its recent robust growth into rapid poverty reduction (Byamugisha, 2013). This underpins the necessity of detailed monitoring at regional and local / country level.

The annual SDGs Reports monitor the progress in achieving the 17 Goals using the targets and indicators as explained above. The recent SDGs Report 2020 presents an overview of progress towards the SDGs before the COVID-19 pandemic started, but also it looks at some of the devastating initial impacts of the pandemic on specific goals and targets. For instance, the report states that, even though the world was not fully on track to end poverty by 2030, the COVID-19 pandemic pushes over 70 million people into extreme poverty. The share of the world´s population living in extreme poverty declined from 15.7 % in 2010 to 10.0 % in 2015. The rate is estimated at 8.2 % in 2019 ending at 6.0 % in 2030. However, due to the COVID-19 pandemic the poverty rate is predicted to reach 8.8% in 2020, representing the first rise in global poverty since 1998 (UN, 2020).

These annual refinements of indicators are included in the indicator framework as they occur (UN, 2017). Furthermore, the global indicator framework is complemented by indicators at the regional and national levels, which are developed by member states of the United Nations.

Hence, it is possible that emerging experiences from around the world could lead to the discovery of more relationships between land governance and gender-related equality in the context of the SDGs as a global development agenda. Worthy of note is that all the SDGs related to land governance are also connected to gender (see goals 1, 2, 5, 11, 13, 15, 16). This relationship exists because land governance is a necessary tool towards putting gender into action to respond to people-oriented land developments. It is possible that the land governance and gender relationship would continue to grow as land issues emerge based on future realities.

4.5 The Role of Land Governance and Gender in Support of the Global Agenda

Sustainable development cannot be achieved without ensuring that women everywhere have equal rights and opportunities to access and enjoy the benefits of land resources. Women's equality and empowerment is integral to all dimensions of inclusiveness and sustainability. Achieving gender objectives (e.g. gender equity and gender equality in natural resource use and land tenure) by 2030 requires action to eliminate the many root causes of discrimination that still curtail women's access to land and the enjoyment of land rights. Making gender vision of development depends largely on how land and natural resources are governed at three critical levels – national, sub-national and local levels of development.

Solutions to the overall global land issues relate to alleviation of poverty, social inclusion and stability, investments and economic development, and environmental protection and natural resource management (to mention a few). These land matters are embedded in the SDGs, and gender responsive land governance plays a key role in achieving them as part of the global vision on development. On this basis, the role of land governance and gender (i.e. gender responsive land governance) relate to the following.

Improving the security of land rights for all. Across many countries in the Global South, people largely follow patrilineal lines of inheritance and succession. Sons benefit as the primary heirs of land plots from their fathers while daughters access land through their fathers, brothers, sons or male relatives. These practices limit the right of women to access land easily, and even when they do access land, it also limits their tenure security on the land.

Secure tenure rights enable poor people to invest in their property and livelihood without the fear of eviction. There is increasing evidence of positive economic, social, and environmental effects of improved tenure security (GIZ, 2019). Secure land rights are also the basis for the function of an efficient land market, assessment, and collection of land tax, and is seen as an incentive to use land and resources in a more sustainable manner. More fundamentally, access to land and the ability to legally defend land rights directly affect the enjoyment of a wide range of human rights. The governance of tenure can play a role in ensuring that practices that limit women's access to land are replaced with practices that support equality in the exercise of tenure rights.

Ending or reducing poverty for all. Poverty is a highly gendered issue. Most of the world's poor are women. Despite some important progress to change this in recent years, in no country have women achieved economic equality with men, and women are still more likely than men to live in poverty. Oxfam (2020) has noted a range of areas where women are suffering compared to men, such as low wages, lack of decent work, unpaid care work and longer working days. Dealing with the above scenario is a herculean task. Yet, it can be done by embracing land governance systems that are responsive to gender issues.

The incentives deriving from security of land rights are a key factor in poverty alleviation. While the importance of land tenure and access to land for agricultural production and for shelter and housing has long been clear, recent research goes beyond this recognition by emphasizing the significance of secure property rights over land as a precondition for sustainable pro-poor economic growth (Deininger, 2004). Good land governance plays a key role in driving this evolution. Furthermore, a change in status from informal to formal can improve the social status of the individual, family or household (GIZ, 2019)

Enhancing food security. The understanding of food security has evolved over the past two decades. Increasing attention has gone to the connections between food security and gender. Other factors of food security (such as environmental, cultural, technical and socioeconomic aspects) have gendered relationships (Quisumbing *et al.*, 1996). Equality principles is a crucial aspect of the solutions since equity in access to land resources by all (both men and women) is also crucial aspects of the food system (e.g. food production, availability, distribution, and access and use). Land governance, when gender responsive, helps to address the constraints facing women land users, especially female farmers. By 2050, the world will need to feed 9 billion people. This will require an increase of 70% in global agricultural production (World Bank, 2014). Good governance of land promotes food security at household, regional and national levels. Especially for rural livelihoods where women play crucial household roles, secure land rights are fundamental for access to credit and investments in long-term sustainable agricultural production (FAO, 2020). This again enables development of sustainable land use policies and control through the land governance institutions.

Attaining gender equity in land rights. Despite the general progress on women´s right, rights to land are not enjoyed equally in many parts of the world. This goes against international human rights and impacts negatively on households and the economy. This issue can only be addressed through the building of inclusive land registration records. According to the report, *Voluntary Guidelines on the Responsible Governance of Tenure of Land, Fisheries, and Forests in the Context of National Food Security (VGGT)*, States should ensure that women and girls have equal rights and access to land independent of their civil and marital status (FAO, 2012). This global recommendation, apart from being a land governance issue, underlines the importance of both land governance and gender in attaining equality.

Improving investment and equitable economic development. The land governance institutions such as land registration, land valuation and taxation, and land use planning and control provide a basic access to credit, and investments towards social and economic development. Urban development, construction works, transport and energy infrastructures, and a range of public services depend on such reliable land governance institutions and spatial data infrastructures with a countrywide coverage.

Achieving sustainable land use management for inclusive urban, peri-urban and rural development. The land governance institutions and connected regulations enable control of existing and future use of land as well as planning and implementation of urban development schemes. In the same way, the land governance institutions provide the key means for dealing with the urban–rural interrelationship and the urban development challenges as stated in SDGs Goal 11 and unfolded in the New Urban Agenda (UN-Habitat, 2016).

Accelerating climate change adaptation and mitigation. This can be achieved to a large extent through sound land governance and administration by including the perspective of possible future climate change and any consequent natural disasters. One of the elements in achieving climate-resilient urban development and sustainable rural land use is the degree to which climate change adaptation and risk management are mainstreamed into two major components of land governance, namely: securing and safeguarding of land rights; and planning and control of land use (Mitchell *et al.*, 2015).

Accomplishing environmental protection and sustainable natural resource management solutions (including land restoration and land degradation neutrality). Land policies and land use regulations relate to a range of different sectors (such as agriculture, forestry, water supply, heritage, costal zones, etc.). They enable sustainable control through permit procedures, and other relevant planning mechanisms. The regulatory frameworks should then ensure environmental protection of urban and rural areas as well as sustainable management of natural resources. The regulatory framework imposed through sound land governance can also determine how people use land in a nature positive manner. When land is used in nature positive ways, it has the capacity to avoid, reduce or reverse land degradation. Hence, land governance enables land restoration and can lead to achieving land degradation neutrality. This scenario explains the tenure-restoration nexus of land degradation neutrality (Chigbu *et al.*, 2015).

4.6 The Wider Global Agenda

The SDGs represent only one of the many global development agendas associable with land governance and gender. Of the many land- and gender-related agendas for global development, four major ones are worth noting: The New Urban Agenda; The Voluntary Guidelines on Responsible Governance of Tenure (VGGTs); The Universal Declaration of Human Rights; and the Paris Agreement on Climate Change.

The New Urban Agenda (NUA) is to be an extension of the 2030 Global Agenda. It is the outcome document agreed upon at the Habitat III cities conference in Quito, Ecuador, in October 2016 (UN-Habitat, 2016). The NUA replaces the former Habitat Agenda: Istanbul Declaration on Human Settlements, from the Habitat II conference, 1996. This former agenda called for adequate shelter for all and sustainable human settlements in an urbanized world and has influenced over 100 countries to adopt constitutional rights to adequate housing. The former agenda was also included in the MDGs Goal 7 with a target of achieving cities without slum. The NUA is a roadmap for building cities that can serve as engines of prosperity and centres of cultural and social well-being while protecting the environment. This is a historic opportunity for change. The New Urban Agenda is also a response to the fact that the majority (55%) of the world´s population now live in urban areas, and that this amount is expected to increase to 68% by 2050 (UN-DESA, 2018). It is recognized that over 70% of the urban growth currently happens outside of the formal planning process and that 30% of urban populations in developing countries are living in slums or informal settlements (FIG/WB, 2010).

Voluntary Guidelines on Responsible Governance of Tenure is now incorporated as part of the global agenda through the Committee on World Food Security's endorsement of the (VGGT) (FAO, 2012). These Guidelines are an international 'soft law instrument' that represents a global consensus on internationally accepted principles and standards for responsible practices. The Guidelines outline principles and practices that governments can refer to when making laws and administering land, fisheries and forest rights. The VGGTs also recommend that safeguards be put in place to protect tenure rights of local people from risks that could arise from large-scale land acquisitions (land grabbing), and to protect human rights, livelihoods, food security and the environment. The Guidelines promote secure tenure rights and equitable access to land as a means of eradicating hunger and poverty, supporting sustainable development and enhancing the environment. Based on the guidelines, a variety of actors can determine whether their proposed actions and the actions of others constitute acceptable practices.

The Universal Declaration of Human Rights (UDHR) (UN, 1948) states the universal rights of human beings based on the principle of respect for the individual – rights that can be enjoyed by everyone simply because of being alive. In relation to land governance, the UDHR states that 'everyone has the right to possess property' (Art. 17) and 'everyone has the right to adequate standard of living including housing, food, clothing' (Art. 25). Article 17 did not make it when transferring the Declaration into binding international law, even though it is recognized at various Conventions on Human Rights at regional level. As for Article 25, the UN interprets this as merely a social right to 'live somewhere in security, peace, and dignity (UN-CESCR, 1991). The right to adequate housing therefore cannot be viewed in isolation from other human rights contained in international covenants (Enemark *et al.*, 2014). The right to adequate housing has become the basis for the UN Centre for Human Settlement known as UN-Habitat that was established in 1978 with a UN mandate to 'promote socially and environmentally sustainable towns and cities with the goal of providing adequate shelter for all' (from the mission statement of UN-Habitat).

Climate change is a cross-cutting issue that relates to both land governance and gender. It is particularly included in the SDGs Goal 13 with some specific targets. However, climate change is also a global agenda issue on its own. It is stated in the Paris Agreement (UN, 2015b). Climate change mitigation refers to efforts and means for reducing the anthropogenic drivers such as greenhouse gas emissions from human activities – especially by reducing emission of carbon dioxide (CO_2) related to land use and transport. These emissions stem from consumption that of course tends to be higher in rich industrialized countries. At the same time, loss of healthy life years because of environmental change is predicted to be 500 times greater in poor African populations than in European populations. (Ezra Klein, 2009). On the other hand, at the national level, the issue of climate change adaptation does not necessarily relate to the inequity between the developed and less developed countries. Climate change adaption is a managerial issue related to means such land administration and land use planning.

4.7 Key Challenges Ahead

Many developed countries have strong land institutions and laws that protect the citizens' relationship with land and provide land administration services to secure and often guarantee land rights. These services directly support land markets that underpin modern economies. In these countries, security of tenure is taken for granted. However, an often-cited estimate indicates that for 70% of the world´s population, especially in developing countries, this is not the case (McLaren, 2015) and in the sub-Sahara region often 90% of land and people are outside the formal systems. The majority of these are the poor and the most vulnerable in society and, without any level of security of tenure, they constantly live in threat of eviction.

Most developing countries are struggling to find remedies for their many land problems that are causing land conflicts, reducing economic development, and preventing their countries from reaching their true potential. Existing investments in land administration and management solutions have been piecemeal and have not delivered the required changes and improvements at scale. The solutions have not helped the neediest; the poor and disadvantaged with no security of tenure. In fact, the beneficiaries of this unsustainable management of land have been the rich, elite and organizations involved in land grabbing. Conventional solutions are not effective within developing countries and it is time to rethink the approaches. Solutions are required that can deliver security of tenure for all, can be quickly developed and are affordable and scalable.

Building Basic and Inclusive Land Administration Systems.

When considering the resources and capacities required for building such simple and inclusive systems and the connected spatial, legal and institutional frameworks in developing countries, the conventional Western-style concepts may well be the end target but not the point of entry. When assessing technology and investment choices, the focus should be on serving the purpose of the systems namely providing security of tenure for all and enabling control of the use of all land, rather than aiming at high-end technology solutions. Such simple systems should meet the needs of society today and can be incrementally improved over time. Building such spatial, legal and institutional frameworks will establish the link between people and land. This will enable the management and monitoring of improvements in meeting aims and objectives of adopted land policies as well as meeting the global agenda.

The recent GLTN publication 'Fit-For-Purpose (FFP) Land Administration – Guiding Principles for Country Implementation' (Enemark *et al.*, 2016) outlines a pragmatic and realistic approach for developing countries that can provide security of tenure for across a country within a short timeframe and at affordable costs. The Guide presents the concept, provides the connected key principles and a generic set of guidelines to be applied in developing countries for building basic and inclusive land administration systems.

The phrase 'fit-for-purpose' is widely used as a quality label for government policies or interventions. The phrase is also commonly used for any intervention or activity that is appropriate, and of a necessary standard, for its intended use. So, the label indicates that this (FFP) approach is appropriate and of a necessary standard for the purpose – namely to provide security of tenure for all and enable control of the use of all land, rather than blindly complying with top-end technological solutions and rigid regulations for accuracy.

Institutional Change

A key challenge relates to the issue of institutional change. Such change may be constrained by many factors such a lack of political will, conflicting interests between various groups in society, and vested interests of key professions and other key stakeholders. Introducing new flexible and fit-for-purpose approaches to building inclusive land administration systems may imply that a range of current land administration functions normally undertaken by specific land professionals become obsolete. Similarly, related activities of the land agencies will change, and new procedures will be applied. Therefore, such new approaches are often seen as disruptive.

Groups of land professionals, such as lawyers, surveyors and planners are highly educated and act as custodians of existing systems. It is therefore no surprise that their professional codes support these systems, and there are many examples of resistance towards change that will challenge their monopolistic position. Similarly, the national land agencies will often defend the existing system and try to keep business as usual, thereby guarding their role and position as experts and the importance of existing regulations and administration. Overcoming these barriers requires that a political focus on the benefits of land to society to be achieved by implementing a new system. This can be done through effective engagement through seminars and open discussions with all relevant stakeholders involved including civil society (Enemark and McLaren, 2019). In this regard, it may be worth recalling a famous quote from the Renaissance by the man who has often been called the father of modern political philosophy and political science:

> It should be borne in mind that there is nothing more difficult to plan, more doubtful of success, nor more dangerous to manage than creation of a new system. For the initiator has the enmity of all who would benefit from the preservation of the old institutions and merely lukewarm defenders in those who would benefit from the new ones.
>
> (Machiavelli, *The Prince*, Ch. 6)

This captures the reason behind why many efforts to make institutional changes in the land governance of many countries (both developed and developing nations) encounter challenges that either derail or delay or scuttle the process. Achieving the SDGs would require institutional changes in the land governance systems of many developing countries. Visionary leadership at both the political and technical levels are crucial preconditions to achieving success.

Natural Disasters and Disease Pandemics

Unexpected circumstances pose serious challenge to achieving the ongoing global agenda through land governance. These include natural disasters and pandemics which, in most cases, happen without the immediate control of humans. Existing evidence show that these disasters (both environmental and disease-related) cause serious problems to land administration systems. Based on World Bank (2009) reports, the tsunami that affected the parts of Indonesia killed over 200,000 in the country. It also led to estimated cost of damage to property and business worth over US$4.4 billion. Furthermore, over 570,000 people were displaced, and at least 250,000 homes and buildings destroyed in Indonesia as the wave swallowed large parts of the coastline. The tsunami damaged infrastructure such as roads, bridges and farms. About 54,000 coastal land parcels in active use (i.e. land use) were washed away or permanently inundated by the tsunami. It destroyed the entire land records system of the affected region because they were not digitized. All of these meant that Indonesia had to start again in building the land administration system of the affected areas. These are the sort of setbacks that can happen due to the occurrence of natural disasters.

Also, disease outbreaks (judging from the COVID-19 or coronavirus pandemic experience) and natural disasters have a unique way of redefining the vision and priorities of pertinent development issues. For instance, the outbreak of coronavirus placed unprecedented challenges on all aspects of human life, including on development priorities. Due to limited resources many developing countries put pandemic at the top of their development priorities. The wealthier countries diverted attention towards the development of vaccines while the poorer countries diverted their limited funds towards containing the pandemic. More so, the dependence on social/physical distancing and work-from-home policies and government-imposed curfews led to less on-the-field activities in various land sector activities. This situation posed a serious problem to land governance. There was no 'enumerable (or an exhaustively describable) set of potential solutions' and no 'well-defined set of permissible operations that may be incorporated' to resolve it (Chigbu and Onyebueke, 2021, p. 4). This describes how pandemics and natural disasters can pose obstacles to land governance.

Whenever and wherever these disasters occur (both disease and environmental disasters), they are bound to have tremendous effect on achieving the land governance visions. The COVID-19 pandemic is already being projected to be a setback with an impact on Agenda 2030 targets unless efforts are doubled to improve the ability of humans to contain pandemics.

Capacity Development

There is now an emerging agreement within the development community that capacity development is the engine of human development. Human, institutional and societal capacity remain critical for designing and implementing strategies towards achieving development objectives including the SDGs.

Capacity development refers to the process through which individuals, organizations and societies obtain, strengthen, and maintain the capabilities to set and achieve their own development objectives over time (UNDP, 2009). Capacity development, therefore, must be seen in a wider context of providing the ability of organizations and individuals to perform functions effectively, efficiently and sustainably. This includes the requirement to address capacity needs also at institutional and even more broadly at societal levels. Capacity development does not imply that there is no capacity in existence; it also includes retaining and strengthening existing capacities of people and institutions to perform their tasks and deliver services.

Responsible and fit-for-purpose land administration systems are the operational component of land governance in support of the global agenda. When building such systems in developing countries the quest for capacity development is fundamental. 'Don't start what you can't sustain': this phrase is particularly relevant for implementing land administration systems at country level. Once established, the systems must be maintained and updated from day one; otherwise, the efforts and investments in building the systems are wasted. The necessary capacity to manage and maintain the systems, therefore, must be developed up front to ensure efficient implementation and effective ongoing maintenance and management (Enemark *et al.*, 2018).

Building knowledge through education, research and capacity development on land governance is essential. Land-related challenges have always posed problems to the achievement of development objectives at national and local levels. Tackling these problems at a technical level requires knowledge from multiple professional and scientific domains for proper solutions. Within the geodetic community, the building of capacities in land governance knowledge provides opportunities for all (both men and women) to participate in development activities. It also enhances the how-to aspect of applying land governance to achieving the SDGs. Building land governance knowledge would enable the education and capacity of land professionals with land management and land governance knowledge and experience from the Global South' (de Vries *et al.*, 2021, p. 123).

4.8 Final remarks

This chapter has sought to tackle several issues. It establishes two critical relationships necessary for making decisions within the land sector projects. It establishes a relationship between land governance and gender, and then a tripartite relationship between the SDGs, land governance and gender. It also identified the components or elements of land governance and gender in the SDGs and presents the roles land governance and gender can play towards achieving the Global Agenda 2030. The chapter analyses the goals provided in the 2030 Global Agenda, as well as the range of targets that can never be achieved without having good land governance and well-functioning countrywide land administration systems in place. Furthermore, it delves into the challenges that could be encountered in achieving the SDGs and covers how all of these relate to other global development agenda.

The SDGs deal with issues related to poverty, hunger, gender, natural resource management, access to energy, sustainable economic growth, resilient infrastructure, inequality, urbanization, climate action, ecosystems and promotion of peace. The key contribution of land governance and gender to the achievement of these goals lies in the improvements in access to land resources, women's land rights, control of land use, climate change mitigation and adaptation, ecosystem management, and reduction in land conflicts. Hence, land governance and gender are very relevant in any development agenda geared towards socioeconomic and environmental development, as well as feeding the growing population located in the world. However, these expected roles of land governance in achieving the SDGs (among many other development agendas) will not be feasible unless there is a shift towards a tenure security and gender-responsive approach in land policy, land administration and management.

The SDGs provide a framework around which governments, especially in developing countries, can develop policies and encourage overseas aid programmes designed to alleviate poverty and improve the lives of the poor. The SDGs also represent a rallying point for NGOs to hold governments to account. In other words, the SDGs are a key driver for countries throughout the world – and especially developing countries – to develop adequate and accountable land policies and regulatory land governance frameworks for poverty reduction, food security, gender and social equity, and sustainable management of urban and rural land use and natural resources.

There is a consensus that governing the people to land relationship is at the heart of the global agenda. Therefore, in developing countries, there is an urgent need to build simple and inclusive land administration systems using a flexible and affordable approach to secure all rights in land and enable control of the use of all land.

Good land governance and management should be seen as a key means of support of the global agenda. If a hypothetical map of the world were generated using gross domestic product as the scale for territorial size, the so-called western regions North America, Western Europe, South Korea and Japan would balloon while other regions such as Africa and Central Asia would almost disappear (UNEP, 2007). The global agenda is very much about bringing this kind of map back to scale through poverty reduction, improving education and health, facilitating economic development, encouraging good governance, and ensuring sustainability. The means of land governance and gender equality (and equity) have key roles to play in this regard.

References

Byamugisha, F. (2013) *Securing Africa's Land for Shared Prosperity. A Program to Scale Up Reforms and Investments*. World Bank, Washington, DC. Available at: http://www.scribd.com/doc/144377306/Securing-Africa-s-Land-for-Shared-Prosperity (accessed 29 July 2021).

Chigbu, U.E. (2021a) The quest for 'good governance' of urban land in sub-Saharan Africa: Insight into Windhoek, Namibia. In: Home, R. (Ed.) *Land Issues for Urban Governance in Sub-Saharan Africa*. Springer, Cham, Switzerland, pp. 17–34.

Chigbu, U.E. (2021b) Tenure responsive land-use planning as a tool for improving quality of life: The perspective of sub-Saharan Africa. In: Martinez, J., Mikkelsen, C.A. and Phillips, R. (Eds), *Handbook of Quality of Life and Sustainability*. Springer, Cham, Switzerland, pp. 17-33.

Chigbu, U.E. and Onyebueke, V.U. (2021) The COVID-19 pandemic in informal settlements: (Re)considering urban planning interventions. *Town Planning Review*, 92(1), 107–114.

Chigbu, U.E., Mabakeng, M.R. and Chilombo, A. (2021) *Strengthening Tenure and Resource Rights for Land Restoration*. UNCCD Global Land Outlook Working Paper. Bonn, Germany.

Deininger, K. (2004) *Land Policies and Land Reform*. World Bank, Washington, DC, USA.

de Vries, W.T., Chigbu, U.E. and Duran-Diaz, P. (2021) Twenty years of building capacity in land management, land tenure and urban land governance. In: Home, R. (Ed.), *Land Issues for Urban Governance in Sub-Saharan Africa, Springer*, Cham, Switzerland, pp. 121–136.

Enemark, S. (2012) *Sustainable Land Governance: Three Key Demands*. Proceedings of the FIG Working Week, Rome, Italy, 6–10 May. Available at: http://www.fig.net/resources/proceedings/fig_proceedings/fig2012/papers/ts03a/TS03A_enemark_5998.pdf (accessed 29 July 2021).

Enemark, S. and McLaren, R. (2019) Secure tenure for all starts to emerge: New experiences of countries implementing a fit-for-purpose approach to land administration. *Proceedings of the 2019 World Bank Conference on Land and Poverty*, World Bank. Washington, DC, USA, 25–29 March.

Enemark, S., Hvingel, L. and Galland, D. (2014) Land administration, planning and human rights. *Planning Theory*, 13, 332–348.

Enemark, S., McLaren, R. and Lemmen, C. (2016) *Fit-for-Purpose Land Administration – Guiding Principles for Country Implementation.* UN-Habitat / GLTN, Nairobi. Available at: https://unhabitat.org/books/fit-for-purpose-land-administration-guiding-principles-for-country-implementation (accessed 29 July 2021).

Enemark, S., McLaren, R. and Antonio, D. (2018) Fit-for-purpose land administration: Capacity development for country implementation. *Proceedings of the 2018 World Bank Conference on Land and Poverty, March*. World Bank, Washington, DC, USA.

FAO (2020) *The State of Food Security and Nutrition in the World.* Food and Agriculture Organization, Rome, Italy.

FAO (2012) *Voluntary Guidelines on the Responsible Governance of Tenure of Land, Fisheries and Forests in the Context of Food Security*. Food and Agriculture Organization, Rome, Italy.

FIG/WB (2010) *Land Governance in Support of the Millennium Development Goals. FIG Publication No.* 45. Available at: http://www.fig.net/pub/figpub/index.htm (accessed 20 November 2020).

Gates, B. (2013) *Annual Letter 2013: Measuring Progress.* Available at: 2019a9734885387.pdf (accessed 18 December 2020).

GIZ (2019) *Secure Land Tenure Rights for All: A Key Condition for Sustainable Development*. Available at: https://www.donorplatform.org/publication-land-governance/secure-land-tenure-rights-for-all-a-key-condition-for-sustainable-development.html (accessed 20 December 2020).

ICLEI (2015) Measuring, monitoring and evaluating the SDGs. *ICLEI Briefing Sheet – Urban Issues,* No. 6, November.

Klein, Ezra (2009) *Your World in Maps: Climate Change Edition. Washington Post*, 18 May.

Landesa (2013) *Gender and Land: Good Practices and Lessons Learned from Four Millennium Challenge Corporation Compact-Funded Land Projects. Landesa Center for Women's Land Rights.* Available at: https://www.landesa.org/wp-content/uploads/Landesa-Gender-Land-Report-MCC-2014.pdf (accessed 20 December 2020).

Machiavelli, N. (1531) *The Prince.* Antonio Blado, Italy.

McLaren, R. (2015) How big is global insecurity of tenure? *GIM International*, November. Available at: http://member.gim-international.com/Geomares/magazine/gim/magazine.jsp (accessed 20 December 2020).

Mitchell, D., Enemark, S. and van der Molen, P. (2015) Climate resilient urban development: Why responsible land governance is important. *Land Use Policy,* 48, 190–198.

Oxfam (2020) *Why the Majority of the World's Poor Are Women.* Available at: https://www.oxfam.org/en/why-majority-worlds-poor-are-women (accessed 20 December 2020).

Quisumbing, A.R., Brown, L.R., Feldstein, H.S., Haddad, L. and Peña, C. (1996) Women: The key to food security. *Food and Nutrition Bulletin,* 17(1), 1–2.

UN (1948) *Universal Declaration on Human Rights.* Available at: http://www.ohchr.org/EN/UDHR/Pages/Language.aspx?LangID=eng (accessed 20 December 2020).

UN (2014) *The Millennium Development Goals Report 2014.* Available at: http://www.un.org/en/development/desa/publications/mdg-report-2014.html (accessed 20 December 2020).

UN (2015a) Transforming our world: The 2030 Agenda for Sustainable Development. Available at: https://sdgs.un.org/2030agenda (accessed 1 July 2021).

UN (2015b) *The Paris Agreement.* Available at: https://unfccc.int/files/essential_background/convention/application/pdf/english_paris_agreement.pdf (accessed 20 February 2021).

UN (2016) *Report of the Inter-Agency and Expert Group on Sustai nable Development Goal Indicators.* Available at: http://unstats.un.org/unsd/statcom/47th-session/documents/2016-2-SDGs-Rev1-E.pdf (accessed 20 March 2021).

UN (2017) *SDG Indicators: Global Indicator Framework for the Sustainable Development Goals and Targets of the 2030 Agenda for Sustainable Development.* Available at: https://unstats.un.org/sdgs/indicators/indicators-list (accessed 20 December 2020).

UN (2020) *The Sustainable Development Goals Report 2020.* Available at: https://unstats.un.org/sdgs/report/2020/ (accessed 20 December 2020).

UN-CESCR (1991) *United Nations Committee on Economic, Social and Cultural Rights, General Comment No. 4, The Right to Adequate Housing.* Available at: http://www1.umn.edu/humanrts/gencomm/econ.htm (accessed 20 November 2020).

UN-DESA (2018) *United Nations Department of Economic and Social Affairs: World Urbanization Prospects.* Available at: https://population.un.org/wup/Publications/Files/WUP2018-Report.pdf (accessed 20 March 2021).

UNDP (2009) *Capacity Development: A UNDP Primer.* Available at: http://www.undp.org/content/dam/aplaws/publication/en/publications/capacity-development/capacity-development-a-undp-primer/CDG_PrimerReport_final_web.pdf (accessed 20 March 2021).

UNEP / GRIID Arendal (2007) *World Economy Cartogram.* Available at: http://www.grida.no/graphicslib/detail/world-economy-cartogram_1551 (accessed 17 February 2021).

UNFPA (2005) *Frequently asked questions about gender equality. United Nations Population Fund.* Available at: https://www.unfpa.org/resources/frequently-asked-questions-about-gender-equality (accessed 20 November 2020).

UN-GGIM (2020) *Framework for Effective Land Administration.* Available at: http://ggim.un.org/meetings/GGIM-committee/10th-Session/documents/E-C.20-2020-29-Add_2-Framework-for-Effective-Land-Administration.pdf (accessed 20 November 2020).

UN-Habitat (2016) *New Urban Agenda.* Available at: http://habitat3.org/the-new-urban-agenda/ (accessed 20 March 2021).

Williamson, I., Enemark, S., Wallace, J. and Rajabifard, A. (2010) *Land Administration Systems for Sustainable Development.* ESRI Academic Press, Redlands, CA, USA. Available at: https://www.esri.com/en-us/industries/government/departments/land-administration/offers/e-book (accessed 14 Sept 2021).

World Bank (2009) *Reconstruction of Aceh Land Administration System (RALAS) in Indonesia. The Implementation Completion and Results Report (ICR) Report.* World Bank, Washington, DC, USA.

World Bank (2014) *Land and Food Security.* Available at: https://www.worldbank.org/en/topic/agriculture/brief/land-and-food-security1 (accessed 20 12 December 2020).

5 Governing African Land in an Era of Instability

Sara Berry*
Department of History, Johns Hopkins University, Baltimore, MD, USA

5.1 Introduction

Governance of any valuable resource is a multifaceted process. People and institutions compete to manage and regulate the ways resources are accessed, used and exchanged, or they collaborate to block others and advance their own position. In doing so, they deploy different systems of authority, applying them to new circumstances, and reshaping them in the process. At least three systems of authority are involved in governing land in Africa today: the state, custom, and what used to be called 'associations' – social structures based on relations of kinship, community, religion or political affiliation. By 'systems of authority', I am referring to changing clusters of people, ideas and practices that make, interpret and attempt to enforce rules, with varying degrees of success. Systems of authority overlap, and individuals within them assert and contest claims on their own account, as well as working to manage and/or control the way other people make and exercise claims. Many individuals participate in more than one such cluster (*de facto* if not *de jure*), and people in each cluster compete, cooperate and contend with one another, working to consolidate and increase their influence and regulate the activities of those around them. Unsurprisingly, the resulting processes of governance are often messy, contentious and unstable.[1]

One of the most sought-after resources in Africa today is land. During the colonial period and after, claims on land became increasingly commercialized in areas where land was in demand, both as a productive resource (for agriculture, mining, hunting and forestry) and as a place of habitation for growing urban and peri-urban populations. As the economic value of land increased, people also began to seek land to hold as a form of wealth. In recent years, increasing demands for land have been reinforced by pervasive economic uncertainty. As demand for land pressed against fixed supplies, land prices rose steadily – in contrast to the volatile market values of machinery, inventories, financial assets, etc. – leading people to seek it as a safety net – a source of relative security in a risky and uncertain world. Because people invest in land as a form of wealth as well as a productive resource, their investments tend to intensify social and market pressures on land, contributing to overall economic instability rather than mitigating it. Subject to multiple, competing claims, land arrangements serve, paradoxically, both as a *source* of instability and as a form of protection *against* it (Berry, 2018).

Pressures on land have also arisen from political as well as market competition. Both state

*Corresponding author: sberry1@jhu.edu

 Land Governance and Gender: The Tenure-Gender Nexus in Land Management and Land Policy (ed. U.E. Chigbu)
DOI: 10.1079/9781789247664.0005

and local authorities have worked to consolidate and/or expand control over territories under their jurisdiction, hoping to strengthen their own hold on power, as well as manage natural resources to gain income for state expenditures or to reward political supporters. In Kenya, Côte d'Ivoire, South Africa and elsewhere, tensions over land have interacted with ethnic and religious animosities, leading to outbreaks of violence in anticipation of national elections.

In the following pages, I reflect on some of the ways African state, customary and non-governmental authorities have interacted in their efforts to govern access to and use of land in conditions of instability.[2] In doing so, I think it is useful to expand the widely used concept of 'legal pluralism' to include not only state and customary laws and institutions, but also social practices and understandings that operate both through and alongside them. Associational structures such as families, communities, religious congregations and others are partly regulated by the state and a variety of customary and informal authorities, but they also go beyond the dictates of both statutory and customary law to shape what people can and cannot do. Often lumped together under the rubric of 'informal' governance, customary systems of authority and what (for lack of a better term) I am calling associational structures are not monolithic. Partly constrained by both statutory and customary law, everyday practices of governance follow dynamics of their own, deviating from and disrupting the intentions of state and customary authorities alike. To understand the way land is allocated, managed and transferred under conditions of economic and political instability, it is important to try to unpack these dynamics, disentangling the various strands of interest, obligation, and loyalty that interact to shape the way land is governed.

The present discussion is organized as follows. After a brief introduction, I discuss the commercialization of land transactions in a context of rising demand, the roles of landholders and land users in investment, land markets and practices of governance, and the way social differences impact and are affected by patterns of land governance. The chapter ends with a brief section on the effects of commercialization on customary land arrangements, followed by a conclusion.

5.2 Commercialization and the Demand for Land

As suggested above, conditions of economic and social instability have fostered the commercialization of land transactions and the development of land markets. Demand for land began to rise in cities and cash crop producing areas in the colonial period and gained momentum after independence. Population growth, agricultural commercialization, and urban expansion all worked to increase the amount of land occupied – for farming, foraging, forestry, mining and building. Following the end of colonial rule, many newly independent states passed laws designed to alter the terms on which land was used or exchanged. Invoking (or establishing) the state's powers of eminent domain, politicians and officials allocated, regulated, and managed land access and use, justifying their actions in terms of 'development' that often failed to materialize. Politicians and bureaucrats also took advantage of their governing authority to accumulate land for themselves. In colonial Kenya, for example, where the appropriation of land by white settlers served as a catalyst for the struggle for independence, the Kenyatta family emerged from that struggle as one of (if not the) largest landholders in the country (Moore, 2018).

In the early 2000s, social and political tensions rose over large-scale acquisitions of land by both international and domestic investors seeking to take advantage of differences between relatively low prices for rural land in Africa and rising global prices of land-based commodities such as minerals, biofuels and staple foodstuffs. Seen as the last global 'frontier' of abundant unused land, Africa – long shunned by international investors as too risky – has begun to attract them in the early 21st century. Working in partnership with African governments, whose leaders often take personal as well as public advantage of laws designed to promote landed investment, corporations and other private agencies have 'grabbed' substantial tracts of African land, intending to use them for large-scale commercial production of staple foodstuffs, biofuels, forests or minerals. Commonly referred to as 'land grabs', large-scale land acquisitions (especially by foreign investors) have occasioned a small avalanche of publications. See, among many others, Cotula (2009), Patnaik *et al.* (2011) and Hall *et al.* (2015).

Not infrequently, perceptions of land as a source of relative economic stability proved illusory in practice. Increased demand has given rise not only to the creation of widespread and increasingly sophisticated land markets, but also to a growing volume of informal (sometimes illegal) transactions, leading to frequent disputes, litigation and social unrest. In some cases, conflicts over land have aggravated ethnoregional and political tensions, erupting in violence at both local levels – dividing families and communities – and in national and regional affairs. Tensions over land were a major factor contributing to the outbreak of civil war in 2003 in Côte d'Ivoire (where conflicts over land in the southern cocoa belt fed into ethnoregional rivalries between candidates for succession to the late President Houphouêt Boigny), to repeated outbreaks of electoral violence in Kenya in the early 2000s, and to genocide in Rwanda in 1994. For details, see Chauveau and Richards (2008); and Elder *et al.* (2014).

5.3 Land 'Reform'

Land acquisitions undertaken to offset the effects of economic, social and political instability often exacerbate them instead. Hoping to attract capital, stimulate development and satisfy 'conditionalities' imposed on borrowers by the World Bank and other international lending agencies, a number of African governments enacted so-called land reforms in the 1990s and early 2000s. Land laws and policies formulated during this period were designed not to redistribute land from large estates to smallholders and the landless, but to formalize land ownership, regulating transactions, registering holdings, and issuing titles or certificates of ownership. People will be more inclined to invest, it was argued, if their rights to land are legally and practically secure. Shaped by this period of land 'reform', policy makers have come to regard land registration and titling as a precondition for development, facilitating transfers of land to more productive uses and promoting investment by expanding the use of land as collateral (Deininger, 2010; Byamugisha, 2013).

In practice, many land reforms have not lived up to their designers' expectations. Using land as collateral to invest in productive equipment is risky. Borrowers who are unable to repay their loans on time may lose their land to foreclosure or face additional financial penalties that they cannot pay – risks that very few people with low and uncertain incomes are willing to run. Titling may provide legal protection for those who have land and enough money and influence to defend their claims, but it also works to dispossess landholders who lack the means to enforce them. Those who are left out lose a key source of livelihood as well as the opportunity to acquire land as an asset – events that further increase inequality, land disputes, and social tension, and work overtime to weaken ties among members of families, communities, and institutions. As Peters explains:

> there is much to support a view of Africa as a continent with many of its people living on the land, without well-defined classes of landed and landless ... [but] a growing body of evidence [shows] intensifying conflict and competition over land ... deepening rifts within and between kin-based, ethnic, and regional groups, and appropriation of land by local and non-local elites.
>
> (Peters, 2004, p. 270)

In short, rising competition over land invites, or requires, governance – to facilitate orderly land transfers, resolve disputes before they get out of hand, and try to channel land toward the most productive uses. In response, both local and national authorities have worked to regulate, manage and adjudicate competing claims to property in the interests of 'development' and social peace. Their efforts not only affect formation and implementation of policy, but also give rise to competition among different authorities seeking to expand their influence and jurisdiction. Such jockeying for power among multiple authorities tends, in turn, to disrupt both the formation and the implementation of governing agendas. In the following pages, I describe some of the changes in governing arrangements made in response to growing pressures on land and discuss their implications for structures of authority and patterns of resource allocation. The discussion focuses primarily on Ghana, citing some comparative cases to illustrate variations across countries (Benjaminsen and Lund, 2012; Manji, 2013).

5.4 Landholders and Land Users

Despite intensive commercialization and increasing legal and administrative regulation of land rights and transactions, the majority of land in Africa remains subject to 'customary' tenure (Deininger, 2010). Under most customary arrangements, land is subject to claims by a number of people: those who hold, buy or inherit pieces of land do not gain exclusive ownership, but membership in a group of people who hold simultaneous, varied, often overlapping rights to use or dispose of the land in question, leading them to renegotiate terms of access and transfer as circumstances change. Commercialization of land held by groups of people tends to spill over into relationships among them, deepening divisions between genders, generations, ethnic groups, etc. rather than transcending them.

In such conditions, people who manage to obtain claims on land may not know just *what* they have acquired. Claiming 'indigeneity' in their area of residence, long-established families turned on their neighbours, insisting that descendants of immigrants were 'strangers', who did not own their land but used it on sufferance from 'indigenes', even though they had lived in their present abode for two or three generations (Boni, 2006). Young people who believed their claims to family land provided them a safety net have returned to their villages after losing urban jobs and incomes under the pressures of structural adjustment, only to find that their elders have sold or leased out all the family land they are not using themselves, leaving their juniors to fend for themselves. Not surprisingly, intergenerational conflict has intensified as a result (see Chauveau and Richards, 2008; Mustapha and Ehrhardt, 2018).

Similarly, wives who were customarily entitled to use land belonging to their husbands' families if their marriages lasted but lost it in the event of death or divorce, have become more assertive in demanding a share of farms or other landed assets that they helped their husbands develop (Kanogo, 1987; Allman and Tashjian, 2000; Davison, 2019). In a recent study of relations between land, labour and marriage in the cocoa belt of southern Ghana, Duncan (2010) found that courts are increasingly supportive of wives' claims. Recognizing the precarious position of women – many of whom have made substantial contributions to their husbands' farms and other forms of conjugal property but are dispossessed by their husbands' families when the husband dies or the husband and wife divorce – some governments have given increasing legislative and judicial support to women's claims. In Ghana, for example, this trend was reinforced by PNDC Law 111 (passed in 1985 by Ghana's last military regime), which mandates that when a man dies, his house, chattels and a major part of his self-acquired assets passed to his wife and children, rather than his matrilineal family.

Many studies report that rates of formal marriage are declining across Africa (see, inter alia, Rodriguez *et al.*, 2015; Pauli, 2019; Popoola and Ayandele, 2019). In Ghana, a recent paper by Beatrice Akua Duncan argues that instead of taking additional wives to augment their supply of labour (as happened for much of the 20th century), farmers are engaging in 'contract marriages' (see section 5.6 below).

Social divisions have also developed between local farmers and immigrant labourers eager to gain land rights in their areas of employment. This trend is exemplified in the tree crop zone of West Africa – notably southern Côte d'Ivoire, where migrants from poorer regions to the north flooded into the southern forest belt from 1946 when France abolished forced labour, and cocoa growing surged. Some migrants gained access to land and established cocoa and coffee farms of their own; others worked for local farmers on a sharecropping basis, gradually acquiring land for themselves. For instance, Côte d'Ivoire's long-reigning President Houphouêt Boigny – whose ruling party benefitted handsomely from the revenue derived from cocoa and other export crops – encouraged immigration, calculating that it would increase agricultural production by expanding the supply of cheap farm labour. Declaring that Côte d'Ivoire's doors were open to all, Houphouêt's party cadres pressured officials to settle local disputes in favour of immigrants, and even allowed them to vote, in violation of the law (Ruf and Siswoputranto, 1995; Akindès, 2004).

As explained above, in the 1980s, the Ivorian economy contracted sharply under the impact of structural adjustment. Newly unemployed urbanites who returned to ride out the recession in their villages, discovered to their dismay that their elders had leased or sold off unused portions of 'family land' to immigrant farmers, leaving little or none for their returning juniors to use. Following Houphouêt's death in 1993, rival politicians cultivated these resentments to recruit supporters, contributing to hostilities that divided the country in the early 2000s, and prevented President Alassane Ouattara from taking office until France sent a military force to rescue him (Akindès, 2004).

Côte d'Ivoire's case was dramatic, but it was by no means the only one. Across the region, tensions between 'indigenes' and 'strangers' over access to land became an increasingly significant source of conflict as supplies of unused land dwindled in the late 20th and early 21st centuries (Chauveau, 2000; Berry, 2001, 2013; Lentz, 2014; Colin, 2017). As conditions of landholding shifted under people's feet, the increasing contentiousness of access, use and control of land has acted as a further source of instability in both economic and social relations.

5.5 Investment

Advocates of titling argue that titles will promote investment by clarifying and securing rights of land ownership, reducing uncertainty, and lowering the risk of making improvements that will not pay off for a long time. Economists predicted that people who hold secure rights of ownership will borrow more money to invest in economic activities, using their land as collateral to secure loans without fear that their property will be foreclosed before they are able to pay off the loans. While the rising value of land undoubtedly enhances its value as collateral, this argument fails to take account of the uncertainty surrounding borrowers' ability to repay loans *on time*. Facing volatile markets and the ever-present threat of bad weather and poor harvests, farmers especially are wary of losing their land to foreclosure if they fall behind in loan repayments. Despite holding state-sanctioned proof of ownership, many people are loath to risk losing their land by using it as collateral, and the anticipated surge in investment has often failed to materialize (Shipton, 2009).

As illustrated by these examples, pervasive economic and political instability combined with rising contention over land have put contradictory pressures on social relationships. As the supply of steady jobs declines and the gap between rich and poor widens, more people need the kind of support that family, community, and other social networks have provided in the past. Such needs are especially pronounced for those without money or connections who find it increasingly difficult to put together a livelihood. As need for family support rises, however, limited, and unstable incomes reduce families' ability to take care of their less fortunate members. This is well illustrated in Maxim Bolt's vivid account of hierarchically intertwined networks among Zimbabwean immigrants employed on a large, commercial farm in South Africa (Bolt, 2015). Meagher (2010) also makes a similar point in her study of tailors and shoemakers in Aba, Nigeria. The resulting tensions spark friction in people's relationships with relatives, neighbours and friends that spill over into the economic and social contexts in which they live.

The resulting pressures are vividly described by Kristen Peterson in her study of the wholesale pharmaceutical trade in Lagos. 'Doing business', she writes, involves 'hustling' – spending large amounts of time moving between suppliers, creditors and customers to build and sustain relationships, negotiate transactions on razor-thin margins, seek loans, and collect outstanding debts quickly enough to pay off their own debts and maintain their creditworthiness. Contrast this with economic life during the Nigerian oil boom of the 1970s, when limited or unreliable means of communication obliged people to maintain economic and social networks by travelling frequently to visit and negotiate with creditors, customers, suppliers and their own relatives. At that time, the Nigerian economy was booming, and such commercial restlessness often paid off – unlike the precarious conditions of recent years, when people operate on narrow margins and 'success' is the exception rather than the rule: see Peace (1978), Guyer (2004), Bolt (2015) and many others. 'Life can revolve around hustling security as well as hustling the money needed to ensure that security' (Peterson, 2014, p. 107), pushing traders into a continuing scramble to generate sufficient cash flow to keep their creditors at bay.

As Peterson shows, traders do not simply enter or inherit networks of suppliers, traders and customers specific to their businesses, but must build them over time. Unlike older conceptions of social networks as kin-based, religious or community groups to which Africans belonged by birth, market networks require continual effort to develop and sustain. Networks may flourish when markets are expanding and their members are successful, only to wither when market conditions decline. As land markets have become increasingly commercialized, land 'ownership' has become more unstable – a product of patronage, hustling and luck rather than a stable artifact of legislation and administrative practice.

Building and sustaining social relationships takes work, requiring investments of time and money that may be difficult to sustain in a volatile economy. For example, a number of studies have shown that rates of marriage have fallen in the last 50 years, for economic as well as social and cultural reasons. As wages have declined, steady employment has become the exception rather than the rule, forcing people to shuttle among workplaces, combining several marginal jobs as they struggle to put together a livelihood. 'The high level of ... mobility is an expression of the pervasive economic insecurities most people have to cope with' (Pauli, 2019, pp. 220ff).

One reason for the decline in formal marriages is that, for many people, weddings have become prohibitively expensive. Like funerals, weddings have come to serve as demonstrations of a family's status and success, rather than a modest ritual declaring the families' commitment to sustaining the relationship when it falters. As Pauli concludes in her study of changing marriage practices in Namibia, 'to marry has become an indicator of elite success' (Pauli, 2019, p. 258). As they grow more elaborate and expensive, Ghanaian weddings are coming to resemble funerals – prolonged and costly rituals that van der Geest (2000) characterizes as investments in family status for the relatives of the deceased.

Young men who lack the resources to hold a creditable wedding are obliged to postpone formal marriage or avoid it altogether. Many couples cohabit instead, often producing children, but breaking up and moving on if the relationship sours. Even formal marriages take time to develop, with relatives of both bride and groom stepping in to solve problems and sustain the marriage when it is in trouble (Cooper, 1997; Allman and Tashjian, 2000). Formal marriage is highly valued, earning a family respect, but breaking up is easier if a couple is not formally joined. Men who cohabit say they appreciate the flexibility of domestic life outside of formal marriage, while increasing numbers of women say they would rather remain unmarried than be stuck supporting an unemployed and abusive husband (Ekejiuba, 2005; Pauli, 2019, pp. 242ff).

In contrast to the rise of informality in marital relationships, economic instability has intensified intra-familial disputes, leading people to resort to litigation when they cannot settle their differences on their own. Inheritance is a case in point. Always a potential subject of family discord, inheritance has become increasingly contentious as people's economic circumstances decline. In Ghana, as elsewhere, courts continue to hear 'customary' evidence on competing claims to inheritance based on oral history, although they prefer to decide cases on the basis of statutory law and documentary evidence. Some years ago, I heard a High Court judge in Ghana overrule a lawyer's objection to testimony based on oral history on the grounds that it was 'nothing but hearsay'. 'Of course, it is hearsay', the judge responded. '*All* traditional history is hearsay. But it is permissible hearsay.'

I do not know whether the judge decided the case on this basis, however. Many of his colleagues try to avoid resting their decisions on oral history, knowing that they can be easily overturned on appeal (Berry, 1997; cf. Shipton, 2007, 2009). As many studies have shown, pervasive economic insecurity has destabilized families, communities and other kinds of social networks. Wives, but also tenants, employees, domestic servants, and others who have long been regarded as having claims on their conjugal or employers' resources if they fulfil their obligations, are increasingly likely to lose them abruptly if jobs are terminated or cohabiting couples break up. Cooper's (1997) subtle analysis of the changing emotional dynamics of marriage among Hausa families in Niger adds nuance to quantitative studies of declining rates of marriage (Pauli, 2019; Popoola and Ayandele, 2019). Widows are especially vulnerable. In principle, widows are cared for by their children or natal families, but in practice they are often ignored by relatives who do not feel bound by custom, or simply lack the resources to take care of them (Allman and Tashjian, 2000; Mutongi, 2007).

5.6 Land Markets and Social Change

African women have long played a major role in agricultural production, both for home consumption and for sale, but gained access to land only through their husbands. If a marriage breaks up, the wife or wives are dependent on their natal families for access to land and other forms of support that may or may not be forthcoming. As the pace of social life becomes more volatile, access to productive resources has become more unreliable. A striking example is the recent rise of 'contract marriage' in the cocoa farming region of southern Ghana. As Duncan (2010) explains, 'contract marriage' is primarily a labour arrangement rather than a mode of family formation. A woman agrees to live with a farmer for 2–6 months, not only assisting with work on the farm, but also providing domestic services in exchange for a cash payment or a share of the season's harvest. For some farmers, 'contract marriages' are preferable to hired labourers whose contributions are limited to work on the farm, without the domestic and sexual services included in a contract marriage. Formalized marriage is respected but may also be regarded as a liability – increasing a widow's chance of inheriting part of a farm that she has helped her husband to develop but depriving his family of part of their land (Duncan, 2010, p. 316). As courts seek to resolve such disputes, they have drawn clearer boundaries between 'self-acquired' and family land, contributing to the individualization of property ownership (Berry, 2021, forthcoming).

Land arrangements and the social relationships that develop around them have been further destabilized in recent years as international investors have become increasingly interested in African land, often acquiring large tracts of land for farming or conservation. Popularly known as 'land grabs', as mentioned earlier, these transactions have had decidedly mixed effects on land users and local economies. Often justified as a necessary condition for investment in infrastructure, equipment and advanced farming methods, land grabs have also displaced small-scale farmers and other rural residents who lack ready access to alternative sources of income. National and local authorities who often profit from these deals argue that land allocated to large and medium-scale investors is uncultivated or 'unused', but fail to take account of alternative forms of land use, such as fallowing or the collection of firewood, medicines and other naturally occurring plants, that are a significant part of local livelihoods (Chimhowu and Woodhouse, 2008; Peters, 2013). Comparing large and medium-sized commercial farms in three African countries (Kenya, Zambia and Ghana), Hall *et al.* (2017) found that both state appropriations of land for plantations and land acquisition by medium-sized commercial farmers increased pressure on land in all but a few of the localities they studied. Surprisingly, perhaps, out-grower schemes – which are often defended as 'win–win' arrangements whereby farmers receive inputs, credit and improved access to markets while retaining their land – also increased pressure on land in two of the countries studied (Kenya and Zambia).

A further source of increased competition and unstable markets for land has been the rising pace of peri-urban expansion around African cities. Because of the high risk of default, mortgages are expensive, and many people are reluctant or unable to take them on. A popular form of investment, construction of houses and/or multi-use buildings is largely self-financed. Structures are built bit by bit, when the investor has a little spare cash, creating cities that grow outward rather than up. Suburban sprawl displaces farms and farmers, exacerbated by the rapid creation of partial structures, as landholders seek to secure their claims to parcels of land by fixing something on them – establishing a foundation, for example, and then adding to it when they can. Many who work in the city reside outside it where housing costs are cheaper, commuting to and from the city daily, and creating a ready market for rental space in peri-urban areas (Berry, 2006).

5.7 Governing Practices: Multiple Rules, Competing Authorities and Lines of Conflict

Eminent domain, science and obfuscation

In addition to enacting laws, African states have used their powers of eminent domain to appropriate private land for 'public purposes', ranging from conservation schemes to 'development'. The process is vividly illustrated in *Atomic Junction*, a recent book by Osseo-Asare (2019). *Atomic Junction* charts the history of a state institution – the Ghana Atomic Energy Commission (GAEC) – to illustrate the scientific ambitions of newly independent African states, and the ways they were often thwarted by financial constraints, international scepticism, and postcolonial politics. Rather than enlighten the public about the Commission's work, GAEC used popular misconceptions about their progress to counteract the effects of increasing competition over land allocated to them by Ghana's first independent government.

Established some distance from the capital city of Accra, the neighbourhood of Atomic Junction filled up rapidly as the city expanded, leading neighbours to encroach repeatedly on the Commission's land. Arguing that the land was needed as a buffer against potential radiation leaks from the nuclear reactor, GAEC fostered the widespread belief that a nuclear reactor had been installed on the site in the early 1960s, although this did not actually happen until 1994 and when it did, the reactor was smaller and much safer than the one GAEC planned in the 1960s.

Gender

In *Atomic Junction*, competition over land centred on differences in knowledge between state-supported scientists and the citizenry that allowed the commission to resist encroachment on unused portions of land allocated for nuclear research and production of energy. Elsewhere, competition over land coincided with other kinds of economic and social difference, helping to sharpen and politicize them. Gender is another source of difference in access to land, both through and beyond conjugal relations. Differences in gender also work indirectly to advance men's power over land while diminishing that of their wives and female neighbours. Often developed far from Africa and applied broadly across the continent, paradigms of rural and agricultural development reach into the daily lives of men and women in African villages, affecting relations between them in sometimes unexpected ways.

In the 1970s and 1980s, international agencies pushed programs of 'Women in Development' (WID) aimed at reducing gender inequalities while promoting agricultural expansion. In a longitudinal study of one village in Gambia, Schroeder describes a WID project that helped women establish small market gardens, growing hand-watered vegetables during the dry season for home consumption and for sale. Male landholders had no objection to women planting gardens on portions of their land, but husbands complained loudly that wives who spent their days tending to their gardens were not available at home to draw water for their husbands' baths or prepare food for his guests. Their tune changed as women brought home income that they had earned from selling their vegetables, while men's income from groundnuts suffered from exhausted soil and falling prices. In a year or two, married men had become advocates rather than opponents of their wives' market gardens (Schroeder, 1999).

By the 1980s, however, rising concern over desertification led international agencies to shift their attention from WID to agroforestry. Encouraged by foreign NGOs, male villagers saw an opportunity to offset declining returns to groundnuts (their principal cash crop) and began to plant mango and other fruit trees, often locating them in or adjacent to women's gardens so that the women could water the trees as they watered their vegetables. As the trees grew, however, they began to cast shade over the gardens, reducing the yields of the cabbages and onions that women grew on their plots. Male landholders emphasized that the women's gardens were temporary; planting permanent tree crops was male landholders' prerogative. Asked whether he planned to drive the women off his land when his trees matured, one of the larger landholders in the village professed innocence. 'I will not drive them', he explained, 'the trees will drive them' (Schroeder, 1999, p. 114).

Rewriting history

As land has become scarce in areas of both annual and tree crop farming, conflicts have broken out not only between men and women, but also between 'strangers' and 'indigenes' – terms used to distinguish descendants of immigrants who migrated to an area a generation or two ago when land was abundant, from those who welcomed them when they first arrived. Increasingly, 'indigenes' argue that since they came first, the land *belongs* to them: later arrivals only used it with their permission. The effect has been to downgrade 'strangers' from established residents to temporary sojourners, subject to displacement if the land is needed by 'indigenes' to use, lease or sell.

An example of the kinds of conflict that may result is Côte d'Ivoire, where immigrants played a key role in the rapid expansion of the cocoa economy from the 1950s. After the French government abolished forced labour in 1946, migrants from drier and poorer regions in central and northern Côte d'Ivoire, Burkina Faso and Mali moved south, working as labourers for established cocoa farmers in the forest zone and, in many cases, acquiring land and developing farms in their own right. By the late 20th century, uncultivated land was scarce and resentment against the immigrants mounted, especially among the descendants of villagers who considered themselves indigenes. As ethnoregional competition mounted over succession to the long-reigning Ivorian President Houphouët Boigny after his death in 1993, conflict between indigenes and strangers intensified, adding fuel to the fires of political contestations that descended into civil war in 2003 (Akindès, 2004; Chauveau, 2006).

Convergence between land access, ethnic identity and conflict has not been limited to Côte d'Ivoire. Lentz has chronicled the long history of territorial expansion by one ethnic group in the border area between northwestern Ghana and Burkina Faso. Led not by chiefs, but by ordinary rural residents, Dagara expanded their control over land by taking their earth shrines with them when they migrated, installing them in new settlements as they moved (Lentz, 2014). In the late 20th century, priests and custodians of earth shrines waged a successful campaign for judicial recognition, placing their authority over rural land in the north on a par with that of chiefs in the south (Kuba and Lentz, 2006; Lund, 2009). Lentz and others have argued that the rearrangement of differential land rights also sharpened ethnic differences in the region. Researchers working in other parts of the continent have reported similar effects (Meinert and Taylor, 2017; Klaus, 2020).

Chiefs and state

Another kind of political contestation furthered by increasing land scarcity has pitted traditional authorities against local officials sanctioned by the state. Despite their very different histories of both colonial rule and independence, both Ghana and South Africa have seen a rise in chiefly power since democratic governments came to power. In both cases, newly elected authorities took legal steps to strip governing authority away from traditional authorities, reducing them to symbols of 'customary' culture. In both cases, chiefs capitalized on growing class and ethnic tensions over land to reinsert themselves into the process of government, claiming 'historical' authority over land and the settlement of disputes. Struggling to mobilize popular support after independence, politicians courted 'traditional leaders', hoping they would mobilize blocs of voters to strengthen or sustain the politicians' hold on power. Especially in South Africa, where chiefs presided over well-established local governing institutions created by the apartheid regime, they were far better prepared to meet residents' needs than newly created local authorities who often lacked basic equipment and services (Ntzebeza, 2005; Comaroff and Comaroff, 2018).

Although Ghana achieved independence decades earlier than South Africa, Nkrumah and many of his successors were also not eager to offend traditional authorities, allowing both chiefs and, later, earth priests to assert their traditional 'oversight' of land attached to their jurisdictions (known as 'stools' in the south, 'skins' in the north). By the early 21st century, chiefs had not only reasserted their authority over domestic land seekers but negotiated land deals with international investors eager to take advantage of booming world markets for biofuels and other agricultural staples. Asked why the government permitted chiefs to do this, officials explained that control over stool land was a chiefly prerogative, and that the constitution prohibits state officials from interfering in 'chiefly affairs' (Government of Ghana, 1992, article 270).

Generations

Economic instability and the rising value of land also led to divisions between generations. Relying on customary land arrangements that treated rural land as belonging to families rather than individuals, many young people left their natal villages to try their luck in cash cropping regions, cities and towns. When African economies shrank – especially in urban areas – under the impact of structural adjustment, many young people returned to their villages to ride out the downturn by farming on their 'family land'. The resulting conflicts were bitter: young people's smoldering resentment undermined their respect for seniors' authority and sometimes erupted in violence (Mathieu, *et al.* 2003; Chauveau and Richards, 2008). Ethnic, generational and gender differences over access to land and employment also permeated extractive industries, especially mining. See, for example, Cook (2011) and Hilson and Hilson (2017).

5.8 Conclusion

Promoted by population growth and by increasing uses of land for economic purposes ranging from farming to urbanization, commercialization of land transactions tends to reinforce the factors that caused it. It has also contributed to a variety of social differences – dispossessing some people while enriching others, widening the gap between richer families and poorer ones, sharpening divisions between genders and generations, and turning neighbours into 'indigenes' and 'strangers'. Social divisions have frequently given rise to conflict, putting strain on social relationships while, at the same time, increasing people's need for them. People invested time and money in sustaining older relationships and building new ones, hoping to strengthen their ability to cope with a turbulent world, with mixed results. Subject to crosswinds of competition and collaboration, land was a focus of frequent contention.

Seeking to manage these tensions while at the same time consolidating their own power and, in many cases, increasing their wealth, governing authorities at both local and national levels became deeply involved in land affairs. Beginning in the 1990s (or, in some cases, the 1980s) many African governments instituted programs of land 'reform' – not to reduce social and economic inequalities, but to attract both international and domestic investment by clarifying and certifying property rights in general, and rights of land ownership in particular. As illustrated by developments in Ghana, Côte d'Ivoire, South Africa and elsewhere, efforts to govern land transactions have had very mixed results – too complex to sum up in one short chapter. Thirty years after the process of land 'reform' got underway, studies in many different parts of the continent do point to some common trends. Efforts to consolidate state (and state elites') power over land allocation have reinforced hierarchical patterns of authority, pulling people away from networks defined in terms of kinship and community towards political patronage (see Meagher, 2010). Rather than streamline processes of governance, however, these pressures have often worked to reinforce both legal and institutional pluralism. Politicians, bureaucrats, judges, chiefs and a variety of local officials and power brokers 'govern' with but also parallel to one another, leading not to more broadly democratic systems of authority, but generating plenty of contention and debate.

Endnotes

[1] The principal systems of land governance in Africa today have emerged since independence, but elements can be traced to colonial and even precolonial times.

[2] Societies have always faced conditions of uncertainty, of course. In focusing on Africa in the present discussion, I do not mean to suggest that political, economic and social instabilities are exclusively African or contemporary.

References

Akindès, F. (2004) *The Roots of the Military-Political Crises in Côte d'Ivoire*. Nordafrikainstitutet, Uppsala, Sweden.

Allman, J. and Tashjian, V. (2000) *'I will not eat stone': A Women's History of Colonial Asante*. Heinemann, Portsmouth, NH, USA.

Benjaminsen, T. and Lund, C. (2012). *Securing Land Rights in Africa*. Taylor & Francis, Hoboken, NJ, USA.

Berry, S. (1997) Tomatoes, land and hearsay: Property and history in Asante in the time of structural adjustment. *World Development*, 25(8), 1225–1241.

Berry, S. (2001) *Chiefs Know Their Boundaries: Essays on Property, Power and the Past in Asante*. Heinemann, Portsmouth, NH, USA.

Berry, S. (2006) 'Natives' and 'strangers' on the outskirts of Kumasi. *Ghana Studies*, 9(1), 25–59.

Berry, S. (2013) Questions of ownership: proprietorship and control in a changing rural terrain. A case study from Ghana. *Africa*, 83(1), 36–56.

Berry, S. (2018) Chieftaincy, land, and the state in Ghana and South Africa. In: Comaroff, J.L. and Comaroff, J. (Eds), *The Politics of Custom: Chiefship, Capital, and the State in Contemporary Africa* (pp. 79–109). University of Chicago Press, Chicago, IL, USA.

Bolt, M. (2015) *Zimbabwe's Migrants and South African Border Farms: The Roots of Impermanence*. Cambridge University Press, Cambridge, UK.

Boni, S. (2006) Indigenous blood and foreign labor: The ancestralization of land rights in Sefwi (Ghana). In: Kuba, R. and Lentz, C. (Eds), *Land and the Politics of Belonging in West Africa* (pp. 160–185). Brill, Leiden, The Netherlands.

Byamugisha, F. (2013) *Securing Land for Shared Prosperity: A Program to Scale Up Reforms and Investments*. World Bank, Washington, DC, USA.

Chauveau, J. and Richards, P. (2008) West African insurgencies in agrarian perspective: Côte d'Ivoire and Sierra Leone compared. *Journal of Agrarian Change*, 8(4), 515–552.

Chimhowu, A. and Woodhouse, P. (2008) Communal tenure and rural poverty: land transactions in Svosve Communal Area, Zimbabwe. *Development and Change*, 39(2), 285–308.

Colin, J. (2017) Contractual practice and land conflicts: the 'plant and share' arrangement in Côte d'Ivoire. *Journal of Agrarian Change*, 17(1), 144–165.

Comaroff, J.L. and Comaroff, J. (Eds) (2018) *The Politics of Custom: Chiefship, Capital and State in Contemporary Africa*. University of Chicago Press, Chicago, IL, USA.

Cook, S. (2011) The business of being Bafokeng: the corporatization of a tribal authority in South Africa. *Current Anthropology*, 52(S3). DOI: 10.1086/657894.

Cooper, B. (1997) *Marriage in Maradi: Gender and Culture in a Hausa Society in Niger*. Heinemann, Portsmouth, NH, USA.

Cotula, L. (2009) *Land Grabs or Development Opportunities: Agricultural Investment and International Land Deals in Africa*. IIED, London, UK.

Davison, J. (2019) *Agriculture, Women and the Land in Africa*. Routledge, London, UK.

Deininger, K. (2010) *Innovations in Land Rights Recognition, Administration and Governance*. World Bank, Washington, DC, USA.

Duncan, B.A. (2010) Cocoa, marriage, land and labor in Ghana: matrilineal and patrilineal perspectives. *Africa*, 80(2), 301–321.

Ekejiuba, F. (2005) Down to fundamentals: woman-centered hearth-holds in rural West Africa. In: Bryceson, D. (Ed.), *Women Wielding the Hoe: Lessons from Rural Africa for Feminist Theory and Development Practice*. Routledge, Oxford, UK, pp. 47–61.

Elder, C., Stigant, C. and Claes, J. (2014) *Elections and Violent Conflict in Kenya: Making Prevention Stick*. United States Institute for Peace, Washington, DC, USA.

Frempong, S. (2004) *The Application of the Law of Intestate Succession and Its Effects on Families*. Institute of African Studies, Legon, Ghana.

Government of Ghana (1992) *Constitution of the Republic of Ghana 1992*. Government of Ghana, Accra.

Guyer, J. (2004) *Marginal Gains: Monetary Transactions in Atlantic Africa*. University of Chicago Press, Chicago, IL, USA.

Hall, R., Scoones, I. and Tsikata, D. (2015) *Africa's Land Rush: Rural Livelihoods and Agrarian Change*. James Currey, Rochester, NY, USA.

Hall, R., Scoones, I. and Tsikata, D. (2017) Plantations, outgrowers and commercial farming in Africa: agricultural commercialisation and implications for agrarian change. *Journal of Peasant Studies*, 44(3), 515–537.

Hilson, G. and Hilson, A. (2017) Mining in Ghana: Critical reflections on a turbulent past and an uncertain future. In: *Aryeetey, E.* and Kanbur, R. (Eds), *The Economy of Ghana Sixty Years After Independence*. Oxford University Press, Oxford, UK, pp. 261–278.

Kanogo, T. (1987) *Squatters and the Roots of Mau*. Ohio University Press, Athens, OH, USA.

Klaus, K. (2020) *Political Violence in Kenya: Land, Elections and Claim-Making*. Cambridge University Press, Cambridge, UK.

Kuba, R. and Lentz, C. (Eds) (2006) *Land rights and the Politics of Belonging in West Africa*. Brill, Leiden, The Netherlands.

Lentz, C. (2014) *Land, Mobility and Belonging in West Africa*. Indiana University Press, Bloomington, IN, USA.

Lund, C. (2009) *Local Politics and the Dynamics of Property in Africa*. Cambridge University Press, Cambridge, UK.

Manji, A. (2013) *The Politics of Land Reform in Africa: From Communal Tenure to Free Markets*. Zed, London, UK.

Mathieu, P., Deville, P.L., Paré, L., Zongo, M., Ouédraogo, H., Baud, J., Bologo, E., Koné, N. and Triollet, K. (2003) *Making Land Transactions More Secure in the West of Burkina Faso*. IIED, London, UK.

Meagher, K. (2010) *Identity Economics: Social Networks and the Informal Economy in Nigeria*. Cambridge University Press, Cambridge, UK.

Meinert, L. and Taylor, D.R. (2017) Questioning boundaries and belonging: Introduction, ASR Land Forum: Land disputes and displacement in post-conflict Africa. *African Studies Review*, 60(3), 7–15.

Moore, J. (2018) Kenya's political turmoil is a tale of fathers and sons. *New York Times*, 20 February. Available at: https://www.nytimes.com/2018/02/20/world/africa/kenya-kenyatta-odinga.html (accessed 17 November 2020).

Mustapha, A.R. and Ehrhardt, D. (Eds) (2018) *Creed and Grievance: Muslim–Christian Relations and Conflict Resolution in Northern Nigeria*. James Currey, Suffolk, UK.

Mutongi, K. (2007) *Worries of the Heart: Widows, Family and Community in Kenya*. Chicago University Press, Chicago, IL, USA.

Ntzebeza, L. (2005) *Democracy Compromised: Chiefs and the Politics of the Land in South Africa*. Brill, Leiden, The Netherlands/Boston, MA, USA.

Osseo-Asare, A. (2019) *Atomic Junction: Nuclear Power in Africa After Independence*. Cambridge University Press, Cambridge, UK.

Patnaik, U., Moyo, S. and Shivji, I. (2011) *The Agrarian Question in the Neoliberal Era: Primitive Accumulation and the Peasantry*. Pambazuka Press, South Africa.

Pauli, J. (2019) *The Decline of Marriage in Namibia: Kinship and Social Class in a Rural Community*. Transcript Verlag, Bielefeld, Germany.

Peace, A. (1978) *Choice, Class and Conflict: A Study of Factory Workers in Southern Nigeria*. Humanities Press, Atlantic Highlands, NJ, USA.

Peters, P. (2004) Inequality and social conflict over land. *Journal of Agrarian Change*, 4(3), 269–314.

Peters, P. (2013) Conflicts over land and threats to customary tenure. *African Affairs*, 112(449), 543–562.

Peterson, K. (2014) *Speculative Investments: Derivative Life in Nigeria*. Duke University Press, Durham, NC, USA.

Popoola, O. and Ayandele, O. (2019) Cohabitation: harbinger or slayer of marriage in sub-Saharan Africa. *Gender and Behaviour*, 17(2), 13029–13039.

Rodriguez, C., Tsikata, D. and Ampofo, A.A. (2015) *Transatlantic Feminisms: Women and Gender Studies in Africa and the Diaspora*. Lexington Books, Lanham, MD, USA.

Ruf, F. and Siswoputranto, P.S. (1995) *Cocoa Cycles: The Economics of Cocoa Supply*. Woodhead Publishing Limited, Cambridge, UK.

Schroeder, R. (1999) *Shady Practices: Gender and Agroforestry in Gambia*. University of California Press, Berkeley/Los Angeles, CA, USA.

Shipton, P. (2007) *The Nature of Entrustment: Intimacy, Exchange and the Sacred in Africa*. Yale University Press, New Haven, CT, USA.

Shipton, P. (2009) *Mortgaging the Ancestors: Ideologies of Attachment in Africa*. Yale University Press, New Haven, CT, USA.

van der Geest, S. (2000) Funerals for the living: conversations with elderly people in Kwahu, Ghana. *African Studies Review*, 43(3), 103–129.

Part 2

Tenure–Gender Dimensions in Land Management, Land Administration and Land Policy

6 Advancing Women's Position by Recognizing and Strengthening Customary Land Rights: Lessons from Community-Based Land Interventions in Mozambique

Julian Quan,* Lora Forsythe and June Y.T. Po
Natural Resources Institute, University of Greenwich

6.1 Introduction

A growing body of research demonstrates the importance of women's ownership of and control over land as a livelihood asset for a range of development outcomes (Quisumbing and Maluccio, 2003; Meinzen-Dick *et al.*, 2019). Previous studies have found consistent associations between women's land rights (WLR) and bargaining and decision-making power on household consumption, spending (for instance on children's education), investment and intergenerational transfers (Federici, 2011; Harari, 2019; Meinzen-Dick *et al.*, 2019). However, in Africa and globally, pervasive gender inequalities exist in the ownership and control of land resources (Doss *et al.*, 2015). These inequalities constrain the potential of development interventions, including those that aim to strengthen women's tenure rights. However, a dearth of data concerning the differential impacts of land reform on women makes it difficult to produce practical recommendations on gender-transformative land governance (de Villiers, 2003; Chigbu, 2020).

This chapter argues that gender-sensitive lessons from recent land programmes and projects are critical to the planning, design and modification of new and continuing efforts of land programmes, to achieve transformative development outcomes, for both women and men. We propose three important considerations for understanding the opportunities and constraints for gender-senstivity in land programmes: (i) the context of gendered land tenure and livelihood systems; (ii) the increase in private-sector agricultural investments for economic growth and national development in Africa, and (iii) the actors and methods involved in delivering land and development programmes to rural communities. Using three recent cases from Mozambique, this chapter explores how these factors shape the interaction between development organizations and local communities creates tension between land programmes and private investors, and women's empowerment in the context of their households and communities. The chapter draws on two locally specific tenure projects and one wider national programme, all of which received financial and technical support from the UK's former development agency, the Department for International Development (DfID). Each intervention aimed to secure customary land rights as an important condition for achieving transformative outcomes in agricultural and natural resource-based development.

*Corresponding author: j.f.quan@gre.ac.uk

DOI: 10.1079/9781789247664.0006

Next, we briefly summarize existing literature on gender dimensions of land tenure in Africa and followed by a description of the national land tenure policy and gendered development context in Mozambique. In Section 6.4, we describe the three cases of land tenure interventions in Mozambique. We identify the impacts of land tenure programmes on women's economic and social development options and consider the dynamic interaction with gendered local livelihood contexts and with agricultural investments and development programmes. We then examine the gendered objectives and methods used by programme delivery organizations, and the immediate and potential longer-range outcomes these interventions have had for women, based on practical insights and available project data. Section 6.5 discusses the impacts of these land programmes on development opportunities for women, the local contexts that influences impacts of land programmes, and the key design and management lessons for tenure projects and programmes to generate gender transformative outcomes. A brief conclusion summarizes lessons learned, the opportunities to apply these lessons in future land tenure interventions, and the implications for programme design and implementing partner's organizational strategies in Mozambique and elsewhere in sub-Saharan Africa.

6.2 Women's Tenure Security in Africa

Common conceptualizations in the women's land rights literature categorize use, control and ownership of land as a bundle of land rights (International Food Policy Research Institute, 2013; Johnson *et al.* 2016). Security of land rights is of particular importance in poverty reduction. Yet the evolving gender and land tenure security literature has been conceptualized and analytically framed in multiple, often ill-defined, categories, making comparisons across studies challenging (Arnot *et al.*, 2011; Meinzen-Dick *et al.* 2019). In practice, land rights, statutory or customary, are applied and sanctioned through formal and informal mechanisms, not only described by a bundle of rights, but also involving 'a bundle of powers', of which women systemically have an inequitable and secondary share (Ribot and Peluso 2003; Chigbu, 2020). While men and women can benefit from land resources without formal or secure land property rights, marginalized groups, such as young widows without children, single mothers, young and non-married men, and migrants frequently face widespread land discrimination and disputes (Holger, 2011). On the other hand, state-level land formalization programmes, for example in Ethiopia and Rwanda, have paid particular attention to ensure that women's names are included in registration documents. However, for formalization of rights to have an impact, a shared understanding among women and men of what formalized rights entail, how these changes can influence on existing local social-cultural practices, and the changes involved is needed (Federici, 2011, Doss *et al.*, 2014, Meinzen-Dick *et al.*, 2019).

Since the 1960s, decades of efforts to formalize land rights have advanced aims of land tenure security unevenly. Since then, proponents of context-informed understanding of land governance have promoted the role of multiple forms of land rights and levels of tenure security in pathways to reduce poverty (Lastarria-Cornhiel, 1997). Statutory acknowledgement of customary land governance and resulting plural legal jurisdiction have highlighted the complexities of implementation and practice of land governance reforms. Policy makers and practitioners are urged to integrate gender-sensitive analysis into the assessment of land governance institutions (Po *et al.*, 2019), and the local power relations that become levers of resource distribution (Daley and Lanz, 2016).

Beyond recognizing the different matrilineal and patrilineal kinship structures that continue to influence contemporary tenure systems, previous research has shown that gender relations had evolved historical and culturally with significant impacts on women's ownership and control of land. For example, Adichie (2018) found that women of the Igbo ethnic group in Nigeria owned property until top-down colonial policies were enacted where male dominance within a conventional Western hierarchy had led to land registration under men's names only. In the eastern part of the continent, Kenyan customary marital practices, such as polygamy (Po and Zipporah, 2016), have continuing impacts on contemporary, customary access to land. Moreover, women's entry into informal and formal land markets have led to an uptick of land registered and secured in their male children's names (Po and Hickey, 2018).

The growing complexity of land tenure security and policy discourse is further compounded by significant pressures of demographic changes, large-scale agricultural land investments, internal migration, and the presence of development agencies, and private companies. For most subsistence land users and small-scale farmers the time and resource-intensive process of acquiring formal tenure security is out of reach. In the interim, communities adapt to less secure access to land and forest resources through less formal institutional, relational, and structural mechanisms (Ribot and Peluso, 2003). For instance, groups have shown resourcefulness and agency to engage in alternative income-generating activities, participate in training in improved agricultural technologies, sustainable natural resource utilization and management, build entrepreneurial and leadership skills, as illustrated in the case studies in this chapter.

6.3 The Land Tenure and Gender Context in Mozambique

Women in Mozambique are disadvantaged by low levels of education, high maternal health risks, pressure to marry at a young age, limited economic prospects, gender-based violence, and discriminatory cultural norms. Although the 1997 Land Law confirms the constitutional principle that women and men have equal rights to occupy, use, and inherit land, in a predominantly patriarchal system, rights to access land are derived from men and women's position in the family. Throughout southern and central Mozambique, under predominantly patrilineal systems, only men inherit land. In much of northern Mozambique, matrilineal inheritance and matrilocal marriage are practised. Although the transmission of land through the female line affords widows greater security, and daughters greater access, land allocation is largely controlled by male relatives and family heads. Across most of Mozambique, typically men use land to produce for the market and have greater access to the most valuable and productive land (Raimundo, undated) while women provide 63% of the agricultural workforce, principally responsible for subsistence, family food production (USAID, 2019).

Constitutionally, all land remains the property of the Mozambican state. However, the Mozambican legal framework permits Mozambican nationals to acquire tenure rights through inheritance, peaceful occupation, or customary channels. Under the 1997 Land Law, which has been regarded as one of the most progressive in Africa (Toulmin and Quan, 2000; Tanner and Baleira, 2006; Norfolk and Tanner, 2007), citizens, associations of small-scale producers, and corporate bodies can enjoy a bundle of land tenure rights (use, access, maintenance and benefit) although they are not allowed to buy and sell land. In other respects, these usufruct tenure rights, known by the Portuguese acronym 'DUAT' (*Direito de Uso e Aproveitamento da Terra*), are equivalent to ownership. Community groups can formally register customary land rights or rights established by occupation of ten years or more, and the law states that where land rights have not been formally registered, oral evidence of neighbours and community members can be accepted as legal proof of established land use rights.

Like most postcolonial states, Mozambique relies on a national cadastral system, organized centrally, which in this case is operated at the provincial level. Most formal land administration functions, such as registration of land rights, are carried out by the provincial cadastral services or by urban municipal authorities. However, the cadastral database has been consistently judged not to be fit for purpose and out of date. In practice, it is primarily local community leaders who uphold customary tenure rights, make land allocations to community members, and resolve community disputes according to locally established customary principles. Although the law recognizes in principle the long-established rights of customary land users, the vast proportion of customary rights held individually and collectively remain largely undocumented, and thus vulnerable to dispossession by the state.

The 1997 Land Law was also intended to stimulate economic development partnerships between rural communities and the private sector. Investors seeking to lease land in Mozambique are legally required to conduct and participate in consultations with host and neighbouring communities to agree on the release of community areas for development, an approach referred to as an 'open borders model' (Norfolk and Tanner, 2007; Quan *et al.*, 2013). Since 2005, Mozambique has experienced a wave of interest in large-scale land acquisition among foreign investors. Between 2005 and 2014, 63 investment projects in Mozambique were identified, totalling over 2.1 million hectares (Schoneveld, 2014), one of the largest areas of land transferred from public and community control into private hands in sub-Saharan Africa. Although the biofuels sector was initially viewed as a main driver of land acquisition (Nhantumbo *et al.*, 2010), biofuel investments have experienced very high failure rates and accounts for only a small proportion of private land allocations. Most investors have focused on grains or horticulture crops (Di Matteo and Schoneveld, 2016), or on the plantation forestry sector, estimated to occupy over 1 million hectares in land concessions, largely in areas otherwise under long-term customary occupation and use. The minerals and extractives sector has also occupied rural land, leading to displacement of customary users and curtailment of existing natural resource dependent livelihoods across significant areas. New public–private spatial development initiatives have further encouraged large-scale acquisition of farmland, together with land allocation for infrastructure development. Several high-profile investments have been implicated in accusations of land grabbing and speculation (Norfolk and Hanlon, 2012; German *et al.*, 2016), with most large private agricultural and forestry investments subsequently failing, amid poor planning and conflicts with local people. Since 2011, contract farming arrangements and support to Mozambican smallholders and producers[1] have received greater policy emphasis however.

The approach of community land delimitation, with associated community development support was promoted and undertaken largely by civil society organizations working in partnership with provincial government, financed by bilateral donors and some international NGOs. The government welcomed this approach as a means of enabling communities to take ownership of development opportunities, and a basis for participation in public-rivate partnerships. Securing land rights on a collective basis offered a legal and cost- effective basis to protect the *de facto* land rights held by communities and their members, but provides no guarantees of tenure security for individuals' land rights beyond the rules prevailing in local customary practice. In the absence of systematic land rights mapping and certification of the rights of individuals (Norfolk *et al.*, 2020), it remains extremely difficult and prohibitively expensive for rural Mozambicans to secure official land titles which requires travel to distant provincial capitals, and compliance with a series of bureaucratic steps, in most cases beyond their means.

Prior to 2015, Mozambique's national cadastre included only official DUAT titles that registered individuals, or commercially oriented smallholders, and corporate bodies granted concessions by government or delimited community land holdings. In 2015, *Terra Segura*, a five-year government programme on land security, was launched with the aim to deliver 5 million DUAT titles. In practice, between 2013 and 2019 a series of donor-supported land administration and rural development programmes delivered approximately 375,000 titles to individual households. Information on the numbers of women and female-headed households who have formalized land rights through *Terra Segura* was not available at the time of writing. With World Bank support, the Mozambican government aims to expand household land registration, strengthen land administration capacity, update the National Land Policy, and revise the existing Land Law, and to strengthen the legal and regulatory framework to enable rural communities to contribute to and benefit from natural resource management. Although official policy recognizes rural communities as key actors in managing land use changes, challenges remain to ensure that women are fully engaged in these processes.

6.4 Case studies

Below we present two local tenure projects and a national land initiative in Mozambique, all of which aimed to strengthen existing communities' land rights as a basis for economic development partnerships. The cases highlight the importance of cultural contexts, livelihood diversification opportunities, and methods of engagement by land programme delivery organizations in transforming gender relations.

Community Land Rights and Women Baobab Harvester Clubs in Manica

In the north of Manica province, highly variable rainfall, frequent droughts and seasonally dry savanna woodlands subject the area to uncontrolled fires. Seasonal male migration for temporary work in regional towns or local logging operations was common. Women were traditionally responsible for household food production. Frequent burning, together with uncontrolled logging were increasing pressure on the resource and the primary livelihoods for women. The Micaia Foundation, an NGO working to support community livelihoods and sustainable natural resources management, runs an impactful project in this fundamentally patriarchal region of Manica province in which polygamy is widely practiced, teenage girls are married off at an early age, and men control household decision making (Kingman, 2018). Women have little access to cash income and are reliant on sales of peanuts and baobab fruits. However, profits from baobab sales were generally marginal due to the low prices paid by traders. Growing demand and profitability of baobab products have raised the importance of women's continued access to and income from baobab, yet this important livelihood avenue for women and their families received little recognition by customary authorities. In recent years, access to the baobab trees, usually in communal areas, is increasingly threatened due to illicit logging, deforestation, and forest fires (Wardell and Fold, 2013; Kingman, 2018).

In response, the project worked to empower women by strengthening their involvement in sustainable trade of baobab products, community decision making, communal land rights, forest management and natural resource planning. Women's baobab harvester clubs were established as a basis for women's in capacity strengthening and participation in land use planning activities. These aimed to protect their access and user rights of baobab in 20 contiguous village land areas. These clubs were then linked to Baobab Products Mozambique or BPM in 2015 to develop new natural resource-based domestic and export value chains. Two lead harvesters from each club were trained in legal procedures required to formalize rights to the resources, basic literacy, numeracy and business skills to manage group sales to BPM, and to train other group members. Micaia also established a registered baobab harvesters association involving all of the village-base harvester clubs, which holds a 20% share in the BPM business and has a significant voice in natural resource and landscape management in the Zambezi valley region.

Micaia's approach was to work with the traditional hierarchy of male community leaders to facilitate cross-community land use planning that would increase the recognition of baobab's value and safeguard resource for women and the community. Detailed forest inventories, land cover and land use zoning maps were also established to identify the largest areas of baobab forest to be considered as common land, and the occurrence of other potentially marketable plant resources. Rather than registering formal DUAT titles to designated village baobab collection zones, the chiefs opted to follow customary practice by allowing harvester groups access to one another's forests to ensure that groups from neighbouring communities can access baobab trees, in a context of considerable local and seasonal variation in baobab productivity.

The project saw several positive impacts on women and their communities. By eliminating intermediary traders, BPM created a lucrative and inclusive market for local baobab harvesters. BPM sells baobab pulp and seed oil directly to certified organic baobab traders and has developed new urban markets for baobab flour. Since partnering with BPM, women had more reliable income, which doubled their previous revenue. Increased cash income enabled small-scale household investments, school-related expenses, access to healthcare services and food purchases during hunger seasons. Almost half the women surveyed by the project reported that they had achieved greater influence over household and community affairs in an otherwise male-dominated context (Kingman, 2019). An active landscape-wide baobab harvesters' association that is led by and largely comprises women, contributed to broader economic development and sustainable natural resource utilization prospects in the community. Micaia's efforts in bringing male community leaders onside with the project directly enhanced women's participation in new economic opportunities, control over their resource rights, and leadership capacity in the community.

Strengthening Customary Land Rights in an Investment Zone in Zambezia

In Zambezia Province, northern Mozambique, land is generally passed down the maternal line and matrilocal marriage is generally practised. Women have somewhat greater control over land than in patrilineal, patrilocal contexts. Although women occasionally act as customary community leaders, these roles are generally occupied by men. In the fertile areas, men and women lead semi-subsistence agricultural livelihoods. Settlement and land holding is increasingly fixed, and historical land use practices, for management of grazing and forest land, agricultural land rotation and fallowing practices, are slowly changing. Population growth and increasing small-scale commercial farming and large agricultural investments have increased demands for land.

In this context, ORAM (Associação Rural de Ajuda Mútua), a national civil society organization (CSO) founded in 1992, led a successful land mapping and registration initiative using participatory methods. ORAM's work supports rural communities in land rights registration, sustainable utilization of natural resources, and agricultural projects. With the support from specialized land service provider Terra Firma, ORAM used digital technologies to document village and household parcel boundaries in 20 communities. The data was incorporated into comprehensive map records and utilized to generate land rights certificates for households.

To enhance gender sensitivity of its programmes, ORAM actively recruited male and female outreach officers from the region to ensure that both men and women in the community participated in interpretation of imagery and maps in relation to their land holdings and features they were familiar with. Participants came to an agreement on parcel boundaries and claims, which in turn created a sense of ownership over the process and results. Importantly, land certificates were issued directly to women, recognizing their customary matrilineal inheritance rights, and securing their land tenure. The initiative recognized and protected women's *de facto* rights, often ignored in land titling processes. Notably, 67% of land parcels (approximately 2100 parcels) were registered solely to women, with a further 3% registered as joint spousal co-titles. Some women co-registered land with their daughters or sisters to ensure that inheritance rights were maintained in the event of death, separation or divorce, as women's family land may be exposed to counterclaims from men (Norfolk *et al.* 2020). Between 2017 and 2019, ORAM supported the mapping and certification of over 66,000 ha of community land and over 10,000 family and individual land parcels.[2]

In addition, the land delimitation process also acted as a key entry point to establish community land associations. ORAM registered 20 community land associations and organized tailored training for women to strengthen their capacity in local land management. As a result, the women and the communities were better prepared when negotiation took place with a plantation forestry investor who was granted a large-scale concession in Zambezia. The delimitation process revealed that there was little 'unused' community land available for investors, as most of the rural land was legally occupied by families and households, or used for communal sacred forests, schools, and roads. Maps and data were shared with the forestry investor, and ORAM was able to identify overlaps between community members' land claims and areas ceded to the company by chiefs and elders through hasty consultation exercises promoted by the government. This helped to establish a basis for communities to negotiate with the company from a position of strength, as their legitimate customary land rights were thoroughly documented. As a result, the company shifted its approach and promoted out-grower partnerships with individual farmers, including women, as an alternative to establishing large contiguous plantation blocks.

Challenges of Organizational Culture and Scale: Enhancing Gender Strategies in Community Land Delimitation

The Community Land Initiative (*Iniciativa para Terras Comunitárias*, or iTC) was established in 2006 to facilitate community and small-scale farmer participation in land delimitation and demarcation processes as defined by the 1997 Land Law. Until 2019, iTC was funded by a group of donors, led initially by DFID and subsequently the Netherlands. It operated as the principal umbrella programme financing rural tenure security interventions. Over a 12-year period, iTC mapped and registered the collective land rights of rural communities and producer associations. In addition, it funded and collaborated with local CSOs and private service providers to deliver a wide range of local projects focused on community development, capacity building, legal awareness, and local land use planning. Begun as a pilot programme in three provinces, the Community Land Initiative gradually expanded to eight of Mozambique's ten provinces. In each province iTC funded, organized, and strengthened the operational capacity of local delivery providers, such as ORAM.[3]

Under pressure from its donors, iTC funded a Gender and Diversity Audit in 2006 to review the status of women's participation and benefits from land delimitation. The audit found a lack of gender expertise and women's participation across iTC, service providers organizations, beneficiaries and government agencies concerning land (Forsythe and Chidiamassamba, 2006). The main recommendations from the audit were to mainstream gender-responsive approaches in community engagement activities to address neglected practical gender needs, such as setting the time and location of community-based trainings that is amenable to child-care and domestic work schedules, generally carried out by women and using local languages and female facilitators. Moreover, the audit underscored the need for further integration of quantitative and qualitative gender-relevant indicators into monitoring and evaluation (Forsythe and Chidiamassamba, 2006). As a result, iTC developed a Gender and Diversity strategy, which underscored the importance of gender-specific outcomes of community land delimitation and identification of lessons learned, routinely at each end-of-funding-cycle review (Forsythe and Chidiamassamba, 2010).

The strategy aims to strengthen women's effective and meaningful participation in iTC activities: secure access to land and resources, training in local land management, strengthen producer organizations, and access to new livelihood opportunities. Gender specialists, hired as consultants, collaborated closely on *mainstreaming* gender into existing iTC community engagement methods and tools[4] (Forsythe and Chidiamassamba, 2010). A cascade training approach was then implemented in 2012 to strengthen capacity among iTC staff and service providers in implementing the strategy. One problem found with the cascade training was that central coordination by iTC was not sufficiently focused on local or provincial gender contexts. Hence, the capacity to generate gender-sensitive outcomes or to capture gender-specific needs through monitoring was also limited (Forsythe and iTC Gender Working Group, 2013). Moreover, the gender mainstreaming approach was only really applied by iTC management of community land rights delimitation processes, as opposed to more transformative and context-specific gender activities focusing on women's rights (e.g. initiatives on women's empowerment or challenging perceptions and gender norms around land inequality). As a result, iTC was more accepting of recommendations that involved pragmatic measures applicable in all contexts, such as reaching out to women in information and awareness campaigns, using local languages, as women are less likely to speak Portuguese, and recruiting female community facilitators where possible. Like Micaia, sensitizing and working with male community leaders was an important activity to promote women's engagement with the Community Land Initiative.

Despite the lack of commitment to gender transformative efforts in iTC, there were some positive outcomes. Between 2015 and 2019, iTC delivered 1049 community land delimitations and 784 collective DUAT titles to small-scale village-based producer associations. Women's participation in awareness campaigns was found to be higher than 30% and participation in community natural resource committees to be 'improving' (EDG, 2014). A DFID project report (2019) found that across the national programme, women's overall representation in community decision-making bodies was 20%, with a similar percentage (21%) occupying leadership positions.

However, there were notable differences across provinces in relation to male labour migration to South Africa. Gender-related improvements were fragmented and depended on location and service provider. For example, women's position in resource management committees were mainly treasurers, with limited inputs to decision making (Topsøe-Jensen *et al.*, 2017). A DFID review of pre-2014 iTC community land delimitations identified a decrease in women's representation in these bodies (DFID, 2019), indicating a need for more sustainable strategies.

DFID (2019) reported 'some success in overcoming some of the traditional attitudes that limit women's participation', but that there was still a long way to go.

6.5 Discussion

In this section, we highlight the lessons learned from the cases presented, focussing on three principal aspects:

- The interplay of land programmes with local livelihoods, land use and tenure systems, population growth, seasonal and longer-term migration, and the gendered socio-economic and cultural contexts in which these take place.
- The influence of broader agricultural development programmes and land-based investments on the land rights, natural resources, and the opportunities available to women.
- The strategies, approaches, and methods used by organizations engaged in delivering land tenure projects for community engagement, land rights mapping, documentation and formalization, and their effectiveness in engaging women and promoting their interests.

Interplay of Land Interventions with Gendered Livelihoods, Tenure Systems and Cultural Practices

Comparing provinces north of the Zambezi river with the south provinces in our first two cases, we find that customary matrilineal or patrilineal inheritance and land allocation practices remain influential on women's access to land. The cases also show the importance of agroecological contexts in shaping livelihood strategies, for example, leading to out-migration or livelihood diversification. Moreover, the presence of land-based investment projects influences the opportunities or barriers that delivery organizations face to facilitate gender transformative change.

In the northern provinces where ORAM works, there are increasingly fixed agricultural holdings within family lands. While customary matrilineal inheritance is practised and women's customary land rights readily enabled their formalization processes to secure women's rights cannot be taken for granted. In fact, the case of iTC suggests that women's *de facto* rights are at risk of being undermined in gender-blind land tenure programmes, resulting in greater barriers for women's access to productive resources and sustainable livelihoods. This is particularly the case in high population areas where competition for resources, including with private investors, is considerable.

In the central province of Manica where Micaia operates, land and natural resource uses tend to be more extensive and more variable. Frequent forest burning, together with uncontrolled logging were undermining the integrity of land-based resources. In this context, given the lack of fixed land holdings, the scope to formalize women's rights to agricultural plots as a basis to develop women's agricultural skills and incomes was limited. Instead, on the basis of secure community land rights over baobab collection areas, there were opportunities to promote sustainable baobab harvesting and forest management. Baobab products became a sustainable off-season source of income, directly increasing the level of respect for women in the communities.

In addition, migration trends have influenced women's land rights security, as seen from iTC's work in different parts of the country. In Gaza province, in southern Mozambique, men are the primary land holders in a patrilineal system, and women's access to land is dependent on husbands and male relatives. However, longer-term male migration, mainly to the mines and urban areas of South Africa or to Maputo, has significantly influenced women's land rights. Women have become *de facto* heads of households and market-oriented farmers. In this context, women's land use was vulnerable to encroachment, and women lacked agency in developing agricultural business: for example, there were cases where women had to wait for their husband's permission to participate in activities. In this context, iTC demarcation of specific land areas for use by women-led and female majority farmer's associations provided women with land security and opportunities to make plans for longer term investments in the land.

The Place of Agricultural Development Programmes, Land-Based Investments and Natural Resource-Based Value Chains in Shaping Outcomes for Women

In Mozambique and elsewhere in Africa, agricultural development programmes and land-based investment have emerged as key factors shaping women's land rights and broader development opportunities. While government programmes increasingly target small-scale commercial farmers, usually men, the private sector is now widely engaged in delivery of agricultural production and marketing support alongside government extension agents. In many cases, this assistance is linked to larger-scale private investments in production, processing, infrastructure and value chain development. However, these approaches require that farmers have prior formal access to land, secured by land title or other forms of legally recognized documentation. Targeting well-functioning farmers groups or individual landowners may, however, risk marginalizing more vulnerable groups. For women without documented land rights, this is particularly problematic. Women may be unable to access credit, even where the land is not used as collateral against loans, or to participate in private-sector-led out-grower or contract farming schemes.

Nationally, iTC's approach to securing rights at community level, wherever possible linked to production support and market development, has offered significant opportunities for smallholders, but was only able to respond to women's economic needs by providing collective title to producer associations in which women were active participants. This was a notable feature of iTC's work in Gaza province, which also built capacity for women-led farmer associations to make productive use of irrigable land areas, formerly occupied by large-scale state farms and cooperatives. To spread the benefits more widely, however, women farmers and female-headed households need opportunities to register their own individual land rights, as, for example, facilitated by IFAD in southern Mozambique under the Terra Segura programme, and linked directly to agricultural development support for promising crops and small-scale livestock production.

Where government had decided that private investment should be the principal driver of economic development, as in the Zambezia case, the use of an independent spatial data platform, as deployed by ORAM for land rights mapping and provision of certificates to land users, offers a practical alternative to recognize both women's and men's customary land rights in the absence of the coverage by official cadastre. However, access to new economic opportunities was largely reliant on support offered by the forestry investor that was also interested in accessing community land for its own purposes. A transformation following the consultations that were hastily arranged by government with unrepresentative and overwhelmingly male groupings of customary leaders, land was handed over for tree-planting without consultation of the actual land users, many of whom were women. Nevertheless, these created widespread demand for land rights documentation by residents. In this context, ORAM's land rights project transformed the situation to one in which the company, anxious to be seen to comply with national law and accepted international principles, was required to negotiate with the legitimate occupiers and users of land parcels, and to engage directly with women counterparts, not only with male community leaders.[5] The project also enabled women to play a significant role in the community land associations it created, and in anticipated negotiations with the investor, which responded by suspending acquisition of new land and shifting to a less ambitious production strategy which it reframed as investment in a sustainable agroforestry landscape mosaic, based on small-scale woodlots and out-grower contracts. The company also doubled its initial investment of US$5 million in a development programme including agricultural extension support, improved seeds, income-generating projects and provision of wells and grain stores reaching approximately 6000 families.

For investments like this, to succeed in making good use, good documentation of customary land rights is necessary to enable the people directly affected, including both women and men, to consent to the new developments and allow their participation in new economic opportunities the investment may create. In regions with lower agricultural potential, where commercial investments and public agricultural development programmes are likely to be absent, such as the north of Manica province where Micaia's project operated, clarification of land and natural resource rights can also support investments in community-based enterprise and livelihood diversification. In this case, where agriculture is subsistence-oriented and women are more reliant on natural resources and off-farm activities for income-generation, Micaia's approach shows how investments in new natural resource-based value chain, such as baobab, can directly benefit women.

Similarly, iTC supported a variety of women-led and mixed associations producing ceramics, handicrafts, honey, cashew nuts or other useful tree products for sale. Such initiatives founded on secure collective rights registered on a village community basis need, however, to be backed by adequate arrangements for land and natural resource use planning, engaging with and influencing traditional resource management practices of male leaders, to ensure that women have clear use and access rights and associated economic opportunities.

Although iTC identified positive outcomes for women from new economic activities like these, linked to community-based land rights formalization, these interventions generally fell short of being transformational. Although iTC projects included assistance to women in producing their own crops or handicrafts, marketing fish or taking up opportunities to produce and market goods traditionally associated with men, such as honey, the organization's *modus operandi* was only to initiate rather than provide sustained support for new local economic initiatives. This meant that the organization felt it could not directly influence gender norms constraining women's independent participation and access to cash returns and benefits, or to ensure that these were fully sustainable and equitable. This contrasts with the more sustained, in-depth and localized approach adopted by Micaia in northern Manica, focused on transforming gender relations, and benefiting from direct collaboration with a commercial business partner working actively to develop new value chains accessible to poor and marginalized women.

Importantly, areas that were particularly restrictive to women's involvement in land-related activities but had positive outcomes for women, particularly in the case of Micaia and iTC in Gaza province, often required separate spaces for in-depth engagement with women – such as through women's groups, associations, and harvester clubs – within the context of broader community support. Programmatic initiatives can make visible women's contribution to household livelihood and social status to create more secure rights for overall community well-being. In this sense simply confirming women's land rights through a formal registration process alone would not be enough. It is necessary to work directly with women and men to promote their awareness of gender roles and norms, and the importance of strengthening women's basic skills and independent livelihoods.

The Central Role of Organizational Culture and Gender-Sensitive Methodologies in Engaging Women

The methods and approaches used by organizations delivering land tenure projects for community engagement, land rights mapping, documentation and registration also provide important lessons in securing women's land rights. ORAM's approach of using initial delimitation of village land holdings as the entry point for household parcel mapping, identification of the relevant customary leaders, and their involvement in training and awareness sessions facilitated the accurate identification of local land rights, involvement of the relevant community members in mapping exercises, as well as wider community discussions, and the formation of community land associations. In practice, women played active roles in these processes. Furthermore, their use of an independent spatial data platforms and hand-held devices for data collection not only promoted an efficient, low-cost mapping process, but also an inclusive one. A detailed, nuanced picture of everyone's land rights could be built up in the absence of any official government land documentation process. ORAM's achievements in registering existing family or individual land use rights has had a notably positive effect in clarification and recognition of women's *de facto* rights to land in a matrilineal region of Mozambique, which were otherwise at risk due to large-scale government-promoted commercial investment.

Micaia's approach of mapping and documenting dispersed community land areas, as opposed to household registration, was a practical approach to securing land rights as in a context in which agricultural land use was not fixed. Micaia sought synergies between better environmental stewardship and women's empowerment, targeting women as principal beneficiaries for their baobab initiative. In a strongly patriarchal context, it was important that Micaia worked with the communities as a whole in the first instance, building trust among community members and increasing awareness of different gender roles regarding land and natural resource use. Facilitators then worked with women to discuss their common circumstances, their roles in the baobab trade, and identify their livelihood and well-being needs. The meetings served as the basis to support the development of women's baobab collectors' clubs and fed into Micaia's wider assessment of the gendered character of local livelihoods and natural resource use across the project landscape. Micaia's approach emphasizes raising awareness of gender differences and demonstrating the economic benefits of promoting women's engagement in land and natural resource management to community leaders and the broader community. This involved expanding and improving the conditions and remuneration of women's work and introducing new skills and organization that not only increased women's incomes and autonomy, but also brought benefits for men and the whole community. Whereas if women's independent entitlements to land, natural resources and income opportunities were the primary focus, the project would have likely met greater resistance among men. As an integral part of community land delimitation of village lands, women's clubs were directly engaged in addition to male community elders, in the identification and mapping of wild produce collection areas. The engagement with the male-dominated hierarchical authority structure to facilitate the full acceptance by the community of the women's baobab business and value chain development work.

In contrast, as a national programme, iTC's facilitated incorporated standardized tools to facilitate community discussions on gender roles and issues. However, service providers lack capacity in understanding how to use that information to design context-specific and tailored solutions to inequalities and monitor progress. This type of capacity needs to develop over the long term, and although the cascade training approach was designed to provide this, iTC lacked capacity to provide direct support or supervision of training conducted at project and community levels. iTC's relatively short-term engagements with local community land formalization projects also constrained continuity and further development of income generating activities. The programme's national scope and centralized planning limited its ability to understand and address deeply entrenched but location-specific gender discriminatory norms and practices. This was compounded by low representation of women and gender expertise within iTC itself and service provider organizations. More importantly, a generalized cultural resistance within a male-dominated organization contributed to views that women were difficult to support and gender norms were too strong to change. Taken together, the cases demonstrated that it requires intensive, long-term engagement with an explicit management objectives and sufficient dedicated field capacity to apply gender sensitive methods at the field level to achieve more transformative outcomes for women.

Furthermore, the extent to which women's participation was meaningful or active is also difficult to discern from the available project data due to constraints in obtaining consistent monitoring data (Topsøe-Jensen *et al.*, 2017). This was a struggle for iTC service providers to evidence. Often service providers would base the number of beneficiaries on community or association population figures, which was not reflective of meaningful engagement. iTC was overly focused on quantitative targets around women's participation, partly driven by donor-set requirements. In turn, the monitoring and evaluation process neglected qualitative measures on how women worked to challenge their status during the iTC community land delimitation interventions.

Despite the significant potential of iTC and its gender strategy which was also formally adopted by the national government in 2018, in practice its principles were diluted leading to limited impact. Underlying this is a political culture within iTC and the land sector, which resist the perceived 'feminization' of what had previously been a very masculine domain. There is a tendency to dismiss the emphasis placed on gender as a westernization of African culture. This issue aside, the two local cases of land projects by ORAM and Micaia, which took place in the same overall Mozambican sociopolitical context suggest that the principal success factors are the capacity to apply locally devised approaches, suitable gender expertise, sustained engagement to understand and influence gender dynamics. As a result, explicit commitments to address gender in these ways are required to achieve more transformational outcomes.

6.6 Conclusion

The interplay of local gender dynamics, demographic change and commercial land investments with land tenure programmes have significant implications for gender and socially and economically related outcomes. In this chapter we have sought to demonstrate three important dimensions that are essential for a gender-responsive impact in land tenure projects and programmes: first, the local livelihoods and customary tenure context, gender relations and migratory dynamics; second, the locally specific gendered impacts of agricultural development programmes and land-based investments; third, and perhaps most importantly, the organizational culture of implementing agencies and the technical approaches used. Together, these interrelated factors are relevant to the development of higher level and operational guidance to improve gender equity in development practice.

Using the three Mozambican cases of land tenure interventions, this chapter illustrates the importance of systematic engagement with both women and men in local communities, and with community leaders in gaining a fuller acceptance of land interventions and fuller understanding of local gendered dynamics. While each case represents a unique combination of existing evolving local context and livelihood practices within distinctive agroecological and development landscapes, they have common features relevant to the broader rural African context. These specific cases also illustrate some key differences between women's positions, rights and opportunities in terms of land access, ownership and decision making, which are at risk in both matrilineal and patrilineal cultural contexts. As a result, it becomes important both to confirm women's *de facto* rights where these are socially recognized, and to clarify and strengthen women's rights and roles in areas where these have traditionally been weaker and dependent on the consent of male relatives or customary leaders.

However, while understanding and responding to the differences between customary practice in matrilineal and patrilineal systems is pertinent, other factors, including increasing population and commercial land use pressures, wider gender power relations in society, gender-blind government policies, and the roles of new actors, including private business and development agencies, tend to have an overriding influence on the realization of women's land rights in rural communities. Attention to women's positions and options, the use of gender-responsive methods to identify gender needs, as well as working with men and male customary leaders is critical to programme success. Strengthening community organizations and making effective links between women's newly clarified land and resource rights, their participation in value chains and the wider economy were found to be necessary and effective for bolstering women's land rights and for women's social and economic empowerment. In addition, the cases illustrate the need to combine expertise on land and gender with capacity to engage with private-sector actors to secure a positive place for women in dynamic investment context.

Although the rationale for linking approaches of securing land rights, conceptually strengthening arrangements for effective land and natural resource governance, and commitment to transformative gender outcomes is clear, this remains challenging to achieve in practice. Poor gender balance and weak incorporation of gender-responsive methods in the staffing of implementing organizations, and general cultural resistance against a perceived feminization of the programme, as found in iTC's operations, proved to be significant constraints. Programme funding, design and delivery modalities employed by donors and development agencies need to prioritize the strengthening of local skills and capacity to engage with complex, diverse and invariably gendered development processes. If this can be done successfully, land programmes can strengthen tenure security, strengthen women's agency in governance and build their participation in new economic projects in multiple and diverse locations.

Effective monitoring of the quality of local outcomes and the ability to learn and design iteratively from longer-term engagements with rural communities are fundamental to scale-out gender transformative outcomes. While there are significant lessons from these cases for the design and delivery of continuing land tenure programmes in Mozambique itself, designing land tenure interventions to create the capacity for context-specific understanding of and engagement with gendered tenure and diversified livelihood systems can provide a way forward for greater transformative change for women's land rights in other African countries.

Endnotes

[1] A Strategic Plan for Development of the Agrarian Sector (PEDSA) targeted a core group of up to 800,000 dynamic small/medium farmers with larger than average land holdings secured mainly on a customary basis.
[2] Although the project was not able to register formal title to each land parcel which requires incorporation in the national cadastre, the data can potentially be used to issue formal DUAT titles by the state. Meanwhile the process of land registration and certification provides individual community members with a first level documentary proof of land rights that has legal force under the 1997 Land Law.
[3] When donor funding ended in 2019, iTC sought to establish itself as an independent national foundation that could work in partnership with the private sector and started to integrate individual household level and community-based land registration and titling.
[4] Gender and diversity learning tools on gender analysis and develop gender-friendly economic-development projects; baseline, monitoring and reporting tools to capture qualitative and quantitative data on gender and diversity indicators; revisions to key iTC operational documents, including the operations manual, social preparation guidelines, proposal evaluation, staff job descriptions, and development of the iTC project monitoring database.
[5] The Voluntary Guidelines on the Responsible Governance of Tenure of Land, Fisheries and Forests in the Context of National Food Security (VGGT) and associated Responsible Agricultural Investment (RAI) principles require identification of a consultation with all legitimate local land holders affected and adoption of a gender-sensitive approach to land governance.

References

Adichie, C.N. (2018) Igbo bu Igbo. *7th Annual International Igbo Conference*, SOAS, University of London, 21 April.

Arnot, C., Luckert, M. and Boxall, P. (2011) What is tenure security? Conceptual implications for empirical analysis. *Land Economics*. 87(2), 297–311. DOI: 10.3368/le.87.2.297.

Chigbu, U. E. (2020) Negotiating land rights to redress land wrongs: women in Africa's land reforms. In: Ochieng, C.M.O. (Ed.), *Rethinking Land Reform in Africa: New Ideas, Opportunities and Challenges*. African Development Bank, Abidjan, Ivory Coast, pp. 156–167.

Daley, E and Lanz, K. (2016) *Gender, Land and Agricultural Development in Africa*. LEGEND Evidence Update 2. ODI, London. Available at: https://landportal.org/library/resources/evidence-update-2-gender-land-and-agricultural-development-africa (accessed 8 July 2021).

De Villiers, B. (2003) *Land Reform: Issues and Challenges: A Comparative Overview of Experiences in Zimbabwe, Namibia, South Africa and Australia.* Konrad Adenauer Foundation, Johannesburg, South Africa.

DFID (2019) Project Completion Review/ Title: MOLA – Mozambique Land Action Programme. Department for International Development, Foreign, Commonwealth and Development Office, London, UK.

Di Matteo, F. and Schoneveld, G.C. (2016) *Agricultural Investments in Mozambique. An Analysis of Investment Trends, Business Models, and Social and Environmental Conduct*. Working Paper 201. CIFOR, Bogor, Indonesia.

Doss, C., Summerfield, G. and Tsikata, D. (2014) Land, gender, and food security. *Feminist Economics*, 20(1). DOI: 10.1080/13545701.2014.895021.

Doss, C., Kovarik, C., Peterman, A., Quisumbing, A., and van den Bold, M. (2015) Gender inequalities in ownership and control of land in Africa: myth and reality. *Agricultural Economics*, 46, 403–434. DOI: 10.1111/agec.12171.

EDG (2014) *Evaluation of the Mozambique Community Land Use Fund. Final Report.* Effective Development Group. Department for International Development, London, UK. Available at: https://assets.publishing.service.gov.uk/government/uploads/system/uploads/attachment_data/file/327645/Mozambique-Community-Land-Use-Fund.pdf (accessed 17 January 2021).

Federici, S. (2011) Women, land struggles, and the reconstruction of the commons. *Journal of Labor and Society*, 14(1), 41–56.

Forsythe, L. and Chidiamassamba, C. (2006) *Gender Audit Report*. iTC internal document. Community Land Initiative and Natural Resources Institute, London, UK.

Forsythe, L. and Chidiamassamba, C. (2010) *iTC Gender Strategy*. iTC internal document. Community Land Initiative and Natural Resources Institute, London, UK.

Forsythe, L. and iTC Gender Working Group (2013) *iTC Cascade Monitoring Report*. iTC internal document. Community Land Initiative and Natural Resources Institute, London, UK.

German L, Cavane, E., Sitoe, A. and Braga, C. (2016) Private investment as an engine of rural development: A confrontation of theory and practice for the case of Mozambique. *Land Use Policy*, 52, 1–14.

Harari, M. (2019) Women's inheritance rights and bargaining power: Evidence from Kenya. *Economic Development and Cultural Change*, 68(1). DOI: 10.1086/700630.

Holger, S. (2011) Intra-household bargaining, gender roles in agriculture and how to promote welfare enhancing changes. *FAO Agricultural Development Economics Division Working Paper 11-10*. DOI: 10.22004/ag.econ.289011.

International Food Policy Research Institute (2013) *Reducing the Gender Asset Gap through Agricultural Development: A Technical Resource Guide*. Available at: http://gaap.ifpri.info/technical-guide (accessed 17 January 2021).

Johnson, N., Kovarik, C., Meinzen-Dick, R., Njuki, J. and Quisumbing, A. (2016) Gender, assets and agricultural development: lessons from eight projects. *World Development* 83, 295–311. DOI: 10.1016/j.worlddev.2016.01.009.

Kingman, A. (2018) Safeguarding the livelihoods of women baobab harvesters in Mozambique through improved land and natural resources governance. *Land Policy Bulletin. LEGEND*, 10 (May), 2–3.

Kingman, A. (2019) Changing household and gender dynamics resulting from baobab business development. *Micaia Reflections, 02*. Micaia Foundation, Chimoio, Mozambique.

Lastarria-Cornhiel, S. (1997) Impact of privatization on gender and property rights in Africa. *World Development*, 25 (8), 1317–1333. DOI: 10.1016/S0305-750X(97)00030-2.

Meinzen-Dick, R., Quisumbing, A., Doss, C. and Theis, S. (2019) Women's land rights as a pathway to poverty reduction: Framework and review of available evidence. *Agricultural Systems*, 172, 72–82.

Nhantumbo, I, Salomão, A. and Cotula, L. (2010) *Biofuels, Land Access, and Rural Livelihoods in Mozambique*. IIED, London, UK.

Norfolk, S. and Hanlon, J. (2012) Confrontation between peasant producers and investors in northern Zambezia, Mozambique. in *the context of profit pressures on European investors. Paper presented at the Annual World Bank Conference on Land and Poverty*, 23–26 April. World Bank, Washington, DC, USA.

Norfolk, S. and Tanner, C. (2007) *Improving Tenure Security for the Rural Poor: Mozambique Country Case Study.* Legal Empowerment Working Paper No. 5. FAO, Rome, Italy.

Norfolk, S., Quan, J. and Mullins, D. (2020) *Options for Securing Tenure and Documenting Land Rights in Mozambique: A Land Policy and Practice Paper*. Natural Resources Institute, University of Greenwich, Chatham, UK.

Po, J.Y.T. and Hickey, G.M. (2018) Local institutions and smallholder women's access to land resources in semi-arid Kenya. *Land Use Policy*, 76, 252–263.

Po, J.Y.T. and Zipporah, B. (2016) Land to feed my grandchildren: Grandmothers' challenges in accessing land resources in semi-arid Kenya. In: Brownhill, L., Njuguna, E., Bothi, K.L., Pelletier, B., Muhammad, L. and Hickey, G.M. (Eds), *Food Security, Gender and Resilience: Improving Smallholder and Subsistence Farming*. Routledge, London, UK, pp. 55–72.

Po, J.Y.T., Saint Ville, A., Rahman, H.M.T. and Hickey, G.M. (Eds) (2019) On Institutional diversity and interplay in natural resource governance. *Society and Natural Resources*, 32(12), 1333–1343. DOI: 10.1080/08941920.2019.1667463

Quan, J., Monteiro, J., Mole, P. and Salomao A. (2013) The experience of Mozambique's Community land initiative (iTC) in securing land rights and improving community land use: Practice, policy and governance implications. Presentation at the World Bank Annual conference on land and poverty. Moving Towards Transparent Land Governance: Evidence-Based Next Steps, 8–11 April. World Bank, Washington, DC, USA.

Quisumbing, A.R. and Maluccio, J. (2003) Resources at marriage and intrahousehold allocation: Evidence from Bangladesh, Ethiopia, Indonesia, and South Africa. *Oxford Bulletin of Economic Statistics*, 65(3), 283–327.

Raimundo I.M. (undated) Women's Empowerment in Mozambique: A Fiction Move or Reality? Unpublished working paper, Open University, Milton Keynes, UK.

Ribot, J.C. and Peluso, N.L. (2003) A theory of access. *Rural Sociology*, 68(2), 153–181.

Schoneveld, G.C. (2014) The geographic and sectoral patterns of large-scale farmland investments in sub-Saharan Africa. *Food Policy*, 48, 34–50.

Tanner, C. and Baleira, S. (2006) *Mozambique's Legal Framework for Access to Natural Resources: The Impact of New Legal Rights and Community Consultations on Local Livelihoods.* Livelihoods Systems Programme Working Paper, 28, FAO, Rome, Italy.

Topsøe-Jensen, B., Calane, A., Ainadine, E. and J. Carrilho (2017) *CTC-COOP / iTC-F mid-term review Final report. NIRAS*. Available at: https://upload.openaid.se/document/mozambique/ctc-coop-itc-f-mtr-final-report-august-2017-revised.pdf.

Toulmin, C. and Quan J. (2000) *Evolving Land Rights, Policy and Tenure in Africa*. DFID/IIED/NRI, London, UK.

USAID (2019) *Mozambique Factsheet: Gender Equality and Female Empowerment*. Available at: https://reliefweb.int/report/mozambique/usaid-mozambique-factsheet-gender-equality-and-female-empowerment (accessed 17 January 2021).

Wardell, A. and Fold, N. (2013) Globalisations in a nutshell: Historical perspectives on the changing governance of the shea commodity chain in northern Ghana. *International Journal of the Commons*, 7. DOI: 10.18352/ijc.361.

7 Women's Insights on Bargaining for Land in Customary Tenure Systems: Land Access as an Individual and Collective Issue

Cynthia M. Caron*
International Development, Community and Environment, Clark University, Worcester, MA, USA

7.1 Introduction

Access to land and livelihood resources is a major focus for donors, policy makers, and development practitioners. The women and land rights scholarship shows that a woman's secure access to land may yield several positive development benefits for her and her family and reduce household inefficiencies (Kevane and Gray, 1999; Johnson *et al.*, 2016). How women gain access to and maintain control over land depends both on existing institutional frameworks and on efforts to change patriarchal relations and practices within the family and across the land governance system. In this chapter, I emphasize *what* women as wives and widows report that they say and that they do in order gain access to land and how they perceive that land relations are changing. I show connections between NGOs and women's rights programming that elucidates mechanisms for social change and highlights the need to address women's land access as a collective problem or issue.

I use qualitative data collected during fieldwork conducted in 2016 in the Zambian capital, Lusaka, and three districts in the Eastern Province: Chipata, Petauke and Nyimba.[1] I conducted 21 key informant interviews with national-level government officials, staff persons from national and local civil society organizations (CSOs) that work on gender and/or land rights, traditional leaders (chiefs, village headpersons and an induna, or chief's advisor), academics, and three focus group discussions with women residing in the Eastern Province. I chose the Eastern Province, as I was familiar with local land rights concerns and several donor-funded, land tenure initiatives taking place there (Sommerville, 2016; Caron and Fenner, 2017). The districts and the villages where focus group discussions took place were chosen in collaboration with the Zambia Land Alliance (ZLA). With the help of an assistant, focus group discussions were conducted in Nyanja. A total of 40 women from either the patrilineal Ngoni tribe or the matrilineal Nsenga tribe participated in group discussions.

The structure of this chapter is as follows. I present the conceptual framework that shaped my investigation and subsequent analysis to show how this chapter contributes to the wider women and land scholarship, followed by a brief

*Corresponding author: ccaron@clarku.edu

DOI: 10.1079/9781789247664.0007

description of the land rights context in Zambia. Thereafter, I describe the methods and methodology before presenting and discussing the results where I emphasize how marital status influences women's experiences. I found that women bargain with men in different ways for land access and that women see lack of access as an individual rather than a collective problem. Recent donor interventions that seek to improve women's land tenure security focus on women as private, rights-holding individuals within the household. While there is evidence that individual women do benefit from such schemes (Sommerville, 2016), donors also might focus on investments in grassroots and women's organizations and networks and leadership development so that women might be more willing to help one another thereby expanding the space for women's collective action.

7.2 Conceptual Framework: Women's Access to Land and Bargaining Power

Econometric analyses demonstrate the economic gains that would result from advances in gender equality and women's property and asset ownership (McKinsey Global Institute, 2019). Academic scholarship and applied research done in the context of international-development interventions confirm the benefits of women's land rights and security of those rights, not only for women themselves, but also for their families (Scalise and Giovarelli, 2020). Studies show that when women own land and have decision making over how to use the income derived from it that they tend to invest in their children's education and family nutrition (USAID, 2016). When women have decision-making power over land, they are more likely than men to adopt agricultural innovations such as new crops and new crop varieties, and planting methods being promoted as part of climate change adaptation and food security strategies (Shibata *et al.*, 2020, p. 7). Quisumbing and Kumar (2014) found that Ethiopian women with the power to manage plots were more likely to plant trees and adopt climate-smart agricultural practices.

For women and nation-states to realize such gains, women need secure access to land. In customary tenure systems, such as in Zambia, women traditionally have secondary rights to land (Spichiger and Kabala, 2014; Caron, 2018a). For women to have secondary rights means obtaining access to land through a male relative as derived through marital status and motherhood. Therefore, secondary rights do not provide women with security of tenure, as access is conditional. Men are primary rights holders accessing land through family or via allocations from chiefs and other authorities (Caron, 2018a). If a husband denies his wife access to land, she can approach the chief for an allocation.

In recent years as part of gender justice agendas and women's rights and empowerment programming, country governments and international donor agencies have sought ways to improve both women's access to land in customary tenure systems and the security of that tenure. Regularization and titling or certification are among these measures (Santos *et al.*, 2014; Sommerville, 2016; Caron, 2018b,c). In Zambia, civil society organizations and donor agencies have piloted certification programs through Traditional Land Holding Certificates issued by chiefs, which recognize land rights for the individual or collectively at the household level. Certificates clarify rights, verify these claims through boundary demarcation, and protect use and inheritance rights as both rights holders and the name of successors are listed on certificate (Caron, 2018c). A woman may be listed as a 'primary' rights holder, which protects her individual rights to that parcel. Certification at the household level clarifies and supports claims of a collective household unit to a parcel of land.

There are several ways to conceptualize land rights. A *bundle of rights approach* specifically places emphasis on access to and use of given resources within the framework of property rights, whereas a *bundle of powers approach* focuses on the ability to control and maintain access to the benefits derived from those resources (Ribot and Peluso, 2003). For Ribot and Peluso, access refers to a bundle of powers represented by the 'multiplicity of ways' through which people derive those benefits that land offers, other than through an externally sanctioned or recognized set of rights. I use the bundle of powers approach as an analytical framework for its emphasis on how 'knowledge, authority, social identities, and social relations can shape or influence access' (Ribot and Peluso, 2003, p. 165). I use the term 'bargaining power' to acknowledge the gendered asymmetries of power within the household that women contend with to access land and to show how women reckon with authority and harness social relations to access land and pursue livelihood goals and greater independence (Agrawal, 1997). Djurfeldt *et al.* (2018), for example, show how women's land rights influence the gendered nature of inter-household decision making and income distribution. Given intra-household power dynamics and the extent to which women experience male dominance in land tenure relations across the life course (Kevane and Gray, 1999; Chigbu, 2019), women may bargain with men first within their household and then possibly within the larger family or community or they may not ask for land at all. Some women may not be willing to suffer the consequences of a failed 'ask', as the maintenance of relations with persons who have a relatively greater bundle of powers may be an important element of other or future access to resources, and they do not wish to risk such access.

The experiences that women in Zambia's Eastern Province narrated to me and that I share below demonstrate whether and how they bargained with men in power for access to land, and the extent to which they come to one another's aid or work collectively on issues of land allocation and distribution. In doing so, I shed some light on bargaining across scale (with other women, chiefs, and in-laws) thereby answering the call of Kevane and Gray (1999, p. 19) that land tenure scholars 'need to look beyond the bargaining that goes on within households'. These stories highlight how women ask for land from men with power both within and outside the household. The illustrative quotes shared below demonstrate how women themselves understand the norms and attitudes that shape their access to land, and how these norms and rule can be bent to create more gender equitable land tenure relations.

7.3 Setting the Context: The Land Governance Structure and Women's Access to Land

Zambia won independence from Great Britain in 1964. The country's population is nearly 18 million inhabitants (World Bank, 2019). Land and natural resources are essential to the rural household economy and form the basis of the national economy. Agriculture supports the livelihoods of over 60% of the country's population, with 54% of women engaged in agriculture (World Bank, 2019). The colonial legacy of a dual tenure system is reflected in two categories of land: state land and customary land. All land and natural resources, including those found on land held under customary tenure, is vested in the President. The Ministry of Lands and Natural Resources manages state land. Traditional leaders, such as chiefs and headpersons, administer customary land according to unwritten customary law, traditional norms and customs.

The government maintains a plural legal system of statutory and customary law. While customary law is valid under the Constitution, it is subordinate to it. Therefore, any customary practice that contradicts or is inconsistent with constitutional provisions is neither legal nor valid, and neither should be implemented nor passed as judgement in local court. Chiefs govern areas held under customary tenure, maintain law, and order in the chiefdom, and ensure that all the subjects have a piece of land to live on and cultivate crops. They are the main point of contact for investors seeking land and together with headpersons generally grant occupancy and use rights to customary land, usually to men, as men are considered the heads of households. A woman then asks her husband or another male relative, as the primary land rights holder, to use a portion of the land allocated to him. Thus, Zambian women have secondary rights to land. Chiefs are not elected, but rather succeed one another based on kinship and membership in a royal family. Chiefs rule for life. Even the government cannot remove a chief from power (Baldwin, 2016).

A woman's access to customary land and the security of that access are contingent upon gendered social relationships. Even in matrilineal-matrilocal systems, where land is passed down through the line of the mother, a woman's access to land is mediated through male kin or traditional authorities (Peters, 2010; Lambrecht, 2016; Chigbu, 2019). In patrilineal areas, a widowed woman needs to move back to her natal village and appeal to her brothers or uncles for access to land (Bessa and Malasha, 2020). In matrilineal groups, where children inherit land through their mother's family, men (maternal uncles) have considerable power. When a man who marries into a matrilineal family dies, his wife's brother and sister-in-law normally take over the property. His children and widow do not inherit the land they farmed and resided upon. His nieces and nephews do.

The 2016 Zambian Constitution attests to the equal worth of women and men, supported by a range of gender-sensitive laws, granting women an equal and legal right to land (Caron, 2018a). The National Gender Policy mainstreams gender across national-level policy and programs. Its gender action plan includes land-sector activities including rights-based awareness raising and training programs for government officials and traditional leaders and public awareness campaigns about a woman's right to own land (Government of the Republic of Zambia, 2002). The 1995 Lands Act authorized the conversion of customary land to leasehold (state) land, with a chief's written approval to convert (Government of the Republic of Zambia, 1995). Once converted and titled, such leasehold land is governed under statutory law and can be sold to others. The 1995 Land Act does not address traditional customs and practices that limit women's ability to own and control land. Recently, several donor-funded interventions such as certification are improving women's land tenure security.

Finally, the country's statutory, Constitutional, legal framework protects a woman's rights as a private, autonomous individual, treating her as somehow separate from the social and community relations she has with extended family. Customary law, on the other hand, situates her within a larger set of familial and kin relations and the traditional hierarchy of chiefs and subjects. Tensions between individual rights promoted in the Constitution and community expectations and obligations that traditional norms and social structures beget create difficult choices for women living in customary tenure systems (Brown and Gallant, 2014). Below I show how women in Zambia's Eastern Province work through normative expectations.

7.4 Methods and Methodology

As a development sociologist and a feminist scholar, I employ an interpretivist methodology, use qualitative methods (Patton, 2002), and focus on nuancing the general category of 'women' (Young, 1994). During fieldwork, a research assistant and I used phenomenological principles to capture how women describe, remember and talk about a social phenomenon they have directly experienced (Patton, 2002): asking for a piece of land. Women also discussed social change taking place in gender relations. As women are not a homogeneous group, I analyzed transcripts by social identities that might differentially structure a woman's experience such as marital status, as marriage is a structural arrangement that mediates land access (Lembrecht, 2016; Chigbu *et al.*, 2019).

With assistance from the Zambia Land Alliance, a translator and I conducted three focus group discussions in Nyanja, two discussions with matrilineal Nsegna women and one discussion with patrilineal Ngoni women. We audio-recorded the 60–90 minute group discussions. The translator then created verbatim transcripts translating our discussions from Nyanja to English so that here I can present women's narrations in their own terms. I reviewed a range of relevant documents on women and land rights published by Zambian NGOs, the Government of Zambia, and the peer-reviewed scholarship on women and land rights to situate the findings within a larger context.

7.5 Findings and Discussion

Under each subheading below, I present findings disaggregated by marital status (married versus widowed women). All married women are in monogamous (not polygamous) relationships. I highlight what women reported they said and did as they bargained for land. When illustrative, I provide longer quotes in alignment with an interpretivist framework to share women's views in their own words. Afterwards I discuss the play between the individual and the collective to emphasize the need for collective, feminist politics to enhance women's land access.

Married Women Bargaining with a Husband: Failures and Successes

Women agreed that it is difficult to ask for land from a husband because he might refuse saying, '*why should we split the field when we are married?*' As one woman in Chipata noted, '*Men refuse to give their wives land purely because of jealousy. They know that if a woman has land, they will use it well in farming and get ahead of them.*' In customary tenure systems where women traditionally have secondary land rights, they may not have a livelihood asset and depend on husbands for funds to cover household expenses.

During discussions, many women narrated the following type of experience:

> I asked for land from my husband ... I told him that it is because when we harvest and sell our produce you don't give part of the money so that I can buy household stuff and clothes for children. He said this farm is not for two people ... the chief only knows me as the owner of this land and that was the end of the conversation.

In this case, the speaker left the matter alone when her husband refused her request. However, other women did not allow similar refusals to end their pursuit for land and followed a few different strategies: (i) use it anyway; (ii) ask the chief for her own allotment; or (iii) borrow land in secret.

One woman undeterred by her husband's refusal decided to use part of his plot anyway, noting:

> My marriage ended because of what has been said here, my husband would refuse to share the money after selling the farm produce and when I asked for land so that I can start farming on my own he refused to give ... saying you did not come with land here. I went ahead and used a portion of it ... he ended up selling everything that I had planted without sharing money with me. The following year, I asked for a piece of land where I planted my groundnuts, my husband went and removed everything (before the harvest). This marked the beginning of marriage failure and today we are no longer together.

Following refusal, a woman might ask the chief for her own piece of land to farm. One research participant did just that, explaining:

> I did ask for land from my husband. He denied ... me. Because this was a family issue, I could not ask anyone to intervene ... He told me that there was no need for us to split the land because we were married. What I did was to ask for land from the chief and I was given [land] for free ... When farming all is well and rosy with ... husbands, but once you harvest and sell that is it. [Women] are not given anything so that they can buy what is needed at home. These are family matters no one dares to take them out of their homes. If you do tell your family members ... and maybe you want to leave your husband, their responses are usually ... 'You have children. How are you going to look after them if you leave?'

While this woman followed an alternative pathway to land (via the Chief), her narration exposes that another alternative, leaving her husband, appeared less possible. Finally, following a refusal, a woman might ask a friend to help her. One middle-aged woman stated:

> A friend of mine lent me a portion of her field to use when my husband refused to give a piece land [to me] and I started having problems with him. My friend made sure her husband didn't find out because she was scared that he would be upset.

These experiences of failure to secure land from a husband reaffirm Mvududu and McFadden's (2001) and Chigbu's (2019) argument that male power (husbands and chiefs) enables women's access. These stories also show evidence of limited women's solidarity in land matters, as these are '*family issues*' and reveal the risks of involving a woman outside the family. The two women kept their land use arrangement a 'secret', which might be necessary since husbands wield so much power over household resource allocation. A husband might consider his wife speaking about this personal matter with another woman as form of betrayal. As chiefs have power and authority over all men and women in a chiefdom, a husband would not challenge a chief's decision to grant his wife a plot of land. When women advise a woman to stay with a husband who denies her access to land, it signals that perhaps it is too risky for a woman to try to survive on her own. Many husbands will grant a wife's request. Sometimes the household expenses argument works, as this exchange from the Nyimba District suggests:

> Research Participant (RP): I asked my husband for a portion so that I can plant other crops that I could sell and buy what I wanted. He gave me.
> Interviewer: How did you ask your husband for land?
> RP: I told him that my kitchen needs pots and plates and I also need to buy children clothes. My thinking is that you give me a portion of

> land so that I can plant maybe sunflower or groundnuts so that when I harvest and sell then I can buy these things. My husband agreed. We [women] usually have challenges with accessing money from our husbands so that we can buy kitchen things ... This is the reason I gave him, saying when I harvest and sell the produce, I will buy clothes, pay school fees, buy plates, pots and other things.

She continued by saying that she did not want land to become 'pompous' rather,

> In my case I wanted land to use so that I can better myself and family. We do things together ... when a problem comes and maybe he has not sold his produce, we can use the money from my produce ... I even bought my husband gumboots so that he is protected from snakes or thorns. Even next year, he will allow me to use the field because he has seen that I am using it well and I am helping at home.

Despite her exuberance, the phrase *'even next year, he will allow me to use the field'* reaffirms dependency on male power for access to land, and in this case, access is conditional on how he perceives her performance, evidence by her statement, *'because ... I'm using it well and I'm helping at home.'* Without access to land, a wife might solely depend on her husband for spending money, re-emphasizing the importance of not risking this relationship. While it is not clear under what conditions a husband might take access away, research participants in the Nyimba District argue that recently they have seen changes in gender relations with respect to household resource allocation. They attribute these changes to two factors: (i) male out-migration; and (ii) awareness raising via radio programming.

Most of the women present shook their heads as an elder woman said, *'we have seen that we women have changed because men have changed, their jealousy has reduced because men were too jealous of women's success.'* Such social change, they argued, happens for a few reasons. First, in areas where most residents are women, the men who stay behind see women successfully manage farms in the absence of husbands and are changing their opinions on women's competency. Second, research participants also noted that weekly radio programming spreading gender-equality messages have an effect. This programming tackles the issue of intra-household income distribution with stories of husbands who bring home friends to find a wife who needs a wash, who is wearing dirty clothes and has not prepared any greens (relish) to accompany a meal. The reason why the woman and her clothes are dirty and there is no relish is because her husband neither gives her money nor does she have ability to earn her own. The lesson: husbands will be either annoyed or embarrassed and will either give access to land or spending money. As a radio call-in show demonstrated, the women agreed that men regularly call in to say they are learning something about how they behave and 'confess' that they will try to change. There are also changing social practices with respect to the treatment of widows.

Widows Bargaining with In-Laws

A wife's status and access to land and other forms of property change when her husband dies. Rights of residence and to marital property in widowhood differ depending on whether a women's tribe is matrilineal or patrilineal. Under patrilineal-patrilocal marriage custom, after marriage the bride leaves her natal village and makes a home with her new husband and his family. Upon the death of her husband, she is generally expected to leave this home and return to her natal village.

As one Ngoni woman in the Chipata District explained: '*When a woman is widowed ..., she usually [returns] to her parent's villages [and asks] for land from the fathers / parents.*' She must return with all her children and start a new life in her natal village. Property grabbing accompanies her dismissal from her marital home. She returns to her native village with few resources to help her rebuild her life.

As one woman explained:

> When we came back from Zimbabwe, my family settled here because this is where my dad came from, I was young then. After my father died, everything was grabbed from my mother; they got the sewing machine, bicycles and many other things, she just remained with suitcases of clothes and pots. My father's relatives told her to go back to her mother's village together with us... children saying, 'the children are yours not ours, our relative is dead'. We left. Now that we have grown and have our own homes, ... now they refer to us as their children and want us.

Women from the matrilineally-organized Nsenga stated that when their husbands die, they are not forced to leave. A widow is required only to share her husband's clothes and some farming tools with her in-laws. She will only be forced to move and forfeit land if she remarries, being told, to '*leave the land for your children, but you go and join your new husband.*'

Just as some women above noted asking for help from other women or the chief when a husband denied giving a share of land, one widow from the patrilineal Ngoni tribe prevented her in-laws from grabbing her marital property by refusing to comply with her in-law's demands and seeking the help of the village headman:

> When my husband died and we were still mourning, his relatives took over the fields we used to farm. When I went to field so that I can start farming, I found they had already used the field. [They] told me to leave and that the field belonged to their family not me, so I went and informed the headman, who then came and sat all of us down. He told them that the field belonged to me since my husband was no more and that if they went ahead to grab the land, the case will be taken to the chief so that he can solve it. After that they left everything for me ... it is two years and I have not had any problems with my in-laws.

Legal aid and women's rights activists in Zambia's capital Lusaka agree that such changes are occurring. Host country governments, donor agencies and non-governmental organizations around the world have undertaken programming to reduce widows' marginalization (Young, 2006). NGO personnel conduct gender-sensitivity sessions with traditional authorities to curtail property grabbing (Caron, 2018a). One Lusaka-based women's rights advocate went as far as to state that '*the topic of property grabbing is less now. Now we are focusing more on wife-beating and child marriage*' (Interview, 19 August 2016), showing that gender-equity concerns remain, even if a harmful practice such as property grabbing appear to be lessening.

Bargaining Across Scale: Involving Traditional Authorities

As noted above, if a married woman cannot convince her husband to share a portion of his land or if a widow is harassed by her in-laws, she may move up the hierarchy to make an appeal to the chief or village headman. Appealing to these other authorities challenge traditional practice, illustrating that traditional familial authority figures might no longer have 'the final word'. Group discussions though reveal that receiving a successful outcome depends on the chief, land availability, and the resources a woman has available to her. One woman provided the following description of the process as she understood it in her area:

> One must go to the chief to ask for land and when you get there you first see the indunas [advisers]. If one wants a field for farming, you must go with two cows that you present to the chief as a present before you speak to him. This gives disadvantages to a lot of women because cows are very expensive. When you are given land for farming you are supposed to pay for it. But if one wants to see the chief for other reasons or land for building a house you only take a chicken as gift for chief.

Women acknowledged differences when asking for land to build a house versus land for farming. While the headman may allocate land to build a structure, only the chief allocates land for farming. Women also noted that with land scarcity, the requirement of in-kind 'payment' (cow, chicken, goat) was increasing, and it was more difficult to acquire land for free. Chiefs do not follow standardized procedures; 'payments' vary across location. For a resource-poor woman acquiring access to land from her chief is not a guarantee.

Bargaining for Land: An Individual or Collective Structural Problem?

Secondary rights and traditional norms complicate women's access to land and keeping that access. While some women noted that traditions are changing, and that they are not necessarily letting traditional power brokers such as husbands and in-laws curtail their access, women who participated in group discussions stated that bargaining for land is a private matter. In general, a married woman will hesitate to ask for assistance from other women when her husband denies her land, as '*everyone [each woman] sorts out their own issues.*' Women face a collective problem, yet there is little collective action. Women have a tradition of collective action including work groups that pound maize and shell ground nuts. Zambian activists are in the process of building 'sisterhood' across the country, pushing women to think beyond gendered expectations and publicly taking on issues that affect women as a social group (Geisler, 1995). One woman and gender rights activist reaffirmed this when she stated that, '*We are building the capacities of women so that they are able ... to stand for themselves ... and stand together*' regardless of party politics and political divides (Interview, 17 August 2016).

The belief that access to land within the family is a private, family problem and not a gender-based, collective problem for women often stops women asking other women for help. Also, an individual woman might be hesitant to intervene in a household situation where there might be larger and unknown issues at stake. The family is both a source of identity and struggle for women. Marriage is often a strategic alliance, and the maintenance of its alliances may be more important than the needs of any one individual woman (Mvududu and McFadden, 2001). As family and kinship are sources of security, women may not wish to compromise these relationships (Kabeer, 2011). Reaching out to other women over a land issue might damage family, social or other livelihood networks (Cleaver, 2009), forcing women to walk the fine line between individual rights and community expectations (Brown and Gallant, 2014). While one woman might help another one in secret, such one-on-one assistance does not address the structural oppression or disadvantages that women as a collective face as secondary rights holders. Donor-sponsored programming to improve land tenure security is only a partial answer.

Land Certification: Improving Individual Tenure Security

Land certification in areas held under customary tenure is a process that includes the marking of plot boundaries and creating a written, ordered list of plot inheritors (Sommerville, 2016; Caron 2018a). Certification helps women consolidate control over land and reduces the conditionality of that access. One woman explained that her household has access to three plots of land; one plot is certified in her husband's name, one in their child's name, and one in her own name. Certification of women's use rights to a plot of land may increase her land tenure security but bargaining or negotiating does not vanish. Husbands and wives still must decide on a plot's subdivision and discuss the order of names on the list of successors. The Zambian Government does not legally recognize land certificates and not all chiefs participate in certification programming, thus certification only has a localized effect. Nevertheless, research participants appreciate the process, but noted that '*the major issue of getting [a] land certificate is that in future we don't know what will happen.*' While certification might secure an individual woman's use rights to a plot of land, it does not fully address women's land access as a collective issue. Women's rights activists together with the National Women's Lobby Group now work at the grassroots level with local women's groups to emphasize that '*you [women] cannot sort out all the issues on your own, individual women need to work together*' (Interview, 17 August 2016).

7.6 Conclusion

In this chapter, I show how women bargain across a male-dominated hierarchy (husbands and traditional authorities) and employ a variety of strategies to gain access to land. By focusing on married women and widows, I avoid conceptualizing 'women' as a homogeneous category and recognize their differential pathways to secure land based on social status. Married women and widows might by-pass the traditional authority of husbands and in-laws, by asking either the village headman or chief for land, noting too that she may require resources that she does not have to acquire that access. I documented why some women think that men provide them land and highlight the mechanisms that women believe influence men's thinking and change gender relations. Finally, I show how women's talk portrays land access as an individual or family issue rather than a structural challenge that women as a collective face in heterogeneous ways.

This chapter makes contributions to feminist politics and development practice. As the international donor community supports country governments to increase land tenure security through individual/privatization measures such as titling, certification, and other means of documentation (Peters, 2010; Sommerville, 2016), it should be mindful of the heterogeneity of women's social identities (e.g. married vs widowed), their experience of social life, and how changes in land tenure regime might create differential outcomes for individual women. Certification of customary land in Zambia started in 2014. It is unclear if women's bargaining strategies might have changed in the context of certified rights. For example, do women need to strongly advocate for themselves to have land certified in their own names? A recent investigation found that women face physical, social and psychological / emotional violence when they ask for their names to be added to certificates or when they try to develop land that is held solely in their own name (Bessa and Malasha, 2020). Research must continue to examine the extent to which certification has improved women's access to and control over land and the strategies that women need to use to do pursue access to land to determine if the certification process is gender equitable (e.g. works the same for men and for women). Since land certification also can stop at the collective, household level, do women in such a household still need to bargain for access to land held within that certified household-holding or are their use rights unquestioned?

While women as a social group are heterogeneous, and there is no singular 'essence' of being a woman, the notion of women as a social collective remains salient for feminist politics (Young, 1994). As Young writes, 'without conceptualizing women as a group in some sense, it is not possible to conceptualize oppression as a systematic, structured, institutional process' (Young, 1994: p. 718). Bessa and Malasha (2020) also found that to defend their certified land rights, Zambian women in land conflicts have appealed, *as individuals*, to NGOs that partner with international donor organizations and to chiefs, indunas, and headpersons to help them defend their certified rights. There appears to be little collective action among women within households or extended families. Rather, there is evidence that older female relatives abuse and threaten younger female relatives who are demanding access to land (Bessa and Malasha, 2020), thereby reproducing gender-discriminatory norms and customs. Government and donor-funded programming that focuses on women's empowerment and mobilization such as rights-based awareness raising, fostering collective networks, and leadership training as well as multi-media programming that is accessible to everyone including men and boys (Caron, 2018b) is vital to creating momentum for more gender equitable resource access and allocation.

Endnote

[1] To protect the identities of the Chiefs, chiefdoms are not listed.

References

Agrawal, B. (1997) Bargaining and Gender Relations: Within and Beyond the Household. *Feminist Economics*, 3(1), 1–51.

Baldwin, K. (2016) *The Paradox of Traditional Chiefs in Democratic Africa.* Cambridge University Press, Cambridge, UK.

Bessa, T. and Malasha, P. (2020) *Gender-Based Violence and Land Documentation and Administration in Zambia: Emerging Lessons from Implementation.* USAID Integrated Land and Resource Governance Task Order under the Strengthening Tenure and Resource Rights II (STARR II) IDIQ, Washington, DC. Available at: https://land-links.org/document/gender-based-violence-and-land-documentation-administration-in-zambia-emerging-lessons-from-implementation (accessed 10 July 2021).

Brown, J. and Gallant, G. (2014) *Engendering Access to Justice: Grassroots Women's Approaches to Securing Land Rights.* The Huairou Commission and The United Nations Development Program, New York, NY, USA.

Caron, C.M. (2018a) Pursuing gender-transformative change in customary tenure systems: Civil society work in Zambia. *Development in Practice*, 28(7), 872–883. DOI: 10.1080/09614524.2018.1480896.

Caron, C.M. (2018b) Creating the 'girl effect': Including boys and men to promote girls' land and asset ownership. *Progress in Development Studies*, 18(4), 223–234. DOI: 10.1177/1464993418786773.

Caron, C.M. (2018c) The projects that are helping Zambian women get better access to land. *The Conversation*, 30 July Available at: https://theconversation.com/the-projects-that-are-helping-zambian-women-get-better-access-to-land-100178 (accessed 10 July 2021).

Caron, C.M. and Fenner, S. (2017) Forest access and polycentric governance in Zambia's Eastern Province: Insights for REDD+. *International Forestry Review*, 19(3), 265–277.

Chigbu, U.E. (2019) Anatomy of women's landlessness in the patrilineal customary land tenure systems of sub-Saharan Africa and a policy pathway. *Land Use Policy*, 86, 126–135. DOI: 10.1016/j.landusepol.2019.04.041.

Chigbu, U.E., Paradza, G. and Dachaga, W. (2019) Differentiations in women's land tenure experiences: Implications for women's land access and tenure security in sub-Saharan Africa. *Land*, 8(22), 1–21. DOI: 10.3390/land8020022.

Cleaver, F. (2009) Rethinking agency, rights, and natural resource management. In: Hickey, S. and Mitlin, D. (Eds), *Rights-Based Approaches to Development: Exploring the Potential and Pitfalls*. Kumarian Press, Sterling, VA,USA, pp. 127–144.

Djurfeldt, A.A. *et al.* (2018) The family farms together, the decisions, however are made by the man – Matrilineal land tenure systems, welfare and decision making in rural Malawi. *Land Use Policy*, 70, 601–610.

Geisler, G. (1995) Troubled sisterhood: Women and politics in Southern Africa: Case studies from Zambia, Zimbabwe, and Botswana. *African Affairs*, 94(377), 545–578.

Government of the Republic of Zambia (1995) The Lands Act, Chapter 184 of the Laws of Zambia. Available at: http://www.parliament.gov.zm/sites/default/files/documents/acts/Lands%20Act.pdf (accessed 10 July 2021).

Government of the Republic of Zambia (2002) *Strategic Plan of Action for the National Gender Policy (2004–2008).* Gender in Development Division, Office of the President, Lusaka, Zambia.

Johnson, N.L. *et al.* (2016). Gender, assets, and agricultural development: Lessons from eight projects. *World Development*, 83, 295–311.

Kabeer, N. (2011). Between affiliation and autonomy: Navigating pathways of women's empowerment and gender justice in rural Bangladesh. *Development and Change*, 42(2), 499–528.

Kevane, M. and Gray, L.C. (1999) A woman's field is made at night: Gendered land rights and norms in Burkina Faso. *Feminist Economics*, 5(3), 1–26.

Lambrecht, I.B. (2016) 'As a husband I will love, lead, and provide': Gendered access to land in Ghana. *World Development*, 88, 188–200.

McKinsey Global Institute (2019) *The Power of Parity: Advancing Women's Equality in Africa.* Available at: https://www.mckinsey.com/~/media/McKinsey/Featured%20Insights/Gender%20Equality/The%20power%20of%20parity%20Advancing%20womens%20equality%20in%20Africa/MGI-The-power-of-parity%20Advancing%20womens%20equality%20in%20Africa.pdf (accessed 29 July 2020).

Mvududu, S. and McFadden, P. (2001) *Reconceptualizing the Family in a Changing Southern African Environment.* Women and Law in Southern Africa Research Trust, Harare, Zimbabwe.

Patton, M.Q. (2002) *Qualitative Research and Evaluation Methods*. SAGE Publications, London, UK.

Peters, P.E. (2010) Our daughters inherit our land, but our sons use their wives' fields': Matrilineal-matrilocal land tenure and the new land policy in Malawi. *Journal of Eastern African Studies*, 4(1), 179–199.

Quisumbing, A.R. and Kumar, N. (2014) *Land Rights Knowledge and Conservation in Rural Ethiopia: Mind the Gender Gap*. IFPRI Discussion Paper 1386. IFPRI, Washington, DC, USA.

Ribot, J.C. and Peluso, N.L. (2003) A theory of access. *Rural Sociology*, 68(2), 153–181. DOI: 10.1111/j.1549-0831.2003.tb00133.x.

Santos, F., Fletschner, D. and Daconto, G. (2014) Enhancing inclusiveness of Rwanda's land tenure regularization program: Insights from early stages of its implementation. *World Development*, 62, 30–41.

Scalise, E. and Giovarelli, R. (2020) *What Works for Women's Land and Property Rights? What We Know and What We Need to Know*. Resource Equity, Washington, DC, USA.

Shibata, R., Cardey, S. and Dorward, P. (2020) Gendered intra-household decision-making dynamics in agricultural innovation processes: Assets, norms and bargaining power. *Journal of International Development*, 32(7), 1101–1125. DOI: 10.1002/jid.3497.

Sommerville, Matt (2016) Mobile Applications for Secure Tenure (MAST): Documenting land rights in Zambia; Burma; Vietnam. *Proceedings of the World Farmers' Organization*, 4–7 May, Livingstone, Zambia.

Spichiger, R. and Kabala, E. (2014) *Gender Equality and Land Administration: The Case of Zambia.* DIIS Working Paper #4. Danish Institute for International Studies, Copenhagen, Denmark.

USAID (2016) *Fact Sheet: Land Tenure and Women's Empowerment*. USAID, Washington, DC. Available at: https://www.land-links.org/wp-content/uploads/2016/11/USAID_Land_Tenure_Women_Land_Rights_Fact_Sheet.pdf (accessed 29 July 2020).

World Bank (2019) Zambia – population total. Available at: https://data.worldbank.org/indicator/SP.POP.TOTL?locations=ZM (accessed 29 July 2020).

Young, I.M. (1994) Gender as seriality: Thinking about women as a social collective. *Signs*, 19(3), 713–738.

Young, K. (2006) Widows without rights: Challenging marginalization and dispossession. *Gender and Development*, 14(2), 199–209.

8 Gender-Sensitivity in Land Management: Trajectory of Housing, Agriculture and Land Ownership in South Korea

Cheonjae Lee*
Global Development Partnership Center, Korea Research Institute for Human Settlements (KRIHS), Sejong-si, Republic of Korea

8.1 Introduction

One of the most significant components of the sustainable development goals (SDGs) is its gender equality indicators. In the last few decades, there has been a surge of interest in promoting gender equality and empowering women to enhance their contribution to national growth, development, and social stability (United Nations, 2014). The gender issues, which are enshrined in international agreements, have grown in importance, coupled with the ongoing feminist movement. To develop a full picture of equality between women and men, there are several important changes which need to be made at different levels. For example: changes in attitudes and relationships, institutional and legal frameworks, economic situations, and political decision-making structures (UN, 2002). Gender mainstreaming is a common strategy which can have considerable impact on the promotion of gender equality. According to the definition provided by United Nations Economic and Social Council (1997, p. 2), gender mainstreaming is:

> The process of assessing the implications for women and men of any planned action, including legislation, policies or programmes, in any area and at all levels. It is a strategy for making the concerns and experiences of women as well as of men an integral part of the design, implementation, monitoring and evaluation of policies and programmes in all political, economic and societal spheres, so that women and men benefit equally, and inequality is not perpetuated. The goal of mainstreaming is to achieve gender equality.

One of the practical advantages of mainstreaming a gender perspective in land management is that it enhances the effectiveness of major public policies. It does this because it institutionalizes gendered practices and norms into the assumptions, structures, processes, outcomes and environments; on the other hand, theoretically it is the process of conceptual transformation from gender-blind to gender-aware to better understand gendered society (Daly, 2005; Walby, 2005). Some of the methodological tools and operational techniques in policy making introduced for gender mainstreaming include gender analysis (GA), gender impact assessment (GIA) and gender budgeting (GB), to mention a few. These tools are relevant to ensure gender sensitivity.

*Corresponding author: cheonjae.lee@krihs.re.kr

DOI: 10.1079/9781789247664.0008

The significant transformation in various policy spheres in South Korea is in line with the global gender mainstreaming strategy. The introduction of the Basic Act on Women's Development in 1995 and the establishment of the Ministry of Gender Equality in 2001 helped the institutionalization of gender policies in South Korea. It also helped to draw the public's attention to the gender issues. To implement gender mainstreaming in the country, a GIA system was first introduced as a key operating mechanism and now covers a range of the quality of life issues for women in the aspects of social welfare, culture, public safety and education (Ministry of Gender Equality and Family, 2020). These remain the most important milestone in the gender politics of South Korea. It also helped in setting up the structures for promoting women's interests and rights (Lee, 2020). Despite its rapid growth of GIA implementation in recent years, Kim and Kang (2016) note that there are challenges in implementing the GIA. Some of these GIA challenges include ambiguity in the legal basis for GIA, weaknesses in organizational capacity, a lack of expertise in implementing GIA, and insufficient amounts of gender-disaggregated data.

According to the Statistics Korea and MOGEF (2020), Korea has experienced a 39.5% increase in the number of single-women households between 2010 and 2019. This indicates that there is a growing trend of single-woman households and they need gender-sensitive or responsive policies to enable them to use their property in the most efficient and effective manners possible. Although gender policy implications have been recognized in many policy domains in Korea, very little is known about the gender perspective of this situation in the land management sector. In the same vein, the discourse level of this issue remains low. Only limited discussions have been undertaken on this issue based on women-friendly urban planning and housing. However, there is a growing body of literature that recognizes the importance of women's access to land and securing land rights (Chigbu *et al.*, 2019; Meinzen-Dick *et al.*, 2019; Doss and Meinzen-Dick, 2020). These body of literature are mostly restricted to the situation in developing countries. The situation in developed countries remains unclear (at least in land management sphere). This chapter focuses on South Korea. In this chapter, we trace the issues that underpin a growing support for gender sensitivity in Korean housing and agriculture policies as well as land ownership aligning, based on the development of awareness of gender in land management.

8.2 The Gender Dimension of Land Management

Gender issues have long been a question of great interest in the field of land management since its early customary practices in Korea. Land management and the profession has traditionally been gender-blind. Land management covers a wide spectrum of concerns including land tenure, land value, land use and land development (Williamson *et al.*, 2010). Many of the core concerns in international policy discourse relates to the SDGs (e.g. targets 1.4 and 5.a) focus on women's land rights (WLR), women's land tenure (WLT) or women's access to land (WAL). Target 1.4 denotes that 'By 2030, ensure that all men and women, in particular the poor and the vulnerable, have equal rights to economic resources, as well as access to basic services, ownership and control over land and other forms of property, inheritance, natural resources, appropriate new technology and financial services, including microfinances.' Target 5.a promises to: 'undertake reforms to give women equal rights to economic resources, as well as access to ownership and control over land and other forms of property, financial services, inheritance and natural resources, in accordance with national laws.'

In line with political frameworks, many technical guidelines have also been proposed with labels denoting gender-sensitive, gender-responsive, gender-inclusive, gender-balanced, gender-equitable, gender-neutral and so on (e.g. by FAO, World Bank, UN-Habitat, etc.). One of these guidelines is the *Voluntary Guidelines on the Responsible Governance of Tenure of Land, Fisheries and Forest* (FAO, 2012), which sets the international standards for ensuring equality in tenure security, land rights and access to land.

Theoretically, securing women's land rights has potential effects in conferring not only economic access as a source of income and collateral for credit. It also confers social access that increases empowerment and participation of women in decision making at both household and community levels (World Bank, 2005). However, in practical terms, gender dimensions should be considering multiple factors. These should include social, cultural, economic, legal and political factors from the household level to the international level. This is important since the institutions that affect women's access to land rights are interconnected and often addressed together in many policy interventions (FAO, 2002). Apart from this interconnectedness, it has several dimensions that must be understood. These include issues related to technology adoption, natural resource management, government services and institutions, HIV risk, improved resilience and empowerment, human capital investment, and intergenerational property transfers, and outcomes such as food security (Meinzen-Dick *et al.*, 2019; Doss and Meinzen-Dick, 2020).

However, there is still uncertainty about how applicable experiences from developing countries are given unique contexts and conditions. In addition, the association between gender and land management is largely determined by specific local conditions. For example, the argument over the customary regimes and norms and weak land governance systems that affect women's access to land (and its associated land rights concerns) rarely takes place in developed countries, where land institutions are well established. Legal pluralism is not usually an issue in the developed countries, too. However, social norms and entrenched systems that make it more difficult for women to purchase land, enter land markets or actively make decisions around how land is used and managed still exist.

With a broader perspective of gender dimension of land management in developed countries (e.g. women's education, employment, safety and participation in spatial planning and urban and regional development) is under discussion in Korea. Therefore, it is important for gender to be recognized as a crucial aspect of sustainable land management, irrespective of whether one is in developed or developing countries. When it comes to Korea's land management, three critical questions emerge in terms of gender perspective as follows: (i) Is there any interest in moving beyond 'gender-aware' to 'gender-responsive' or 'gender-transformative'?; (ii) How does gender matter in land management?; (iii) What might a gendered land management practice achieve? The following section of this chapter presents how the awareness of the gender dimension of land management in Korea has developed and is being reflected in specific case studies.

8.3 Initiatives in Support of Gender-Sensitivity in Land Management in Korea

'Women-Friendly Cities' Programme

In Korea, discussions have spread internationally on the need for gender perspective (in support of the role of women) in spatial development, especially in the urban environment. In the same vein, the demands of regional polices in Korea to facilitate and promote the women's safety and rights has increased. To meet the residents' growing demands, Iksan City (and several other local governments) signalled its willingness to establish a women-friendly city in 2009. As of 1 July 2015, the 'Women-Friendly Cities' programme had a legal ground to take effect based on the provisions of the *Framework Act on Gender Equality*. According to Article 39 Paragraph 1 of the *Framework Act on Gender Equality*, 'Women-Friendly Cities' is defined as 'areas where women and men equally participate in regional policies and development processes, and policies are operated in a way to ensure the empowerment of women and their care and safety.' This offers a new model for local governments that implement the women's policy at the regional level. The overall aim of the program is to improve the quality of life by promoting existing urban and regional policies together based on gender-sensitive perspectives. In other words, women-friendly cities programme is about mainstreaming gender in regional policies (MOGEF and KWDI, 2017).

The scope of *women-friendly cities programme* is relatively broad, being primarily concerned with the alignment of existing women's policies and various related projects in the vicinity. It also includes regional specialization programs associated with women-friendly cities (MOGEF and KWDI, 2015). Under an agreement between local governments and the MOGEF, the project evaluates, and then designates competent cities as women-friendly cities every year. At the start of the programme in 2009, only two cities were designated to be the first women-friendly cities in Korea. As of 2019, 92 cities have been recognized as women-friendly cities because of their integration of gender measures into the regional governance policies and operating in gender-sensitive administrative policies. However, it is worth noting that the geographic distribution of these cities does not exactly tell us about lingering social norms in Korea that might be less friendly to gender-sensitive land and housing policies. Due to the population concentration of metropolitan areas in Korea (50% of the total population), many local authorities in the metropolitan regions have shown interests in women's safety and rights to housing, and thus many women-friendly cities are clustered in the north-west of Korea where the capital city of Seoul is located.

The main goal of creating women-friendly cities is to: (i) lay the institutional foundation for all administrations to carry out gender-inclusive work; (ii) expand women's economic and social participation; (iii) promote the safety of the community; (iv) create a family-oriented environment; and (v) strengthen women's capacity to engage in community activities (MOGEF and KWDI, 2016). Meanwhile, to enrich the quality of women-friendliness in cities rather than to merely increase the size and numbers of cities being designated, the programme provides education for government officials and citizens to understand the concept of women-friendliness cities. They also conduct training for policy makers to strengthen their practical skills. Moreover, it also supports the cities with a pool of cost-free consultants (comprising of experts from various fields, including women's policies, urban planning, and women's rights organization) to design and implement projects for regional gender-friendliness. In addition, the programme calls for good practices on the work-and-life balance, women's active economic presence and wraparound care. It also engages in the discovery and award of honours to cities that contribute to women-friendliness. In areas where situations perform poorly, they are forced to reset their programme to make necessary improvements (MOGEF and KWDI, 2016).

'Safe Housing' Schemes for Single-Woman Household in Seoul

Some of the operational components of the land management include the functions of managing the building of new physical infrastructure, the implementation of construction planning and change of land use through planning permission and granting of permits (Williamson *et al.*, 2010). In 2014, the Seoul Metropolitan Government first supplied 'safe housing' for single women household within the Cheonwang urban development project area where the development restriction zone was released. These newly constructed and designed rental housing schemes were meant for many low-income single-woman households, including university students and young professionals. The model of this public rental housing in Seoul is based on consumer-customized scheme that caters for the safety and lifestyle of single-person household women who are more likely to be exposed to crime.

Characterization of safe housing for single-women households is important for our increased understanding of what elements of the buildings (and its surrounding) that must be taken into consideration. The key priority factor considered lies in the safety of both the inside and outside buildings. It also ensured more practicality in use, as well as easier access for women. For example, unmanned home-delivery systems are installed in these houses (right next to the entrances), and they are designed in such a way that meter readings are only done from the outside. This means that it is possible for the meter readers to read the gas, electric and water meter from outside the buildings to reduce unnecessary private contact, in the case that women do not want them to come into their homes. Moreover, double doors (with the card readers) are installed to protect residents from outsiders and there are window guards and covers to prevent theft. CCTVs are installed throughout the buildings, including their main entrances, elevators, and corridors on each floor. Alarm bells and motion sensors are also installed for households to enable people to contact the security office or police stations in the case of emergencies. This makes it possible for the women to have 24-hour access to the building with the confidence of feeling safe within, and when they are away from home. Furthermore, the buildings are designed to ensure that parking lots and stairways are visible from the security offices on their first floors to minimize blind spots in public spaces (Seoul Metropolitan Government, 2014).

This Korean model of safe housing is based on the premise that community spaces play a pivotal role in ensuring that single-women households interact with their neighbours freely without barriers. Communal laundry rooms are in the basement floors. These are in-built open (multi-purpose) spaces meant to serve as key components for community cohesion and engagement. It also has residents' lounges on various floors to offer panoramic views of neighbourhoods to enhance their sense of familial warmth and kinship and promote communal living. The buildings are lightly painted, and their walls also painted with light red, green and yellow colours. There are also reception areas for visitors and a day-care centre incorporated with a local community centre, to aid in the problem of insufficient child-care facilities in the cities/region (Seoul Metropolitan Government, 2014).

Concerning the requirements for accessing these housing units, some criteria are put in place to ensure that only women of a certain socioeconomic class can enjoy them. In Seoul, out of a total of 96 houses (with 14-square-metre rooms), 70% are allocated as general type housing by the Seoul Metropolitan Government. However, 30% are allocated (as a matter of priority) to economically and socially marginalized groups. The former applies only to the single-person homeless females who are registered residents in Seoul. Applicants are required to demonstrate that they have been working at small and medium-sized enterprises (SMEs) for more than 6 months. A deposit of KRW 7,360,000 (approximately US$6550) is compulsory. A monthly rent of KRW 120,000 (approximately US$107) is the least expensive of the rental prices. Overall, the Seoul metropolitan government guarantees and supports these schemes to make it easier for low-income single-women households to have access to housing at a significantly lower price/rent in comparison to the market values. Applications can be made only on the internet and within a given period per year. Evaluation for qualification is on a points system based on criteria such as incomes, homelessness, work conditions and the total asset (including land, buildings, and motor vehicles).

'Urban-to-Rural Migrant Women' Support Programmes

The Minister of Agriculture, Food and Rural Affairs (MAFRA) first announced 'master plans for female farmers (2000–2005)' in 2000. Since then, they have re-formulated the master plans every five years. Recently, there is a rural women's policy team put in place and dedicated to establishing policies for female farmers. This has been established within MAFRA, and forms part of the framework of action for supporting urban-to-rural migrant women. In addition, the fourth master plan for female farmers (2016–2020) in Korea was implemented after reviewing the previous plans in coordination with female farmers' organization, local governments and expert groups (MAFRA, 2020a). Since 2015, the Support of Female Farmers and Fishermen Act contributes to the realization of policies and provides legal grounds for the formulation of master plans for female farmers. Its important policy agenda here emphasizes: (i) improving the ability to run an agricultural business; (ii) enhancing the status of female farmers; (iii) ensuring maternity rights, improving child-care conditions, and promoting the quality of life of female farmers. These interventions are intended primarily for fostering and developing the rights and capabilities of female farmers. They are, therefore, limited to supporting the early settlement for urban-to-rural migrant women.

Urban-to-rural migrant women can have difficulties in Korean cities due to societal biased views against women, as well as their rural life. Although female farmers account for more than half of the farm population and play significant role in various functional aspects, there still exists strong patriarchal culture. This trend is like those of developing countries (see Chigbu, 2013a,b,c). It is indicative that even in developed economies, women continue to face challenges of gender equality and perceptions. To overcome these challenges, many capacity building programs were launched in Korea to provide chances for education and access to the female farmers from multiple agencies. These rural migrant women opportunities are embedded in initiatives such as: Woman Farmer Leadership Academy; Woman Agricultural and Food Trade Leadership Training; Basic Course for Returning Woman Farmers; Accounting for

Woman Farmers; Family Management Agreement Education and Education on Woman-Friendly Farming Machines, etc.

To increase the quality of life of women farmers, local governments in Korea are encouraged to initiate a 'woman farmer centre' that primarily functions in providing child-care, after-school learning for children in farming villages, grievance counselling, educational and cultural activities, and other non-regular programmes. In other words, the woman farmer centre can be deemed as an interim support for ensuring rural women's welfare in an era of urbanization. The budget for the centre is born by local governments on average of KRW 120 million (US$106,864) as of 2019, excluding budgets related to other forms of burden to individuals. As of 2019, a total of 39 women farmers' centres were operational across the country. Article 13 of the 'Support of Female Farmers and Fishermen Act' and the Article 3 of enactment ordinance stipulate the establishment and operation related to the woman farmer centre' (MAFRA, 2020b).

Use of Gender-Disaggregated Data on Land Ownership

Since 2017, gender-based classification on the 'status of individual land ownership' were officially announced by the Ministry of Land, Infrastructure and Transport (MOLIT). A previous 'cadastral statistics' was unable to provide estimates on how much land women and men actually own. Until recently, the central and local governments have shown little interest in adding a land-based gender classification or indicator that depicts or represents the level of inequality or change in status in the economic sector between men and women (Lee, 2016).

Based on data from the Statistics Korea and MOGEF (2020), it is possible to reflect on gender-disaggregated data on land ownership issues to understand the trend of women-and-men power balance in land-related decisions. The statistics on land ownership prior to 2017 categorized individual landowners based on their age and residence only. However, engaging in gender-disaggregated data on land ownership is becoming a common global trend. International organizations such as the United Nations pay attention to the data on land ownership for the recognition of women's land rights and tenure security. Based on the Statistics Act in Korea, gender classification is a principle when compiling statistics. Every national agency intending to produce new statistics, is expected to obtain prior approval from the commissioner of the Statistics Korea on the matters such as name, kind, purpose, subject of survey, methods of survey, statistical chart on distinction of sex. Gender classification of the statistics may only be avoided if there is a compelling reason not to do so and must be in consultation with the MOGEF. The 'status of individual housing ownership', which is like the 'status of individual land ownership', has been gender-disaggregated since 2012. Various classifications of gender-disaggregated data on housing ownership are organized by age, residency, number of housing holdings, equity and disability. Although it is still at its infancy stage (i.e. classifying statistical data on individual land ownership), it is meaningful that there are indicators of how much women have access to land as one of the most important assets.

When it comes to the housing ownership, women only accounted for 44.4% of the whole country in 2018 and there is a tendency that the proportion of women owners will continue to increase. More than half of the housing ownership still tend to be registered in the name of men (55.6%) rather than women. This is a trend normally attributed to developing countries (see Chigbu, 2020; Doss and Meinzen-Dick, 2020), but which is evident in Korea. The mean estimate of women's land ownership in Korea in 2019 was around 44.0%. We assume that the difference of housing and land ownership between women and men can be explained by the balance of power over household decision-making in purchasing a house and land. It is important to bear in mind that the statistics on land ownership are based upon land and ownerships registered in the cadastre; whereas those of housing ownership are based on housing-related administrative data such as officially announced prices of housing by MOLIT, building register, property tax, population, households, and housing information from the census.

8.4 Reflections on the Learning Points on Gender and Land Issues in Korea

Several learning points are derivable from the gender- and land-related programmes (and initiatives) in Korea presented in this chapter.

The women-friendly cities program ensures that local government cooperate with the central government (MOGEF) to change the institutions, spaces and decision making to create a gendered community in both urban and rural areas. One of the most significant interventions to emerge from this case is that governance (re-)arrangements and legal provisions have been made to force all government departments to consult with the competent authorities on gender equality when planning and designing policies related to jobs, education, safety, roads and urban planning. Moreover, there are also voluntary guideline meant to be used to improve the women's spatial proximity to the public spaces and infrastructure in support of women's empowerment and community participation in administrative decision making. This indicates that the women-friendly cities program at the governmental level has matured to the point where gender perspectives can work and be strengthened within Korean society.

According to the Statistics Korea and MOGEF (2020), the single-women households (approximately 3.1 million households) account for nearly half of the total households (50.3%) in the country. This indicates that the single-women households outnumber single-men households. The perception of vulnerability to crime, particularly from women, remains high (57.0%) compared to 44.5% for men. Therefore, the introduction of 'safe housing' schemes for single-women households in Seoul is essential based on these sociodemographic factors. In addition, housing inequality begins with many sociodemographic problems that lead to crimes against women households. Single-women households feel insecure, and this leads to a high cost of housing for better locations and conditions. What stands out in this housing scheme is that the elements of crime prevention design through environmental design (CPDED) have been considered. It is important to note that the buildings are designed with both safety and comfort in mind for women, as well as to secure women's housing rights in urban environment.

The support programs for urban-to-rural migration women focuses on the elevating the status of women farmers to be socially respectable, along with improving their social and economic well-being. It also allows the women farmers' to actively engage with policy makers and participate in the development process. The programmes are gender responsive because it incorporates the women farmers' needs in the changing agricultural environment in rural regions (with revisions done every 5 years). It also provides a new private–public-partnership (PPP) model on women empowerment through the multiple capacity building programs in the agricultural sector and allows to engage marginalized groups such as youth and elderly farmers (as well as married migrant women in rural areas).

Although generating gender-disaggregated data on (documented) land ownership is still in its infancy, it represents a first step towards tracking the long-term impacts of (in)equitable distribution of wealth on women's access to land and property as well as to credit. The appropriate use of the data can help provide solid evidence on the true state of land and property gap between women and men. Such data will allow for appropriate steps to closing the gaps that exists. Openness and transparency of gender-disaggregated data are key ingredients for building a gendered land management in practice and is the only way towards achieving a gender-neutral (but also gender-inclusive) society in Korea.

8.5 Conclusion

So far, very little is available in the literature about the question of how gender perspective has implemented in land management, especially in the developed countries where less attention has been paid in understanding the men-and-women situation in property and land based empowerment. The examples presented in this chapter demonstrate a strong interest in the part of governments and the private sector to respond to women's needs and to provide services/structures for women in Korea. However, more still need to be done. More land rights and tenure-oriented discourses should be considered in land and gender-related policy making. Questions related to how easy or difficult it is for women farmers to acquire/lease land should be asked and investigated. For instance, are the lands that women own smaller or less valuable than are those of men?

The biggest revelation of this chapter is that the gendered land management practice put the cross-cutting issues on the discussion table, especially focusing on urban planning, housing, rural development, and land administration. Based on the experience in Korea, it suggests that gender mainstreaming in land management can be achieved in the following ways: (i) governance (re-)arrangements in spatial decision making; (ii) smart-infrastructure concepts aligned with female elements and preferences; (iii) private–public partnership (PPP) on women empowerment; and (iv) openness and transparency of gender-disaggregated data. However, several important limitations also need to be considered when trying to adopt (or adapt) the Korean experience elsewhere. First, on the surface, all the projects and programs for gender sensitivity in land management demand bottom-up and community-driven decision making, but there still exists some top-down culture and state-directed approach in practice for aligning implementation to legal procedures. Second, the central and local governments consider to make project performance a priority rather than making the programmes (quality) better. Lastly, the government brought gender awareness into the policies and budgets of all agencies (gender-responsive budgeting), allocation and implementation pathways can be problematic. Korea is yet to reach full awareness on these gender matters because there is still a lack of gender awareness in many government departments.

This is the first study that has presented evidence for how gender perspective has been supported and implemented in land management in the Korean context. The revelations of this chapter have several important gender implications for future land management practice. The study is important in furthering the understanding of gender mainstreaming in land management and related issues in a global context that embrace not only developing countries but also the developed countries. Therefore, it is recommended that further research be undertaken to develop and understand the issues of land administration and cadastral processes, land use management and the legal and policy framework for owning or leasing land and housing in ways that benefit men and women equally.

References

Chigbu, U.E. (2013a) Territorial development: Suggestions for a new approach to rural development in Nigeria. PhD thesis, Technical University of Munich, Germany. Available at: http://mediatum.ub.tum.de/doc/1136728/document.pdf (accessed 25 May 2021).

Chigbu, U.E. (2013b) Fostering rural sense of place: the missing piece in Uturu, Nigeria. *Development in Practice*, 23(2), 264–277. DOI: 10.1080/09614524.2013.772120.

Chigbu, U.E. (2013c) Rurality as a choice: Towards ruralising rural areas in sub-Saharan African countries. *Development Southern Africa*, 30(6), 812–825. DOI: 10.1080/0376835X.2013.859067.

Chigbu, U.E. (2020) Negotiating land rights to redress land wrongs: Women in Africa's land reforms. In: Ochieng, C.M.O. (Ed.), *Rethinking Land Reform in Africa: New Ideas, Opportunities and Challenges*. African Development Bank, Abidjan, Ivory Coast, pp. 156–167.

Chigbu, U. E., Paradza, G. and Dachaga, W. (2019) Differentiations in women's land tenure experiences: Implications for women's land access and tenure security in sub-Saharan Africa. *Land*, 8, 22. DOI: 10.3390/land8020022.

Daly, M. (2005) Gender mainstreaming in theory and practice. *Social Politics: International Studies in Gender, State & Society*, 12, 433–450.

Doss, C. and Meinzen-Dick, R. (2020) Land tenure security for women: A conceptual framework. *Land Use Policy*, 99, 105080.

FAO (2002) *Gender and Access to land.* Food and Agriculture Organization of the United Nations, Rome, Italy.

FAO (2012) *Voluntary Guidelines on the Responsible Governance of Tenure of Land, Fisheries and Forests in the Context of National Food Security / CFS Committee on World Food Security*, Food and Agriculture Organization of the United Nations, Rome, Italy.

Kim, D.-S. and Kang, M. (2016) Rapid Growth – what's next for gender mainstreaming? Analyzing the gender impact assessment system in Korea. *Journal of Women, Politics & Policy*, 37, 168–189.

Lee, J.-Y. (2016) How many women's lands? *Gender-disaggregated data on land ownership is coming up*. Available at: https://www.yna.co.kr/view/AKR20161125099700003 (accessed 30 October 2020).

Lee, S.-H. (2020) Beyond the policy rhetoric: The limitations of gender mainstreaming in South Korea relating to women and childcare. *Social Policy and Society*, 19, 379–395.

MAFRA (2020a) *The 2020 Master Plans for Women Farmers.* Ministry of Agriculture, Food and Rural Affairs. Government of South Korea, Seoul, Korea.

MAFRA (2020b) *Policy Databook for Woman Farmers*. Ministry of Agriculture, Food and Rural Affairs. Government of South Korea, Seoul, Korea.

Meinzen-Dick, R., Quisumbing, A., Doss, C. and Theis, S. (2019) Women's land rights as a pathway to poverty reduction: Framework and review of available evidence. *Agricultural Systems*, 172, 72–82.

MOGEF (2020) *The 2019 Analysis Report on Gender Impact Assessment.* Ministry of Gender, Equality and Family. Government of South Korea, Seoul, Korea.

MOGEF and KWDI (2015) *Guideline for Women-Friendly Cities.* Ministry of Gender, Equality and Family and Korea Women's Development Institute. Government of South Korea, Seoul, Korea.

MOGEF and KWDI (2016) *Best Practice of Women-Friendly Cities.* Ministry of Gender, Equality and Family and Korea Women's Development Institute. Government of South Korea, Seoul, Korea.

MOGEF and KWDI (2017) *The 2017 Standard Manual on Women-Friendly Cities*. Ministry of Gender, Equality and Family and Korea Women's Development Institute. Government of South Korea, Seoul, Korea.

Seoul Metropolitan Government (2014) *Seoul Supplies the First 'Women's Safety Housing' with 96 Households in Chunwang.* Government of South Korea, Seoul, Korea.

Statistics Korea and MOGEF (2020) *2020 Women's Life in Statistics.* Government of South Korea, Seoul, Korea.

United Nations (2002) *Gender Mainstreaming: An Overview*, United Nations Publications, New York, NY, USA.

United Nations (2014) *2014 World Survey on the Role of Women in Development*. United Nations Publications, New York, NY, USA.

United Nations Economic and Social Council (1997) *Mainstreaming the Gender Perspective into all Policies and Programmes in the United Nations System*. United Nations Economic and Social Council, New York, NY, USA.

Walby, S. (2005) Gender mainstreaming: Productive tensions in theory and practice. *Social Politics: International Studies in Gender, State & Society*, 12, 321–343.

Williamson, I., Enemark, S., Wallace, J. and Rajabifard, A. (2010) *Land Administration for Sustainable Development*, ESRI, Redlands, CA, USA.

World Bank (2005) *Gender Issues and Best Practices in Land Administration Projects: A Synthesis Report.* World Bank, Washington, DC, USA.

9 Analysing Non-Legal Barriers to Land Ownership by Women

Katriel Marks* and Rhonda Phillips
Purdue University, West Lafayette, IN, USA

9.1 Introduction

In every region of the world, women perform large amounts of labour in agriculture. Often, this is their main source of income. However, their ability to access that land is all too often tied to their relationships with males, especially husbands (Wangari, 2016). In the case that a husband passes away or a marriage dissolves, women are at a high risk of losing their access to land, and in the process, their livelihood. Despite many countries having laws that allow women to own and inherit land, these laws are commonly overlooked. The benefits that women experience when they can own land can be numerous. Increased levels of women's land ownership are correlated with higher levels of food security in communities (Hallward-Driemeier *et al.*, 2013). Beyond simply serving as an asset and a means of food production, land can also be used as collateral for accessing credit (SIDA, n.d.). It also increases negotiating power within relationships and may empower women to have more say in child-bearing. When they own their own land, women are not tied to potentially abusive relationships for their livelihood and may often have higher levels of self-esteem. However, it should be noted that within some cultures, women having independence can result in abuses as males take it as a sign of disrespect. It is not an easy terrain to traverse given these complicating cultural and societal aspects of seeking more economic empowerment for women. Despite these and other challenges, analysing and addressing barriers to women's land ownership can help encourage the economic, social and political empowerment of women across the developing world.

This chapter explores barriers to women's land ownership. It investigates the potential factors behind why women's rights to own land are often ignored despite laws permitting women to own and inherit land. Measures of gender equality are correlated, as presented in the World Economic Forum Global Gender Gap Index 2020 (economic participation and equality, educational attainment, health and survival, and political empowerment) to percentages of land held by women in a nation. Commonalities between case studies on women's land ownership around the world are discussed as well.

9.2 Context of Women's Land Ownership

Globally, women perform around 43% of farm labour, although the exact percentage varies

*Corresponding author: katriel.marks@gmail.com

 Land Governance and Gender: The Tenure-Gender Nexus in Land Management and Land Policy (ed. U.E. Chigbu)
DOI: 10.1079/9781789247664.0009

between regions (FAO, 2011). Rural women in the developing world typically spend between 30% and 70% of their time on farm-related activities. If processing and preparing of food is included in that statistic, women spend around 60–80% of their time on agriculture and food-related activities. Despite their heavy involvement in agriculture, women are often deprived of the right to own land. The Food and Agriculture Organization of the United Nations (FAO) reports that on average, only around 18% of landowners in each nation are women; this statistic varies from around 0.8% in Saudi Arabia to 50.5% in Cape Verde (FAO, 2020a).

Owning land benefits women in many ways: it can provide a level of income security, increase their bargaining rights in the family and community, and help women accumulate capital (SIDA, n.d.). Many banks will lend to women only if they possess land or another form of capital, meaning that land can help women access credit. Land ownership can allow a woman to be less dependent on male relationships and can empower her to improve her own economic, social and political standing (Silliman, 1996). Women in the developing world often have lower levels of participation in labour markets and experience wage discrimination, meaning that they have fewer chances to increase their economic standing outside the home (FAO, 2011). Further, having secure access to land via ownership enables women to have a better chance of feeding their families, whether growing food or generating income via the land. Especially in rural areas, the phenomenon of food deserts continues to be an issue, where small communities may not have access to resources for provision of healthy and nutritious food (Thomas, 2020).

Additionally, women are expected to perform many other household tasks that take much of their time, such as obtaining water, firewood and other resources, as well as caring for children. For rural women, improving the equity of land ownership may represent a good way to increase their socioeconomic standing and hopefully improve their quality of life. Increasing the ability of women to own and control land, which in turn impacts their livelihoods, may be a route to encouraging more 'caring economies'. These are essentially economic systems that include compassion, empathy and more equitable approaches to sustaining livelihoods. Since suffering is often directly tied to economic well-being, policies and actions integrated into structures of business, organizations and communities for lessening suffering and increasing both equity and access to women could have significant impacts (Kocaoğlu and Phillips, 2017).

As of 2010, women and men had equal rights to own and manage property in 112 countries (Almodóvar-Reteguis, 2019); 75 countries had placed at least some restrictions on women's property rights. The Middle East and North Africa tended to be the most restrictive, particularly around inheritance, while Europe and Central Asia had no property rights restrictions for women in any nation. In many of the nations where women's land ownership is restricted, access to land is acquired through *usufruct rights* – a woman must have a relationship with a man who owns land, usually a father, brother, or husband (Wangari, 2016). Typically, her access to that land ends when that relationship ends for any reason, be that death, disagreements, getting married or getting divorced. The land then reverts to a male. Having access to land is only the first aspect of ensuring women's land ownership rights, however. Even when women have the right to legally own land, they often lack the ability to control it and earn income from it. This is due to traditional customs of farming, decision-making and earning an income being considered masculine activities, whereas the care-taking aspects of agriculture are considered feminine. Thus, the issue of women being able to own and use land is not only about legal ownership rights, but also connected to their ability to sustain livelihoods to improve economic well-being as well as meeting basic needs for food for themselves and their families.

9.3 Legal Aspects

Many nations in the developing world recognize varied forms of law, such as constitutional and statutory law, customary law, and religious law (Rünger, 2006). Constitutional and statutory law covers the entire nation and is enforced through a national legal system, whereas customary and religious laws tend to be localized and enforced less formally. While almost all nations analysed by the FAO Legal Assessment Tool prohibit gender-based discrimination in their constitutions, fewer declare that customary law is superseded by this constitutional ban, and even fewer place religious law beneath constitutional law (FAO, 2020b). In many countries, customary and religious laws may discourage or not allow women to own property while constitutional law does allow women to own land. Women who live in countries where constitutional and statutory law does not supersede customary and religious law are likely unable to own property due to local restrictions and are not able to appeal to national courts. Those who live in countries where constitutional and statutory law does override customary and religious law still must face enormous barriers to enjoy their right to own property. Illiteracy, threats, and lack of money could easily strip women of their ability to petition the courts for their right to own or inherit land.

At the international level, almost all countries (except Iran, Holy See, Niue, Palau, Somalia, Sudan, Tonga and the United States) have ratified the Convention on the Elimination of all forms of Discrimination Against Women (CEDAW) by the United Nations (UN OHCHR, 2014). CEDAW includes language to guarantee women equal rights to own and administer property, as well as to guarantee equal access to credit, equal rights in the dissolution of marriage, and in all legal proceedings (UN OHCHR, 1979). Because CEDAW is an international treaty, it is legally binding to all signatories. However, similarly to domestic law, CEDAW is not enforced in a meaningful way in many countries.

9.4 Non-Legal Barriers and Global Themes

The non-legal barriers that restrict women from owning land are numerous and often seemingly immutable. One study focusing on Khwisero Constituency, Kakamega County in Kenya found that the largest barrier to women's land ownership in that area was a lack of information (Wangari, 2016). Although land could legally be held jointly in the country, only 15% of households were aware of this. Land institutions in the county were not telling residents that land could be held jointly or by women. To make matters worse, Kenya's female illiteracy rate is significantly higher than the male illiteracy rate, meaning that women have a much lower chance of finding this information from sources other than word of mouth. Because of this, women often had many questions about land ownership and legal rights. Due to a cultural constraint on asking questions in front of men, they were unable to learn about their legal rights to own land.

Similarly, a study of the women in the Luhya Community in Kakamega County, Kenya found that there was a large amount of cultural resistance to women owning land (Mwagae, 2013); 49% of the community found it unacceptable for women to own land, and less than 12% said that women have equal rights to inherit and own land. For many, this was a difficult issue to discuss. Over one-fifth considered women's land ownership to be a taboo subject. In this community, women's land ownership was denounced at a moral level. Emphasizing the depth and permanence of these beliefs, the author stated, 'Many are "soaked" in strong retrogressive cultural beliefs that deem it immoral for women to own land and other land-based resources' (Mwagae, 2013). The enforcement and violence of this belief leads to women being forced off their land if their husbands pass away or divorce them. This study also cited low literacy rates and low incomes as reasons women did not own land. In this case, although women are provided the constitutional and statutory rights to own land, culture, illiteracy, and low incomes form a trap that is difficult for women to escape.

In Ghana, women face both legal and non-legal barriers to land ownership. Ghana's constitution allows legal pluralism, meaning that constitutional, statutory, customary, and religious law are all valid in the country (Rünger, 2006). Because of the complicated nature of Ghana's legal system, women seeking to gain legal rights to property are at a marked disadvantage. Like the women in Kenya, Ghanaian women often have lower incomes and lower literacy rates than men. For many women, facing a complicated, cumbersome legal system to the low level of resources at hand is an unachievable task. Beyond the rights to land itself, women also faced legal battles around marriage and sharecropping. In some communities, the common form of marriage did not involve the wife joining the husband's family, meaning that even if a husband wished to leave land to his wife, the woman would not be legally recognized as a valid inheritor. In case of divorce, women typically did not receive land. Additionally, if a woman was involved in a sharecropping arrangement with a relative or landowner, it was very easy for the owner to change the details of their agreement at any time because these agreements were typically only verbal. Women in Ghana could inherit land, but still faced large legal barriers to large-scale land ownership. Just as in Kenya, the non-legal issues of low literacy rates, low incomes and cultural resistance exacerbated the tedious process of navigating the national legal system.

Saudi Arabia has the lowest women's land ownership rate in the world at a mere 0.8% (FAO, 2020a). However, Sharia law, of which Saudi Arabia's legal system is based, provides women full legal rights to own land (Almazi, 2016). Due to a cultural belief that men are responsible for caring for their families, men inherit twice as much property than women. While this provides men an unfair advantage, low levels of education for women and an expectation for married women to remain in the domestic sphere has often led women to turn over their inherited assets to their husbands. In this way, customs allow men to retain almost absolute control of the country's land. Women in Saudi Arabia also face similar non-legal barriers to those seen in Kenya and Ghana – low levels of education, low levels of economic participation, and cultural rejection of women increasing their own socioeconomic standing. In Saudi Arabia, customary law has completely superseded both statutory and religious law to the detriment of women.

While women in Latin America have less stringent customary law than their Saudi Arabian counterparts, they still must negotiate a legal and social system that discourages them from owning land. Historically, although women could own land, their husbands were able to choose whether to title the land jointly or individually because they were legally the head of the household (Deere and León, 2003). As a result, most land was titled only in the male's name, and in the case of divorce, he would receive all the land as his own. As agricultural reforms swept the region in the 1970s, many laws were written with language that presumed most agricultural producers were male. Deere and León also found that women had substantially less bargaining power in international markets. Historically, women were forced to buy smaller plots of land at higher prices than men. Across the region, men owned larger and higher-quality pieces of farmland than women.

9.5 Themes from Across the Globe

Across the globe, themes begin to emerge. While there are differences between regions, many women face large, multifaceted barriers to owning land. Women consistently confront lower levels of education and higher illiteracy rates. Improvement in women's education access has been 'linked to a reduction in infant and childhood mortality, socio-economic development, community development, physical and mental well-being' (Merriam, 2016, p. 71). Lack of adequate education proves a barrier to accessing information about land ownership and navigating a legal system. Women often have lower levels of income, making it difficult to purchase land or pay any necessary legal fees to own land. In some cultures, their communities and families may be strongly opposed to women's land ownership, deeming it taboo and morally wrong. These case studies highlight the need for continued investment in women's education, as higher levels of education would improve literacy rates, legal understanding, and probably raise women's incomes. Investing more in women's education, however, requires a shift in cultural thinking surrounding gender roles. If women can obtain higher levels of education, they may also be deemed worthy of owning their own land. To truly change broad legal and cultural mindsets about women's land ownership, women must be included and represented in legislative bodies. Women in land governance would be likely to address some currently invisible issues in land ownership, such as a lack of disseminated information or adjacent legal issues such as considering males the legal head of the household.

In several of these cases, land ownership or agricultural labour have been gendered male. Rooij argues that the gendering of agriculture and farming continues to higher levels of agricultural development and agricultural policy, as typically farmers are gendered male and farm technology strives to be larger and stronger (Rooij, 2005). To spur true organizational change, Rooij argues that national ministries of agriculture should shift from an often technically intensive focus with splintered sub-organizations to a broader, more integrated structure with gender equality as a core commitment. Changes and commitments towards gender equality from national level organizations could help influence long-standing cultural institutions to consider new ideas.

9.6 Analytical Approach

This analysis uses data for the measures of gender equality from the Global Gender Gap Index 2020, and data for the percentage of land owned by women were from the FAO. Data from the Global Gender Gap Index 2020 were correlated with the FAO's data on percentage of total landowners who are female. The four sub-indices: (i) economic participation and opportunity; (ii) educational attainment; (iii) health and survival; and (iv) political empowerment all factor into the overall Gender Gap Index. The sub-indices are comprised of the following indicators:

- Economic participation and opportunity: Women's labour force participation rate, wage equality for similar work, estimated earned income, percentage of female professional and technical workers, and the percentage of female legislators, senior officials, and managers.
- Educational attainment: Literacy rate, enrolment in primary education, enrolment in secondary education and enrolment in tertiary education.
- Health and survival: Sex ratio at birth and healthy life expectancy.
- Political empowerment: Women in parliament, women in ministerial positions, and years with a female head of state.

The factors within each sub-index are given different weights based on their perceived importance. For example, under educational attainment, percentage of females enrolled in primary school is weighted heavier than percentages of women in higher education. The overall Gender Gap Index is then calculated by a simple average of each sub-index score.

The Gender Gap in Voter Turnout data was published in a report by the International Institute for Democracy and Electoral Assistance (2016). It simply measures the difference between the percentage of men and the percentage of women who answered 'yes' to the question, 'Do you always vote in national elections?' If a higher percentage of women answered 'yes', a nation would have a positive gender gap, and a negative one if a higher percentage of men responded 'yes'. This measure was added to measure political participation more fully by women in communities. Although likely not as powerful, voting may be a way for women to influence their governments without having to overcome the stricter social and cultural barriers to political office. The FAO's percentage of women landowners' data is simply calculated by dividing the number of female landowners in a nation by the total number of landowners in that nation.

9.7 Results

It would be plausible to expect to find a high correlation between women's education levels and women's land ownership due to the need to read and sign documents as well as navigate complex legal systems to increase land ownership. Additionally, it may be expected that women's political empowerment and women's land ownership would be highly correlated. For women to be elected or nominated for public office, they must be well-educated and highly respected by their communities – two factors which would increase land ownership. In turn, they are more likely to understand the need for women's land ownership and shape legislation to assist other women in securing land rights. Other factors of gender equality will likely be correlated, but perhaps less strongly.

Somewhat surprisingly, none of these factors showed strong correlation. Table 9.1 shows results from the correlation analysis on the overall Gender Gap Index, the four sub-indices, and the percentage of women landowners. None of the sub-indices had a strong level of correlation with women's land ownership. This is likely because many of the variables that impact land

Table 9.1. Correlation analysis

	Gender Gap Index	Economic participation and opportunity	Educational attainment	Health and survival	Political empowerment	Gender gap in voter turnout
Gender Gap Index	1.00					
Economic participation and opportunity	0.721	1.00				
Educational attainment	0.553	0.212	1.00			
Health and survival	0.275	0.208	0.156	1.00		
Political empowerment	0.784	0.241	0.239	0.150	1.00	
Gender gap in voter turnout	0.541	0.487	0.398	0.452	0.338	1.00
Percentage women's land ownership	0.357	0.476	0.304	0.335	0.060	0.391

Source: Compiled from data from the Global Gender Gap Index 2020 and Food and Agriculture Organization of the United Nations (FAO), 2020 Gender and Land Rights Database – Statistics, http://www.fao.org/gender-landrights-database/data-map/statistics/en/.

ownership are not represented in the Gender Gap index, such as legal barriers and the amount of land available in each area. Additionally, gendered land ownership data was only available for around 90 countries, and the gender gap voter turnout data was only available for 31 of the countries with land ownership data.

Economic participation and opportunity did have a moderate level of correlation, with an R-value of 0.48. One possible explanation for this would be that for many of the indicators to be higher in this category, the cultural stigmas against women working and advancing themselves socioeconomically must be overcome. The case studies reviewed from Kenya, Ghana and Saudi Arabia revealed a cultural aversion to women working as well as women owning land, suggesting that these two factors are related. In many ways, women's participation in labour markets may be an equivalent to owning land for women outside of rural areas or outside of the agricultural sector. Normalizing women's participation in labour markets may be an important concurrent step to normalizing women's land ownership. See Fig. 9.1 for the scatter plot of this relationship between economic participation and opportunity with percentage women's land ownership variables.

Educational attainment had a mild level of correlation with women's land ownership, with an R-value of 0.30. This sub-index included the literacy rate for females, which was noted by several authors as a major barrier to land ownership. However, the literacy rate for females was weighted very low compared to the other factors within the educational attainment sub-index. Enrolment in primary education was heavily weighted. In theory, high levels of enrolment in primary school should increase literacy rates. Further, the quality of education may be highly variable. Although the educational attainment sub-index did not produce a high level of correlation, education is likely still critically important to land ownership as it is necessary for reading

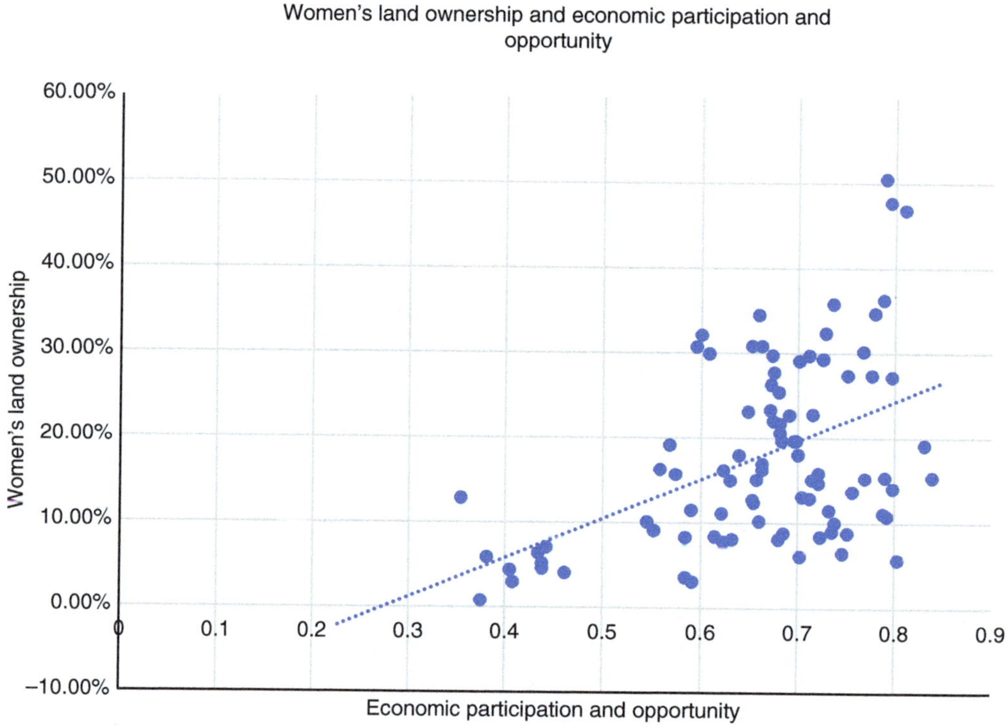

Fig. 9.1. Economic participation and opportunity (compiled by authors from data from World Economic Forum, 2020 and FAO, 2020a).

legal documents and navigating a complex legal system. See Fig. 9.2 for the scatter plot of the relationship of educational attainment and women's land ownership percentages.

Health and survival also had a mild level of correlation with women's land ownership, with an R-value of 0.33. This sub-index is dominated by the ratio of females to males at birth. For most nations, this is essentially even, leading to a high health and survival score. The only other factor in the sub-index is healthy life expectancy in years. This misses a key aspect typical healthcare challenges for rural women – access to health care and distance to a healthcare provider. Of all sub-indices, health and survival is the least logically related to women's land ownership. However, higher health and survival scores for women may signal increased cultural respect for women, which in turn could possibly impact other factors of land ownership. See Fig. 9.3 for the scatter plot of health and survival and women's land ownership percentages.

Notably, Political empowerment had a very weak correlation with women's land ownership, with an R-value of 0.06. This may partially be because of the way the political empowerment sub-index was calculated, which was entirely based on the percentage of women in high-level elected and ministerial positions. See Fig. 9.4 for the scatter plot for political empowerment and women's land ownership.

In nations which are slow to accept women in the workforce or receiving higher education, electing, or nominating women to these high offices may be much more of a stretch than allowing women to own land. For this reason, the Gender Gap in Voter Turnout data was included for additional analysis for considering political empowerment. Voter turnout yielded a higher correlation with women's land ownership with an R-value of 0.39. While this is still a mild level of correlation, it shows that higher percentages of women voting may influence their rights to own land. See Fig. 9.5 for correlations of voter turnout and women's land ownership.

The overall Gender Gap Index had a mild level of correlation with an R-value of 0.36. However, as visible on the scatter plot of women's land ownership and Gender Gap Index scores, the trend line for this variable is steep. Although each individual sub-index likely does not cover the specific aspects of gender equality necessarily for equality in land ownership, the index overall may begin to approximate a critical yet difficult aspect of the non-legal determinants of land ownership –

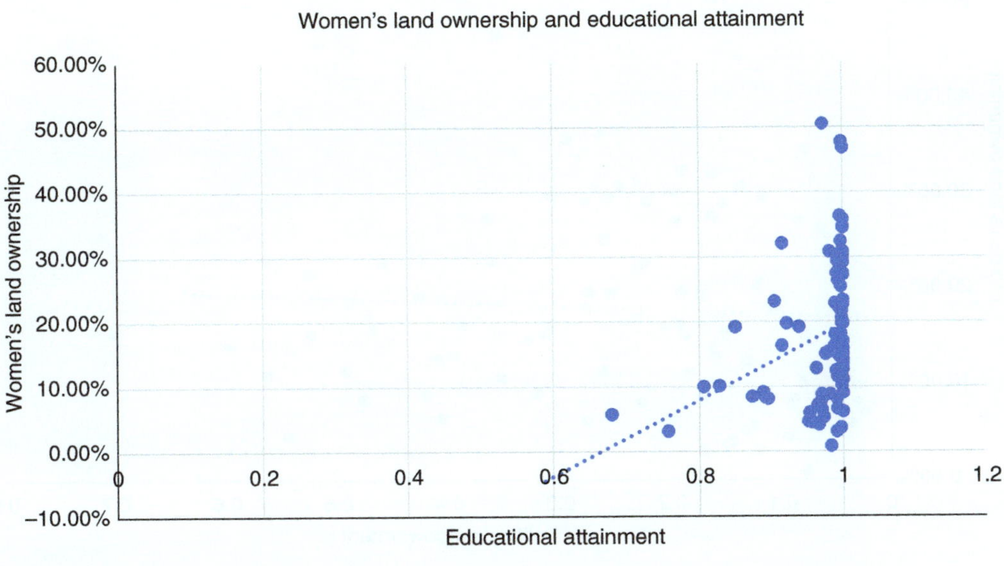

Fig. 9.2. Educational attainment (compiled by authors from data from World Economic Forum, 2020 and FAO, 2020a).

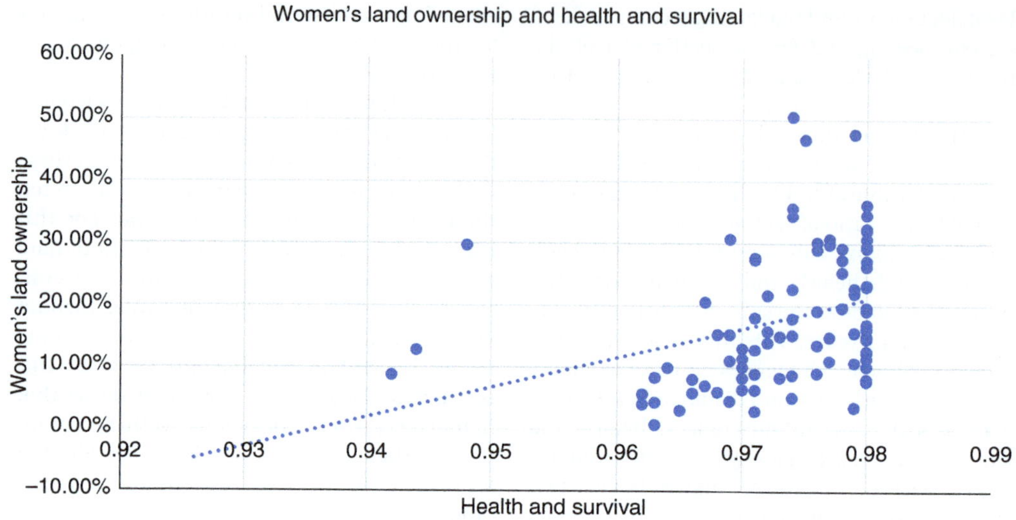

Fig. 9.3. Health and survival (compiled by authors from data from World Economic Forum, 2020 and FAO, 2020a).

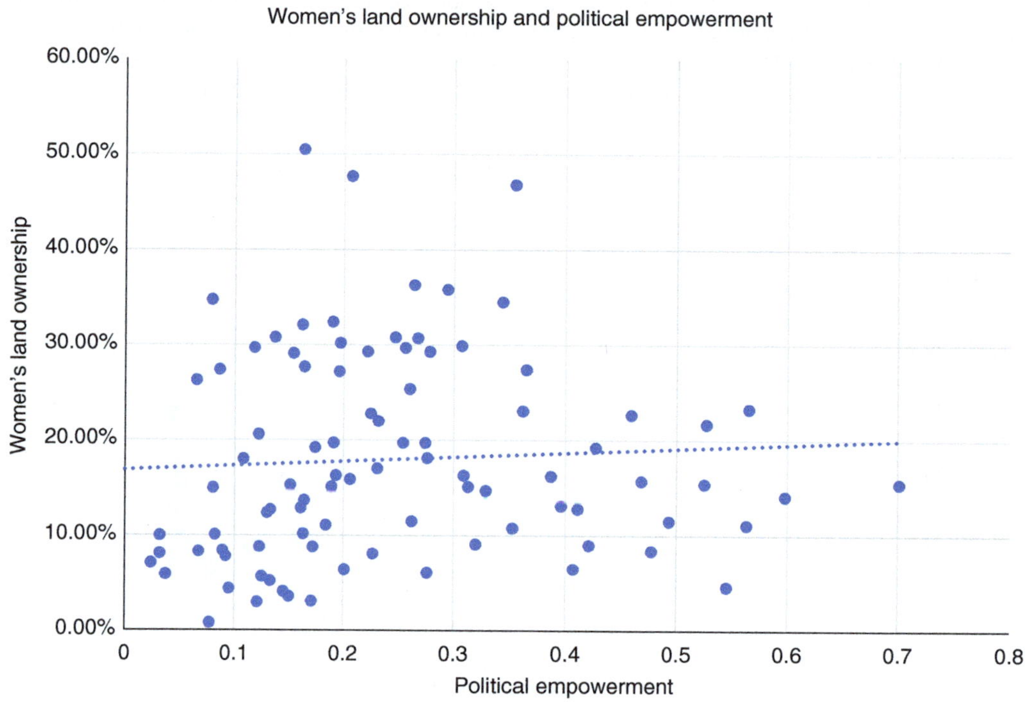

Fig. 9.4. Political empowerment (compiled by authors from data from World Economic Forum, 2020 and FAO, 2020a).

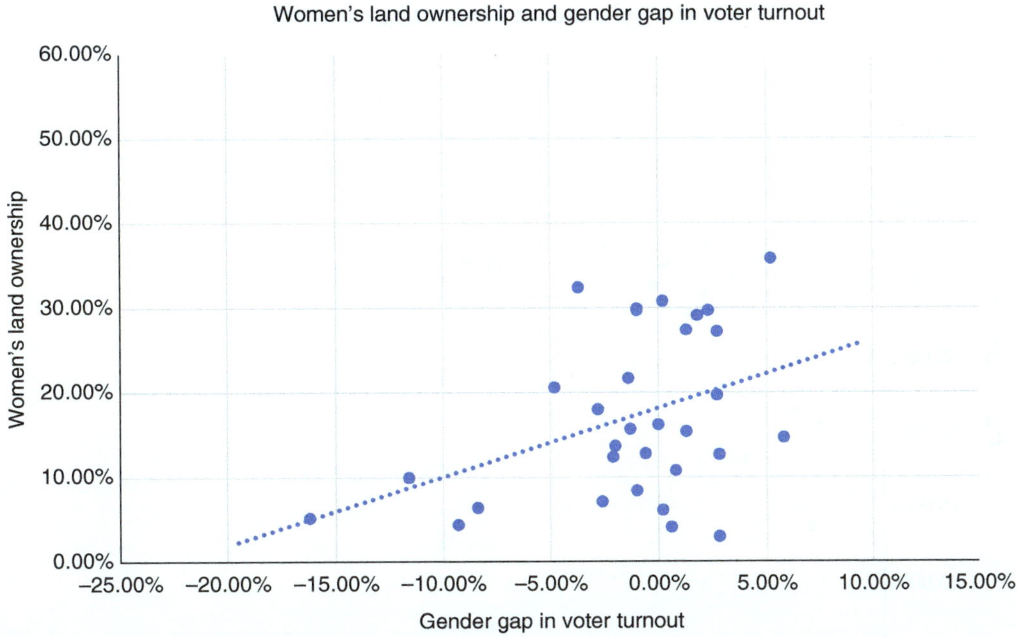

Fig. 9.5. Voter turnout (compiled by authors from data from World Economic Forum, 2020 and FAO, 2020a).

how a society views its female members. A society with an overall favourable, respectful view of women will score highly on the Global Gender Gap Index even if the specific characteristics measured are not directly related to land ownership. However, that cultural level of respect should cause factors more closely associated with women's land ownership to be higher, even if they are not included in the Global Gender Gap Index. Following are scatter plots for women's land ownership and each sub-index as well as the overall Global Gender Gap Index as well as women's land ownership and gender gap in voter turnout (see Fig. 9.6).

From these scatter plots, it is evident that data from the educational attainment and health and survival sub-indices are skewed. Because of this, these sub-indices may not provide truly accurate results as to how educational attainment and health impact women's land ownership. The cultural dimensions, along with other non-legal barriers need further investigation, especially in terms of those countries where data are not readily available or measured in ways that reflect women's ability to be landowners.

9.8 Policy Implications

From this analysis and exploration, it seems clear that increasing economic participation and opportunity would at least somewhat influence women's land ownership. For nations, this means allowing women to join the workforce if they so choose and barring discrimination in the job hiring process. It implies ensuring equal pay for equal work and encouraging women to pursue careers in technical fields. Many of the case studies referenced a lack of income and lack of access to credit as key financial barriers to land ownership, and these issues must also be addressed to increase land ownership among women. Often, these issues have roots in culture as it is difficult or taboo for women to work outside the home or have a full-time job in many cultures. Making strategic organizational changes, like those suggested by Rooij, may help create more inclusive economic and social institutions for women.

Similarly, increasing literacy rates and knowledge of their rights should be a priority for nations. Almost all case studies referenced illiteracy and lack of knowledge, as well as a lack of access to knowledge, as key barriers to women's land ownership. Improving education would also

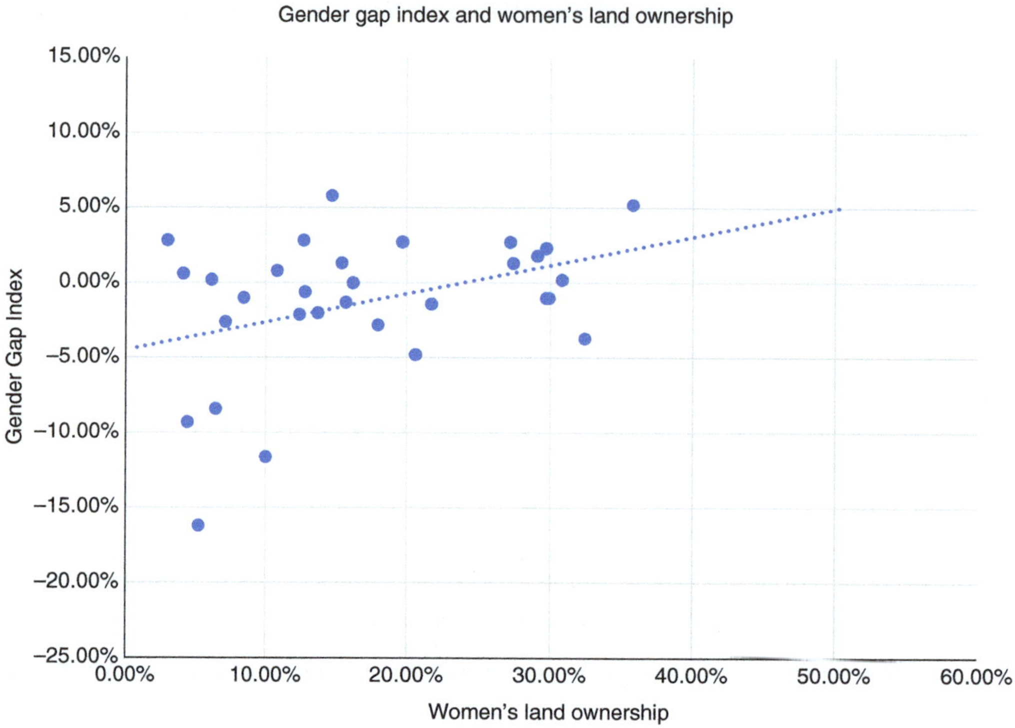

Fig. 9.6. Land ownership and Gender Gap Index (compiled by authors from data from World Economic Forum, 2020 and FAO, 2020a).

improve economic participation and opportunity, as women would have more marketable skills to earn an income outside of agriculture if they so wished. Like the economic factors, these factors are also deeply ingrained in culture, as it is common for cultures not to value women's education, thus leading to lower literacy rates. Strategically improving education for women at the national level would both allow women to achieve higher literacy rates and create positive organizational change for women. It should be noted that societal and cultural hurdles can exist preventing women from obtaining more education; these barriers need addressing along with economic factors to help gain improvement in education obtainment and opportunity.

Additionally, large multinational non-governmental organizations (NGOs) and intergovernmental organizations (IGOs) should be aware that the factors affecting gender equality in rural areas is often different than those affecting gender equality in urban areas. While the Global Gender Gap Index may appropriately measure gender equality in urban areas, it misses key aspects for rural women, including distance to healthcare facilities, time necessary to gather supplies such as water and firewood, and unpaid agricultural labour. Specific gender equality indices for rural populations would provide further insight into how to spur rural development and women's land ownership.

As well as improving education and addressing institutional equity, nations should encourage women to participate in their governments through voting and running for political office. While women may face social and cultural barriers to voting, they are likely much more likely to be able to vote even in societies which may not readily accept women in elected positions. Even though they may not achieve descriptive representation in their governments, they can at least vote for those who will substantively represent them and the changes they would like to see. However, much like land ownership itself, voting or running for office depends on women having access to education and being unhindered by social norms.

9.9 Conclusion

At its core, many of the barriers that women face around land ownership can be traced either indirectly or directly to lower social status and cultural standing in countries across the globe. A lack of education, access to information and credit stem from economic institutions which do not place women on an equal footing to men. Broad cultural change is needed to truly bring equality to women's land ownership. However, culture can be very engrained and slow to change. Having processes in place that help embed support and reduce barriers to women owning land is crucial. Processes can in turn change how things are done, and once a part of governance systems, can then influence cultural change. There are many other numerous policies and actions available to communities and nations to aid women in gaining equality in land ownership, but also more broadly for improving status and standing. These include development of indicators to track and gauge progress at the community and regional levels. It is easier to see progress if it can be measured over time to assess what policies and actions had the intended effect. And while the sources utilized as part of this chapter are indicators, there are issues with scale and scope, as discussed. It may be that indicators developed at the community or state/provincial/regional level can better reflect what is occurring in those areas and respond more quickly with needed policy action.

Communities and countries should increase women's education to increase literacy rates and provide information about land ownership rights. Additionally, every effort should be made to improve women's economic participation and opportunities, as this helps women build capital. At the national level, countries should consider restructuring key organizations to place gender at the centre of their work and should encourage women to vote. Slowly but surely, these actions should help to change the exclusive institutions that bar women from owning land, and in turn, contribute to healthier, wealthier communities.

References

Alazmi, W.H. (2016) Women's rights to accessing and owning land in the United States, Saudi Arabia, Brazil, and South Africa. MA thesis. Ball State University, Muncie, IN, USA.

Almodóvar-Reteguis, N.L. (2019) Where in the world do women still face legal barriers to own and administer assets? World Bank Blog, 18 June. Available at: https://blogs.worldbank.org/opendata/where-world-do-women-still-face-legal-barriers-own-and-administer-assets (accessed 30 April 2020).

Deere, C.D. and León, M. (2003) The gender asset gap: Land in Latin America. *World Development*, 31(6), 925–947.

FAO (2020a) *Gender and Land Rights Database – Statistics.* Food and Agriculture Organization of the United Nations. Available at: http://www.fao.org/gender-landrights-database/data-map/statistics/en/ (accessed 30 April 2020).

FAO (2020b) *Gender and Land Rights Database – Legal Assessment Tool.* Food and Agriculture Organization of the United Nations. Available at: http://www.fao.org/gender-landrights-database/legislation-assessment-tool/en/ (accessed 30 April 2020).

FAO (2011) *The Role of Women in Agriculture*. Food and Agriculture Organization of the United Nations. Available at: http://www.fao.org/3/am307e/am307e00.pdf (accessed 30 April 2020).

Hallward-Driemeier, M., Hasan, T. and T. Rusu, A.B. (2013) *Women's Legal Rights over 50 Years.* Available at: http://documents.worldbank.org/curated/en/312581468338398063/pdf/WPS6616.pdf (accessed 30 April 2020).

International Institute for Democracy and Electoral Assistance (2016) *Voter Turnout Trends Around the World.* Available at: https://www.idea.int/sites/default/files/publications/voter-turnout-trends-around-the-world.pdf (accessed 27 July 2020).

Kocaoğlu, M. and Phillips, R. (2017) Exploring caring economics and alleviating suffering. In Anderson, R. (Ed.), *Alleviating World Suffering – The Challenge of Negative Quality of Life*, pp. 423–430. Springer, Dordrecht, The Netherlands.

Merriam, S. (2016) Gender equity and community well-being. In: Kee, Y., Lee, S.J. and Phillips, R. (Eds), *Social Factors and Community Well-Being*, Springer, Dordrecht, The Netherlands, pp. 71–86.

Mwagae, E.W. (2013) Factors hindering realization of women's land rights. MA thesis. University of Nairobi, Kenya.

Rooij, S. (2005) Institutional capacity building for women's empowerment. *EJPAU* 8(3) #30. Available at: http://www.ejpau.media.pl/volume8/issue3/art-30.html (accessed 27 April 2020).

Rünger, M. (2006) *Governance, Land Rights and Access to Land in Ghana – A Development Perspective on Gender Equity*. Available at: https://www.fig.net/resources/proceedings/fig_proceedings/accra/papers/ts01/ts01_02_ruenger.pdf (accessed 30 April 2020).

SIDA (n.d.) *Quick Guide to What and How: Increasing Women's Access to Land.* Available at: https://www.oecd.org/dac/gender-development/47566053.pdf (accessed 29 April 2020).

Silliman, J. (1996) Reviewed work: a field of one's own: Gender and land rights in South Asia by Bina Agarwal. *Land Economics*, 72(2), 269–273. Available at: http://www.jstor.org/stable/3146971 (accessed 30 April 2020).

Thomas, T.D. (2020) An exploratory study of food deserts in Utica, Mississippi. In Phillips, R., Trevan, E. and Kraeger, P. (Eds), *Research Handbook on Community Development*. Edward Elgar Publishing, Cheltenham, UK, pp. 290–300.

UN OHCHR (1979) *Convention on the Elimination of All Forms of Discrimination against Women.* UN Office of High Commission on Human Rights. Available at: https://www.ohchr.org/en/professionalinterest/pages/cedaw.aspx (accessed 29 April 2020).

UN OHCHR (2014) *Status of Ratification Interactive Dashboard – Convention on the Elimination of All Forms of Discrimination against Women*. UN Office of High Commission on Human Rights. Available at: https://indicators.ohchr.org (accessed 30 April 2020).

Wangari, I.J. (2016) Factors influencing land ownership by women: Case of Khwisero Constituency, Kakamega County, Kenya. MA thesis. University of Nairobi, Kenya.

World Economic Forum (2020) *Global Gender Gap Index Report 2020*. Available at: http://www.weforum.org/docs/WEF_GGGR_2020.pdf (accessed 30 April 2020).

Part 3

Applications and Experiences: Techniques, Strategies, Tools, Methods and Case Studies

10 The Evolvement of Land Consolidation in Rural China from the Perspective of Governing Tension between Construction Land Expansion and Farmland Protection

Xiaobin Zhang*[1] and Yanmei Ye[2]
[1]*Lanzhou University, Lanzhou, China;* [2]*Zhejiang University, Hangzhou, China*

10.1 Introduction

Land consolidation serves as a very critical instrument for rural development for countries in Europe, Africa, South Asia and in China. Land consolidation has become a national strategy in China since 2008 (Land Consolidation Center of Ministry of Land and Resources, 2014). Forms of land consolidation, problems trying to be solved by land consolidation and methods implied in land consolidation are determined by political, social and economic context and legal system, thereby varied across countries. Nevertheless, there is still basic consensus over the original and fundamental function of land consolidation: It is the most important tool to ameliorate land fragmentation. Land consolidation usually is defined as the planned readjustment of the ownership of land parcels with the aim of forming larger and more rational land holdings (King and Burton, 1983; Pašakarnis and Maliene, 2010). Land consolidation is becoming a more complex and comprehensive instrument, goals such as improving the infrastructure and the implementation of developmental and environmental policies are gradually attached to land consolidation projects, but to conquer land fragmentation remains the focus of land consolidation in most of the countries. Simple land parcel exchange remains the basic and important form of land consolidation (FAO, 2003). This is not the case in China though. China is one of the most severe land-fragmented countries. According to the survey of FAO, the average holding size in China is only 0.67 ha and scattered across five places in 2003 (Demetriou, 2014), and the fragmented situation has not been improved since then as reported by Ministry of Agriculture of China in 2013 (Gu *et al.*, 2017). However, land consolidation in a modern sense was introduced to China in 1980s not to ameliorate farmland fragmentation, but to contain the decline of farmland (Huang *et al.*, 2011). In general, land consolidation in China is also to resolve the conflicts between economic development and food security as it is in other countries, but in specific, to provide more farmland at the same time of rapid construction land expansion in the context of unprecedented urbanization has always been the focus of the institutional function of land

*Corresponding author: zhangxiaobin@zju.edu.cn

 Land Governance and Gender: The Tenure-Gender Nexus in Land Management and Land Policy (ed. U.E. Chigbul)
DOI: 10.1079/9781789247664.0010

consolidation in China. The farmland area added by land consolidation is the paramount indicator for assessment through the whole development process of land consolidation in China. This separates land consolidation practice in China from other countries because farmland managed by a household is usually reduced after land consolidation due to infrastructure occupation. The underlying reason lies in the tension between extreme scarcity of farmland resource and the largest population in the world, especially given the decline of farmland in 1980s. Despite its severity, land fragmentation was not the top issue on the agenda when land consolidation was introduced – the rural labour surplus relieved the impacts of land fragmentation. Nowadays, land consolidation has also evolved into a more integrated policy tool aiming at rural revitalization and boosting poverty alleviation, institutional path dependence leads to the situation that land fragmentation amelioration is still peripheral. This chapter first elaborates how land consolidation in rural China evolves from the perspective of governing the tension between farmland protection and construction land expansion. It then explains how land consolidation gradually injects resilience in the rigid land use planning system along with the development of urbanization. Then it traces the incentive mechanism of local government officials to guarantee land consolidation implementation. Finally, challenges faced by the current land consolidation institution and practice in China are presented.

10.2 Evolvement of Land Consolidation

To protect the extremely scarce farmland in the unprecedented urbanization process, China has launched the most stringent land use and planning institution. Land use is strictly regulated by a land use general plan and land use annual plan. The former is a general plan which regulate land use in planning area in each period (usually 15 years), where not only scale of different types of land use, but also spatial layout is strictly controlled by land use quotas such as the total scale of urban and rural construction land, farmland area reserved, and basic farmland protection area. The land use plan consists of five levels – national, provincial, prefecture, county and town level – where land use at the lower level ought to be planed according to the upper level plan. In the period of the land use general plan, land use is more precisely controlled by the land use annual plan, which is an instrument for central government to determine annual land use and spatial layout. In this system, quotas for local land use are determined from the upper level land annual plan, and land use must be in accordance with quotas provided in the plan. One of the overarching goals of this land use planning institution is to protect farmland from arbitrary occupation, and it creates an urban–rural dual land system. The only way to change rural farmland into urban construction land is for the government to expropriate farmland (Shi and Tang, 2020) (Fig. 10.1).

As shown in Fig. 10.1, construction land needed by the local area for urban development is controlled by the land use general plan and quotas are assigned from central government to local government annually. And under the current situation, only after farmland is expropriated by government can it be developed into construction land and further be leased to private developers. In this system, land consolidation is not only an imperative tool to fulfil tasks of the land use and planning institution, but also gradually to bring resilience into it to adapt to the ever-changing economic and social environment. From the perspective of governing the tension between farmland protection and construction land expansion, land consolidation has evolved through three stages (Fig. 10.2). Land consolidation was introduced in 1980s and until 1998 land consolidation institution was formally established by the amended land administration law (Land Consolidation Center of Ministry of Land and Resources, 2014).

In this infancy stage, land consolidation is to achieve the stringent Requisition-Compensation Balance of Farmland (RCBF) (Gengdi Zhanbu Pingheng) policy and has set the basic pattern for the succeeding development of land consolidation. In the second stage, the policy of Linkage between Urban Land Increasing and Rural Land Decreasing (LULIRLD) (Chengxiang Jianshe Yongdi Zengjian Guagou) was proposed and gradually established as a basic land use policy accompanied by the flexible land quotas in land planning

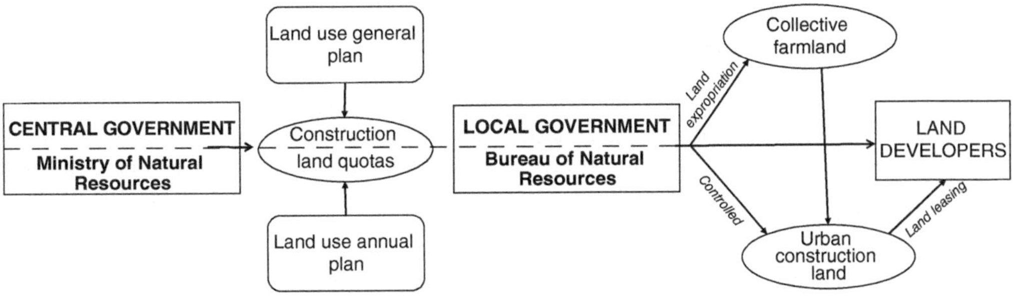

Fig. 10.1. The process of changing rural farmland into urban construction land (Authors' illustration).

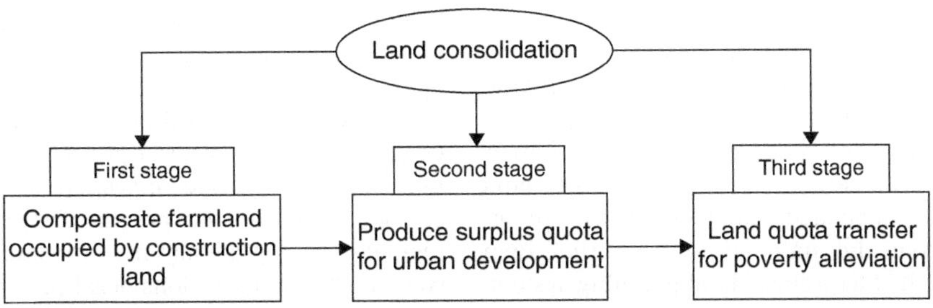

Fig. 10.2. Evolution of land consolidation in China (Authors' illustration).

system. Land consolidation, except for still serves to provide more farmland, not only helps to mitigate the rural hollowing problem but also brings adaptability into the rigid land use planning system. Recently, as in other countries, land consolidation has become more and more multifunctional and comprehensive, and it is also on the brink of entering the landscape-ecological-oriented stage (Yan *et al.*, 2015). In this stage, land consolidation serves to balance economic development at large scale and national level and boost poverty alleviation by allowing land quota transactions across regions.

Linking Land Consolidation with RCBF Policy

China is undergoing unprecedented urbanization in terms of speed and scale, leading to the surge of construction land and reduction of farmland. The loss of farmland was uncontrolled in the early 1980s; consequently, the total area of farmland in China decreased from 99.5 million ha to 96.2 million ha from 1978 to 1985 (Zhou *et al.*, 2020), which threatened the food security of the world's largest population. To stop the unplanned occupation of farmland, land consolidation was introduced in the 1980s as a critical instrument to provide more farmland, at the same time guaranteeing economic development. It was introduced originally through pilot projects with the help of Western European countries such as Germany. Two basic policies, namely RCBF and Construction of High Standard Basic Farmland (CHSBF) (Gao Biaozhun Jiben Nongtian Jianshe), were launched into the land use planning system, of which land consolidation was the core part. Land consolidation has gradually become formal and become a national strategy in China in 2008.

In this stage, the task of land consolidation is to realize the rigid land use planning system. In the Chinese land regulating system, to ensure that farmland will not be reduced is of paramount importance. To this end, any farmland occupied by construction land must be provided somewhere else with the same quantity and quality within the same region. The most symbolic indicator of this system is the provision of the 150-million-ha bottom line of farmland, which requests that farmland area in China can never be less than this figure. Specifically, quotas of total area of urban–rural construction land

and construction land added are set in the planning area and cannot be exceeded, while total area of farmland reserved, basic farmland protected, and new farmland provided to compensate those occupied by construction land added are rigidly stipulated as well. In this system, farmland newly provided, and the construction of high standard basic farmland are both count on land consolidation, through development of unused land into farmland, eliminating land ridge or reclamation of abandoned construction land. The function of land consolidation in this stage is presented in Fig. 10.3.

As shown in Fig. 10.3, construction land area is constrained by land use planning system in the planning period. Total construction land area equals to construction land status quo plus construction land added in the need of urban or rural development. As mentioned above, land quotas are calculated, regulated and then designated from the national level to the town through the hierarchical land planning system. Farmland cannot be reduced in the planning period according to the plan, but construction land added usually must occupy farmland, which must be compensated by farmland with the same quality and quantity according to the RCBF policy. Land consolidation is the instrument for farmland provision. Another mission for land consolidation in this stage is to improve the quality of existent farmland under the regulation of CHSBF policy. Land use in the whole society is planned and calculated without resilience by the central government, it has the obvious characteristic of planned economy and social engineering. Under such circumstances, land consolidation is also land-engineering oriented, which means that the main task of land consolidation is only to construct agricultural infrastructure and other critical work such as land reallocation is left behind, because its missions are merely to provide more farmland and improve quality of farmland. Specifically, the missions are fulfilled through land levelling engineering; hydraulic engineering; road engineering and ecological protection engineering; and road networks, irrigation and drainage canals provision are the core part. The projects are regulated by a gradually mature system which consists of five institutions: legal person institution; biding institution; supervision institution; contract institution; and announcement institution (Liu and Zhao, 2017).

In summary, to govern the tension between farmland protection and construction land

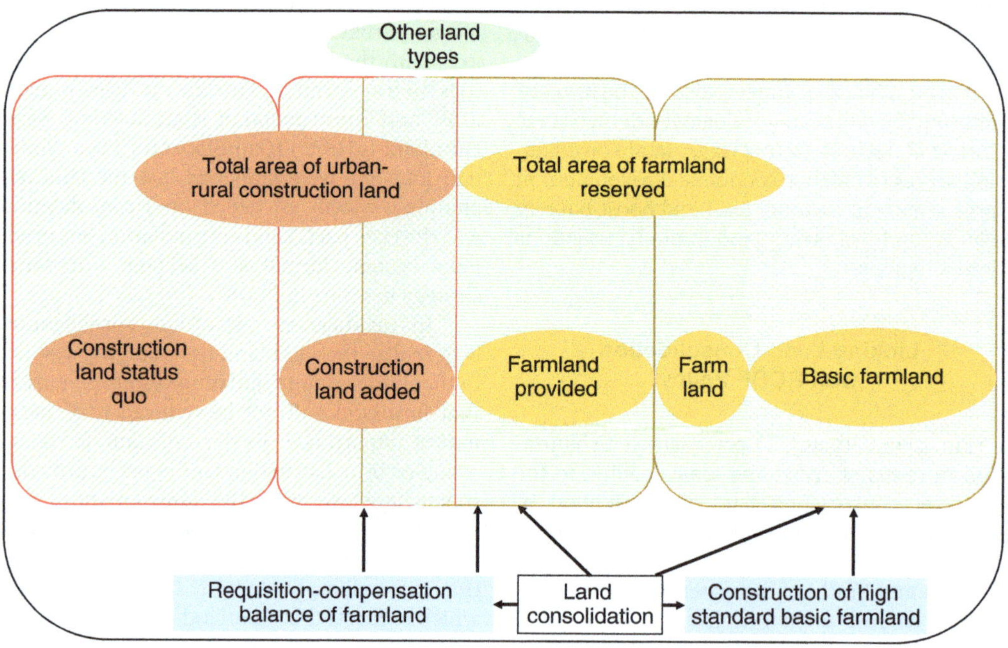

Fig. 10.3. The function of land consolidation linked with RCBF and CHSBF (Authors' illustration).

expansion, land consolidation in the first stage, through providing more farmland and improve the quality of farmland, is a crucial cog to fulfil tasks of the local rigid land use planning designated from the upper level. However, the precisely calculated land quota can hardly adapt to the ever-changing economic-social environment, and the needs of urban construction land often greatly exceeds quotas provided by the land use general and annual plan in developed regions. For example, according to Wang (2002), in a county in Zhejiang province, the land quota of construction land added designated in the land use general plan (1997–2010) is 134.5 ha, while the actual need of new construction land is 739.9 ha. The gap is huge between planned land quota and the actual need. Land consolidation can only enlarge farmland according to the rigid quotas, and so is powerless to deal with this problem.

Applying Land Consolidation in LULIRLD

A new way to solve the problem of inadaptability of land use planning with the economic-social environment was proposed and gradually became the basic policy in China`s land management system, which is LULIRLD policy, and this brings land consolidation into its second stage in terms of balancing construction land and farmland under context of urbanization.

The surging demand of land in urban area is inevitable given industrialization and urbanization. Also, people from rural areas flow into cities, creating a need for residential land. Strangely, the outflow of the rural population does not lead to a decrease in rural residential land as expected. On the contrary, total rural residential land and total housing area continue to increase with the expansion of urban construction land while the rural population decreases (Fig. 10.4), together leading to the decrease of farmland and the rural hollowing problem (Long *et al.*, 2012; Liu *et al.*, 2014). According to Yu *et al.* (2018), the increase of rural residential land is mainly due to the demand for houses after marriage, improving the living environment.

Nonetheless, the disordered expansion and inefficient use of rural construction land provide opportunities to solve the problem of insufficient supply of urban construction land. In many villages, there is the potential to gain more farmland through reclamation of rural residential land. The LULIRLD policy was proposed to assemble rural construction land at the same time to provide more quotas of urban construction land in the planning period. The policy stipulates that under the urban–rural dichotomy system of land use, the urban construction land increases must be equal to the rural construction land

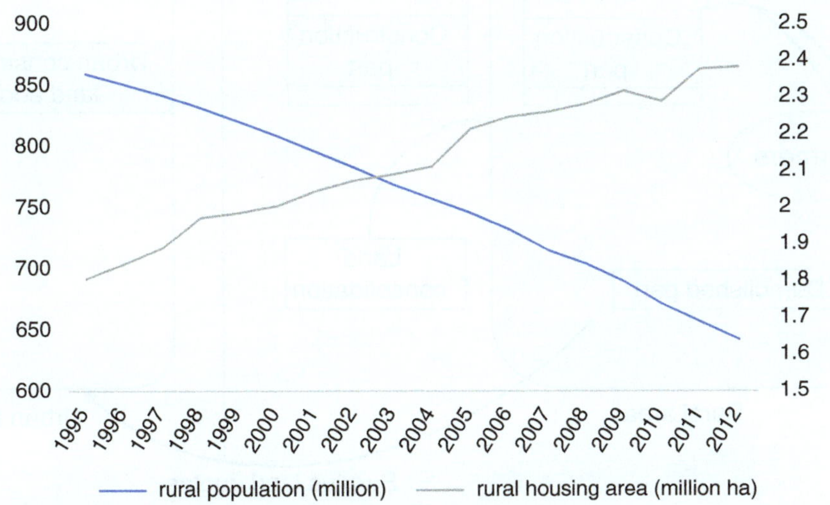

Fig. 10.4. Change of rural population and rural housing area from 1996 to 2012 (Authors' illustration, based on data from National Bureau of Statistics of China, 2019).

decreases, where the decrease of rural construction land is realized through land consolidation. The operational logic of land consolidation in this stage is presented in Fig. 10.5. The exploration of using farmland gained through reduction of rural construction land to exchange for land quota of urban construction land emerged in Zhejiang, Sichuan and Chongqing. The legitimacy was first recognized by central government policy Decision of the State Council on Deepening Reform and Strict Land Management in 2004. Then in 2008, it was formally regulated by the policy The Management Measure for the Pilot of Increasing vs Decreasing Balance of Urban–Rural Construction Land.

Through land consolidation, the disordered and inefficiently used rural construction lands are organized into more compact and efficient land parcels, which eventually can provide more farmland. And these newly added farmlands can be turned into surplus land quotas, which can be used in urban area to make up the gap between needs of urban construction land and the construction land quotas designated by the original plan. Specifically, LULIRLD policy is also implemented through land consolidation projects. In those projects, there are usually two separated but linked parts: the demolished part and the construction part. In the demolished part, rural construction land is consolidated into farmland through land consolidation projects, farmers who situated in the area originally will have to move into new residential area, which is the construction part. In the construction part, new buildings are constructed to be inhabited by farmers originally lived in the demolished part. Because land use is more intensive in the construction part, there is more construction land reclaimed into farmland than new construction provided for farmers` living. Therefore, surplus land quotas are created to be transferred and used in urban area. This process is often regarded as development right transfer in China (Wang and Tao, 2009). The utilization of those land quotas is not necessarily after them being created by land consolidation projects, therefore, the surplus land quotas are often called turnover quotas for they are pre-borrowed (Tan, 2014).

Figure 10.6 shows a land use map of a land consolidation project based on LULIRLD policy implemented during 2015–2018 in Guangdong Province. As shown, a total area of 2.42 ha of rural residential land is planned to be reclaimed into farmland, and the farmers who originally lived there will move into the construction part in the same village, where the land use type is

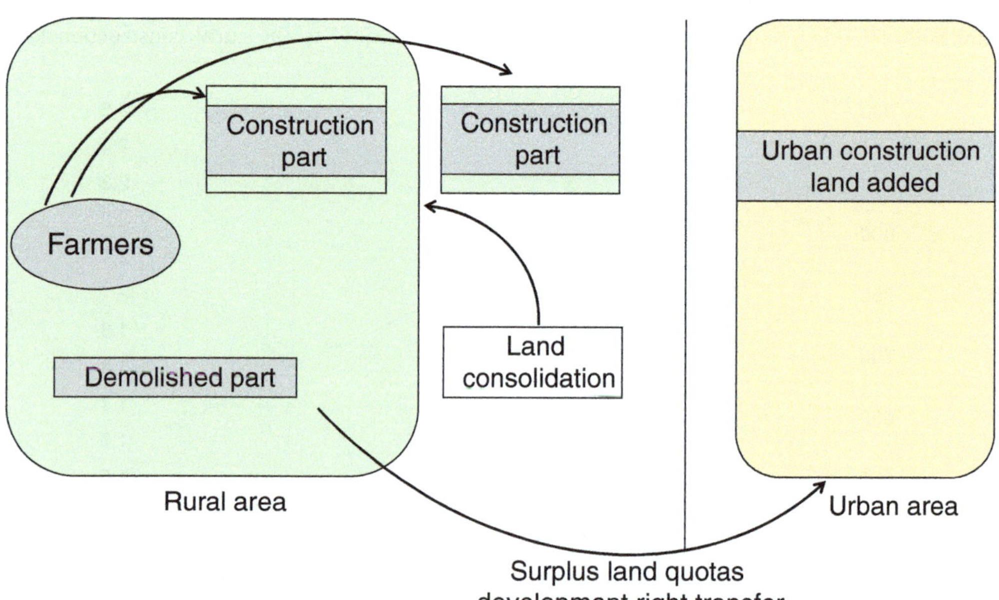

Fig. 10.5. The logic of land consolidation implementation under LULIRLD policy (Authors' illustration).

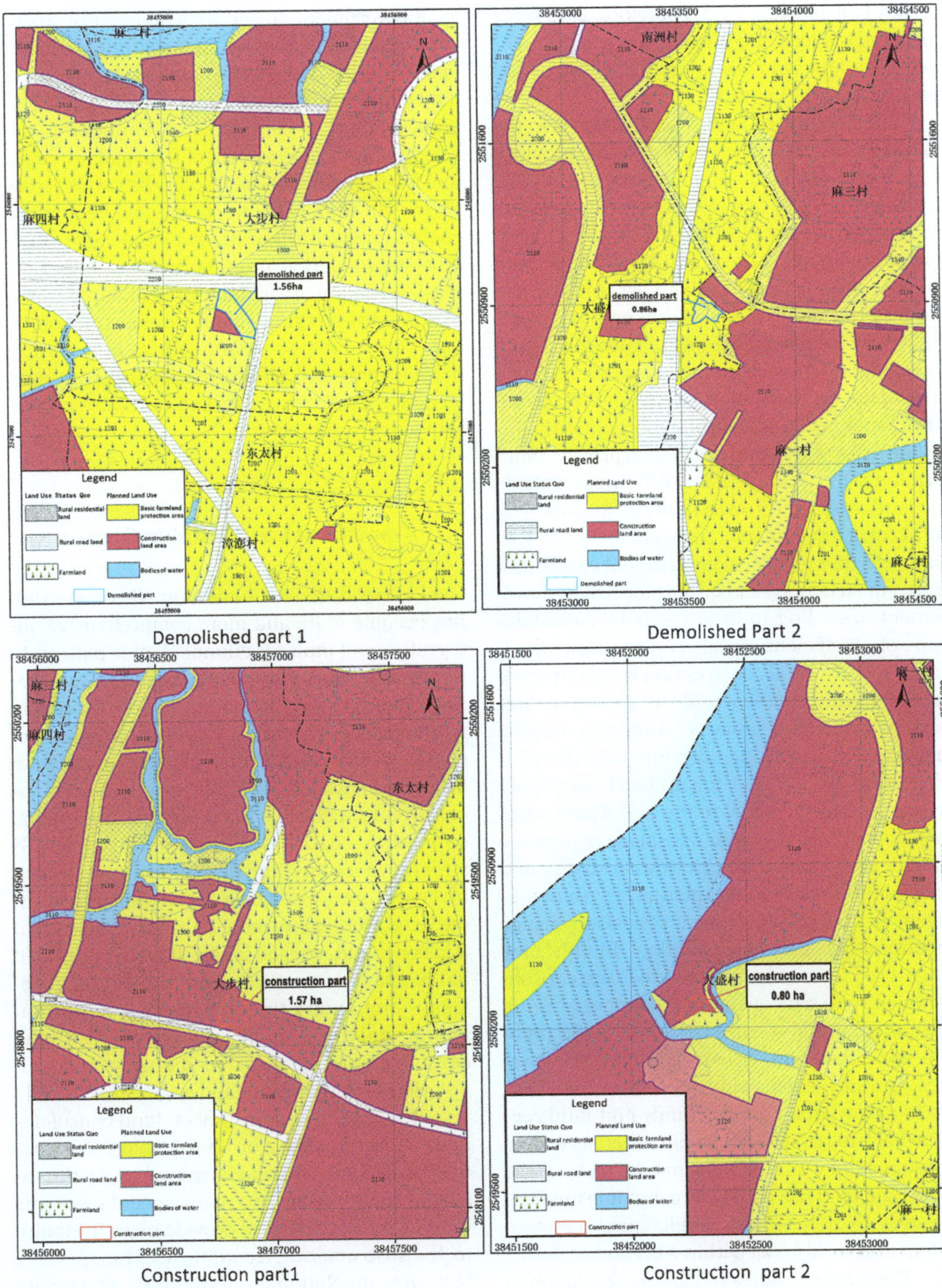

Fig. 10.6. Land use change in a LULIRLD project (Authors' illustration, based on data from the Chinese Government Information Disclosure Directory, 2020).

already construction land. Therefore, 2.42 ha of farmland is added after the project, which can be converted into land quota used as construction land in the same county.

The function of land consolidation is in the following aspects different from the previous stage. Land consolidation linked with RCBF and CHSBF is the only tool to mechanically execute and realize the target of rigid land use general and annual plan. In the first stage, through land consolidation, more farmland is provided according to related plans to make up those occupied by construction land. Therefore, land consolidation projects were focused on undeveloped land and farmland itself. In the second stage, however, land consolidation not only fulfils the tasks of the land use plan to provide more farmland, but also creates land quotas outside the land use plan through land consolidation of rural construction land. The significance of this change is that now local government can obtain more construction land quotas for urban development according to local needs by consolidation of inefficient rural construction land. Consequently, rural construction land is the core part of LULIRLD policy and the corresponding land consolidation projects. Although surplus land quotas are also included into land use plan after 2009 (Tan, 2014), it is still up to local governments to decide how many and where rural land consolidation should take place to produce surplus land quotas, which brings flexibility and adaptability into land use planning system and incentives to local government officials to engage in promoting land consolidation. In this new stage, broader areas are connected. The consolidation of rural settlements, improvement of living environment and solving rural hollowing problem are linked with urban development: rural area provides surplus land quotas to urban area while urban area provides funds and land revenue back to rural development. Therefore, land consolidation was only a cog to fulfil tasks of the local rigid land use plan before, but it is now imperative to a balanced development between urban and rural areas within a certain region.

There are still limits of land consolidation in this stage. As it in the first stage, providing more farmland is still the core task of land consolidation in stage, although improvement of living conditions of farmers is also the aim of land consolidation projects. To gain more surplus land quotas, local government official sometimes consolidates rural residential areas without soliciting farmers` opinion. Although land quotas of construction land can be transferred from rural area to urban area, it is strictly confined and cannot be transacted. However, endowment of farmland resources and level of economic development varies across regions in China. There are regions having not enough potential to provide more farmland through land consolidation projects, while in other regions farmland are abundant. Forbidding transaction across regions confines the function of land consolidation coordinating urban–rural development and govern tension between construction land expansion and farmland protection in a broader scope.

Transfer of Land Surplus Quotas

Land consolidation in China, as in other countries, has become more and more comprehensive, integrative and multifunctional. A new pattern to implement land consolidation called comprehensive land consolidation in the whole region (Quanyu Tudi Zhengzhi) has been proposed recently, which goes further in integration than former comprehensive land consolidation. It focuses on functions of the whole planning area, optimizing spatial structure and layout. It stresses coordinating development of urban and rural areas as a whole unit, assembling separated engineering into more integrative projects. In addition, land consolidation has incorporated landscape construction and protection, ecological and nature resource reserve, and stimulating rural revitalization as its goals. Also, land consolidation begins to be industry and value-oriented rather than land engineer oriented.

Under such circumstances, land consolidation continues its function on governing construction land expansion and farmland protection in a more resilient way. Two management measures were enacted in 2018 to provide more flexibility to the instrument. According to Management Measures on National Coordination of Supplement Farmland Across Provinces, for developed provinces which have limited farmland, the task of providing more farmland according to RCBF policy can be burdened by other provinces with abundant farmland in exchange for development funds. And Management Measures on Adjustment across Provinces of Surplus Land Quotas allows land quotas produced by land consolidation projects to be transacted, in a broader region across provinces.

Specifically, province-level municipalities and provinces with extremely scarce farmland can apply to central government that the mission of providing farmland to be fulfilled by other provinces through national coordination. However, for province-level municipalities the application must be on account of urban development or infrastructure construction, and for provinces it must be for major construction projects in principle limited to transportation, energy, water conservancy and military national defence. The province-level government should pay funds for farmland supplement after approval. The fund should be included in transfer expenditure of public budget from provincial finance to central finance, which must serve to poverty alleviation and rural revitalization. And farmland occupied will be provided by other provinces (usually poverty struck), through land consolidation projects.

In the meantime, land quotas produced by rural construction land consolidation can be used in a broader regional scaling up to national level. But areas which can transfer out surplus land quotas are limited to be certain deeply impoverished regions, such as Tibet, and impoverished counties. Provinces which buy these land quotas have more construction land to meet their needs of economic development while payments will help ameliorate poverty in those impoverished regions. A unified price standard for land quotas is set by the state.

Therefore, in this stage, land consolidation endows the land use planning system more resilience by allowing land quotas being transferred in a broader region, and steers the land use system to incorporated multiple targets such as poverty alleviation and improvement of unbalanced regional development on national level. In those developed regions where farmland is extremely scarce, the system provides new opportunities for their development while poor regions also benefit from this system. Impoverished regions can gain plenty revenue through creation and selling land quotas, eventually improving economic development and living environment of people there. However, transaction of land quotas is still strictly limited and regulated, not through market mechanism. Some scholars believe the permission of transferring land quotas is only about politics of poverty alleviation rather than to establish free land market (Xia, 2019).

10.3 Supporting Mechanism for Land Consolidation Implementation

This section explains how land consolidation in China is promoted. As mentioned above, the original and overarching goal for central government to introduce in land consolidation is to stop the trend of farmland loss induced by urbanization and industrialization, eventually to guarantee food security. However, this is against the interest of local government officials for they need more construction land for local development. In addition, with the continuous development of land consolidation, aims such as improving farmland quality, ecological protection and landscape construction, rural revitalization and poverty alleviation are gradually being taken into consideration by the central government. And eventually, the central government seeks to promote welfare for the whole society through land consolidation. However, according to principal-agent theory, government on lower level does not necessarily have the same interests, and therefore not the same aims, as upper-level government on implementation of land consolidation, while the actual promotion and implementation of land consolidation rely on behaviour of local government (Gui, 2014). For local government officials, their main concerns are career prospects, which is closely linked to economic development indicated by GDP, and social stability. A balanced development on broader scope or food security is not in their original concern either. Consequently, a mechanism should be designed to guarantee that local government has an incentive to promote and implement land consolidation in a way as the central government expected.

The arrangement of every land consolidation project must be based on the land consolidation plan drawn up and approved beforehand. There are four levels of the land consolidation plan: national; provincial; prefecture-level; and local (county), drawn up by the corresponding level of government. Land consolidation on each level serves different purposes. The national plan provides strategic guidance. The provincial plan is the nexus between national plan and plans on lower levels, assigning tasks from the national plan and providing instructions for the lower level plan. The prefecture and local plans are the direct basis for the arrangement of land consolidation projects in terms of scale, timing, and location etc. (Zhang and Ye, 2016). Making up the land consolidation plan must be according to the land use general and annual plans. In two aspects, land consolidation is mandatory for lower level governments. First, according to RCBF policy, governments from provincial level to county level have responsibility to supply farmland for those occupied by newly added construction land according to land use annual plan, and the performance on farmland provided through land consolidation will be appraised by upper level government. Second, an area of high standard basic farmland constructed through land consolidation is also in the system of career appraisal. And for specific land consolidation projects, there is a check procedure before completion which addresses mainly on are and quality of farmland provided, quality of infrastructure constructed. For governments that meet the requirement, there will be rewards like more financial support for land consolidation, and for those that don't, there will be a penalty such as a fine or to stop the procedure for conversion of agricultural land to construction land and land expropriation in the next year. In this way, land consolidation is linked to local government officials` career promotion.

Another mechanism to guarantee local government to implement land consolidation is the financial support from central government. There is a special section of the public budget of central government for land consolidation, funded by the new construction land use fee and land reclamation fee. The fund will be allocated to local government to promote implementation of land consolidation through land projects. The implementation of land consolidation projects, especially high standard basic farmland construction projects, major land consolidation projects and farmland destructed by disaster reclamation projects, usually depends on funds distributed by the central government (Gui, 2014; Liu and Zhao, 2017). This is especially the case for poor areas. As mentioned above, the allocation of the special fund for land consolidation takes into consideration local governments` performance on land consolidation the year before. Therefore, financial support not only provides necessary fund for local government, but also encourage local government to engage in land consolidation by linking distribution with performance.

Another mechanism to stimulate local governments to engage in land consolidation is to link land consolidation with economic development. Specifically, since the establishment of LULIRLD policy, land consolidation has created surplus land quotas for urban construction, which are critical for urban and economic development. Local government officials now have a strong motivation to engage in land consolidation, for local economic development is the most important indicator in the appraisal system for their achievements. Also, in impoverished regions, surplus land quotas can be sold to raise more funds for regional development. Figure 10.7 shows how local government officials are urged to engage in land consolidation.

In this system, governments dominate the whole process of land consolidation, and local

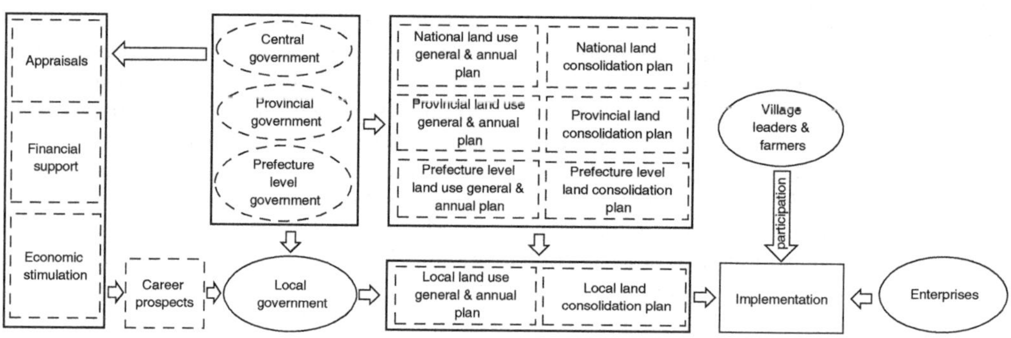

Fig. 10.7. The mechanism in China to promote and implement land consolidation (Authors' illustration).

governments are at its core. Village leaders, farmers and enterprises can participate in land consolidation, but generally land consolidation projects are implemented through a top-down mechanism. As mentioned above, land consolidation is implemented mainly through formal projects, which are consist of complicated formalities and often need massive investments beyond villages` capacity. Therefore, farmers and village leaders are gradually excluded from land consolidation implementation, playing an inconsequential role in many projects (Liu and Zhao, 2017). Recently, there have been experiments with self-organization of land consolidation by farmers and the private sector in designated pilot areas (Tan and Heerink, 2017), but for most of the projects, governments still play the leading role.

10.4 Implications and Drawbacks

The Implications

Land consolidation in China has made great achievements: 4.6 million ha of farmland was provided through land consolidation from 2001 to 2015 according to the National Land Consolidation Plan (2016–2020), which effectively constrained the decline of farmland. Not only has farmland area increased, but also farmland quality has been improved through land consolidation: the quality of farmland has been upgraded to a higher level in land consolidation areas. The provision of agricultural infrastructure greatly improves production conditions, which eventually improves agricultural production efficiency with yield per unit area increased by 10–20%. Therefore, land consolidation has been remarkably conducive to guarantee food security under context of rapid urbanization. And since the proposition of LULIRLD policy, it has also achieved significant results in solving the rural hollowing problem: 155,800 ha of inefficient rural construction land was consolidated into more compact and intensive land during 2011 to 2015, and more importantly, farmers` living conditions have been improved correspondingly. Surplus or turnover land quotas created in this process not only provide more space for urban development, but also serve as a source of land revenue, providing funds for rural development. Land consolidation has made a great contribution to poverty alleviation and rural revitalization in China.

The introduction and evolution of land consolidation in China has shown that the function of land consolidation does not have to be confined to the amelioration of land fragmentation, even in its original form, but can be tailored to address the urgent issues faced by a certain country. Generally, to ameliorate land fragmentation is the paramount task of land consolidation in many countries in its early stage and simplified form. However, despite the fact that land fragmentation in China is severe, it is a secondary consideration to scarcity of farmland. The situation in China is unique in the following aspects. First, China is the most populous country in the world, while farmland is scarce: 20% of the world` population live on only 7% of the world's farmland. Second, urbanization in China is unprecedented, inducing urban construction expansion and aggravating tension between construction land and farmland. Finally, when land consolidation was introduced to China in the 1980s, land fragmentation is not an obstacle for agricultural production, because there was abundant rural labour supply. Therefore, land consolidation in China was tailored into an instrument to supply more farmland and to improve quality of farmland rather than aiming at ameliorating land fragmentation, which solves unique land use problem in China in a targeted way.

Another lesson drawn from the Chinese experience is that except for the well-recognized functions such as land fragmentation amelioration, landscape construction, providing more farmland or improvement of farmland quality, which directly optimize land use structure and improve land use efficiency, land consolidation in China shows another critical function of land consolidation in land governance, which is to bring resilience in land use planning system. The original land use planning system in China was very rigid, having characteristics of planning economic and social engineering, land consolidation played a significant role to functionalize the system by focus on land engineering. But more importantly, land consolidation breaks through its role as only a link to guarantee farmland supplement according to land use general and annual plan. Through rural construction land consolidation producing surplus construction land quotas, it endows local government officials with autonomy in land resource allocation. No matter whether the aim of this process is land politics or land market, it is certain that land consolidation brings resilience into the original land use planning system, which makes it more adaptable to the fast-changing economic-social environment and facilitates the coordination of unbalanced development in a broader scope.

The Drawbacks

Land consolidation institution and implementation in China also have some drawbacks. The development of land consolidation has fallen into path dependence. As illustrated above, when land consolidation was introduced to China, land fragmentation was not an obstacle then because there was abundant rural labour supply. Along with rural immigration, land fragmentation has gradually begun to hinder agricultural production. However, land consolidation continues its original development path, focusing mainly on infrastructure construction, and the amelioration of land fragmentation as land consolidation` basic function, has rarely been taken seriously, especially in government-dominated land consolidation projects. Solving the problem of land fragmentation mainly relies on land registration and land transfer, which incurs many problems such as the huge transaction cost in land transfer or mandatory land transfer, because land consolidation as a critical link is missing in this process.

Another problem in land consolidation implementation is the neglect of farmers, especially in farmland consolidation. Government domination and the address of formal procedures and infrastructure construction have formed a vicious spiral which eventually excludes farmers from participation in land consolidation: The implementation of land consolidation mainly relies on local government officials: they only focus on aspects which can be easily assessed, such as farmland area increased and infrastructure constructed. Land consolidation is largely about infrastructure construction and has to be implemented through formal projects, which entails complex formalities and huge investments, and has to be implemented by local governments. Although land consolidation is to help farmers to get better agricultural and living conditions, in many projects, farmers rarely participate and are indifferent regarding land consolidation (Liu and Zhao, 2017). In such a situation, the construction of infrastructure in land consolidation often does not solicit farmers` opinions and the outcome is divorced from the actual needs of agricultural production. It is not uncommon that infrastructure constructed in land consolidation is abandoned soon afterwards.

It is worth noting that there has been exploration of self-organization in both farmland consolidation and rural construction land consolidation for many years. Self-organized farmland consolidation usually focuses on ameliorate land fragmentation and more than 1.33 million ha of farmland has been concentrated through land reallocation in self-organized projects (Pan, 2014), which is complementary to government-dominated projects. In self-organized land consolidation projects, rural social governance is at its core. How (and what) collective action among village leaders and famers is achieved is critical to the success of the project. Also, the role of government in self-organized land consolidation and how to incorporate it into the current system of land consolidation in China remain to be studied.

10.5 Conclusion

This chapter illustrates the evolution of land consolidation in China from the perspective of construction land expansion and farmland protection in the context of rapid urbanization. Also, we explain the supporting mechanism which stimulates governments at a local level to engage in land consolidation promotion and implementation. Land consolidation in China, unlike in most other countries, does not originate from an instrument aiming at land fragmentation amelioration, but was introduced to supplement farmland occupied by construction land. By linking construction land requisition and farmland compensation, land consolidation becomes an imperative tool to functionalize the rigid land use plan in its first stage. Then by linking urban construction land increasing with rural construction land decreasing and further permission of land quotas transaction across regions, land consolidation changes the stringent nature of land use plan in China, brought resilience into the system. As we can see, the initiative of local governments in local development and land resource allocation has been exerted by using land consolidation to create surplus land quotas. Land consolidation has made great achievements regarding farmland supply, solving the rural hollowing problem and improving farmers` living conditions. But on the other hand, local knowledge at the village level has not been fully exploited. Local government officials, pursuing career promotion, seek to expedite land consolidation projects focusing mainly on land engineering. The problem of land fragmentation often remains to be solved after land consolidation projects finish.

To summarize: land consolidation in China was originally adjusted into an engineering-oriented tool to realize the aim of social engineering. It is necessary and conducive, with the help of administrative instructions, to control the decline of farmland. Along with the change of socioeconomic environment, land consolidation has evolved to make the land use planning system more flexible and adaptable in China, but the social governance aspects of land consolidation still need to be further addressed. Decision making should take full account of different stakeholders' interests and bottom-up participation is also necessary.

References

Chinese Government Information Disclosure Directory (2020) *Announcement on the 'Implementation Plan of Dabu Village Project Area (2015–2018).'* Available at: http://www.dg.gov.cn/zwgk/zfxxgkml/myz/ghjh/zxgh/content/post_934846.html (accessed 17 December 2020).

Demetriou, D. (2014) *The Development of an Integrated Planning and Decision Support System (IPDSS) for Land Consolidation.* Springer, Cham, Switzerland.

FAO (2003) *The Design of Land Consolidation Pilot Projects in Central and Eastern Europe.* Available at: http://www.fao.org/3/Y4954E/y4954e00.htm (accessed 7 July 2020).

Gu, T., Ji, Y. and Zhong, F. (2017) The sources of economies of scale in China's agricultural production. *Chinese Rural Economy*, 2, 30–43.

Gui, H. (2014) Project system and analysis of rural public goods supply: taking land consolidation as example. *Cass Journal of Political Science*, 4, 50–62.

Huang, Q., Li, M., Chen, Z. and Li, F. (2011) Land consolidation: An approach for sustainable development in rural China. *AMBIO*, 40(1), 93–95.

King, R. and Burton, S. (1983) Structural change in agriculture: The geography of land consolidation. *Progress in Human Geography*, 7(4), 471–501.

Land Consolidation Center of Ministry of Land and Resources (2014) History of land consolidation and rehabilitation in China. In: The Land Consolidation Center of Ministry of Land and Resources (Ed.), *Blue Book of Land Consolidation: Research Report on Land Consolidation and Development in China No. 1.* Social Science Literature Publishing House, Beijing, China, pp. 1–79.

Liu, X. and Zhao, C. (2017) Rural land consolidation's engineering construction and its causes. *Chinese Rural Economy*, 7, 15–28.

Liu, Y., Fang, F. and Li, Y. (2014) Key issues of land use in China and implications for policy making. *Land Use Policy*, 40, 6–12.

Long, H., Li, Y., Liu, Y., Woods, M. and Zou, J. (2012) Accelerated restructuring in rural China fueled by 'increasing vs. decreasing balance' land-use policy for dealing with hollowed villages. *Land Use Policy*, 29(1), 11–22.

National Bureau of Statistics of China (2019) *China Statistical Yearbook 2019*. China Statistics Press, Beijing, China.

Pan, X. (2014) Land reallocation in land consolidation facilitates factor allocateon. *Farmers' Daily*, 21, 1.

Pašakarnis, G. and Maliene, V. (2010) Towards sustainable rural development in Central and Eastern Europe: Applying land consolidation. *Land Use Policy*, 27(2), 545–549.

Shi, C. and Tang, B. (2020) Institutional change and diversity in the transfer of land development rights in China: The case of Chengdu. *Urban Studies*, 57(3), 473–489.

Tan, M. (2014) Strict control and incentives: evolution of linking decrease of arable land with increase of construction land and its local implementation. *Social Science in China*, 7, 125–142, 207.

Tan, R. and Heerink, N. (2017) Public and self-organized land readjustment in rural China – A comparison. *Journal of Rural Studies*, 53, 45–57.

Wang, H. (2002) *Land System in the Process of Urbanization: A Case Study of Zhejiang Province.* Zhejiang University, Hangzhou, China.

Wang, H. and Tao, R. (2009) On Zhejiang pattern of development right transfer and transaction: the institutional origin, operation modes and implications. *Management World*, 8, 39–52.

Xia, Z. (2019) Land policy in poverty alleviation and the predicament of Xian's development model. *Beijing Culture Review*, 6, 109–116, 143.

Yan, J., Xia, F. and Bao, H.X.H. (2015) Strategic planning framework for land consolidation in China: A top-level design based on SWOT analysis. *Habitat International*, 48, 46–54.

Yu, Z., Wu, C., Tan, Y. and Zhang, X. (2018) The dilemma of land expansion and governance in rural China: A comparative study based on three townships in Zhejiang Province. *Land Use Policy*, 71, 602–611.

Zhang, X. and Ye, Y. (2016) Land reallocation in land consolidation: A Chinese mode and its future direction. Conference paper, FIG Working Week. 2–6 May, Christchurch, New Zealand.

Zhou, Y., Li, Y. and Xu, C. (2020) Land consolidation and rural revitalization in China: Mechanisms and paths. *Land Use Policy*, 91, article 104379. DOI: 10.1016/j.landusepol.2019.104379.

11 Discourse on Women and Land Tenure in Ghana: Does a Matrilineal Land Tenure System Make a Difference for Women?

Nancy Kankam Kusi,*[1] Frank Mintah,[2] Valentina Nyame,[3] Uchendu Eugene Chigbu,[4] Menare Royal Mabakeng,[4] Barikisa Owusu Ansah[5] and Walter Dachaga[6]

[1]West Africa Civil Society Institute, Accra, Ghana; [2]Kwame Nkrumah University of Science and Technology, Ashanti, Ghana; [3]Youth Advocates Ghana, Nsawam, Ghana; [4]Namibia University of Science and Technology, Windhoek, Namibia; [5]Leibniz University of Hannover, Hannover, Germany; [6]Technical University of Munich, Munich, Germany

11.1 Introduction

Globally, women have made huge contributions to socioeconomic development (in terms of human capital). The sheer number of females – approximately 49% of the world's population (United Nations, 2017) – represents a potential for social and economic emancipation in all spheres of a nation's economy. However, research has shown that women's inability to fully contribute to development is a result of patriarchal inclinations that fail to promote gender equality (Chigbu, 2019a). In effect, women remain underrepresented in social, economic and political decision making about the ownership, control and utilization of resources. This situation is evident in many countries of the Global South, including Ghana (Ameyaw *et al.*, 2019; Chigbu, 2019b). Land is one crucial resource where there is disproportionate access in favour of the male gender (Chigbu, 2015, 2020; Chigbu *et al.*, 2019).

The study presented in this chapter is contextually centred on women's land rights within the Asante tribe of Ghana. The study area is Kumasi, which is in the central part of the Ashanti Region in Ghana. Kumasi is made up of predominantly Asante (a people who constitute more than 80% of its population) (Ghana Statistical Service, 2014). The research followed a case study based discourse analytical approach. By popular opinion, matriarchy means female authority. The discourse investigates this proposition. A mix of literature, interviews, and historical data was necessary for gathering data. All data focused on understanding the matrilineal and 'matriarchal' system among the Asante in the context of women's access to land and property. It also puts emphasis on whether there have been any changes in how land is accessed

*Corresponding author: nancykankam@gmail.com

 Land Governance and Gender: The Tenure-Gender Nexus in Land Management and Land Policy (ed. U.E. Chigbu)
DOI: 10.1079/9781789247664.0011

and used. The strength of these methods is in their ability to trace the power struggles and dynamics underlying customary land tenure governance and politics (Chigbu, 2021). Theoretically, it unravels why there is a deviation from conventional wisdom on matriarchy as a promoter of women's land right. A starting point to grasping this knotty issue is to understand what matriarchy or matrilineality entails in the context of customary land tenure.

11.2 Matriarchy and Matrilineality in Land Tenure Context

Matriarchy and Matrilineality

Matriarchy refers to the sociopolitical rule or governance of the woman in a family or a society (Bamberger, 1974). The historical orientation of this concept can be traced to the work of Bachofen on 'Mother's Right – Das Mutterrecht' in 1861 (Bachofen, 1861). Bachofen's Mother's Right theory was founded on the idea of the mysterious natural and biological relationship between the mother and the child (Bamberger, 1974). Bachofen believed that primitive societies were characterized by the availability of goods, social democracy and group marriage, which he argued were controlled by women even before the emergence of paternity (Burston, 1986). His theory advanced in the 19th century into a system of non-patriarchal society where women rule and have dominion (Farrar, 1997).

Although Bachofen's theory has long existed in anthropological works, her concept of the rule of women was not well received in literature (Burston, 1986). Scholars like Diop (1989) disagreed with Bachofen's ideology and in turn argued that matriarchy is influenced by the social system and not from any relationship between the mother and the child. According to Goettner-Abendroth (2004), Bachofen's concept was unclear in definition and was dismissed based on the theory focusing on emotions, hence providing room for misinterpretation. The controversy, debates, abuse and distortion of Bachofen's theory on matriarchy presented doubts in many scholars on the true existence of any society which is dominated and ruled by women (Mann and Goettner-Abendroth, 2013).

In recent years, works by Mann and Goettner-Abendroth (2013) and Goettner-Abendroth (2017) have disputed the conception of the inexistence of any matriarchy by providing a clearer definition of the concept. In her argument, Goettner-Abendroth (2018) redefined the matriarchal concept as a non-patriarchal and female dominated system but a women-centred egalitarian society based on equality, consensus building, gift giving, peace building and negotiation. This modern concept of matriarchy is feminist-driven and involves a social system where the mother/woman is the head of the family and exerts power and influence, and occupies a ruling position (McGee, 2015).

Matrilinity does not necessarily equate matriarchy, although they are sometimes linked together like in the works of McGee (2015). Matriarchy is about power and authority women hold in a society while matrilineal is a line of decent or kindship from the mother (Fortunato, 2012). Matrilineal principles operate in the domain of inheritance, succession to office, authority, and marital residence (Richards, 1950). People from matrilineal societies trace their lineage from their mothers, maternal cousins, aunts, uncles, and grandparents (Kutsoati and Morck, 2016). Unlike patrilineal cultures where a man's children are part of his lineage, in the matrilineal system, children belong to their mother's kin. For the man, only his sister's children join his lineage (Hartung, 1985). A woman's children are crucial in the growth of her lineage. Hence according to historical accounts, extramarital affairs by the women are not criticized and sometimes women could marry more than one man (Hartung, 1985).

Generally, in matriarchal societies, families live together according to the matrilineal principles (Goettner-Abendroth, 2018). The relationship between matrilineal and matriarchy can be traced to the origin of the concept. Based on Bachofen's work, matriarchy and matrilineal coexisted in the primitive society when mothers initiated monogamous marriages and descent traced from the female lines (Burston, 1986). Diop (1989) on the other hand established that matriarchy is the advanced stage of matrilineal decent when a woman gains power and authority as through her lineage. However, not all matrilineal societies are matriarchies in practice, as argued by Cohen (1977). It is therefore important to distinguish social systems that practice both matriarchal and matriliny from those that practice either one of them. The study, therefore, defines matrilinity as a social system where descents and line of inheritance are traced through the maternal lines, and matriarchy as a system whereby females have power and influence in social organization (Goettner-Abendroth, 2017).

Matriarchal and Matrilineal Land Tenure Systems: A Global Historical Perspective

Matriarchal cultures are practised in different regions across Africa, America, and Asia (Ferrara, 2007). Globally, matriarchal, and matrilineal systems are governed by customary practices and land tenure systems which are customarily arranged. Properties which include land are owned collectively by all members of the kinship or decent and are transferred through successive inheritance. The matrilineal principles are used as the criteria to define the right to access, use, and control, and transfer land (Holy, 1996). These rights are different under customary norms, rules and practices in matriarchal and matrilineal regions across Africa, America and Asia (Ferrara, 2007).

Globally, women hold rights to own and use land in the matrilineal societies. For example, in the old Iroquois Native American society, women controlled the use of land and were favoured in land tenure arrangements (Hurtado *et al.*, 2000). Similarly, women in *Mosuo* matrilineal society in China are key players in land tenure arrangements. The rights to land ownership are given to female members of the lineage (Wang and Morais, 2014). Likewise, in Malawi, women hold right to all lands in their mother's line (Pauline, 2010). However, women in matrilineal societies are not necessarily guaranteed rights to ownership and inheritance. In some instances, customarily matrilineal land tenure system and patriarchal influence weaken the security of tenure of other members in the matrilineal descent. Patriarchal influence aside, the interplay of demographic changes, (peri)urbanization and the monetization of land continues to erode the default scholarship that posit matrilineal and matriarchal societies as better catalysts of women land tenure (Owusu Ansah and Chigbu, 2020), and renders legitimate and supposed matrilineally empowered women landless in their own land (Dachaga and Chigbu, 2020). Upon revealing theoretical positioning of matrilineal and matriarchy concepts from the global perspectives, the following section presents how matriarchy and matrilineal systems are practised in Ghana Asante society.

11.3 Matrilineality and Matriarchy: Local Narratives on the Asantes of Ghana

The Asantes are six Akan communities (clans) in Ghana that migrated from the basin of Pra and Offin rivers up north because of the political instability among the Denkyira and Akwamu in the 17th century (Akyeampong and Obeng, 1995). Upon settling, the six communities joined together and formed the Asante Empire with a strong centralized political system where the 'Asantehene' (the king) and *'Asantehemaa'* (the queen mother – who is the mother or sister of the king) rule as heads of the empire. The Asantes established their state in a forest region full of gold and kola (Akyeampong and Obeng, 1995). They were warlike and fought to expand their territories from the north, south through to the west of Ivory Coast (Wilks, 1993). In the 1800s, the Asante Empire was conquered by the British; however, the Asante fought to regain their autonomy in 1900. In recent times, Asante occupy the central part of Ghana (Ashanti Region) with Kumasi, the second largest city, as its capital. The Asante have held onto their traditions and culture through times and up to now, is one of the most recognized strong socio-political organizations in Ghana (Asiama, 1997).

The authority of females has always remained an integral part of traditional African political system, and the Asante are no exception. Like the Yoruba kingdom (Smith, 1988) and Mande groups (Hoffer, 1974), women held top political offices in Asante matriarchy (Farrar, 1997).

The position of female leaders is noticeable, and has survived through historical transitions from traditional status, through colonial and postcolonial periods. Among the Asante, the female matrilineal and matriarchal role can be traced back to their history. According to Akyeampong and Obeng (1995), Kumasi was discovered by *Adu Nyame Bofuo* (a man) who bought it from the initial owner who was a woman. This political authority of females is embodied in the institution of 'queen mothership', discussed by most Afro-anthropologist within the context of matriarchy (Farrar, 1997).

Asante's matrilineal descent (abusua) was headed by a female elder (*Obaa Panin*) and a male elder (*Abusuapanin*). In the political society, Asante were ruled by a King (*Ohene*) and queen mother (*Ohemaa*). This leadership structure was termed by Okonjo (1976) as a dual-sex political system. The two were positioned side by side at all levels of the Asante authority hierarchy, from the state to the village level (Stoeltje, 2012). To a wider extent, some scholars (Rattray 1969; Diop, 1989) have indicated that the *Ohemaa* was the most powerful personality of the Asante state. The thrones of the King (*Ohene*) and queen mother (*Ohemaa*) use ancestral stools to symbolize their power and authority (Stoeltje, 2012; Owusu-Mensah, 2014). Unlike in *Bura/Pabir* of Nigeria where queen mothers gain prominence from their relationship with the chief (Cohen, 1977), Asante's queen mothers had autonomous power obtained from the stool through the matrilineal lineage (Aidoo, 1977). She was a co-ruler with joint responsibility with the king in all situations and can rule alone even in the absence of the king as a monarch (Farrar, 1997). Accounts of the prominent roles of an Asante queen mother were captured in works of Wilks (1993) and Farrar (1997). Although men occupy the frontiers of the Asantes matriarchal and matrilineal system, the society is generally women-centred. Men were placed in political positions primarily to lead wars and perform all ancestral rituals that women cannot perform (Akyeampong and Obeng, 1995). In fact, according to Rattray (1969), male-occupying stools would not have been necessary if women could lead wars and escape the menstrual taboo surrounding the ancestral stool. While queen mothers in some African countries like Nigeria are just ceremonial titles (Farrar, 1997), a queen mother in Asante is not a ceremonial name. They hold power and authority in political administration, a line of inheritance and succession, decision making and governance.

This account of Asante social organization presents an example of a society that practised both true matriarchy and matrilineal system which is investigated in its present context in relation to land in this chapter.

11.4 Land Tenure among the Asante

Land among the Asante was and is still being managed under customary practice. Customarily, land is communally owned and does not belong to an individual. Hence, all members of a landowning family or community (irrespective of their gender) are entitled to have access to land for various purposes as permitted by predefined norms. Such land can be acquired through conquest, cultivation of vacant land, exploration by hunters or given as gift. It is believed that land is a valuable inheritance from the ancestors to the present generation which must be protected to secure the interest of posterity. It therefore embodies the interest of the ancestors, the present and unborn generations. This made the selling of land prohibited as such an act will constitute a disloyalty to the ancestors and disbanding of the hope of future generations. Even in recent times, monies paid in land transaction to the chief is traditionally considered as 'drink money', which is used to consult the land deity, although in the currently highly monetized land market, the 'drink money' almost equates the actual economic value of the land.

Essentially, according to customary beliefs land is considered a deity rather than an object and as such it is associated with customary practices such as the offering of mashed yam, egg and fowl before cultivation of farms, and pouring of libation during special occasions and observing sacred days (Asiama, 1997). These practices were done to propitiate the land deity to ensure fertility of the land. More specifically, land is referred to as the '*Asase Yaa*', which represents the femininity of land, signifying its ability to support agriculture and produce food to sustain human survival. This is strongly linked with the role of women in child-bearing (giver of life through blood line) and managing the household. The importance of land to the socioeconomic and political organization of society therefore serves to emphasize female recognition and power in the Asante society.

In Ghana, about 80% of the land is under customary ownership (Bugri and Yeboah, 2017). This indicates that traditional authorities exert greater control in land allocation. All lands in the Asante kingdom are vested in the 'stool' which embodies the spirit of the wider community comprising the dead, present and future, hence, the occupants of the stool (Chiefs) hold authority over land in trust for the people (Bugri and Yeboah, 2017). Among the Asante, the Asantehene (also called *Otumfour*) holds the allodial title to lands within his jurisdiction. The day-to-day administration of land is undertaken by designated chiefs within the constitute communities in contact with family heads. The interest of the family just as the individuals is usufructuary, and the right of use and inheritance devolves through the maternal lineage. At the family level, the *'Abusuapanin'* together with *'Obaa Panin'* and other elderly members of the family oversee the management of land to satisfy the female descent which constitute the family. Women are represented in the allocation of land to members of the family and in most cases, they help to clarify issues of kinship related to family lineage. This position of women in land management is further interrogated using the following a discourse analysis on the subject.

11.5 The Ideal Place of the Woman in Asante Matriarchal/Matrilineal Society

The Woman as a Political Authority in Asante Matriarchy

Contrary to widely held assertions about female power as superficial, the Asante queen mother wielded real political authority and in the case of destoolment or demise of a chief, she assumed the position of the chief (the *Omanhene* or *Odikro*, her male counterpart) (Brempong, 2007). More importantly, the selection of a king or chief fall within the authority of the queen mother. When the stool of the king or chief is vacant, she is responsible to appoint a suitable successor within her lineage and clan who is vetted by the council of kingmakers (Asiama, 1997; Owusu-Mensah, 2014). Rattray (1969) added that: 'Having chosen the chief, the queen mother sends a message to the sub-chiefs and elders who now discuss the nominee', and when they have agreed (which they usually do, no one can be put on the stool against whom the queen mother gives her veto) the queen mother is informed. The power held by the *Ohemaa* in the process of choosing an heir to the stool is based on the background that women are the founders of the Akan clans (Boaten, 1992). This implied a high level of power and acceptance of the queen mother, and for that matter, female authority, which clearly contradicts Cohen's (1977) assertion that African 'queen mothership' was only ceremonial and does not sanction political power in practical terms.

In essence, the queen mother also presides over a council of female stool holders with whom she governs the social systems of females within the society (Rattray 1969; Farrar, 1997). The queen mother possesses jurisdiction over a court where various disputes related to females, and in some cases, males, were and are adjudicated. She oversees the performance of various traditional rites such as birth and puberty rites and serves to instil morality among the younger generation, especially females. The power of the queen mother accords her substantial influence in the decision-making process. These female stool holders participate in all legislative processes as well as land distribution. Her importance in decision making is confirmed by her social status as the epithet of wisdom whose council is very paramount. Hence, the saying *'Yenkobisa aberewa'* (let us go and ask the old woman) (Stoeltje, 2012). There is no doubt that decisions within the Asante traditional council are highly influenced by the queen mother. These provide substantial evidence of female political power, in other words, matriarchy, in the Asante society.

Women and Inheritance in Asante Matrilineal System

The Asante system of inheritance is based on the matrilineal lineage. This therefore confers greater importance and attachment to one's extended family of the mother lineage, other than the conjugal family, as the source of social, spiritual and economic support. As part of the wider Akan ethnic group, the Asante belief that the female blood is the medium through which the family spirit transcends from one generation to another, and as such, children obtain their blood and very existence from their mothers (Nave, 2016). Children therefore belong to their maternal lineage, and not that of their father's (Fenrich and Higgins, 2001). Hence, one's extended family is traced from the maternal lineage through which inheritance is practised.

This system places women at the centre of the Asante family system, as they determine kinship and inheritance. The woman can inherit property including land from her mother, aunties, and sisters, while her children can also inherit from her and her siblings (aunties and uncles) (Asiama, 1997; Gedzi, 2012). Usually, males inherit from males, while females inherit from females, though this is not always the case (Gedzi, 2012). Within this context, when a person dies intestate, the property devolves to his or her uterine family (Kutsoati and Morck, 2016). Since the line of inheritance revolves around the woman whose descent inherit the property, she stands to benefit and secure the interest of her uterine female offspring. Ollenu (1962) states emphatically that contrary to assertions about women's frail ability to inheritance, among the Asante (as well as other Akan groups), the mother is the real successor, and her status is critical to the inheritance process. While wives and children cannot directly inherit property from the man (because they do not belong to his uterine family) they can inherit self-acquired properties that are willed (*nsamansew*) to, or offered as gifts from their husbands, albeit their claim to property from their own maternal or uterine family is undeniable.

The Asante Woman in Marriage and the Relation to Matrilineal Property

Marriage was considered an important aspect of the Asante social system due to its inherent potential to secure the posterity of the maternal lineage. The role of the woman as central to protecting the lineage and inheritance made her important in marriage, and in this respect, the man served as a facilitator. Marriage therefore did not mean the subjugation of the female power or interest, but the channel to ensure the posterity of the female lineage and matriliny. Considering this, the loyalty of the mother remained in the conjugal family, essentially, it was directed towards her children and uterine family. Hence it was understood that whatever property she acquired in marriage went to her uterine family, and was not tied to the marriage. Therefore, this imposed a necessary responsibility on the woman not to be dependent on the man, but to be industrious. As a result, a woman could cultivate food crops alone, she must cultivate cash crops with her husband (Asiama, 1997). When the farmland was obtained from the woman's family, the property remained that of the woman's, but properties made by the man during marriage remained tied to the marriage.

In postcolonial times, there have been various contestations on properties acquired in marriage between the man's conjugal family and his uterine family, when the man dies intestate (Gedzi, 2012). This has resulted in various reforms particularly the intestate succession law. Based on this, customary practices render the spouse and children vulnerable, with no property inherited. However, it is worth noting that in the Asante matrilineal system, women's access to land and property from their uterine family served as a form of social security, and as capital which they could develop as their own during marriage.

11.6 The Beginning of 'Matriarchy Crisis'

From a traditional view, Asante land tenure system played a crucial role in emphasizing women's place in the socicty as well as access to land. An Asante woman enjoyed a dual advantage of ownership and control of her personally acquired land plus any other land belonging to her 'abusua' (family) or tribe (Asiama, 1997). Within this context, Asante matrilineal family was a sociopolitical entity hinged on tight social ties, collective gains, and alliance to lineage. Commitment to lineage was at the core of Asante matriarchy, rarely, was a woman autonomous, 'single' or isolated from her roots (Mikell, 1997). However, through the unravelling of history, the values and culture of Asante land tenure have been subject to renegotiations, reinvention and restructuring. Asiama (1997, p. 225) noted that 'modern economy and the surge of urbanization' stresses the traditional land regime and is weakened by the revived preference for conjugal family, religion, commoditization of land, education and Western culture. This study agrees with Asiama's (1997) view on modernization, further highlights the start of 'matriarchal crisis' among the Asantes emanating from colonialism.

Generally, the colonial system of production was shaped by gender. Since plough cultivation was the major approach to agricultural production, women were marginalized because comparatively, 'man-power' was superior (Akyeampong and Fofack, 2014). Through religion, monogamous and conjugal family inclinations were encouraged often leading to the weakening of extended family ties and individualism. The contours of the British colonial education system were also biased towards the males. Generally, the British colonialists, influenced by their patriarchal origins, were either unaware or ignored the Asante matriarchy in favour of what best suited their objective. In Rattray's (1969) book, *Ashanti*, he expressed surprise of his earlier ignorance of Ashante's matriarchy even though he had worked as a British agent and anthropologist in Kumasi. In a quest to receive clarity from his local informants (Asante elders), they replied: 'The white man ... has dealings with and recognizes only the men; we supposed the European considered women of no account, and we know you do not recognize them as we have always done' (Rattray, 1969, p. 84).

The 'cash-crop revolution' began within the 19th century when the British traders sought to trade in 'legitimate' goods such as cocoa, palm oil, groundnut and other raw products to feed the industrial market (Ludlow, 2012). During this period, agricultural labour became even more gendered. While male labour was utilized in the production of cash crops, subsistence or food cropping was female-gendered (Akyeampong and Fofack, 2014). Within the Asante matrilineal system, strong kinship ties meant that the women were less likely to be mobile and thus, better suited for subsistence farming. Backing this conclusion, Fage (1979, p. 329) noted that cash crops were 'most effectively produced and marketed ... by hosts of enterprising small men, who could respond freely and quickly to varying stimuli of work market forces'.

In consequence, the effect of colonization and the period of modernization that followed had a significant influence on Asante matriarchy. La Ferrara and Milazzo (2017) challenge the view that the matrilineal system is breaking down because of contemporary economic settings. They argue that most parents would obligingly pass on their family lands to their children other than their sister's child because of increasing economic hardships. The Asante (extended) family system is gradually decaying while its position is being replaced by the nuclear family. This implies that a postcolonial Asante woman is no longer guaranteed of land security from her family or community and more likely to face the harsh realities of gender inequalities. We argue that the continuous interplay of cultural negotiations within the traditional matriarchal regime have caused a drastic transformation, which we refer to as 'matriarchal crisis', in Asante land tenure system which have fuelled unequal access to land. Since Asante matriarchy is essentially linked with the domains of kinship and matrimony, any shift from the traditional regime requires a social repositioning to negotiate the shift over time. In the Asante case, failure to realize the shift has formed the basis for several other factors which weaken female power in the matriarchal system.

11.7 Weakening 'Female Power' and Land Access in the Matriarchal System

Amid what we describe as matriarchal crises, a pertinent question to ask in the matriarchal–patriarchal dichotomy of women empowerment is: do the sociopolitical, matrimonial, inheritance and cultural powers ascribed to women by matriarchal systems translate into land use decision powers? does this make a significant difference in women land tenure and access from other systems? The answer to this question is to the negative: contrary to *a priori* scholarship, our analysis of the Asante matrilineal system subscribes to a scholarly stance that women in matriarchal systems are suffering a literature paradox of secure land tenure and access in matrilineal societies, where under the disguise of matriarchy they suffer the perceived ills of patriarchy. This is consistent with scholarship in Zambia that there appears to be no difference in changes in land access between women living in matrilineal versus patrilineal villages as they both risk losing their land rights to land to male counterparts (Chapoto *et al.*, 2011). Reasons for this phenomenon among Asantes in this case are the weakening power of women in matriarchal systems which are aggravated by social structures, cultural stereotypes, urbanization, land privatization and succession laws.

The Verbal Abuse: Social Stereotypes of Women in Land Ownership are Disempowering

The Asante, like other Ghanaian societies, have inherent social stereotypes that influence and characterize women's status in society. Largely, these stereotypes espouse male superiority and underscore women's subordination. These stereotypes have been partly influenced by the manner of gender socialization inherent in the cultural settings. At an early stage, the adolescent Asante child is taught to identify and imbibe the polarized gender norms of society. Whereas females are taught to assume more domestic duties, the males take up more dominant roles. Women consider it their responsibility to take care of the house (including cooking, caring for children, and keeping the house clean) and as such, it is incumbent on them to raise their girl children likewise. Considering the belief that child-bearing and raising children are the most prominent contribution of the Asante woman to her family, this reinforces her attachment to the family and housekeeping roles, within which her identity is seen. Meanwhile, parents raise their male children to assume greater responsibility including holding and managing property. Respondents to interviews asserted that both males and females have equal inherent abilities for high achievements. However, they also ascribed male superiority as a 'win' for women since the success of a woman is usually shrouded in association with men. This is confirmed by the saying *'Obaa animuoyam ne aware3'*, literally meaning, 'The glory of the woman lies in marriage' (see Table 11.1). Hence, there is a belief that a woman is not complete without a man. This perception is also rooted in the ideology that women were created as helpmates for men, which was affirmed by both men and women groups interviewed. Due to such conventions, women must accept male superiority and become submissive to them, which is recognized as the character of a 'good' wife or woman. This was endorsed in a statement by one male respondent: 'in fact, *I hate women who are quarrelsome! A woman should show dignity to her husband by adhering to his views and not challenging him'*. This does not mean that women do not have the right to make their own decisions; however, in the case of critical decisions making as related to properties, men hold 'the authority of final say'.

These perceptions have been echoed in various Akan proverbs and folk tales which expresses women subordination in society. These portray women to be inferior, difficult, demanding or, weak, and not able to defend themselves without a man. Considering the Asante's background in matriarchy and matriliny, one would think the narrative about female subordination would have been different. Though other proverbial sayings depict positive characterization of women, it is worth noting that these highlight their motherly characters (compassionate, epitome of wisdom, caring, originators of family and society), but do not give them equal social recognition as compared to their male counterparts. In effect, these negative depictions of women as expressed in proverbial sayings and social norms (as seen in Table 11.1) are passed on from generation to generation, influencing social perspectives about women in perpetuity.

These stereotypes show a negative attitude towards women's access to land. Social perceptions describe women's access to land as more qualitative (to produce food, have space for living) than quantitative (number of plots, their distribution and scale of production). It was remarked that as a woman acquiring large plots of land was not necessary, but all that is needed is just what is adequate to be able to cater for or feed themselves and their children. In some cases, women even preferred that men (either their brothers, sons or husbands) take charge of inherited land or other properties to conceal their identity as the actual owners. This statement was affirmed by a woman traditional

Table 11.1. Akan proverbs expressing female subordination (based on authors' interviews).

Proverbial sayings	Implications to land
Ɔbaa tɔ tuo a, etwere ɔbarima dan mu (When a woman buys a gun, it is kept in the man's room)	Property belonging to the woman is kept under the control of the man.
Ɔbaa mpempem a, ɔbarima na ɔhw3 ne soɔ (No matter how rich a woman is, it is still the man who takes care of her)	
Akokɔ be3ra nim adekye3 nanso ɔbisa firi akokɔnini ano (The hen knows when it is daybreak, but she waits for its announcement from the cock)	The woman must consult the man in decision making concerning acquisition of land and other properties, and the man should have the final say.
S3 ɔbaa y3n odwan a, ɔbarima na ɔtɔn (When a woman rears a sheep, it is the man who sells it)	The man has rights to oversee, manage and deal with transactions concerning the woman's property.
S3 ɔbaa to tuo a, etwere ɔbarima bo (A woman fires a gun only from the chest of a man)	Any milestone achieved by the woman is made on the superior abilities of man. Hence, women cannot independently own, build or acquire property unless supported by a man.
Ɔbaa tɔn nyaadowa na ɔntɔn atuduro (A woman sells garden eggs but not gun power)	There are social limitations on what women can do. They are more successful serving in supportive roles than in authoritative roles that demand the exercise of power.
Obaa animuoyam ne aware3 (The glory of the woman lies in marriage)	The woman is more respected when she is married. Having been associated with a man, receives the social recognition to have access to land which is controlled by cultural norms.
Ɔbaa de3, wode3 ne mukaase (The woman's place is the kitchen)	Women's rights in land are limited to their use rights and they are not to meddle in other affairs such as control and management of land.
Mmaa p3 d3 kyiri ka (Women like to enjoy themselves but do not want to pay any debts)	Women desire to obtain benefits from land but are unwilling to commit resources or take risk associated with managing it. Hence, they only seek use rights, as the rights of ownership, transfer or sales are exercised by men.
Mmarima nni fie a na akyakya yi ne to kyere maa (It is only when there are no men that the hunchback can expose his back to women)	Without a man, the woman lacks security in terms of land acquisition and management.
S3 Enimma nsae, Wofase nni ade3 (When there are surviving brothers of a deceased man, it is unlikely that his sister's child will inherit)	Women shall not be deemed fit to administer family lands so far as there are men.

leader who said that '*Ɔbaa tɔ tuo a, etwere ɔbarima dan mu*' (meaning: Whatever is owned by the woman is held under the domain of the man and so men manage our properties). Usually, women who do not conform to such social stereotypes are seen in a negative light. In the case of acquiring land, it is essential that the woman seeks the service of her husband or a respectable man to lead her in consulting traditional authorities. This is considered as socially more respectful and appropriate. If these perceptions are held, women are not encouraged to exercise their right of securing land or property ownership as their achievement must be associated with the man. These negative attitudes towards women also serve to impose social barriers which make the land acquisition process more complicated for women, contributing to their landlessness.

The Emergence and Prevalence of the 'Male Matriarchy'

Asante matriarchy in recent times can best be described as a blind matriarchy, ruled by men. Asante men are now exercising the highest authoritative and governing power. Men are charged with all responsibilities and the executive power to control economic assets and family resources including land. This practice in Asante society of recent is described in this study as a 'male matriarchy'. Though women in authorities are still recognized in Asante traditional settings, they are only effective in the judicial context (power to appoint and sanction), the highest powers are still held by men. Women rulers are overshadowed by their male counterpart to the extent that, females in Asante's matriarchy of recent ages have become powerless.

Asante matriarchy and matrilineal systems have turned into a mere female line of descent. Comparatively, men are favoured in terms of inheritance owing to the above-mentioned social stereotypes about women. In confirming this position, some respondents put it this way: 'in our family, men lead the family. When there is any problem, you will need the man to lead you to resolve the problem. For example, when we have land issues, or our children are getting married, the man leads the family' (woman, Kumasi). Adding to this, another respondent stated:

> when there are emergencies, we call for help from men (in Twi: *mmarima mmera oo, mmarima mmera oo*). This is because the men have courage to face difficult situations. Because of this, men are very important in every family. And that is why they are our family heads.
>
> (Elderly woman, Kumasi)

This account corresponds to Ferrara's (2007) assertion that the first son of an Asante woman is the head of the household/clan. Family lands – considered as an ancestral trust for the living, the death and the unborn (Mends, 2006) – are first inherited by the clan head followed by his brother and nephew. Land-related decisions are managed by men. The chief is the highest authority in land tenure arrangement. Females in this matriarchal society still need the final consent of their male counterpart in making decisions relating to land. Although property ownership and access to land are fundamental to economic survival, women in the Asante society have limited rights over the control and transfer of land and property (Korang-Okrah, 2015).

Largely, the study found that Asante women are key promoters of this 'male matriarchal' practices. They appoint male heirs (clan head) and chiefs and then give them autonomous power and authority to rule and manage land. In addition, they preserve and protect men rights in matriarchal society. The queen mother virtually acts the motherly role to retain kinship in her lineage. In so doing, she accepts and respects all decisions of the chief. These male matriarchal practices embraced and promoted by females in the Asante society have resulted in the vulnerability and landlessness of Asante women.

The Monetization of Communal Land

Aside from the social prejudice against women, another major factor accounting for their landlessness is the lack of adequate capital. Ghana is in an era of neoliberal capitalism induced by an unprecedented rapid urbanization and market demand for resources (Yaro, 2012). Historically, more than half of the country's population live in urban areas: hence, the competing demand for urban land is unavoidable. In the case of Kumasi, the second-largest city, the population grew from 346,000 in 1970 to surpass 1 million in 2000 and approximately 1,730,249 in 2010 (Ghana Statistical Service, 2014). The increasing population pressure coupled with the concentration of private capital in Kumasi have led to increasing demands for land. As demand continues to increase, the scarcity of land in the city has introduced pertinent evolutions in indigenous land tenure practices. There is a clear shift from the communal notion of land as 'our land' to a more individualistic approach that takes the stance of 'my land'. This phenomenon can be seen from the cases of Esereso and Adum (all suburbs in Kumasi).

After the initial subdivision of residential land at Esereso in 1985, members of the community only had to present bottles of Schnapps to the traditional custodian (chief) to obtain leasehold rights while 'strangers' paid about GH¢4 for the same rights. However, In Adum – Central Business District of Kumasi – an acre of land in 1960 was priced at GH¢50, by 1973 it increased to GH¢164 and has currently galloped to the ranges of GH¢ 600,000 to GH¢1,850,000. This is probably the highest price ever in Kumasi because the agglomeration of economic activities in Adum makes it the most expensive locality in

Kumasi. However, increasing land value is a common trend among all the suburbs. Relatively higher land values are influenced by the comparative advantage of locations with regards to social amenities, infrastructure, markets and other pull factors.

The commoditization of land within the city has induced opportunism into the hitherto egalitarian Asante society. The 'abusua' and indigenes who form the primary owners of communal lands are in constant competition with financially endowed 'strangers' for the rights to use their own land. The winner of this competition is usually obvious, not the owners but 'strangers' with the ability to meet the requirements of the market-driven land tenure. In effect, the market-driven land tenure has had a negative effect on women's ability to access land, because there is a higher prevalence and severity of poverty among women than men (Awumbila, 2006).

11.8 Conclusion

This chapter highlights that matriarchy and matrilineal social orientations are not inherent guarantees of women's access to land but can reinforce male dominance over land ownership, control, and access to land. It notes that social structures and norms are subject to change and, in this instance, colonialization and modernization have acted as the two key influencers in reshaping Asante matriarchy. We argue that the continuous interplay of cultural negotiations within the traditional matriarchal regime have caused a drastic transformation in Asante land tenure system which have fuelled unequal access to land. In effect, a postcolonial Asante woman is no longer guaranteed land tenure security from her family or community and more likely to face the harsh realities of landlessness. The chapter does not assume equal access to land hitherto but notes that the inequality gap has been further widened by the weakening of 'female power' in the matriarchal social system.

The chapter recognizes that the apparent weakening of matriarchy is driven by an ingrained social ideology that stereotypes male superiority and female subordination. In response, women are not encouraged to exercise their right of securing land or property ownership, except through men (either husbands, brothers or uncles). This reinforces a 'blinded' male matriarchy, where women themselves solidify male superiority over land by favouring male heirs over women and supporting men's autonomous control, power and authority to manage land. These social prejudices have imposed pertinent barriers to women's land access and contribute to their landlessness. The chapter further notes that the unequal access to land is aggravated by women's inability to compete in the current market-driven land tenure due to relatively high rates of poverty. Due to these critical challenges, the story of women regarding their access, right and ownership to land remains pessimistic – a fate caused by others and accepted by women. However, the narrative can be different.

Women are in a better position of confronting these inequalities than any other actors. They may be restricted by socioeconomic factors but together can be a powerful force that can rally their needs and concerns to a bigger audience. Even as a single entity, each woman can act as a change agent in her immediate family and community by confronting sociocultural practices that discriminate against them, their daughters and other females. By interrogating social systems, whether matriarchy or patriarchy, women will be able to identify the norms and practices that work to their disadvantage to campaign for change. This has been a key aspect this study sought to investigate. While recognizing women power in negotiating for their land access, the role of men as allies cannot be overemphasized. Male dominance has been entrenched in most cultures in sub-Saharan Africa, which have afforded them privileges over women, including land access. It is therefore important that men recognize that unequal access to land not only exploits women but also limits the ability of households and community to enjoy improved living conditions. Similarly, there is the need to tackle the patriarchal ills of women's land tenure not only from the patriarchal–matriarchal trajectories, but also directing policy towards specific differentiations and actions among women which either disempower other women or endorse patriarchal dominance in land tenure and access. Hence, we all are responsible to addressing this injustice towards women, be it men, communities, scholars, governments, feminists and non-governmental organizations.

References

Aidoo, A.A. (1977) Asante queen mothers in government and politics in the nineteenth century. *Journal of the Historical Society of Nigeria*, 9(1), 2.

Akyeampong, E. and Fofack, H. (2014) The contribution of African women to economic growth and development in the pre-colonial and colonial periods: Historical perspectives and policy implications. *Economic History of Developing Regions*, 29(1), 42–73. DOI: 10.1080/20780389.2014.923154.

Akyeampong, E. and Obeng, P. (1995) Spirituality, gender and power in Asante history. *The International Journal of African Historical Studies,* 28, 481–508. DOI: 10.2307/221171.

Ameyaw, P.D., Chigbu, U.E., de Vries, W.T., Mwesigye, S.P. and Yeboah, E. (2019) *Women and Customary Land Tenure: Emerging Developments and Ways Forward in Savelugu, Ghana.* World Bank Conference on Land and Poverty, 24–29 March, Washington, DC, USA.

Asiama, S.O. (1997) Crossing the barrier of time. The Asante woman in urban land development. *Africa. Rivista di studi e documentazione*, 2, 212–236.

Awumbila, M. (2006) Gender equality and poverty in Ghana: Implications for poverty reduction strategies. *GeoJournal*, 67(2), 149–161. DOI: 10.1007/s10708-007-9042-7.

Bachofen, J.J. (1861) *Das Mutterrecht* [The Mother Right]. Elis, The Epizephyrian Locrians, and Lesbos.

Bamberger, J. (1974) The myth of matriarchy: Why men rule in primitive society. *Women, Culture and Society,* 263–280.

Boaten, N.A. (1992) The changing role of Queen Mothers in the Akan polity. *Research Review*, 8 (1 and 2), 90–100.

Brempong, A. (2007) *Transformations in Traditional Rule in Ghana (1951–1996).* Institute of African Studies, Accra, Ghana.

Bugri, J.T. and Yeboah, E. (2017) *Understanding Changing Land Access and Use by the Rural Poor in Ghana.* IIED, London, UK.

Burston, D. (1986) Myth, religion and mother right. *Contemporary Psychoanalysis*, 22(4), 666–687.

Chapoto, A., Jayne, T.S. and Mason, N.M. (2011) Widows' land security in the era of HIV/AIDS: Panel survey evidence from Zambia. *Economic Development and Cultural Change*, 59(3), 511–547.

Chigbu, U.E. (2015) Repositioning culture for development: Women and development in a Nigerian rural community. *Community, Work & Family,* 18(3), 336–352. DOI: 10.1080/13668803.2014.981506.

Chigbu, U.E. (2019a) Masculinity, men and patriarchal issues aside: How do women's actions impede women's access to land? Matters arising from a peri-rural community in Nigeria. *Land Use Policy,* 81, 39–48. DOI: 10.1016/j.landusepol.2018.10.033.

Chigbu, U.E. (2019b) Anatomy of women's landlessness in the patrilineal customary land tenure systems of sub-Saharan Africa and a policy pathway. *Land Use Policy*, 86, 126–135. DOI: 10.1016/j.landusepol. 2019.04.041.

Chigbu, U.E. (2020) Land, women, youths, and land tools or methods: Emerging lessons for governance and policy. *Land*, 9, 507.

Chigbu, U.E. (2021) The quest for 'good governance' of urban land in sub-Saharan Africa: Insight into Windhoek, Namibia. In: Home, R. (Ed.), *Land Issues for Urban Governance in Sub-Saharan Africa Springer*. Cham. Switzerland, pp. 17–34.

Chigbu, U.E., Paradza, G. and Dachaga, W. (2019), Differentiations in women's land tenure experiences: Implications for women's land access and tenure security in sub-Saharan Africa. *Land*, 8(2), 22.

Cohen, R. (1977) Oedipus Rex and Regina: The Queen Mother in Africa. *Africa,* 47(1), 14–30.

Dachaga, W. and Chigbu, U. E. (2020) Understanding tenure security dynamics in resettlement towns: Evidence from the Bui Resettlement Project in Ghana. *Journal of Planning and Land Management*, 1(2), 38–49.

Diop, C.A. (1989) *The Cultural Unity of Black Africa*. Red Sea Press, Trenton, NJ, USA.

Fage, J.D. (1979) West Africa since 1800 – History of West Africa. *Journal of African History*, 20(1), 135–136.

Farrar, T. (1997) The Queen Mother, matriarchy, and the question of female political authority in precolonial West Africa monarchy. *Journal of Black Studies,* 27(5), 579–597.

Fenrich, J. and Higgins T.E. (2001) Promise unfulfilled: Law, culture, and women's inheritance rights in Ghana. *Fordham International Law Journal,* 25(2), 259–341.

Fortunato, L. (2012) The evolution of matrilineal kinship organisation. *Proceedings of the Royal Society B*, 279, 4939–4945.

Gedzi S.V. (2012) Women's property relations after intestate succession PNDC Law 111 in Ghana. *Research on Humanities and Social Sciences*, 2(9). Available at: https://www.iiste.org/Journals/index.php/RHSS/article/view/3144 (accessed 15 July 2021).

Goettner-Abendroth, H. (2004). Matriarchal society: Definition and theory. In: Vaughan, G. (Ed.), *The Gift, Il Dono: A Feminist Analysis*. Meltemi editore, Athanor, Rome, Italy, pp. 76–85.

Goettner-Abendroth, H. (2017) Matriarchal studies: Past debates and new foundations. *Asian Journal of Women's Studies,* 23(1), 2–6.

Goettner-Abendroth, H. (2018) Re-thinking matriarchy in modern matriarchal studies using two examples: The Khasi and the Mosuo. *Asian Journal of Women's Studies*, 24, 3–27.

Ghana Statistical Service (2014) *2010 Population and Housing Census Report: District Analytical Report, Kumasi Metropolitan.* Ghana Statistical Service, Accra, Ghana.

Hartung, J. (1985) Matrilineal inheritance: New theory and analysis. *The Behavioural and Brain Sciences*, 8, 661–688.

Hoffer, C.P. (1974) Madam Yoko: Ruler of the Kpa Mende Confederacy. In: Rosaldo, M.Z. and Lamphere, L. (Eds), *Women of Tropical Africa.* Stanford University Press, Stanford, CA, USA, pp. 173–187.

Holy, L. (1996) *Anthropological Perspectives of Kinship.* Pluto Press, London, UK.

Hurtado, A., Iverson, P. and Paterson, T. (2000) *Major Problems in American Indian History: Documents and Essays.* Houghton Mifflin, Boston, MA, USA.

Korang-Okrah, R. (2015) "It's only by God's Grace": Capturing Ghanaian (Akan) widows' perspectives on risk and resilience. *Journal of the North American Association of Christians in Social Work*, 42(1), 7–27.

Kutsoati, E. and Morck, R. (2016) Family ties, inheritance right and successful poverty alleviation: Evidence from Ghana. In: Edwards, S., Johnson, S. and Weil, D.N. (Eds). *African Successes, Volume* II*: Human Capital.* University of Chicago Press, Chicago, IL, USA, pp. 215–252.

La Ferrara, E. (2007) Descent rules and strategic transfer. Evidence from matrilineal groups in Ghana. *Journal of Development Economics*, 83, 280–301.

La Ferrara, E. and Milazzo, A. (2017) Customary norms, inheritance, and human capital: Evidence from a reform of the matrilineal system in Ghana. *American Economic Journal: Applied Economics*, 9(4), 166–185.

Ludlow, H. (2012) Ghana, cocoa, colonialism and globalisation: Introducing historiography. *Yesterday & Today*, 8, 1–21. DOI: 10.1109/8.761072.

McGee, K. (2015) The impact of matriarchal traditions on the advancement of Ashanti women in Ghana. In: B. Taylor (Ed.), *Listening to the Voices: Multi-Ethnic Women in Education.* University of San Francisco, San Francisco, CA, pp. 1–10.

Mann, A.B. and Goettner-Abedroth, H. (2013) *Matriarchal Studies*. Oxford University Press, Oxford, UK.

Mends, T. (2006) *A Study on the Customary Land Tenure System and Its Impact on Urbanisation. Case Study: The Peri-Urban Accra, Ghana*. ITC, Enschede, The Netherlands.

Mikell, G. (Ed.) (1997) *African Feminism: The Politics of Survival in Sub-Saharan Africa*. University of Pennsylvania Press, Philadelphia, PA, USA.

Nave, C. (2016) One family: Defining kinship in the neighbourhoods of Kumasi, Ghana. *Journal of the Royal Anthropological Institute,* 22(4), 1–17. DOI: 10.1111/1467-9655.12492.

Okonjo, K. (1976). The dual-sex political system in operation: Igbo women and community politics in mid-western Nigeria. In: Hafkin, N. and Bay, E. (Eds), *Studies in Women in Africa: Social and Economic Change*, Stanford University Press, Stanford, CA, pp. 45–58.

Ollennu, N.A. (1962) *Principles of Customary Land Law in Ghana*. Sweet and Maxwell, London, UK.

Owusu Ansah, B. and Chigbu, U.E. (2020) The nexus between peri-urban transformation and customary land rights disputes: Effects on peri-urban development in Trede, Ghana. *Land*, 9(6), 187. DOI: 10.3390/land9060187.

Owusu-Mensah, I. (2014), Politics, chieftaincy and customary law in Ghana's fourth republic. *Journal of Pan African Studies.* 6(7), 261–278.

Pauline, E.P. (2010) 'Our daughters inherit our land, but our sons use their wives' fields': Matrilineal-matrilocal land tenure and the new land policy in Malawi. *Journal of Eastern African Studies*, 4(1), 179–199.

Rattray, R.S (1969) *Ashanti.* Oxford University Press, London, UK.

Richards, A.L. (1950) Some types of family structures amongst the Central Bantu: Characteristics of matrilineal kinship organisation in Central Africa. In: Radcliffe-Brown, A.R. and Forde, D. (Eds), *African Systems of Kinship and Marriage*, Oxford University Press, London, UK, pp. 207–251.

Smith, R. S. (1988) *Kingdoms of the Yoruba*. University of Wisconsin Press, Madison, WI, USA.
Stoeltje, B.J. (2012) Asante queenmothers; A study in identity and continuity. *Journal of Theatricalities and Visual Culture*, California State University, Los Angeles, CA, USA.
United Nations (2017) *World Population Prospects: The 2017 Revision, Key Findings and Advance Tables.* United Nations, New York, NY, USA.
Wang, Y. and Morais, D.B. (2014) Self-representations of the matriarchal other. *Annals of Tourism Research,* 44, 74–87.
Wilks, I. (1993) *Forest of Gold: Essays on the Akan and the Kingdom of the Asante.* Ohio University Press, Athens, OH, USA.
Yaro, J.A. (2012) Re-inventing traditional land tenure in the era of land commoditization: Some consequences in peri-urban northern Ghana. *Geografiska Annaler, Series B: Human Geography,* 94(4), 351–368. DOI: 10.1111/geob.12003.

12 The Gender Dimensions of Land Tenure Reforms in Ethiopia 1995–2020

Stein T. Holden*

School of Economics and Business/Centre for Land Tenure Studies, Norwegian University of Life Sciences, Ås, Norway

12.1 Introduction

Ethiopia is a unique country in Africa in several respects. It is about the only country that has never been colonized. It has a long and well-documented history through written records and archaeological and historic monuments and buildings. Land has had a central role in the control of power and for the survival of its people for hundreds of years under challenging climatic conditions with recurrent droughts. On the other hand, Ethiopia shares some characteristics with other countries such as a patriarchal culture with strong male dominance. This chapter aims to assess how women's land rights have changed in Ethiopia over the last 25 years. Ethiopia embarked on the largest land reform process in terms of land registration and certification in any African country, starting in 1998. This started as a home-grown low-cost reform in one region and was implemented as a broad-scale participatory process without modern tools within ten years in the four largest regions of the country (Deininger *et al.*, 2008). The reform therefore was implemented primarily in the highlands of the country where smallholder agriculture dominates while the more arid lowlands dominated by pastoralism largely were left untouched by the reform. From 2014 the country scaled up a 2nd Stage Land Registration and Certification (LR&C) that utilized modern tools and provided parcel-level certificates with maps and names of all land holders.

It is important to recognize some of the historical context and regional variations in the areas that were strongly affected by the reform. Some of this heterogeneity is summarized in section 12.2. In section 12.3 I outline the traditional positions of women in the highlands and their situation just before the reform was implemented. New land laws were introduced in the country just before the reform was implemented, including a federal land law (proclamation), followed by regional land laws and regulations that opened for some variations across regions. Sections 12.4 and 12.5 highlight specific gender-related elements of the new land laws and assess the extent to which these were implemented and known and respected on the ground, by land administrations, and the court system responsible for enforcing the law and handling land-related disputes. Sections 12.6 and 12.7 look at the gender impacts of the 1st Stage LR&C and section 12.8 at the 2nd Stage LR&C, before drawing attention to some important future challenges.

*Corresponding author: stein.holden@nmbu.no

 Land Governance and Gender: The Tenure-Gender Nexus in Land Management and Land Policy (ed. U.E. Chigbu)
DOI: 10.1079/9781789247664.0012

12.2 Historical Context: Feudal Times to 1974

The dominant tenure systems during the recent feudal time were the private property and church land in the south and the *gult*, *rist* and *chiguraf goses* systems in the north of the country. However, it is important to recognize the spatial and temporal heterogeneity in these tenure systems that I can barely scratch the surface of here.

Southern Ethiopia

Land rights in Southern Ethiopia were close to private property rights and were distributed in an inequitable way depending on historical events (Adal, 2002). Such land could be sold or exchanged. The system was dominated by absent landlords and tenants. For example, Cohen (1974) reported findings by national surveys undertaken by the Central Statistical Office with 37–73% of the smallholder farmers being tenants and 10–40% of the landowners being absentee owners who controlled 12–48% of the land, with the ranges showing the variation across locations.

Northern Ethiopia

In contrast, in Tigray in Northern Ethiopia there were two customary tenure systems in the highland areas. The most well known is the *rist* system, which has existed for a long time and gained importance with increasing population pressure and involved inheritance of land within the family. The other system, *chiguraf goses* (*shena* in some areas) may have emerged during the 19th century and facilitated land access through membership in a community but without inheritance within the family (Bauer, 1973; Bruce, 1976; Weldu, 2017). This system facilitated land access to immigrants and was used in areas with excess land. People who had temporarily migrated could get land again when they returned. The system lost popularity when land was getting scarcer, and land was reserved for residents in the *rist* system through bequeath of land within the family. The *chiguraf goses* system was combined with a system called *quenchi* and meant equal sharing of land. Land was redistributed to obtain equal sharing of land and committees were established to ensure equal sharing and allocating land of equal size also to immigrants. With increasing population pressure and in-migration the resistance against this increased and the *rist* system had become dominant before the 1974 revolution. In periods with a lot of migration and abundant land *chiguraf goses* had provided advantages over the *rist* system. The *rist* system gave priority to the anterior landholders and resulted in less egalitarian land distribution.

Both systems implied a dominance and favouring of men over women for land access. *Chiguraf goses* allocated land to those with a whip or oxen and men were those cultivating the land with oxen. While the system addressed landlessness, it allocated less land to single women while women with children got as much land as male-headed households. *Gult*[1] land in the north was more like the land system in the south of the country. The emperor Haile Selassie was overthrown by the Derg military regime in 1974 and a radical land reform was introduced taking land from the land-rich and distributing use rights to land in an egalitarian way with emphasis on household needs and ability to cultivate.

During the Derg period (1974–1991) an egalitarian land distribution was emphasized through a strong control by the state. A system with land redistribution was introduced to maintain the egalitarian distribution of land and to provide land to newly formed households. With the disappearance of excess land, land had to be redistributed from the relatively more land-rich to the landless or land-poor households. This resulted in more tenure insecurity (Alemu, 1999; Holden and Yohannes, 2002; Deininger and Jin, 2006). The weak use rights and growing tenure insecurity became important drivers of the later tenure reforms, starting in 1998 in the Tigray Region, that aimed to strengthen the tenure rights and tenure security of rural land holders.

12.3 Traditional Positions of Women

Women in Ethiopia traditionally have a weaker position than men within households as well as in society overall, as the Ethiopian culture is patriarchal and men are regarded as heads of households, except in the case of single, divorced and widowed women with separate households and no husband. Women rarely take up leading positions in society and typically stay at home and are responsible for taking care of children and household chores. The husbands are also traditionally responsible for the farming activities while women only help with certain farming activities such as planting, weeding and harvesting. Ploughing was always done by men and this is believed to be due to their upper body strength. The position of men as household heads and responsible breadwinners implied that they were the main decision makers in farming. In a study in Oromia and SNNP regions in Southern Ethiopia, Holden and Tefera (2008) found that 27–46% of the women stated that they were participating in land investment and production decisions and 23–37% were involved in decisions regarding use of farm income.

The patriarchal Ethiopian societies implied that when land was passed from one generation to the next, it was typically with a patrilineal and patrilocal system implying that the sons received the land from their parents and the wives moved to the home of their husband's family upon marriage. Unmarried daughters could stay with their parents and possibly also get some land if they remained unmarried. In cases of divorce the wife may not receive any of the land unless she has children and would then have to return to her own family, where she may still be given some land. Widows with children were typically allowed to keep the land to farm it with their children, but often they also had to rent the land to their in-laws (Holden and Bezabih, 2009).

The traditionally weak position of women is also illustrated by the marriage system with arranged marriages. Even in parts of Southern Ethiopia, kidnapping marriages were quite common until recently. Holden and Bezu (2014) found that 6% of a sample of married women in SNNP and Oromia regions were married after having been kidnapped.

Ethiopian agriculture is dominated by oxen-ploughing systems and ploughing with oxen is considered a male task. Female-headed households that lack adult male labour therefore commonly have problems cultivating their land and typically resort to renting out much of their land to male-headed households with oxen, mostly with sharecropping contracts. The implication is the reverse-tenancy system with poor (often female-headed) households lacking oxen and male labour renting out their land to typically male-headed households with oxen and surplus male labour. Still, however, it is a frequent finding that land productivity on owner-operated land is lower for female-headed than male-headed households (Holden *et al.*, 2001; Bezabih *et al.*, 2016). Such households typically lacked oxen and male labour which were important for their farming ability.

Holden and Bezabih (2009) also found that land productivity on land sharecropped out by female-headed households was lower than land productivity on land sharecropped out by male-headed households. They attributed this productivity differential to female landlord households being less able to select efficient tenants and being more likely to rent out their land to inefficient in-law tenants, in line with anecdotal evidence that in-laws take control over land of female landlords. This is evidence of their tenure insecurity and weaker bargaining power and limited ability to screen, select and evict tenants before land certification was implemented in Ethiopia, contributing to lower land productivity and welfare losses for their households.

When it comes to inheritance of land within families, Holden and Tefera (2008) investigated this in Southern Ethiopia and found that the oldest son was most likely to inherit land, but also unmarried sons are likely to inherit land from their parents while daughters were much less likely to inherit land, even if they were unmarried. They also investigated the sharing of land for divorced persons and found that men were most likely to get all land and women were most likely to get no land upon divorce before the new land laws were passed. Polygamy is quite common in Southern Ethiopia. Holden and Tefera (2008) found that polygamous wives were likely to have some land of their own, but they were less likely to have participated in public information meetings about the land reform than monogamous wives.

12.4 Land Laws: Are They Ensuring Gender Equity?

Ethiopia introduced new land laws (proclamations) and regulations, first at federal level and then at regional level, allowing for some differentiation in the laws across regions, but without contradicting the federal land laws. These laws provided the basis for the land registration and certification reforms in each region and were also followed up by more detailed regional regulations. While land registration was implemented in the name of the head of household in Tigray region, joint registration of husbands and wives were implemented in the Amhara, Oromia and SNNP regions. In the SNNP region they also tried to include the pictures of husbands and wives in the household level certificates. Two important elements of these laws were the equal sharing of land by husband and wife upon divorce and the required consent from the spouse in case of renting part of the family land to outsiders.

Holden and Tefera (2008) found just after the implementation of joint land certification that most men and women expected to share the land equally upon divorce, which demonstrates a clear break with the tradition that men in most cases retain all the land. More than 60% of the wives also expected to keep the whole family land if the husband were to die. In the past it was common that in-laws took the land or required the widow to marry the brother of the late husband to be able to stay on the farm. We were told a story by local land administrators about a case where the widow refused to remarry within the family of the late husband and found another man and had a child with him. The in-laws then came and killed the newborn baby.

In SNNP region the land law was modified such that land brought into marriage by a person would also be individual property in the case of divorce. Since men traditionally inherit and wives upon marriage move to the husband's home, this modification of the law may render wives landless upon divorce and cause continued landlessness of women. However, the joint land certification process included the names of wives on the land certificates of married households, indicating that their husbands did not claim individual land rights even though they brought most of the land into their families. However, it remains uncertain how this will affect the next generation. It is possible that men will claim individual rights to land when marrying.

Kumar and Quisumbing (2015) concluded that the Family Law (Code) together with the land registration has contributed to more favourable outcomes for women in asset distribution after divorce with possible long-term distributional and welfare implications. They found that women's perceptions on the right of women to share land equally upon divorce has been strengthened from 1997 to 2009.

12.5 Is the Knowledge and Practice of the Law Granting Gender Equity?

Knowledge of and respect for the law are fundamentally important for laws to have an impact. For laws that are expected to influence within-household decision making it is important that this knowledge penetrates down to the household level and that household members understand and respect the law. It may take long time from a law of this kind is enacted until it is known and respected at the local level. Many laws or elements of the laws may never become well known or respected. Knowledge of and respect for the law is needed at all levels and especially among staff in the land administrations and the court systems dealing with land dispute cases.

A study in Oromia and SNNP regions of the early gender impact by Holden and Tefera (2008) provided baseline information about the position of women within households as well as their knowledge of the recent land laws regarding gendered land rights. About half of married men and women were aware of the new land laws and that land should be shared equally by husband and wife upon divorce; 35–64% (cross-community variation) of the wives and 32–53% of the men were aware that women had the right to deny their husband permission to rent out family land. The knowledge of other aspects of the law was poorer among both men and women. The joint land registration and certification may have contributed to this higher awareness of the gender aspects of the law. When asked whether men and women agreed with the joint certification of husbands and wives and equal sharing of land, 75–82% of the women and 70–82% of the men agreed to joint certification, and 68–87% of the wives and 53–77% of the husbands agreed with equal sharing of land upon divorce.

To what extent is the court system ruling according to the law in land dispute cases? 'It is those with mobile phones who win the cases in the courts', said a woman in a focus group discussion in Sashemene, Oromia Region (Holden and Tefera, 2008). Mobile phones may represent status but also influence and ability to communicate and connect to local administrations and court judges. Other women who had taken their lost cases from the kebele court to the district court and won the case, faced the problem that the administration at the kebele level did not help them enforce the decision of the district court so they did not get back their land despite the ruling (Holden and Tefera, 2008).

In our studies of land conflicts in the Oromia, SNNP and Tigray regions we hired law students to review many woreda court decisions regarding land disputes to identify the nature of such disputes and the decisions made by the judges.[2] One of the things they assessed was whether the court decisions were made according to the land laws. The students found that the law was not typically followed in many such cases. The law, and especially recent changes in the law, were typically not well communicated to or known about by local court judges. Even the knowledge of the land laws was very poor among kebele and woreda land administration representatives (Holden *et al.*, 2009; Holden and Ghebru 2016a; Holden *et al.*, 2016). In the case of Tigray, we found that this was good for female-headed households who were breaking the law and renting (sharecropping) out more than 50% of their land because they were not capable of managing the land themselves. There was confusion not only at the local level, but also at higher levels whether the land law restriction of not being allowed to rent out more than 50% of one's land applied to sharecropping as well as to fixed rent contracts. However, when we dug deeper into the sentiments of the different types of agents, land administration representatives were also more likely to rule that female-headed households not able to farm the land themselves should be allowed to rent out all of it without losing their land (Holden *et al.*, 2016). This shows that the law is not always followed, and this can even sometimes be to the advantage of women. These findings also show that there is a need for more training of land administrations and court judges so that they get updated on the content of the land laws and implementation rules that were changed and updated several times during the first ten years of implementation of land registration and certification.

12.6 Land Registration and Certification: First Stage and Gender Equity

The 1st Stage Land Registration and Certification (LR&C) started in 1998 in Tigray Region and was more than 80% completed by 1999 in the highlands of the region where smallholder agriculture dominates and most of the population lives, when the war with Eritrea broke out. The process was run without any donor support and was an extremely low-cost and participatory process with paper-based documentation and no use of computers. Neighbourhoods walked the fields together and demarcated land parcels and for every parcel the neighbouring parcel holders were registered and jointly agreed on the parcel borders. Areas were measured with local tools (rope). Parcels were organized under households in the registry and household level certificates were issued in the name of the household head, listing the plots, their size, location, land quality, and names of neighbour parcel owners. With husbands being heads of households, this system implied that most land was registered in the name of male heads and one may fear that this could lead to weaker land rights of women within male-headed households and through inheritance to more skewed and gender distribution of land.

Dokken (2015) assessed the land distribution of female-headed versus male-headed households after the 1st Stage LR&C in Tigray based on a stratified random sample of households and found that female-headed households had 23% less land on average than male-headed households. Holden and Tilahun (2020) made a similar calculation based on complete land registry data for 11 communities and found that female-headed households on average had 27% less land than male-headed households. On average, family size is smaller for female-headed households so when assessing land per capita the land per capita was 5–8% lower for female-headed than male-headed households.

In the Amhara, Oromia and SNNP regions, 1st Stage LR&C started from 2003–2004 and names of both husbands and wives were included on the land certificates. In SNNP, photos of husbands and wives were also included on the certificates. These changes were stimulated by a growing gender awareness and donor support in these regions. These interventions appear to have strengthened women's land rights and decision-power within households in these regions.

Melesse *et al.* (2018) assessed the effect of joint land certification on women's empowerment in the Amhara region. They constructed a comprehensive index to capture women's empowerment in multiple dimensions, being a combination of seven sub-indices. Joint land certification was positively correlated with the overall and six of the sub-indices indicating a strong association between joint certification and women's empowerment. The surprising finding was that the sub-index most closely related to land, involvement in land-related decisions, was not significantly correlated with joint land certification. They also found that uncertified women were less likely to be literate and lived further away from their parents than certified women. While the results from their cross-section data indicated that women were empowered in areas that had been certified compared to in uncertified areas, the empowerment indices were low in all areas, demonstrating that there is still a long way to go before women are equally empowered to men. However, it may take time for the effects to penetrate household decision making, which is largely influenced by cultural norms.

Holden and Tefera (2008) assessed the early impacts of land certification and found a tendency of increased involvement by wives in land-related decisions soon after the joint land certification had taken place in their study areas in Southern Ethiopia. Only 3–6% of men and women at that time (2007) believed that joint land certification would lead to more involvement of women in land-related decisions within households. In a follow-up study of the same sample by Holden and Bezu (2013, 2014) five years later, wives had become more involved in farm management decisions and particularly in crop choice and land rental decisions. They found a substantial improvement of women's empowerment over the period 2007–2012. Husbands who preferred the traditional weak position of women hindered the empowerment of their wives while more generous husbands[3] had more empowered wives who more actively participated in land-related decisions within the household. Holden and Bezu (2014) found that the proportion of wives who claim all their land rights increased from 41 to 72% from 2007 to 2012. They also found evidence of awareness effects and intra-village social process effects that jointly had contributed to strengthen the involvement of women in land-related decisions. This indicates that with time the effect of the land tenure reform on women's empowerment has increased. The extent of change varies from household to household and depends on personal and community characteristics.

Another finding in our studies in Southern Ethiopia were that the position of polygamous wives was strengthened by the land law and land registration and certification, in a process of negotiations. First, the husband should only have the name on the certificate with the first wife, while second and additional wives should have their own certificates without the name of the husband. The polygamous men refused to accept this, and it was agreed that their names should also be on the certificates with their additional wives. Later a rule was also introduced for the sharing of land in case a husband wanted to take another wife. He would then have to share his half of the land with the second wife without influencing the land share of his first wife. This law should reduce the incentives to marry additional wives and it is worth following up to study what has happened about the implementation of these laws.

12.7 What are the Productivity and Welfare Effects of Strengthened Land Rights for Women?

Holden and Ghebru (2016b) outline the relations between tenure reforms, tenure security and food security of households and some of the complexities of identifying these links. Quite a few studies have investigated the links between land certification, tenure security and land productivity and investment in Ethiopia. Holden *et al.*

(2009) used household farm panel data from Tigray and found that land certification had increased investment in tree planting and land certification and enhanced land productivity. Holden *et al.* (2011) showed that land certification had enhanced tenure security particularly for female-headed households who had become more willing to rent out their land. Holden and Ghebru (2013) showed that land certification had particularly enhanced the consumption welfare of female-headed households and Ghebru and Holden (2013) showed that this contributed to improved food security of their children as evidenced by an improvement in their body mass index.

Bezabih *et al.* (2016) used household farm panel data from the Amhara region and found that land certification also had enhanced tenure security, land rental market participation and land productivity, particularly so for female-headed households. Muchomba (2017) used household panel data from the four first regions that implemented 1st Stage LR&C and looked at male-headed households and whether it made a difference whether the head of households received certificates (Tigray region) or whether the spouses received joint certificates (Amhara, Oromia and SNNP regions). He assessed welfare effects in terms of household expenditures on healthcare, homegrown and purchased foods, clothing, and education. Among the interesting findings were that joint certification and perceived tenure security among women were positively associated with expenditure on clothing for women and girls and negatively for men and boys, pointing towards strengthened bargaining power of women. Another interesting finding was that head-only certification (Tigray) was associated negatively with the probability of illness which is consistent with the finding of Ghebru and Holden (2013) that certification enhanced the nutrition status of children in that region. Joint land certification was also positively associated with the value of homegrown foods which is consistent with the finding of Holden and Bezu (2013, 2014) that women got more involved in land-related decisions such as crop choice and land renting decisions. Women put more emphasis on self-sufficiency in food production and therefore were more reluctant to rent out land in Southern Ethiopia where joint certification was implemented. Muchomba (2017) found that expenditure on education was negatively associated with joint certification possibly indicating that women put less emphasis on education relative to that of men.

12.8 Land Registration and Certification: Second Stage and Gender Equity

The 2nd Stage LR&C has ensured close to equitable gender distribution of documented land rights. We do not know the degree to which this has had an impact on within-household decision making and such impacts are likely to vary a lot from no impact at all to a strong recognition and involvement of wives into household land-related decisions. We know little about the actual local processes regarding whose names were included on the land registries and certificates. There are cases in Tigray where there are alarming indications that names of persons who had been dead for many years appeared on some parcel level certificates and people received a bunch of certificates for their plots but were unable to tell which certificate belonged to each of their plots. However, I have no basis to assess how common such problems are. There is room for a lot more research on the real on-the-ground impacts of the 2nd Stage LR&C. I expect much heterogeneity even though the process has been standardized from the top down.[4] Pre-existing heterogeneities are likely to lead to heterogeneity in the interactions between the standardized top-down approach and local heterogeneities. For example, the quality and timing of 1st Stage LR&C may matter for the incremental effects of the 2nd Stage LR&C. The variation in the gender emphasis in the 1st Stage LR&C has implications for the incremental effect of the gender emphasis in the 2nd Stage LR&C. Some areas were never reached with 1st Stage LR&C, some areas experienced piloting of approaches that were closer in design to the 2nd Stage LR&C, such as pilot areas funded by SIDA, USAID, GTZ and FINNIDA, and other areas were exposed to 1st Stage and 2nd Stage LR&C reforms with varying distance apart and of different quality.

Holden and Tilahun (2020) combined 1st Stage and 2nd Stage LR data to assess gender distribution of land in Tigray where the distance between to two reforms is the largest. It is also an interesting case from a gender perspective because the 1st Stage LR&C only issued certificates and registered the land in the name of heads of households. Some have worried that such an approach could lead to more gender discrimination (Whitehead and Tsikata, 2003; Joireman, 2008; Lavers, 2017). The 2nd Stage LR registered all holders and issued parcel-level certificates and by combining 1st and 2nd Stage LR data from the same communities in Tigray, Holden and Tilahun (2020) were able to assess the extent to which male household heads registered the land only in their own name as that was done in the 1st Stage LR. Based on complete land registry data from 11 municipalities (*tabias*) and 31,500 farms they found in the 2nd Stage LR that 48.8% of the land was registered to women and with little variation across communities. This may be a result of the top-down emphasis in the 2nd Stage LR to include especially wives but also other household members in the parcel-level land registries. It could, however, also be influenced by the relative strong role of women in communities in Tigray that also may be due to women's active participation in the armed struggle against the Derg regime. Lavers (2017) also notes that the previous ruling party, Ethiopian People's Democratic Revolutionary Front (EPRDF) while fighting against the Derg, emphasized enhancement of women's rights, and promoted land registration to improve women's tenure security and land access. It is difficult to separate the effect from land registration and certification from other parallel processes that have strengthened women's positions in the Ethiopian society. Donors, media, women's associations, political parties, government bodies, civil society more broadly, and the growing awareness and acceptance in the minds of Ethiopian men and women are all likely to have had an influence in one way or another.

12.9 Future Challenges

Continued rapid population growth in rural areas is a major challenge to future land access for all in Ethiopia. Landlessness is growing and farm sizes shrinking (Holden and Tilahun, 2020). This tends to erode the constitutional right of all rural residents without another livelihood option to access land for subsistence. With the recent land laws also stipulating minimum farm sizes, this also restricts inheritance rights of children living on small farms. It also restricts the opportunity to share land equally among spouses upon divorce. Co-management of land among divorced parents and children on small farms is also challenging. The result may be disguised fragmentation.

Given the growing landlessness and inheritance rules and the need for alternative livelihoods for youth, we may wonder whether women are at a disadvantage in non-farm employment. Recent studies of a large sample of resource-poor rural youth that have been eligible to join youth business groups and have been allocated rehabilitated communal lands have female members that on average have fewer assets, lower incomes and less education than male members (Holden and Tilahun, 2019). They are also much less likely to own a mobile phone and to become group leaders or group board members (Holden and Tilahun, 2018). This shows that young women in Ethiopia continue to be disadvantaged and are among the most resource-poor and vulnerable. There is a need for more targeted policies to give them equal opportunities in the ongoing rural as well as rural-urban transformation processes.

The recent dramatic political and military conflict that erupted in November 2020 in Tigray Region between the central Government and the Tigray People's Liberation Front (TPLF) was strongly influential from 1991 to 2018, when Abij Ahmed became Prime Minister. It has had an enormous impact on the rural households living in this part of Ethiopia. At the time of writing this chapter more than 50,000 refugees have crossed the border to Sudan and there is a high likelihood that the outcome will be a long civil war and political instability. With locust swarms having caused great damage to the recent harvest, and supply and communication lines being blocked due to the conflict, the civilian population is suffering and is in urgent need of help from outside. Ethnic conflicts are on the rise in several parts of the country and threaten the political stability and strong economic growth that has been achieved in the last 20 years, and which resulted in large welfare improvements with land reforms playing an important role in this process. It is very sad to see how some stupid decisions by political leaders in a short period of time can create so much damage with long-term negative effects for the people they were given the authority to take care of.

Endnotes

[1] *Gult* rights to land were given to the ruling elite for their loyal service and gave them the right to impose taxes on those cultivating this land. The *gult* right does not include the right to cultivate but a *gult* holder may have cultivation rights (*rist* rights) for part of the *gult* land.

[2] Men take up almost all positions in local land administrations and court systems in Ethiopia. There have been attempts to include a minimum number of women in the community level Land Administration Committees in relation to the implementation of land registration and certification based on such requirements being included in the implementation rules.

[3] We had attitude questions which revealed a lot of local variation among local men related to their wives becoming more involved in household decision making.

[4] There is some variation in implementation approaches as well, depending on who the donor is, regional law variations, alternative technical and administrative solutions chosen.

References

Adal, Y. (2002) *Review of Landholding Systems and Policies in Ethiopia under the Different Regimes*. Ethiopian Economic Policy Research Institute Working Paper, Addis Ababa, Ethiopia.

Alemu, T. (1999) Land tenure and soil conservation: Evidence from Ethiopia. PhD dissertation, Göteborg University, Göteborg, Sweden.

Bauer, D.F. (1973) Land, leadership and legitimacy among the Inderta Tigray of Ethiopia. PhD dissertation, University of Rochester, Rochester, NY, USA.

Bezabih, M., Holden, S. and Mannberg, A. (2016) The role of land certification in reducing gaps in productivity between male-and female-owned farms in rural Ethiopia. *Journal of Development Studies*, 52(3), 360–376.

Bruce J. (1976) Land reform planning and indigenous communal tenure: A case study of the Chiguraf Gwoses in Tigray, Ethiopia. PhD dissertation, University of Wisconsin-Madison, Madison, WI, USA.

Cohen, J.M. (1974) Ethiopia: A survey on the existence of a feudal peasantry. *Journal of Modern African Studies*, 12(4), 665–672.

Deininger, K., Ali, D.A., Holden, S. and Zevenbergen, J. (2008) Rural land certification in Ethiopia: Process, initial impact, and implications for other African countries. *World Development*, 36(10), 1786–1812.

Deininger, K. and Jin, S. (2006) Tenure security and land-related investment: Evidence from Ethiopia. *European Economic Review*, 50(5), 1245–1277.

Dokken, T. (2015) Allocation of land tenure rights in Tigray: How large is the gender bias? *Land Economics*, 91(1), 106–125.

Ghebru, H. and Holden, S.T. (2013) *Links between Tenure Security and Food Security: Evidence from Ethiopia*. CLTS Working Paper No. 2/2013. Center for Land Tenure Studies, Norwegian University of Life Sciences, Ås, Norway.

Holden, S.T. and Bezabih, M. (2009) Gender and land productivity on rented land in Ethiopia. In: Holden, S.T., Otsuka, K. and Place, F.M. (Eds), *The Emergence of Land Markets in Africa: Impacts on Poverty, Equity, and Efficiency*. Routledge, London, pp. 179–196.

Holden, S.T. and Bezu, S. (2013) *Joint Land Certification and Intra-Household Decision-Making: Towards Empowerment of Wives?* CLTS Working Paper No. 13/2013. Centre for Land Tenure Studies, Norwegian University of Life Sciences, Ås, Norway.

Holden, S.T. and Bezu, S. (2014) *Joint Land Certification, Gendered Preferences, and Land-Related Decisions: Are Wives Getting More Involved?* CLTS Working Paper No. 6/2014. Centre for Land Tenure Studies, Norwegian University of Life Sciences, Ås, Norway.

Holden, S.T. and Tefera, T. (2008) *From Being Property of Men to Becoming Equal Owners? Early Impacts of Land Registration and Certification on Women in Southern Ethiopia*. UN-Habitat, Nairobi, Kenya.

Holden, S.T. and Tilahun, M. (2018) Gender Digital Divide and Youth Business Group Leadership. *CLTS Working Paper No. 5/2018.* Centre for Land Tenure Studies, Norwegian University of Life Sciences, Ås, Norway.

Holden, S.T. and Tilahun, M. (2019) Gender Assessment of Youth Business Groups: Female Participation and Characteristics. *CLTS Working Paper No. 6/2019.* Centre for Land Tenure Studies, Norwegian University of Life Sciences, Ås, Norway.

Holden, S.T. and Tilahun, M. (2020) Farm size and gender distribution of land: Evidence from Ethiopian land registry data. *World Development*, 130, 104926.

Holden, S.T. and Yohannes, H. (2002) Land redistribution, tenure insecurity, and intensity of production: A study of farm households in Southern Ethiopia. *Land Economics*, 78(4), 573–590.

Holden, S., Bezu, S. and Tilahun, M. (2016) *How Pro-Poor Are Land Rental Markets in Ethiopia?* CLTS Report No. 1/2016. Centre for Land Tenure Studies, Norwegian University of Life Sciences, Ås, Norway.

Holden, S.T., Deininger, K. and Ghebru, H. (2009) Impacts of low-cost land certification on investment and productivity. *American Journal of Agricultural Economics*, 91(2), 359–373.

Holden, S.T., Deininger, K. and Ghebru, H. (2010a) Impact of land registration and certification on land border conflicts in Ethiopia. Annual Conference on Land Policy and Administration, 26–27 April, Washington, DC, USA.

Holden, S.T., Deininger, K. and Ghebru, H. (2011) Tenure insecurity, gender, low-cost land certification and land rental market participation in Ethiopia. *Journal of Development Studies*, 47(1), 31–47.

Holden, S.T. and Ghebru, H. (2013) Welfare impacts of land certification in Tigray, Ethiopia. In: Holden, S. T., Otsuka, K. and Deininger, K. (Eds), *Land Tenure Reform in Asia and Africa – Assessing Impacts on Poverty and Natural Resource Management.* Palgrave Macmillan, London, UK, pp. 137–161.

Holden, S.T. and Ghebru, H. (2016a) Land rental market legal restrictions in Northern Ethiopia. *Land Use Policy*, 55, 212–221.

Holden, S.T. and Ghebru, H. (2016b) Land tenure reforms, tenure security and food security in poor agrarian economies: Causal linkages and research gaps. *Global Food Security*, 10, 21–28.

Holden, S.T., Otsuka, K. and Place, F.M. (Eds) (2010b) *The Emergence of Land Markets in Africa: Impacts on Poverty, Equity, and Efficiency*. Routledge, London, UK.

Holden, S. T., Shiferaw, B. and Pender, J. (2001) Market imperfections and land productivity in the Ethiopian highlands. *Journal of Agricultural Economics*, 52(3), 53–70.

Joireman, S.F. (2008) The mystery of capital formation in Sub-Saharan Africa: Women, property rights and customary law. *World Development*, 36(7), 1233–1246.

Kumar, N. and Quisumbing, A.R. (2015) Policy reform toward gender equality in Ethiopia: Little by little the egg begins to walk. *World Development*, 67, 406–423.

Lavers, T. (2017) Land registration and gender equality in Ethiopia: How state–society relations influence the enforcement of institutional change. *Journal of Agrarian Change*, 17(1), 188–207.

Melesse, M.B., Dabissa, A. and Bulte, E. (2018) Joint land certification programmes and women's empowerment: Evidence from Ethiopia. *Journal of Development Studies*, 54(10), 1756–1774.

Muchomba, F.M. (2017) Women's land tenure security and household human capital: Evidence from Ethiopia's land certification. *World Development*, 98, 310–324.

Weldu, A. (2017) Chiguraf goses: An evolved land-share land tenure system in Enderta Province. *Journal of Social Sciences*, 3(2), 113–119.

Whitehead, A. and Tsikata, D. (2003) Policy discourses on women's land rights in sub–Saharan Africa: The implications of the return to the customary. *Journal of Agrarian Change*, 3(1–2), 67–112.

13 The Paradox of Islamic Land Governance and Gender Equality

M. Siraj Sait*[1] and M. Adil Sait[2]
[1]*Royal Docks School of Business and Law, University of East London, London, UK;* [2]*Department of Geography and Environment, London School of Economics and Political Science, London, UK*

13.1 Introduction: Land Governance and Islamic Land Perspectives

Land governance perspectives have been evolving over the last two decades and more. As Borras and Franco (2010, p. 2) note, in their discussion on contemporary land discourse and the issue of developing pro-poor land policies:

> The term and notion of land governance has gained currency within mainstream agencies in recent years, and generally means the most efficient way of administration of land issues, such as cadastres, land titling, and so on (see, for example, FAO 2006; but see Palmer 2007 for an excellent overview). As generally understood today, land governance is therefore a matter of technical and administrative governance, rather than a matter of democratizing access to and control over wealth and power.

This perspective on land governance emphasizes the role of state and non-state actors in the regulation of the functioning of land management practices rendered in the Foucauldian concept of 'governmentality' (Dean, 2017). Indeed, the concept of governance has emerged by way of research on institutional frameworks and mechanism and understandings of how these 'rules of the game' (see North, 1990) impact economic growth and development outcomes. More generally, governance mechanisms have come to be critical to policy framings and invariably to the success of social and economic interventions (Rhodes, 2007; Bevir, 2010). Hence, the concept of global land governance has stemmed from the objective of implementing land policies to improve tenure security, and access to land rights through strengthening institutional capacities (Palmer *et al.*, 2009; Deininger *et al.*, 2011). This prompts a focus on the 'continuum of land rights' encompassing formal and statutory tenure regimes as well as faith-based, customary and informal land practices that for a variety of reasons remain unrecognized (Payne, 2001; Lemmen *et al.*, 2015).

Land governance is drawn from both formal and informal systems and processes, with governmental and non-state actors accommodating faith- based perspectives and actors where they exist. Given the size of the Muslim population – for example, more than one-third of Africa – and its long historical engagement with land issues, the corpus of Islamic land law as well as the implementation framework keeps resurfacing. The relationship between Islamic and secular land laws as well as Islamic and generic land governance is competitive, volatile and fractal. Thus, Islamic law principles can occur within Islamic or universal governance, for example, customary, informal, or alternate systems. Equally,

*Corresponding author: S.Sait@uel.ac.uk

 Land Governance and Gender: The Tenure-Gender Nexus in Land Management and Land Policy (ed. U.E. Chigbu)
DOI: 10.1079/9781789247664.0013

an Islamic faith-based governance framework can absorb customary and secular norms. Islamic land laws adapt custom as one of its acknowledged sources. The examples of Kenya, Tanzania, Nigeria, Senegal and Somalia below demonstrate the various combinations and manifestations of these trade-offs and negotiations. Universal and Islamic laws are not neat categories but are effervescent and reforming, conjuring hybrid and multilayered models. The outcome is legal pluralism and continuum of land rights evoked though a responsive and embracing governance approach that matures beyond labels and political choices, responding to the needs of the communities seeks to improve access to land through fit for purpose land systems, administration, management and policy.

Examples of extant Islamic land practices are often found when an informed query is undertaken, but the yield is not exclusively Islamic but coexists with other customary, informal and statutory regimes in an evolving 'web of land tenure'. Whether identified as sociohistoric residual practices or simply as custom rather than faith-based concepts, Islamic land tenure and governance begs the question of relevance. To what extent are Islamic principles capable of being developed into pro-poor, gender and age responsive, professional land tools that can be deployed supplementally in the pursuit of achieving the global land rights agenda, as prompted by international human rights norms or the Sustainable Development Agenda? Yet, the quest for Islamic land law and governance and governance seeks not simple pragmatic land indicators and solutions, but adopts sociohistorical memories, evokes spiritual and social meanings of land, and responds to community priorities often dismissed as archaic and counter-intuitive remnants in a modern world. The study of a unifying Islamic land paradigm, mapping influence of faith-based land practices onto governance patterns has only recently emerged through theoretical and applied research on land rights across the Muslim world. As Sait and Lim's seminal work, *Land, Law and Islam*, notes (2006, pp. 4–5), this endeavour cannot be simplified or generalized:

> Resident in over 57 Muslim-majority countries (member states of the Organization of Islamic Conference, OIC), or as significant minorities in the West and from China to Russia, there are an estimated 1.2 billion Muslims amongst the world's population. Though Muslims see themselves as a universal community (Umma), they are, in fact, divided into several nationalities and, contrary to popular assumptions, only 20 per cent of Muslims reside in the Arab world. They include many different ethnic groups and speak dozens of languages, including Arabic, Turkish, Urdu, and Persian. The lived experiences of Muslims – reflecting various socio-economic conditions, political affiliations and religious practices – cannot be essentialized or simplified.

Land debates in both Muslim communities and societies arise out of combinations of specific faith-based practices, cultural norms, and historical processes leading to regional and context-specific understandings of Islamic land dimensions. Beyond well-documented Islamic perspectives on governance and administration (see Iqbal and Lewis, 2009; Drechsler, 2013), there has been insufficient examination of how Islamic land perspectives intersect with the relatively new land governance frameworks. For example, in the case of Muslim women's land rights – in pursuit of gender equality and women's empowerment – discussion on Islamic and customary practices has focused primarily on property rights, inheritance and interplays between women's civil and political rights and socioeconomic rights. Missing is an exploration of how they relate to institutionalized land governance regimes – a notable gap in the current literature (Sait, 2013b, 2015). Thus, this article focuses on the complex interrelationship between Islamic land laws, contemporary land governance and gender equality debates.

In deconstructing Islamic land perspectives to reframe 'Islamic' land governance evolving Islamic perspectives come into play. This chapter first gives a background to the influence of Islamic land practices on contemporary land policy framed through its relationship colonial land administration, followed by an examination of its interaction with customary and statutory land rights regimes, in the broad context of Islam land debates and practices across diverse African contexts. This then leads to a discussion on the critical role of gender in understanding the operation of Islamic land perspective in practice, as well as the need for 'Islamic' land governance perspectives to situate contemporary realities in the context of 'legal pluralism'. Attention is then paid to the specific role of Islamic land practices in diverse African countries – using the examples of Kenya, Tanzania, Nigeria, Senegal and Somalia. Together these perspectives highlight that even though there is no stand-alone 'Islamic land governance', in many ways Islamic land principles, tools and practices do continue to hold influence among Muslim communities juxtaposed with semi-formalized land governance systems. Yet, paradoxically, 'Islamic' land perspectives are not easily disentangled from their contexts, significantly impacting on their application and use as in the gender and land debate.

13.2 Placing Islamic Land Perspectives into Historical Context

The nature and scope of Islamic land perspectives can only be explained through the diversity of experiences and culture as an outcome of their precolonial and colonial legacies. This marks the divergence between uninhibited modern land law drafting and the Islamic and customary norms look back to the origins and sociohistorical meanings to validate their choices and notions of success. Across the Muslim world, Islamic pasts have shaped contemporary approaches to land such as in Egypt (Ottoman), Iran (Safavid), Pakistan (Mughal), Nigeria (Sokoto Caliphate), Indonesia (Aceh Sultanate) and Kyrgyztan (Kokand Khanate). In each case, land was a priority and an integral part of governance structures. Islam interacted variously with local formulations of land and governance; often suffusing custom (*adat*) and Islamic law (*Sharia*) and seeking reforms (Dupret *et al.*, 1999). In the large Ottoman Empire various Islamic land laws and Kanun (secular laws) blended through policies, codified much later into the 1858 Ottoman Land Code which recognized private, public, communal, empty and endowment lands widely constructed even beyond Ottoman territories for centuries. However, contemporary Islamic land consciousnesses are modified by their complex encounters with colonialism. By the mid-19th century, along with its contemporaries, Habsburg Austria and Romanov Russia, Ottoman and Muslim states were losing out to new colonial powers Britain, France and, after 1870, Germany. Though Turkey itself avoided being colonized, many of its territories and that of other Muslim regimes were occupied. As Robinson points out (1999b, p. 398): 'By the 1920s the British Empire embraced substantially more than half the Muslim peoples of the world. For much of the twentieth century Britain was the greatest influence over their development.'

While modernizing land regimes in their new territories, the British creatively and selectively sought legitimacy from the Muslim populace and support of Muslim elites by accommodating Islamic principles or Muslim practices in part. Colonial administrators struck a variety of deals with Muslim power brokers, over the continuation of Islamic land principles, protection of Islamic practices as 'custom' or their absorption into colonial laws to suit their interests. While the British highlighted Islamic individual tenure in Kenya, they preferred Muslim customary law in Nigeria (Sait, 2013a). Most colonial regimes let Islamic systems operate as supplementary, informal, or private law. For example, the Italians in Somaliland considered Italian law to be supreme but in practice yielded to a combination of Sharia and custom (see Contini, 1969).

Even France, with its uncompromisingly secularist ideology at home, projected itself as a 'Muslim power' in Africa (Robinson, 1999a) and a successor to the Ottomans. For example, Aristide Vallon, the French Governor of Senegal (1826–1897) and a proponent of assimilation, saw Islam as private, custom, and not openly challenging to French culture and laws: taming Islam was an important civilizational and political message. In practice, both custom and Islamic law (the *Maliki Risala*) were the basis of customary land law and were accepted by the colonial administration, the *Chefs de Canton* who had wide discretion in dealing with land matters (Meek, 1946). The French were more tolerant of Islamic cities and land tenures in Morocco and Tunisia, but not in Algeria where they repudiated Islamic tenures and nationalized endowments (*waqf* or *Habous*) (Powers, 1989). The divergence in colonial responses to Islamic urban systems and land administrations was shifting political and revenue considerations. Despite contributions of Islamic land practices to improving property rights, the colonial roots of land inequality arose from comparative cross-colonial multivariate frames (Frankema, 2010). The twin objectives of the colonial land enterprise were invariably the modification of Islamic land laws and the dismantling of the Islamic governance structures.

Islamic cities and land relations were interrupted or modified through colonialism. For example, when the Europeans scrambled for Africa in the 1880s, a formidable obstacle to their control and transformation of its people and land tenure system was Islamic. British, French, Dutch, Italian colonizers and, to a lesser extent, Germans, Spanish and the Belgians initially adapted or tolerated earlier Muslim and customary urban and land policies. Acemoglu *et al.* (2001) argue that European colonial responses to Mughal, Inca and Aztec empires differed due to a variety of factors, particularly native population density and the efforts needed and risks to be taken to bring about radical changes. However, over time they wrestled with obdurate Ottoman legacies and left a varying but deep imprint of their modernizing influence on Muslim urbanism that was generally continued by post-colonial states. In China, the Qing dynasty (1644–1912) allowed the operation of Islamic land law in Xinjiang and other Muslim-populated areas until it was secularized by the communist regime (Cassel, 2012). In each case, the methodology was to immobilize the local governance structures which then were helpless in resisting assaults on authentic practices.

In the communist bloc, Pravilova (2011) outlines how the Russians pursued communist ideology and Western conception of property rights purging 'Islamic models of landholding as a deviation', thereby dismantling Islamic tenures in Central Asia and the Caucuses. Landa (1995) refers to how the Soviets explained their forms of state property (*kolkhoz*) and family or community property (*avlod*) to Muslims as corresponding to Islamic concepts of land tenure and social justice. The Dutch East India Company (Verenigde Oostindische Compagnie; VOC) created the dualism of customary (*adat*) (which contained Islamic principles) and Western land laws in Indonesia through their Dutch Indies Agrarian Law (*Agrarische Wet*). However, the Basic Agrarian Law 1960 sought to address this dualism by considering land as a 'gift from god' and requiring *adat* needs to conform to Islamic law. Islamic land principles themselves could be interpreted and managed selectively to serve colonial economics pursuits, but the land governance that sought to promote an equitable, fair and ethical framework remained a challenge.

Muslim conquerors, traders, missionaries and scholars spread the highly sophisticated Islamic land framework, collating customary norms and modernist reforms creating hybrid model and legal pluralism through successive colonial waves. African countries – such as Kenya, Tanzania, Nigeria, Senegal and Somalia – engineered innovative compromises that camouflaged Islamic land rights within secularization, informalization and modernization of land practices (see Sait, 2013a). Often the surviving tenures lost their Islamic label but not their objective or character. Hanretta (2009) argues that conventional research methods, derived from colonial misunderstandings, prevented an appreciation of Muslim intellectual history and its contributions in Africa. As in the discredited trope to find the 'Islamic' city in Urban studies, the land researchers tied themselves in knots to find a single uniform experience of 'Islamic' land perspectives, oblivious to its understated influence through a mixture of faith-based, custom-driven, and adaptive statutory regimes. Islamic land dimensions often sustained Islamic land governance through interwoven narratives on Islamic land practices and community led outcomes. Islamic land governance itself turned local with religious and customary actors often remaining unrecognized under the radar of formal systems. The extent to which faith-based actors were excluded or accepted depended not only on their agency and power, but on whether they could persuade the modern land systems of their continuing relevance or at least – where they asserted symbolism or tradition – their harmlessness to vital land rights objectives.

13.3 Islamic Land Law and the Gender Paradox

Islamic land law is constituted through derivations of urban planning priorities, land use principles, architectural preferences, gender codes, social structures, dispute mechanisms and Islamic land inheritance (Ben-Hamouche, 2011). Supporters as well as detractors of Islamic law note the cauldron of Islamic land law, property rights and gender equality. Abu-Lughod

(1987) in her critique of Orientalist constructions of the 'Islamic city' appreciated the symbiotic relationship between Islamic law and custom, through her historical evaluation of Muslim urbanism. Abu-Lughod (1987, p. 172) writes that the three distinctive elements that 'set in motion the processes that give rise to Islamic cities' are the legal and spatial construction of neighbourhoods based on class and economic differentials; the system of property rights that limited the role of the State in land use and disputes; and gender segregation accompanying codes on women's conduct. Abu-Lughod (1971) also wrote extensively about the Muslim world through a comparative historical lens, explain and examined the sociopolitical and cultural forces driving historic cities such as Cairo as living resilient entities. The Islamic land scholarship failed to identify an appropriate sociohistorical methodology.

Kostof (1991) and others focused on property law, society, and gender in demystifying Islamic urbanism. Islamic land laws were intimately connected to Islamic urban planning. Yet, sceptics such as Kuran (2003) argue that notwithstanding the positive aspects of Islamic law, the decline of Middle East economies was not due to colonialism, location, geography or cultural attitudes, but weaknesses in Islamic institutions. According to Kuran, three bottlenecks kept back progress of Muslim communities: Islamic law of inheritance inhibiting capital accumulation; the lack of an Islamic legal concept of corporation undermining business enterprise; and the ubiquitous *waqf* (endowment), which locked vast resources into unproductive organizations for the delivery of social services. Further, Kuran's (2012) update prompted contrasting reviews popular press (Sardar, 2011). In contrast, Chapra (2008) argues that a diversity of Muslim perspectives – secular, religious, intellectual and political – influenced Islamic law. While Kuran does not blame Islam or deny that Islamic law worked sufficiently well until the latter Ottoman period, he interrogates how Islamic law works in the modern world. Kuran's theories are not about land or even Middle East's economic competitiveness, but the workings of Islamic inheritance, land tenures and institutions in practice.

Since the 1980s, critical re-engagement with the modern manifestations and implications of tradition and religion in the Muslim built environments has increased. The arguments have moved beyond debunking Orientalist essentialism and debates over whether or not an 'Islamic city' prototype exists and offer fresh perspectives on various themes from various Muslim centres (Raymond, 1994). Among the hundreds of researchers are distinguished contributions from Hakim (1994), Akbar and Shaw (1988), Ben-Hamouche (2009), Omer (2008), Elsheshtawy (2008), Bianca (2000), O'Meara (2007) and Bennison and Gascoigne (2007) – which collectively reflect upon the diversity of themes, geography and multidisciplinary engagement with the role and influence of Islamic perspectives on society. From architects and planners, to lawyers, anthropologists, geographers, archaeologists, economists, sociologists, political scientists, land professionals, urban historians, gender specialists and youth experts, contemporary discourse has been shaped by diverse voices.

In contrast to the abundant raw material on Muslim urbanism, legal scholarship on Islam and land has been scarce, despite some valuable inputs from other fields. The term 'Islamic land governance' is not even recognized by google. This gap seems to be driven by the predisposition that no sufficiently delineated body of 'Islamic land law' exists independently of Muslim practices as custom. Islamic land governance seems a non-starter since the relatively land governance has not explored the origins or the continued relevance of custom and practice in Muslim settings. A key question is whether land customs or urban systems of Muslims can be studied without reference to Islamic land law and practices. It is demonstrable that Islamic land law has emerged as a distinct field which cannot always be subsumed within an all-encompassing 'custom, informal and alternative' category. As Sait (2013a) writes, in the context of African countries, where one-third of the continent's population are Muslims (p. 92):

> No country in Africa – or in any other part of the world – can claim to follow Islamic land law exclusively. Customary norms and successive waves of colonialism, modernisation and reform have created legal pluralism and hybridity in Muslim countries too. Yet no country with significant Muslim populations is without the influence of Islamic land laws or principles, official or informal, however varied, or mutated.

> As Islamic land law evolved in Africa it often interlocked with customary, colonial and statutory systems pollinating its distinctive concepts that are discernible even today.

Modern law reforms or codes have changed the label, visibility or format of Islamic land law but have not extinguished it. The author's own experience with countries such as Afghanistan, Iraq and Somalia demonstrate that secular interventions in land matters that marginalize could miss key opportunities in advancing innovative, pro-poor and gendered land tools (Sait, 2013b). Property and land rights of Muslim women cannot be disconnected from discussions over Islamic land law. For example, Sait and Lim (2006) proposed a pioneering 'compensatory' gender equality approach linking various property flow systems to make up for lesser Islamic inheritance shares for women. The reasoning was based on the case that even though inheritance shares for Muslim women are lesser by *Qur'anic* decree there is no prohibition under Islamic law for women to acquire equal, or greater, property rights in other ways.

With reference to Muslim women's land and property rights, two significant observations emerge from the literature. First, key Islamic legal materials generally support Muslim women's right to acquire, hold, use, administer and dispose of property and her home irrespective of marital status. Second, Muslim women have historically exercised property and land rights, supported by law, state and legal courts and institutions. However, a gap between the Islamic theory of female property ownership and Muslim customary practice often persists. For example, case materials on joint marital property and matrilineal communities rework jurisprudential possibilities and gender stereotypes on Islamic inheritance rules are a key mechanism providing access to land for a broad range of beneficiaries (Sait, 2013a, 2015). However, where women's land rights through Islam can be elaborated, the absence of an appropriate land governance often renders its implementation toothless.

There is no practitioners' guide to pluralist Islam land law with readymade technical plans for project design and programme implementation (Sait, 2008). To do so would be premature because Islamic land tools need development, debate, and discussion before they can be scaled up and replicated. As Sait (2013b) notes, a series of Islamic land tools have been deployed in post-conflict contexts:

> In some cases, Islamic mechanisms are straightforward and enjoy sufficient demand and the necessary support. However, other Islamic tools are complicated, and a series of activities and outputs may be needed before the tools are ready for implementation. It might be necessary to clarify and disseminate doctrines, convert them into policy or laws, create institutions or procedures, generate capacity through training, and develop strategies for design, implementation, monitoring, and evaluation. The use of Islamic tools may involve a wide range of stakeholders, from policy makers and land professionals to representatives of civil society, including women, researchers and trainers, experts on Islamic land law, and traditional Muslim scholars, as the Global Land Tool Network is pursuing.

Despite the lack of alignment between Islamic land perspectives and contemporary land governance, there is a relatively well-developed understanding by scholars of the scope, nature and role of Islamic law in shaping land, property and urban development. Islamic land law has been an evolving area of research, mediating its relationship with customary and statutory regimes. As the wider discourse evidence, Islamic perspectives have been utilized and discussed in a variety of ways: from secular, religious, intellectual and political, to a more broad-based multidisciplinary engagement that departs from faith determination of tenure to connected to choices and quest for land rights in community and society. Muslim communities often fall back upon faith-based informal principles and local governance as default – both consciously and unconsciously – for improving access to land and property but also sustaining coherence and continuity. The cultural hybridity of Islamic law poses specific problems regarding how to interpret and assess the potential use and abuse of faith in the context of land rights and tenure security, especially given the predominance of gendered features and norms at the root of Islamic practices.

Although women's land and property rights are not inherently disadvantaged by Islamic land law, they are conceived of differently in the context of inheritance, marital property and ownership, and require a disentangling of patriarchal norms to arrive at gender equality outcomes. Yet, it can also offer marginalized groups of Muslim women key opportunities to access land rights that otherwise many are not open to them given wider societal issues (Tempra *et al.*, 2018). Though Islamic land governance framework to materialize women's land rights seems like the answer to a prayer, there are three inherent challenges to this project. First, women's property rights claims often occur in patriarchal settings where customary or traditional authorities potentially favour minimalist or even gender-deprecating interpretation. Second, a gender-responsive land governance for equal or equitable land rights is predicated on greater female participation in decision making or arbitration of land rights. Finally, Islamic land governance must be a choice among competing mediums for Muslim women pursuing their Islamic rights rather than Islamic land governance complicating the quest for Islamic rights. As Muslim women have learnt, there is no natural correlation between Islamic rights and Islamic land governance, and sometimes their rights are better realized through formal land governance.

13.4 Legal Pluralism, African Land Law and the Role of Islamic Land Governance

Islamic land concepts interact with modern sociolegal conventions at multiple levels, framed through legal pluralism. Defined as a general theory of norms and legality, legal pluralism emphasizes the coexistence of different sets of rules, practices and norms that often emerge from varied historical and social interactions (see Twining, 2009). Islamic principles, practices and approaches have had a dominant influence on customary practices as well as governance models, variously clashing or being appropriated by nation states seeking to administer their own land policies. The nature of interactions between colonial powers and their subjects – with its large geographical, historical, and cultural variations – proposed not only revision of the varied legal frameworks, but also modernist land administration systems, many of which continued to persist even when independence was achieved (Merry, 1991). This conflict between different legal frameworks continued but the ideas of Islamic land law were folded into consensual local governance with Islamic values and multi-stakeholder relationships (Sait and Lim, 2006).

In African countries generally, Islamic land law informed distinctive customary practices with its faith-based land tenure contributing to legal pluralism, hybrid models and informal dispute mechanisms across the continent (Sait, 2013a). For example, in colonial coastal Kenya, Swahili customs Mijikenda (Pouwels, 2002; Loimeier and Seesemann, 2006), with Islamic judges (*Qadis*) playing an institutional role in ensuring demarcation and transfer of individually owned commercial and residential land. Yet, due to the interrelationship between the Islamic principles and African customary practices, the British colonial administration failed to recognize their unique land rights and practices as they did not conform to norms of Islamic land law seen in other parts of the Muslim world (Ghai and McAuslan, 1970). This shift to secularization led to the eclipse of Islamic land actors such as judges (*qadis*), religious leaders (*imams*) and endowment managers (*wakf*), and land came to be controlled by the State. However, religious actors often joined the ranks of village chiefs and administrators were possible.

Colonial administrators also co-opted Islamic property regimes to suit their own interests in controlling land. For example, they acknowledged the principles of revival of dead land (*mewat*) – which under Islamic land law can be acquired by the state or individuals for the purpose of revitalization if unused for 12 years (Cooper, 1980). Other rationales were also part of the decision to send indigenous groups to 'native reserves' – while Arabs and Swahilis, governed by Islamic law were able to register land and property rights. Racism – in the form of preference for the Arab or Persian (*Shirazi*) class and later Indian migrants was key to the fraught and piecemeal transformation of the region's land tenure regime (Leo, 1984). British colonial efforts often led the separation of Islamic and customary tenure from the formal system with complicated results (Hamidin, 2000; Brennan, 2008). One of them was that customary tenure lost its sanctity and became transactional, and the Islamic land governance was diluted and twisted more easily to newly created colonial land managers in the garb of customary institutions.

The experience in Tanzania of Islamic land law has been novel – with the designation of all land as 'crown' or public land under the German and then British colonial administrations (James, 1971). This focus on government centralization of land through 'rights of occupancy' rather than private property – and post-independence national ideology of *ujumaa* (pulling together) reflected a different use of Islamic land law and African customary practices to support socialism (Westerlund, 1980; Yusuf, 1991). While customary tenure was recognized, a dualistic system of land governance evolved, whereby rights granted by the state were functionally superior to customary rights in land. Islamic law was formally displaced in Tanzania – with the de-recognition of Western and Islamic individual property rights – but Islamic land principles were more broadly blended with customary practices. For example, the Sultan of Zanzibar held the right to confiscate unused land under Islamic land law, the Tanzanian government gives perpetual, transferable occupational land rights subject to caveats surrounding misuse or abandonment of land (Okello, 1967; Lodhi, 1986).

Islamic law has been viewed as a vital source of land law in Tanzania – particularly Zanzibar – with the continuation of some tenure states such as Islamic endowments (*waqf*), with accommodations and protections for Islamic inheritance practices if land is in productive use (Fair, 2001). Although rights of individual occupancy transfer are innovative, under Tanzanian land law these rights are recognized when they are both registered and approved. Although private property is not recognized, an active property market supported by mortgage, pledge or sale of land and property rights exists (Shivji, 1998). Debate over privatization of land and customary formulations continues, but Tanzania emphasizes how Islamic land concepts can be interpreted and used variably to achieve specific aims. For example, inheritance of land too is subject to a use-it-or–lose-it policy.

Northern Nigeria's experiences with Islamic land law can be contrasted with those in parts of East Africa. The Sokoto Caliphate (1809–1906) instituted classical Islamic land law, with Kano and Sokoto being among the oldest and largest centres of Islam in West Africa (Abdullahi and Humza, 2003). Land classification, regulation and taxation was guided by the nature of land (occupied or unoccupied), land use, and the status of the owner, with five land categories: individual group ownership (*mamulka*); state land (*amiriyya*); common land (*matruka*); dead land (*mawatoi*) or God's bush (*dajin Allah*); and Islamic endowments (*waqf*) (Sait and Lim, 2006). In this application of Islamic law – like the 1858 Ottoman Land Code – the individual rights are subject to land being put to productive and responsible use. Sources of Islamic land law for the Caliphate were the Qur'an and consensus (*ijma*) – with key feature of land policies being protection of lands (hima), grant over virgin lands (*iqta*), and state ownership of mineral rights with leasing based on condition of mining royalties (Jumare, 1995; Loimeier, 2011). These Islamic principles were converted into Nigerian practices through a hybrid land governance.

Annual tributary land taxes were payable by non-Muslims (*zijya*) alongside more general tax of farm produce (*Kharaj* or *kudin-al-barkar kasa*), and charitable levy (*zakat*). However, innovations to traditional Islamic land law under the Sokoto Caliphate included introducing processes for renewing land tenure and rights, extending the concept of Islamic endowments (*waqf*), recognition of the difference between urban and rural land, and dead land (*mewat*) (Evans, 2016). However, with the advent of British rule all land became either public or crown land, and private ownership was de-recognized in 'community lands' Islamic land law and inheritance continued but of Islamic legal systems. This created multiple different systems of tenure and administration – with not only Islamic law and courts headed by Islamic judges (*alkali*) alongside British property law, and customary practices into which Islamic land practices suffused owing to community-based land administration – impacting on continued formulations of land rights in Nigeria (Pierce, 2005). Islamic land governance came to be seen as a historic relic and Nigerian land governance drew from the British model while embracing legal pluralism.

In contrast to this legacy of continued interaction between Islamic land law and customary practices in Northern Nigeria, the case of Senegal highlights how in the case of Francophone West Africa, Islamic land law has interacted with imperatives of secularism. While Aristide Vallon, the French Governor of Senegal allowed Islam to persist in Senegal as custom – during colonial rule French scholar-administrators developed the theory of 'Black Islam' (*Islam noir*) to emphasize the supposed inferiority to African Islamic practices to those found in the Arab world (Robinson, 1988; Triaud, 2000). By racializing the practice of Islam, Islamic leaders (*marabouts*) were forced to resist colonial policies by promoting them as customary practices – including in application of Maliki law (*Risila*) in land matters. Despite being enmeshed within customary land systems there were conflicts between these and Islamic land practices, though in practice both were accepted by the *Chefs de Canton* as the French failed to their attempt to register customary land use rights (immitriculation) (Behrman, 1970). The French thereby ensured that whatever Islamic land principles endured, they would be governed through secular or universal systems.

With independence from France, the 1963 constitution did not have any specific provisions relating to customary or Islamic law. Rather, these were later embedded in social practices relating to Islamic family and land law, with the resulting 1973 Family Code abrogating customary practices in favour of recognizing Islamic law. This system has attempted to simplify the country's complex land tenure system – recognizing existing land rights subject to a two-year registration period but instituting a system of 'commautes rurales' to administer land. Therefore, under this system, the predominance of state land ownership and secularization of land law have been combined with Islamic land practices and customary norms that are not officially part of the national tenure regime (Freudenberger, 1994; Golan, 1994).

Finally, Somalia exemplifies how Islamic land practices can operate at societal level even in the face of state collapse. Somali customary law (*xeer*) survived British colonial rule and continues to be an essential part of the land practices and dispute resolution mechanisms (Norton, 2008). Prior to its independence in 1960, Somalia's land tenure system was defined by its combination of customary practices with collective land tenure (in the form of the *Salihiya tariqas*), used as an organizational framework for agricultural and spiritual communities – implementing many aspects of Islamic family and land law including in relation to dead land (*mewat*), inheritance, and adhering to Islamic economic perspectives. Yet, by the 1970s, modern Somali reformers argued for the 1973 Unified Civil Code and then the 1975 Land Reform Act, which technically abolished customary tenure in the country, viewing it as backward (Unruh, 2001; McAulsan, 2013)

While attempting to modernize the model of informal collectives, the reforms failed to cater to the rights of pastoralists and others – alongside bureaucracy, corruption, rigidity and mismatched resources meant these policies failed to deliver. Given its history, customary land tenure in Somalia appears to be chaotic – yet its persistence underscores the extent to which statutory land tenure regimes have been constructed in ways that are often oppressive and contributes to political turmoil (Van Notten, 2005; Powell *et al.*, 2008). Since 1991, the situation in Somalia has resulted in frequent confiscation and denial of property and land rights, in the absence of formal institutions that foster and regulate cooperation, customary practices (*xeer*) and Islamic land perspectives offers a local appeal – especially when village elders can help foster dispute resolution, or a local jury (*xeer-beegti*) can help resolve property and land disputes given mutual self-interest. Islamic land governance yields to a hybrid system that responds to the unique context and specific needs of its people.

13.5 Conclusions: Addressing 'Islamic' Land Governance and Gender Equality

The curious case of Islamic land perspectives in the context of African countries highlights the prospects and tensions in acknowledging distinctive Islamic land occurrences as part of the Islamic land governance or more broadly hybrid land governance regimes. Muslim customary land norms recall its history and context to produce land systems that appear more effective on the ground (Jones-Pauly, 1998; Kironde, 2000). These sociohistorical patterns mapping faith-based tenure contribute to additional types of land and property rights regimes that potentially increase access to land for women and marginalized groups. Examples from Kenya and

Tanzania to Nigeria, Senegal and Somalia highlight that Islamic land perspectives cannot be seen as either homogeneous or existing in a vacuum. Shaped in various forms by customary practices, classical Islamic law, as well as colonial-era policies, Islamic land perspectives highlight the need for appropriate land governance. The paradox of 'Islamic' land governance is that while Islamic law has often been invisible and sometimes dismissed, it is an additional useful lens in rethinking the role of faith in land governance. The compelling and volatile relationship between Islamic land practices and governance query whether Islamic tenures need religious informed land governance to be effective.

Islamic land law can be doctrinal or resilient as a set of ideas, but Islamic land governance borrows from enduring land principles as well as the well-acknowledged generic Islamic ethos. In Kenya, Islamic land law was used to strengthen private property rights while certain indigenous peoples had their land rights taken way, while in Tanzania it was to do the opposite in helping solidify national land ownership with creation of rights of occupancy and use. In both cases, Islamic land principles were posed as customary discourse mediated through colonial land governance which acknowledged custom. Northern Nigeria traditional Islamic land norms inherited from the Sokoto Caliphate, but colonial policies delegitimized customary and religious tenure. The British reconstructed the modern land system which undermined Islamic and customary rights. Senegal dealt with similar challenges by adopting Islamic land law through a customary framework, though post-independence secularist land governance has been deployed to undermine the influence of religion on land. Meanwhile, in Somalia, customary and Islamic tenure was officially abolished, but Islamic and customary land governance supported dispute resolution and peace-building efforts, especially in addressing land conflicts.

Varied Islamic land strategies have been utilized to fit varied sociopolitical interests. In the case of Muslim women's land and property rights – Islamic land law offers potentially additional pathways to increase access to land and tenure security for marginalized groups of women and girls, but to rely on Islamic land governance could equally struggle to overcome gender inequality norms and continued patriarchal attitudes preventing access to land. All Islamic land tools – including *waqf* (endowments), *Mewat* (dead land) and others – are in theory gender responsive, inclusive and non-denominational, and often the beneficiaries of such tools are disadvantaged groups of women who otherwise would not have recourse to access land. As Sait (2013b, p. 498) makes clear, it is necessary to distinguish between customary practices and Islamic land law:

> generally, in Muslim societies, Islamic law offers far greater rights for women than customary practice. A striking example is the property rights of widows, which are vital in post-conflict and post-disaster situations. Judgements in inheritance cases after the tsunami in Aceh [Indonesia] saw the sharia courts grant more rights to widows than traditional courts. When widows' property rights are violated in Afghanistan and Somalia, it is a triumph of customary practices over Islamic norms.

Islamic perspectives have the potential to be gender responsive but require increased attention to practical ways of augmenting women's land rights in a faith-based society. The nature, scope and applicability of Islamic land practices and tools conjure the highly heterodox and fragmented nature of existing Islamic land practices. Possible benefits of reframing 'Islamic' land governance is to rethink how land policy makers, professionals, experts and scholars consider the relationship between Islamic land law and governance. Gender-responsive governance is key to deliver women's land rights from whatever source. So far, the current treatment of Islamic land law focuses for obvious reasons on the predominant issues of land rights through the prism of property and inheritance – especially for Muslim women – and need to provide mechanisms and appropriate land governance for gender equality.

Strong arguments have been made to harness innovative but traditional Islamic land tenures to empower women and disadvantaged groups. Yet, the case for Islamic land governance has not been made and perhaps is unnecessary. Islamic land tenures are not being explored because they are religious but because of their functional utility, beyond anthropological or theological interest. The Islamic land governance argument is weak because, despite historical narratives, its nature and scope are unclear.

While it is possible to construct one in theory, with Islamic concepts of justice, fair distribution, dispute resolution, negotiation and *shura* (participation), these are already in play in Muslim countries as part of pluralist and hybrid land governance systems. The fear, whether or not unwarranted, is that Islamic land governance would not be able to accommodate all actors and serve the universal consensus on land rights for all. Past Islamic governance models may not be appropriate for multicultural, larger and diverse societies with complex land issues. Therefore, Islamic land tenure requires further exploration especially through the legal pluralism lens but there is little scope for promoting Islamic land governance. Instead, the question is how good land governance can secure equitable land rights for all, through all means including Islamic and faith-based land tenures.

Islamic land principles need to be tooled to facilitate local level change, urban revitalization and engaging with Muslim communities through a vital cultural, social and faith-based language that can help redress problematic legacies arising from acontextual and ahistorical land policies. Theoretically, projecting or constructing 'Islamic' land governance can refocusing attention on the relationship between Islamic land law, customary practices, and land administration, regulation, and management of land in Muslim contexts. However, there are not exclusively Muslim or Islamic solutions, and in any case, there is no one-size-fits-all approach. Romanticizing religion, history or culture will not transform land rights, a careful consideration of its potential benefits or risk of each intervention could strengthen access to land. The resonance of Islamic land principles in several contexts does not reflect a return to the past or superiority of faith-based tenure, it offers lessons on sustainability, enduring values and often community-based governance. Instead, we need to go beyond formal and customary/cultural dichotomies in recognizing how modern approaches to land governance can reconnect with faith-based tenure systems in the context of legal pluralism.

References

Abdullahi, H.J. and Hamza, I. (2003) Women and land in Northern Nigeria: The rights. In Wanyeki, L.M. (Ed.), *Women and Land in Africa.* Zed Books, London, UK.

Abu-Lughod, J.L. (1971) *Cairo: 1001 Years of the City Victorious*. Princeton University Press, Princeton, NJ, USA.

Abu-Lughod, J.L. (1987) The Islamic city – historic myth, Islamic essence, and contemporary relevance. *International Journal of Middle East Studies*, 19(2), 155–176.

Acemoglu, D., Johnson, S. and Robinson, J.A. (2001) The colonial origins of comparative development: An empirical investigation. *American Economic Review*, 91(5), 1369–1401.

Al-Hathloul, S. A. (1981) Tradition, continuity and change in the physical environment: The Arab-Muslim city. Doctoral dissertation, Massachusetts Institute of Technology, Cambridge, MA, USA.

Behrman, L.C. (1970) *Muslim Brotherhoods and Politics in Senegal.* Harvard University Press, Cambridge, MA.

Ben-Hamouche, M. (2009) Complexity of urban fabric in traditional Muslim cities: Importing old wisdom to present cities. *Urban Design International*, 14(1), 22–35.

Ben-Hamouche, M. (2011) Fractal geometry in Muslim cities: How succession law shaped morphology. *Nexus Network Journal*, 13(1), 235–251.

Bennison, A.K. and Gascoigne, A.L. (Eds) (2007) *Cities in the Pre-Modern Islamic World: The Urban Impact of Religion, State and Society.* Routledge, London, UK.

Bevir, M. (2010) *Democratic Governance.* Princeton University Press, Princeton, NJ, USA.

Bianca, S. (2000) *Urban Form in the Arab World: Past and Present.* Institut für Orts-, und Regional- und Landesplanung, Eidgenössische Technische Hochschule Zürich, Zürich, Switzerland.

Borras Jr, S.M. and Franco, J.C. (2010) Contemporary discourses and contestations around pro-poor land policies and land governance. *Journal of Agrarian Change*, 10(1), 1–32.

Brennan, J. R. (2008) Lowering the sultan's flag: Sovereignty and decolonization in coastal Kenya. *Comparative Studies in Society and History*, 50(4), 831–861.

Cassel, P.K. (2012) *Grounds of Judgment: Extraterritoriality and Imperial Power in Nineteenth Century China and Japan.* Oxford University Press, Oxford, UK.

Chapra, M.U. (2008) Ibn Khaldun's theory of development: Does it help explain the low performance of the present-day Muslim world? *Journal of Socio-Economics*, 37(2), 836–863.

Contini, P. (1969) *The Somali Republic: An Experiment in Legal Integration*. Frank Cass & Company, London, UK.

Cooper, F. (1980) *From Slaves to Squatters: Plantation Labour and Agriculture in Zanzibar and Coastal Kenya, 1890–1925*. Yale University Press, New Haven, CT, USA / London, UK.

Dean, M. (2017) Governmentality. In: Turner, B.S. (Ed.), *The Wiley Blackwell Encyclopedia of Social Theory*. John Wiley & Sons, Hoboken, NJ, USA.

Deininger, K., Selod, H. and Burns, A. (2011) *The Land Governance Assessment Framework: Identifying and Monitoring Good Practice in the Land Sector.* World Bank, Washington, DC, USA.

Drechsler, W. (2013) Three paradigms of governance and administration: Chinese, Western and Islamic. *Society and Economy*, 35(3), 319–342.

Dupret, B., Berger, M. and Al-Zwaini, L. (Eds) (1999) *Legal Pluralism in the Arab World*. Brill, Leiden, The Netherlands.

Elsheshtawy, Y. (Ed.). (2008) *The Evolving Arab City: Tradition, Modernity and Urban Development.* Routledge, London, UK.

Evans, R. (2016) Gendered struggles over land: Shifting inheritance practices among the Serer in rural Senegal. *Gender, Place & Culture*, 23(9), 1360–1375.

Fair, L. (2001) *Pastimes & Politics: Culture, Community and Identification in Post-Abolition Urban Zanzibar, 1890–1994.* Ohio University Press, Athens, OH, USA.

FAO (2006) Good Governance in Land Tenure and Administration. *Land Tenure Studies No. 9*. Food and Agriculture Organization, Rome, Italy.

Frankema, E. (2010) The colonial roots of land inequality: geography, factor endowments, or institutions? *The Economic History Review*, 63(2), 418–451.

Freudenberger, M. S. (1994) *Land Tenure, Local Institutions and Natural Resources in Senegal Madison.* Land Tenure Centre, University of Wisconsin, Madison, WI, USA.

Ghai, Y.P. and McAuslan, J.P.W. (1970) *Public Law and Political Change in Kenya: A Study of the Legal Framework of Government from Colonial Times to the Present.* Oxford University Press, Oxford, UK.

Golan, E.H. (1994) Land tenure reform in the peanut basin of Senegal. In: Bruce, J.W. (Ed.), *Searching for Land Tenure Security in Africa.* Kendall/Hunt Publishing Company, Dubuque, IA, USA, pp. 231–249.

Hakim, B. S. (1994) The 'Urf' and its role in diversifying the architecture of traditional Islamic cities. *Journal of Architectural and Planning Research*, 11(2), 108–127.

Hamidin, A. (2000) Unfinished business: the implementation of land titles ordinance in coastal Kenya, 1908–1940s. Doctoral dissertation, School of Oriental and African Studies, University of London, London, UK.

Hanretta, S. (2009) *Islam and Social Change in French West Africa: History of an Emancipatory Community (No. 110)*. Cambridge University Press, Cambridge, UK.

Iqbal, Z., and Lewis, M. K. (2009) *An Islamic Perspective on Governance*. Edward Elgar Publishing, Cheltenham, UK.

James, R.W. (1971) *Land Tenure and Policy in Tanzania*. East African Literature Bureau, Nairobi, Kenya.

Jones-Pauly, C. (1998) *Old Problems and New Ideologies in Land Reform in Tanzania in Land Tenure in Development Cooperation: Guiding Principles*. Deutsche Gesellschaft für Technische Zusammenarbeit GmbH (GIZ), Bonn, Germany.

Jumare, I.M. (1995) Land tenure in Sokoto Sultanate Northern Nigeria. PhD thesis, York University, York, UK.

Kironde, J.L. (2000) Understanding land markets in African urban areas: the case of Dar es Salaam, Tanzania. *Habitat International*, 24(2), 151–165.

Kostof, S. (1991) *The City Shaped: Urban Patterns and Meanings Through History.* Thames and Hudson, London, UK.

Kuran, T. (2003) The Islamic commercial crisis: Institutional roots of economic underdevelopment in the Middle East. *Journal of Economic History,* 63(2), 414–446. Available at: https://sites.duke.edu/timurkuran/files/2016/10/kuran-islamic-commercial-crisis.original.pdf (accessed 19 July 2021).

Kuran, T. (2012) *The Long Divergence: How Islamic Law Held Back the Middle East.* Princeton University Press, Princeton, NJ, USA.

Landa, R.G. (1995) *Islam v Istorii Rossii* [Islam in the History of Russia]. Vostochnaya Literatura, Moscow, Russia, pp. 203–205.

Leo, C. (1984) *Land and Class in Kenya*. University of Toronto Press, Toronto, Canada.

Lemmen, C., Du Plessis, J., Augustinus, C., Laarakker, P.M., de Zeeuuw, K., Saers, P. and Molendijk, M. (2015) The operationalisation of the 'continuum of land rights' at country level. 16th Annual World Bank Conference on Land and Poverty 2015. World Bank, Washington, DC, USA.

Lodhi, A.Y. (1986) The Arabs in Zanzibar: From sultanate to peoples' republic. *Institute of Muslim Minority Affairs. Journal,* 7(2), 404–418.

Loimeier, R. (2011) *Islamic Reform and Political Change in Northern Nigeria.* Northwestern University Press, Chicago, IL, USA.

Loimeier, R. and Seesemann, R. (2006) *The Global Worlds of the Swahili: Interfaces of Islam, Identity and Space in 19th and 20th-Century East Africa.* LIT Verlag, Münster, Germany.

McAuslan, P. (2013) *Land Law Reform in Eastern Africa: Traditional or Transformative? A Critical Review of 50 Years of Land Law Reform in Eastern Africa 1961–2011.* Routledge Revivals, London, UK.

Meek, C.K. (1946) *Land Law and Custom in the Colonies*. Oxford University Press, Oxford, UK.

Merry, S.E. (1991) Law and colonialism. *Law & Society Review*, 25, 889.

North, D.C. (1990) *Institutions, Institutional Change and Economic Performance*. Cambridge University Press, Cambridge, UK.

Norton, G. (2008) *Land, Property, and Housing in Somalia. Land and Water Digital Media Series.* FAO, Rome, Italy.

Okello, J. (1967) *Revolution in Zanzibar*. East African Publishing House, Nairobi, Kenya.

O'Meara, S. (2007) *Space and Muslim Urban Life: At the Limits of the Labyrinth of Fez*. Routledge, London, UK.

Omer, S. (2008) Towards understanding Islamic architecture. *Islamic Studies*, 47(4), 483–510.

Palmer, R. (2007). *Literature Review of Governance and Secure Access to Land.* Department for International Development, London, UK.

Palmer, D., Fricska, S. and Wehrmann, B. (2009) *Towards Improved Land Governance*. Land Tenure Working Paper 11. UN-HABITAT and FAO, Nairobi, Kenya and Rome, Italy.

Payne, G. (2001) Urban land tenure policy options: Titles or rights? *Habitat international*, 25(3), 415–429.

Pierce, S. (2005). *Farmers and the State in Colonial Kano: Land Tenure and the Legal Imagination.* Indiana University Press, Bloomington, IN, USA.

Pouwels, R. L. (2002) *Horn and Crescent: Cultural Change and Traditional Islam on the East African Coast, 800–1900.* Cambridge University Press, Cambridge, UK.

Powell, B., Ford, R. and Nowrasteh, A. (2008). Somalia after state collapse: Chaos or improvement? *Journal of Economic Behaviour & Organization*, 67(3–4), 657–670.

Powers, D.S. (1989) Orientalism, colonialism, and legal history: the attack on Muslim family endowments in Algeria and India. *Comparative Studies in Society and History*, 31(3), 535–571.

Pravilova, E. (2011) The property of Empire: Islamic law and Russian agrarian policy in Transcaucasia and Turkestan. *Kritika: Explorations in Russian and Eurasian History*, 12(2), 353–386.

Raymond, A. (1994) Islamic city, Arab city: Orientalist myths and recent views. *British Journal of Middle Eastern Studies*, 21(1), 3–18.

Rhodes, R.A. (2007) Understanding governance: Ten years on. *Organization Studies*, 28(8), 1243–1264.

Robinson, D. (1988) French 'Islamic' policy and practice in late nineteenth-century Senegal. *Journal of African History*, 29(3), 415–435.

Robinson, D. (1999a) France as a Muslim power in West Africa. *Africa Today*, 46(3), 105–127.

Robinson, F. (1999b) The British empire and the Muslim world. In Brown, J.M. and Roger Louis, W.M. (Eds), *The Oxford History of the British Empire Volume* 4. Oxford University Press, Oxford, UK, pp. 398–420.

Sait, M.S. (2008) The relevance for Islamic land law for policy and project design. Conference on New Challenges for Land Policy and Administration. World Bank, Washington, DC, USA.

Sait, M.S. (2013a) Women's property rights in Muslim matrilineal communities. *Journal of Islamic State Practices in International Law*, 9(1), 1–35.

Sait, M.S. (2013b) Unexplored dimensions: Islamic land systems in Afghanistan, Indonesia, Iraq, and Somalia. In: Unruh, J. and Williams, R. (Eds), *Land and Post-Conflict Peace Building.* Earthscan/UNEP/ELI, New York, NY, USA.

Sait, M.S. (2015) Rethinking Muslim women's equal rights: Faith, property and empowerment. In: Lennox, C. (Ed.), *Contemporary Challenges in Securing Human Rights*, University of London, London, UK, pp. 121–126.

Sait, M.S. and Lim, H. (2006) *Land, Law and Islam: Property and Human Rights in the Muslim World*. Zed Books, London, UK.

Sardar, Z. (2011) The long divergence: How Islamic law held back the Middle East. *The Independent* (UK). Available at: https://www.independent.co.uk/arts-entertainment/books/reviews/long-divergence-how-islamic-law-held-back-middle-east-timur-kuran-2196199.html (accessed 12 February 2021).

Shivji, I.G. (1998) *Not Yet Democracy: Reforming Land Tenure in Tanzania Dar es Salaam*. International Institute for Environment and Development, London, UK.

Tempra, O., Sait, M.S. and Khouri, R. (2018) *Women and Land in the Muslim World: Pathways to Increase Access to Land for the Realization of Development, Peace and Human Rights.* GLTN/UN-HABITAT/UEL, Nairobi, Kenya.

Triaud, J.L. (2000) Islam in Africa under French colonial rule. In Levtzion, N. and Pouwels, R. (Eds), *History of Islam in Africa.* Ohio University Press, Athens, OH, USA.

Twining, W. (2009) Normative and legal pluralism: a global perspective. *Duke Journal of Comparative & International Law*, 20, 473.

Unruh, J.D. (2001) Somali rural property rights: Whither the future. *Journal of the Anglo-Somali Society*, 30, 38–39.

Van Notten, M. (2005) *The Law of the Somalis*. Red Sea Press, Trenton, NJ, USA.

Westerlund, D. (1980) Ujamaa na dini. A study of some aspects of society and religion in Tanzania, 1961–1977. *Acta Universitatis Stockholmiensis. Stockholm Studies in Comparative Religion Stockholm*, 18, 1–198.

Yusuf, I.S. (1991) Islam and African socialism: A study of the interactions between Islam and Ujamaa socialism in Tanzania. PhD thesis, Temple University, Philadelphia, PA, USA.

Part 4

Land Governance, Gender and Tenure Innovations

14 Transforming Legal Status of Customary Land Rights: What this Means for Women and Men in Rural Africa

Liz Alden Wily*
Van Vollenhoven Institute for Law, Governance and Society, Leiden Law School, Leiden, The Netherlands

14.1 Introduction: Objective, Approach and Presentation

This chapter provides an overview of land tenure reform, which should, in theory, prove a potent trigger towards equitable land relations between men and women in the customary land sector. This has been progressively underway in Africa since the 1990s. Broadly, a common objective is to release customary rights from their historical subordination as occupancy and use rights on presumed unowned lands, and much of which land remains vests in governments as owner-custodians. Or, where national laws have treated customary rights more equitably, a principal aim of reforms is to increase their security by these rights to be registrable without their extinction and conversion into statutory private rights. In short, this new phase of African land reform could signal the end of 70 years of intended disappearance of customary tenure as formally advised by the East African Royal Commission in 1955 and core elements of which were also adopted by France in respect of its own African possessions (Hesseling, 2009).

This is not to say that contemporary tenure reform has lost either the titling or land market imperatives of those earlier privatization land reforms (Bruce and Migot-Adholla, 1994). Both drivers still apply but in altered form, necessitated by strikingly new legal recognition of customary rights as property rights, and concomitant recognition that this community-based tenure system is, after all, a useful framework for securing majority rural land rights. Expectedly, not all African Governments are equally supportive or engaged in this transformation. More progressive laws also face government pushbacks as recognition of customary holdings widely encroaches upon lands which governments have become used to considering their own as later described.

Nevertheless, the emerging new land reform project is well-launched in Africa, and is more meaningful for tackling the overlapping and competing state and community land interests. For, as this chapter aims to show, the more progressive land laws on the continent quietly reconstruct the very meaning of property in land, after a history of subordination of customary rights which goes back much further than colonization. They also alter the legal mechanics through which rights in land may be defined, regulated and administered in a potentially irreversible thrust enhancing devolution to the grassroots. Communities themselves acquire revitalized form as viable sociopolitical entities in the African society. Inter alia,

*Corresponding author: e.alden.wily@law.leidenuniv.nl

 Land Governance and Gender: The Tenure-Gender Nexus in Land Management and Land Policy (ed. U.E. Chigbu)
DOI: 10.1079/9781789247664.0014

their members must come face-to-face with practised inequities, including in their gender relations. While this last impact is the target of this exploration, the primary objective of this chapter is to critique contemporary land law reformism as a foundation from which more equitable gender land relations may be fostered. Space does not allow examination of whether this is being delivered in practice or not. Fortunately, good examples are provided by other chapters in this book.

A strictly legal lens is adopted here. The content and implications of new land laws are used as the most articulate and binding basis of national intentions. New constitutions are examined for the extent to which they anchor new tenure and gender equity paradigms. Sources for this chapter are both literary and practice-based in the form of desk study and field work by the author over many years of working in tenure reform as a scholar and practitioner in several continents. This predominantly includes substantial work in ten African states and remoter contributions to policy and legal change in a number of others in both Anglophone and Francophone Africa.

Presentation is in four parts. Part 14.2, following this Introduction, focuses on locating African customary tenure in its state-making context, colonial or otherwise, as most instrumental in shaping its scope and legal treatment. Terminology is clarified including needed distinctions between customary and community lands, and customary and communal landholding. Part 14.3 reviews the substance of contemporary tenure reform in Africa, opening with a snapshot of global land reforms, a source of pressure, precedent and support. Radical paradigmatic leaps which some home-grown African reforms are arriving at are described. Part 14.4 highlights legal provisions in new land laws aimed to equalize the roles of men and women as owners, co-owners and decision-makers within the customary land sector. Part 14.5 draws conclusions.

14.2 Context: Customary Tenure in the Modern Day

Unpacking Context and Terms

Customary tenure refers to the means through which rural communities define and govern the rights to lands and resources of their members within known local geographic domains. Paradigms in Africa range from permanent village settlements comprising mainly private household plots governed under customary norms, to large territories wherein only a tiny proportion of the area is allocated to housing and farming by individual members. Pastoral domains are most complex, in that these comprise several layers of possession in reference to home and remote seasonal pastures, rights of transit, water and grazing as customarily established between the two areas; and areas various other resource-sharing arrangements, including effective suspension of exclusive possession and use during severe droughts and animal epidemics ('Without rain, no land is private': Maasai proverb) (Herrera *et al.*, 2014).

In contrast, forest and arid land hunter-gatherer communities (or 'bands') hold exclusive rights in common to single vast territories within which they roam to maximize resource sustainability. Perimeter boundaries rarely alter, well-known to themselves and to neighbouring bands if invisible to the outsider (Freeman and Anderies, 2015). Among settled farming communities, which comprise the majority of communities in Africa, customary domains are anchored by homesteads each of which inheritable parcel is acquired or allocated to member families for their exclusive occupation and use. These 'private' lands in the customary sector normally exclude communal rangelands, forests and swamplands, governed under different community rules. Overlap of interests occurs between the two, most noticeably in temporary farming use through shifting cultivation of otherwise communal lands (Alden Wily, 2007). While the extent of community commons varies, and most have seen shrinkage over the last half century, it is strangely rare for a contemporary rural community to have no common land at all, even in the most densely populated Africa country of Rwanda.[1]

Overall, physical common property in the customary sector exists at two levels; communities tend to own ultimate possession of the land or soil (directly, or as its temporal occupants). They, or their chosen or self-appointed leaders, allocate derivative rights to this shared property, in the form of inheritable and exclusive access and use rights to families, under defined practises or rules. In the case of commons such as pasture, community ownership and use rights are more immediately aligned as communal lands. 'Communal lands' may also confusingly refer to a whole domain or to some parts of it. This also embodies recognition that customary tenure is also a community or communal land *governance* system; community ownership and governance are generically inseparable. Their divorce predictably hollows out the system.

Customary and State Land Law

From a legal perspective, customary tenure is distinct from state tenure in that the rules of one derive principally from the community, and the rules of other derive from governments. In substance they influence each other. As state law determines the status of customary law, significant reconstruction occurs. Popular support is ultimately key to adherence in both regimes; remotely so in respect of state law, more immediately felt in customary law. The influence of religious law is also historically and presently important especially where Islamic law (Shari'a) is constitutionally declared the source of all law (as in Sudan, Mauritania, Western Sahara, Somalia and Libya), and a primary source of law in 12 other states. In a continent where 45% of Africans are Muslims, this influence is both tangible and intangible; as Sulitstyarini *et al.* note (2018), deciphering distinct origins in especially customary and Shari'a law can be futile.

Customary Tenure as Community Tenure

While customary tenure is the dominant vehicle of community-based tenure, it is not alone. Hybrid arrangements evolve. For example, Afro-descendant communities in Latin America often recreated the essence of African tenure several centuries after their arrival as they expanded into hinterlands after the end of slavery (Guerena, 2016). A number of governments have devised community tenure systems without building on customary tenure. The most famous example is the 1 million rural land collectives which cover two-thirds of China's land area today, wherein each community governs its own state-allocated domain of mixed private and communal properties (Wang *et al.*, 2015). These and the community land collectives of Vietnam and Cuba, and systems recreated following the break-up of the Soviet Union in 1991 in several countries, closely resemble foundational norms of customary tenure if not their more distinctive local practices. Those foundational norms include (i) entrenched linkage of self-defined social groups with a definable geographic areas; (ii) community governance as ultimately dependent upon consensus for adherence, as described above; (iii) formulation of distinctive individual/family and communal rights to parts of the domain attaining characteristics of private and collective rights and areas; and (iv) such divisions responding to the logic of land type, land use and remoteness, but adjusted in their distribution over time by the exercise of hierarchical privileges, traditional or otherwise, including via individual accumulation of wealth and power.

Global practice now favours the use of community lands to embrace the mixed diversity and commonality of community-based property systems today. I have chosen here to use the term customary tenure, both in cognizance that this remains the major form of community systems in Africa and elsewhere, and because this is the major system practised in Africa, and the term is well known. This includes countries where customary tenure has been formally abolished, usually to rid the system of feudal relations, especially in Asia (Alden Wily, 2009). In Africa, Egypt, Libya, Eritrea and Mauritania have outlawed customary tenure, in the last instance due to sustained enslavement under its norms. All but Libya have since found it necessary to create new community-based systems to satisfactorily manage rural land relations. Several African states recognize customary tenure as lawful but reframe their source of governance under elected community governments instead of traditional authorities (Senegal, Guinea, Ethiopia, and Tanzania), or via registered cooperatives or collectives (Tunisia, and Algeria). Without exception, all community land systems in Africa have a foundation in customary tenure.

The Famed Adaptability and Pragmatism of Customary Tenure

As implied above, customary tenure is a misnomer in that many of its rules and practices are neo-customary or entirely new, acquired or devised by living generations, or imposed by state laws. The substantial literature shows the inherent flexibility of the system, including the argument that customary tenure is as much the product of colonialism as of tradition (Ranger, 2012; Diala and Kangwa, 2019). There can also be no doubt that that this trend is driven by class formation, and pressures exerted by elites and chiefs. As local land values soar, land shortage, degradation, migration, globalized access to Africa's lands, and interventionist laws, increase. Other factors include the social change agendas of land reforms, and now those of the present reform (Ochieng, 2020). Much study has been focused on the reconstructive impacts of land titling as the pillar of reformism in postcolonial Africa (Bromley, 2008, Sjaastad and Cousins, 2008), and more recent globalized neoliberalism (McAuslan, 2013). Chimhowu (2019) suggests that neoliberalization has produced a 'new customary tenure'; one that is market-friendly, legible and inviting to investors. This is indeed so, especially where reforms are truncated, as illustrated later.

Nevertheless, such appealing theses may ignore the importance of communal lands to communities in circumstances where cultivated lands are so minimal (and minimal even generally in Africa, at 13% of its land area) (FAO, 2018). Changing conceptions of property in land may also be missed in over-focus on titling, a tool which can be applied in very different ways. From the 1950s this was designed to individualize and register peasant holdings under statutory entitlements to bring more land into the marketplace, inter alia, producing mass legal landlessness of wives and capturing millions of hectares of unfarmed community commons by governments (Lastarria-Cornhiel, 1997). From the 1990s, collective titling has been promoted, not least as a hedge against involuntary privatization and loss of vast uncultivated lands to governments or aligned elites. There can also be a tendency to mistake where continuity in the customary sector lies; less in its changeable and manipulable norms as so well documented by Peters and Kambewa (2007), Ubink and Amanor (2008) and Berry (2020), as in its structural norms as described earlier. In short, one must ask: has customary tenure ever *not* been 'new', made and remade from time to time? Is not its structural resilience as a framework for local control over land rights, its inherent adaptability and practicality, the more lasting sources of its persistence into the present?

The Scope of Customary Lands and Land Tenure Today

Finally, as context, community lands are not a small matter. Whether customary, neo-customary, hybrid or state created in their nature, these systems regulate 5–6 billion hectares, or half the planet's land area (RRI, 2020). While *c.*3 billion people live within this domain, most of whom cultivate at least some land, community/customary lands mostly comprise rangelands, forests of all types, swamplands and mountainous areas – the nature of which is more naturally communal than individual and logically historically owned by groups rather than individuals.[2] Settlements and farms may anchor a community and its area but, excepting very fertile terrains, these tend to absorb only a tiny percentage of each community's area. Communities vary in size but probably number around 5 million discrete entities. These include 200 million rural Afro-descendants in the Americas, 400 million community members who identify as Indigenous Peoples with ancient histories of possession, and around 2 billion members of communities with old but less ancient occupation and possession in especially Africa and Asia. There are in addition possibly 500 million members of purpose-built land cooperatives or collectives, principally developed to counter mass landlessness and land poverty under feudal regimes or to advance fully devolved rural land tenure and administration (Alden Wily, 2018).

The Customary Land Estate in Africa

A significant part of the global community/customary land estate exists in Africa. I have cautiously estimated this as around 2 billion hectares or 78% of the continental land area, based on official country data or through a methodology adopted by the community land mapping facility, LandMark where data are lacking (Alden Wily, 2015). The results concur with newer analyses which are arrived at by sampling

(RRI, 2020). As is the case globally, the customary estate in Africa is predominantly comprised of rangelands, woodland/forests and swamplands, and a substantial area of desert land customarily owned claimed by desert pastoralists in the north.

14.3 Contemporary Land Reform

The Global Picture

Tenure reform is a global project with a shared outstanding target to belatedly reform the national law status of customary rights. Each country has its own prompts, but many are shared. I pick out those which are remarkably common: new awareness and attention to social justice; acknowledgement that customary systems have nowhere near disappeared as expected and are more practical and useful than conventionally acknowledged; that the applicability of individualization has its limits in terms of resource types; land markets do not necessarily flourish in consequence, nor reduce conflicts; international financing, development assistance, and UN-led commitments impliedly or directly demand new approaches to the majority rural poor; the domino effect of good examples; political changes in an era since the 1980s of pronounced aims of devolutionary democratization including citizen empowerment at one end of the spectrum and adjustment in the roles of governments at the other; and, last but far from least, the dying throes of postcolonialism and clearer perceptions as to what in the colonial yolk needs disposing of. Space does not allow the above to be elaborated on (or other triggers not listed), a subject of scholarship in its own right. However, two facts need exposing here at explaining why current reforms take the routes they do, and why this has become a global project.

First, while evidence of community-framed land relations goes back thousands of years past (Earle, 2017), modern state-making lies firmly at the heart of the ideology of indigenous systems as incapable of producing property, along with the need for rulers and elites to secure the lands they wanted; a useful norm developed in the City State of Rome to control its own plebeians and the subjects of its expanding Empire. The same norms were put to work as the basis of evolving civil and common law towards the making of the feudal European state (North *et al.*, 2009). The principles were subsequently refined to service extractive capitalism in foreign climes through control of vast new markets, and the capture of labour, lands, and resources to grow the home country (Hobsbawm, 1994). Resulting colonies operated on revitalized feudal-like supremacy in which the State became the majority landlord, defining rights according to its own interests. To limit rebellions, this required peaceable occupancy of natives to feed themselves (homesteads) but whose lands needed to be available as required (McAuslan, 2007). The related second fact is more startling; every corner of the world was affected so that only ten or so of today's 196 modern states entirely escaped European colonization.[3] This helps explain the commonality of notions of private property across the globe – and eventually, as seen today – belated advancement into remedy in respect of indigenous property systems encountered including their invaluable common lands. The logical indicator of success is how far customary rights are now legally recognized as property interests state to state. Sampling suggests that land laws by 2015 state land laws recognized 18.7% of global land area as community property or as public lands formally designated for exclusive community use (RRI, 2015). This was revised upwards in 2020 to 26.3% (RRI, 2020).

My own study of 100 national land laws proportionately sampled from all regions found that most countries (73) do now recognize that customary/community systems produce property rights (Alden Wily, 2018). To cite some key findings of that study; 53% of the 73 laws examined were first enacted since 2000, signalling the overall newness of this trend. All 73 laws provide for a community to be recognized as an owner of land to the maximum extent permitted in that country. This in turn necessitates introduction of a new class of registrable ownership, distinct in attributes from private ownership, but granted the equivalent legal force and protection. Just over half of the 73 laws require formal survey and registration of each community property to activate legal recognition. The remainder accept that customarily owned properties already exist and will be protected as such. However, as the exact boundaries of each community property are unknown, laws equally encourage case-by-case adjudication, mapping and registration of these lands and their owners to enhance protection.

Generally, community land in these states is recognized as comprising a mix of privately held homesteads and shared lands, also common in the African sample. There are other countries where constructs for collective ownership is provided only for common lands, that is, excluding permanently settled villages and cultivation, such as widely provided for in Central Asian countries from Mongolia to Uzbekistan. A surprising finding was how ubiquitous community-owned lands are in Europe; these exist either because of sustained if uneven support over centuries for collective ownership of forests and rangelands (e.g. Sweden, Ireland, Austria, Switzerland), or in the instance of Spain, Portugal and Romania, its reactivation in recent decades to provide more effective protection of these assets than their nationalization last century was able to deliver.

In the process of the current tenure reforms, the convention that property in land only exists if it is a saleable commodity is widely abandoned, in addition to presumption that only an individual person or a corporate entity, plus the state itself may be identified as owners. New typologies of indefeasible property which include estates which may be declared owned in perpetuity but indivisible or alienable have emerged. More uniquely, some laws place mirror conditions on the State itself, prevented governments from seizing or extinguishing granted native or community title or their right to impose new land uses (eg. mining) without the informed consent of owners (e.g. provided for in Colombia, Chile, Panama, Nicaragua, Australia and Vanuatu, among others).

This does not mean that all governments uphold their own laws, as the globally condemned instance of Brazil's worsening failure to protect indigenous lands in the Amazon shows, exacerbated by State encouragement of commercial logging, ranching and mining (Nature, 2020). Formulation of responsible investment guidelines by international finance organizations, and court rulings are slowly improving terms for communities and their land rights in extractive, conservation, and compulsory acquisition laws, including in Africa (Alden Wily, 2020). For example, Kenya's new Mining Act, 2016 requires community consent prior to mining exploration and consent to community management and benefit-sharing agreements if mining is then pursued. A court ruling in South Africa in 2018 directs that consent means consent not consultation (UNEP, 2020). Globally, demand is rising that the new Convention of Biological Diversity to be finalized in Glasgow in 2021 agree to extend the coverage of Protected Areas to 30% of global lands only on the basis of safeguards which identify and protect community possession of affected areas (MRG *et al.*, 2020).

Land Tenure Reform in Africa

Tenure reform in Africa descends from a mix of trends in the early 1990s; post-civil war demands, demands for structural adjustment including in land markets required by international lending agencies, and political reforms including adoption of multipartyism. This was also an era launching globally influential social reformism, including around the rights of indigenous peoples, numerous UN-led protocols, and a surge in demands for protection of human rights. The advance of a new era is most tangibly captured in a wave of new constitutionalism; 50 of 55 states have introduced new national constitutions since 1990. Of interest here is that a number of these upgrade the position of customary tenure. Most do so indirectly through new articles on the status of customary law, the roles and powers of traditional authorities, new provision for compensation for untitled lands at compulsory acquisition, and new bills of rights where positive discrimination is obligatory in respect of disadvantaged or indigenous communities and women. Most of the 17 newest constitutions directly address customary tenure. For example: 'All land in Kenya belongs to the people of Kenya collectively as a nation, as communities and as individuals'; 'Land in Kenya is classified as public, community or private'; 'Community land shall vest in and be held by communities' (Constitution of Kenya, 2010, Articles 91 and 63 (1)). And: 'The land tenure system in South Sudan shall consist of public land, community land and private land. Community land shall include all lands traditionally and historically held or used by local communities and their members' (Constitution of South Sudan, 2013, Article 171).

New land laws follow, or more rarely appear without constitutional changes (e.g. Tanzania, Liberia) or new land policies (e.g. Uganda). New national land laws since 1990 number 36 in 55 African states (65%). Around 30 of these positively affect customary land tenure (83%). The newest laws (since 2015) are from Togo, Liberia, Kenya, Malawi and Mali, and Tunisia. South Africa, Ghana and Sierra Leone have pertinent draft bills in hand directly affecting customary lands, improving on already positive constitutional provisions. Comparable community-focused land laws are also in development in Niger, Chad, Senegal, Madagascar, DRC and, allegedly, in the Central African Republic and Cameroon.

Among the 30 laws which reform rural tenure, 12 most comprehensively recognize customary property and its community governance: Burkina Faso, Tunisia, Ghana, Mali, Liberia, Benin, South Sudan, Uganda, Tanzania, Kenya, Malawi and Mozambique.

These are also laws which demonstrate innovations in how a community is registrable as an owner. While establishing that communal as well as individual or family customary ownership, was registrable, Uganda's Land Act, 1998 devised Communal Land Associations as the preferred means for this, albeit dramatically simplifying the terms and conditions stipulated in South Africa's Communal Property Associations Act, 1996. Tanzania broke new ground with its Village Land Act, 1999 by, first, reinforcing an earlier enactment of 1975 that even if elected, a village government could not own community lands, even in trust, but neither should it be assumed that the entire village land area was common property. It provided therefore for the land administrator, the village government, to first define and record community lands in Part A of the Village Land Register, and only then proceed to identify and register family and individual parcels in the remainder of the domain. Neighbouring Kenya eventually created a procedure in which the community first registers itself, through comprehensively listing every member in a Community Land Register, to be updated annually, and this being submitted along with other information for recognition. The community then proceeds to apply for the adjudication, survey and registration of its land, along with certification of derivative occupancy and exclusive rights within the property as issued to families or individual for houses and farms. This snapshot from one region illustrates a wider effort around Africa (e.g. Liberia, Benin, Burkina Faso) to dramatically reduce the costs, inaccessibility, bureaucracy, and often years taken for communities to secure collective entitlement through complex incorporation procedures under earlier generation laws before the 1990s.

African land laws have also been more precise in developing institutions for community land governance than arguably seen in other regions, and again with close attention to maximizing inclusion in decision making and minimizing bureaucracy in a bid for wider uptake and sustainability. Women always gain, although rarely do provisions require equal representation of women and men as decision makers, more like 33 percent. I will elaborate a little more under section 14.4 on gender.

Returning to generalized intra-Africa comparisons, other new land laws but with more limitations than exhibited in the 12 states listed above, have been enacted in 18 states (Angola, Lesotho, Botswana, Sierra Leone, Gambia, Nigeria, Guinea, Ethiopia, Algeria, Niger, Senegal, Madagascar, Republic of Congo, Zambia, Comoros, Namibia, Ivory Coast and South Africa). Some fall short by failing to provide for registrable community ownership (e.g. Botswana, Zambia), or recognize community properties but exclude forest resources (e.g. Angola, Madagascar). Still others fail to provide viable routes for registration of collective lands as touched upon above, requiring conversion of customary rights into leasehold or other forms devised and controlled by government (e.g. Ivory Coast, Zambia, Lesotho).

Most limitations exist in the remaining 21 countries where customary tenure is important in Africa (that is, excluding four island states where customary tenure no longer exists or never existed). Rwanda, like Burundi, allows customary farm and house ownership to be grounds for non-customary individual entitlement but makes no provision for collective entitlement. Indeed, their new land laws of respectively 2005 and 2011 co-opted valuable and scarce valley marshlands and forested lands to State ownership in curiously revisionist strategies. There is also reluctance in some countries to amend the subordinate role of customary tenure beyond lawful occupancy and use rights (Sudan, Zimbabwe, Guinea Bissau, Equatorial Guinea) or to encourage Kings to devolve ownership to their subject customary communities (Morocco, Eswatini).

Problematic Application of the Law

Many informational, logistical and financial shortfalls impede uptake and application of new land laws by communities. Nevertheless, the single commonest complaint is around weak political and administrative will. Review in 2016 by NGOs in DRC, Gabon, Cameroon, Senegal, Ghana and Nigeria identified this as the major impediment to change (ACRN, 2016). Review by civil society representatives in Mozambique, Madagascar, Kenya, Uganda, Namibia, Botswana, Mauritania and the Central African Republic similarly identified this as the most obstructive factor (Alden Wily, 2017). This was highest in slow willingness of governments to regulate their own, or investor and third-party invasion of untitled community lands for dubious public purposes. To use Kenya as an example, reluctance to apply the Community Land Act (2016) has resulted in a 'land rush' of sorts. This takes various forms, such as rushed gazettement of 70 new Public Forests out of community lands in 2017, followed by a 2018 amendment to the Forest Conservation and Management Act (2016) disabling the right of communities to ask parliament to revise boundaries (CLAN, 2020a). Rendille and Samburu pastoralist communities have been forced to go to court in 2020 to limit loss of thousands of hectares of community lands they claim has been 'grabbed' by the Kenya Defence Force, much of which land they fear will end up in the hands of private military personnel and other elites. Pokot pastoral communities secured an injunction in March 2021 against an internationally well-funded wildlife conservation agency creating conservancies on their lands without adequate consultation. Pastoralists are still in court after ten years of protesting the establishment of commercial windfarms on their lands (CLAN, 2020b).

Roadblocks to liberation of community property may also be erected by traditional authorities where they correctly fear new laws will curtail their claimed ownership over their subjects' lands, entrenched over years of colonial and postcolonial government support. Zambia's chiefs are well known as the principal roadblock to finalization of a national law policy of which drafting begun in the mid-1990s. Malawi's chiefs petitioned the President against giving his consent to the Customary Land Act, delaying its enactment until 2016 following adjustments assuring them more powers. In Namibia, the vesting of control in a limited number of paramount chiefs in the Northern Communal Lands has stymied efforts to enable communities within each of these tribal lands to secure their customarily exclusive access to adjacent rangelands as their collective property, while commercial cooperatives, in which chiefs are key members, are achieving this. Ghana's powerful chiefs have had a century to consolidate their allodial title over customary lands, a privilege which limits vesting title in unfarmed lands in the community. Presently, the equally entrenched powers of Sierra Leone's 190 chiefs, only partly limited by creation of elected councils in 2004, is the main challenge for communities to see the draft Customary Land Rights Bill of 2020 approved. Inter alia, while providing for family lands, Sierra Leone's draft bill proposes that shared lands are directly vested in community members in common, a paradigm successfully adopted in neighbouring Liberia.

14.4 Gender Provisions in New Land Laws

All African constitutions outlaw discrimination by gender: 22 of 55 constitutions state this minimally under articles outlawing discrimination based on race, religion, ethnicity, gender, etc. The remaining 33 constitutions (60%) treat women's rights directly. Around half do so in brief statements such as 'The State has a duty to see the elimination of all forms of discrimination against women and to assure them protection of their rights in all domains of private and public life' (Government of Chad, 1996). Some are more proactive, such as pledging to promote the representation of women in all state institutions (Equatorial Guinea in 2012), eliminating sexual violence (DRC in 2014), or protecting a spouse's property held before marriage (Liberia in 1996). Thirteen other constitutions adopt broader agendas (Egypt, Ethiopia, Ghana, Kenya,

Malawi, Republic of Congo, Senegal, South Sudan, Sudan, Swaziland, Uganda, Zambia and Zimbabwe). This paucity is possibly a function of different drafting traditions among Lusophone, Francophone, Arab-Islamic and Anglophone Africa. Ethiopia's Constitution (1995) is among the most precise and expansive, ranging from committing to maternity leave with full pay for women, prohibition of harmful customs which oppress or cause bodily or mental harm, to assuring women an equal right with men in the acquisition, administration, control, transfer and inheritance of land (Article 35). It also pledges to see the historical inequality and discrimination suffered by women considered through affirmative action.

Scrutiny of land laws is more rewarding on women's land rights. Still, these remain sub-optimal despite the plethora of international protocols, guidelines, programmes and development targets since 2000. This latterly includes Sustainable Development Goal 5a seeking increased legal stipulation on equitable gender access, ownership and control of land including over natural resources by 2030. In 2015 the African Union declared a goal of 30% of all registered land being in a woman's name by 2025. Recognition widely exists that 'gender parity is a precondition for Africa's development' (Chigbu, 2020) but less easy to deliver in law. This is apparent in cross-country studies which find countries vary widely in the legal attention they give to gender equity in land relations, and gaps too slowly closing in matters of house and farm ownership, inheritance, decision making, and control over investments and sales (Slavechevska *et al.* 2017; Ghebru, 2019). While Rwanda stands out as most legally proactive across the board in imposing gender equity, other states stand out in particular respects; for example, in introducing spousal consent requirements for sale of land (Uganda in 1998), establishing spousal co-ownership as the default (Tanzania in 1999), formally adopting community level dispute resolution into rural land governance (Tanzania in 1999, Kenya in 2016), enabling women to secure title without male consent (Nigeria in 1978, Madagascar in 2005). Nevertheless, as Ghebru concludes even where gender parity is on the agenda and proactive legal measures are embedded, a minority of rights are yet registered in the names of women as individuals or jointly with their spouses, and where even the leading cases of Ethiopia and Rwanda hover around 20%. Wealth and class exacerbate difficulties of closing gender gaps (Chigbu *et al.* 2019).

There remains a strong tendency in studies to focus on women's entitlement to houses and farms, critical, inter alia, in triggering livelihood investment and security (Chamberlain *et al.*, 2015). However, as more new laws addressing community-based frameworks for property are enacted, more reference is being made to women's rights in communal tenure and governance. One study is the Rights and Resources' examination of 400 land and forest laws to determine women's rights in 30 countries, including 11 countries in Africa (RRI, 2017). While rangelands were not covered, forests may be assumed as a fair proxy for legal treatment of all communal assets. RRI's study found a sub-optimal level of statutory affirmation of rural women's rights against eight indicators across the 30 countries, but African laws were singled out as most positive. Required participation of women in dispute resolution procedures was also highest in Africa. The last is significant considering the elemental role which community level dispute resolution plays in sustaining governance within the land sector. Rural women in Africa in communities fare less well in provisions for inheritance and voting rights. Nevertheless, legal progress was considered sufficiently positive by RRI to conclude that laws which expressly acknowledge that community-based tenure systems 'provide the greatest protection for women' (2018, p. 2). A number of other studies have begun to concur. The World Resources Institute finds on the basis of its own global studies that 'Women are disproportionately affected when title formalization excludes common resources. Rather than individual titling, indigenous women call for full recognition of their collectively held lands' (Salcedo-La Vina, 2020). FAO's guide on achieving SDG indicators also now stresses the need to consciously ensure equal gender access, control and ownership of communal lands (FAO, 2018).

Word limits prevent illustrative legal clauses being laid out, but I would point interested readers to the newest community land laws of Malawi, Kenya and Liberia as discernibly increasing requirements for equitable land rights for women and their participation in decision making. Kenya's law, for example, is particular on the unlawfulness of excluding women and girls from community land registers, requires the two-thirds gender law to be applied in formation of land committees, and prescribes a sufficiently high quorum of attendance at decision-making community assembly meetings to necessitate adult women attending.

14.5 Conclusions

Tenure Reform as a Trigger to Women's Empowerment

Of course, a legal lens has immense limitations; what the law says, if and how it is applied, and how its terms are adopted by affected populations, vary widely. Nor does legal land security prevent the land losses, displacement and dispersal, and other damages wrecked upon communities by especially commons grabbing. Press articles and research articles increasingly show how women, more than men, are ultimately most affected (e.g. Liberia Observer, 2016; Haller *et al.*, 2019; Kropiwnicka and Van Paassen, 2020). Their cases also illustrate the empowering effect of tenure reform affecting the periphery in raising women's awareness of their rights and community rights, contributing to their own voice and the solidarity of communities in challenging illegality and injustices. Such studies also bring forth reality that women's rights and dependence upon shared lands are often most impacted by what Haller *et al.* refer to 'commons grabbing' by commercial-scale encroachment. Women's empowerment is a common response to tenure reform in general. This is witnessed in the plethora of women's land empowerment and action groups which arise in consequence, country to country (Kropiwnicka and Van Paassen, 2020). An inadequately explored implication conveyed by findings of Ghebru *et al.* (2019) and more recently Feyertag *et al.* (2021) in their studies of women's perceptions of land security, is that the more aware women are of reforms the more concerned they are to secure formalization of their lands. An example of this is the rising demand of pastoral women in Kenya to be fully included in discussions on community land reform by county governments (Wairimu, 2021). This is significant in light of the deeply embedded customary exclusion of pastoralist women until the present in landholding and land governance, evident in the continuing difficulties which men in pastoralist communities are presently finding in even adding the names of women and girls to the community land registers (CLAN, 2020a).

Difficulties Putting Collective and Women's Rights Back in the Box

This chapter has shown how widely tenure reform is underway in Africa, and as visibly, a work in progress which could last decades. I have laid emphasis here upon its almost 'revolutionary' attack on entrenched notions of property, as individual and existing only as granted or approved through state procedures and definitions of property as always fungible and in practice regularly biased to male household heads. While much older in origins and practice, this became the adopted orthodoxy for most of the world through colonialism, and its subordination of indigenous property systems. It is tempting to locate African and global reformism as the last throes of anticolonialism, for as the late Okoth-Ogendo, a famed land law scholar, used to say, 'the land issue is the last colonial question to be resolved'. Yet the belated remedy through present reforms gives pause for thought. For the cutting edge of reformism is pragmatic; the most progressive interventions impliedly concede after substantial postcolonial experience that the indigenous customary regime has survived the onslaught of privatization with cause and appears to have a rational purpose which can longer be ignored. Additionally, by land reforms extending rights recognition to women, families and communities, titling is acquiring its rightful role as a tool, correctly ending assumption that titling equals individualization, and conversion of customary rights into non-customary entitlements.

It may also be observed that contemporary reforms 'rebel' in resisting the wholesale pursuit of the land privatization project, as so influentially advised, and demanded by international lending agencies. As a long-time observer of the changing land policies of the IMF and especially the World Bank, it was clear by the late 1980s in

Latin America and from the 1990s in Africa, that neoliberal structural adjustment conditions were only partially acceptable. In the event, unusually, those institutions were forced to follow the home-grown positions of progressive borrower states. Helpfully, they and many other agencies and donors advocate more strongly every year for the rights of communities to own lands and resources collectively. The upshot has been that more and more governments indicate by their strategic choices that individualization, while logical in the housing, farm and business sectors, there is a preference to build upon what exists as more relevant and sustainable in the majority land dependent sector. The plea of Hull *et al.* (2019, p. 21) to begin 'with an honest interrogation of belonging' towards successful land reform in Southern Africa resonates.

Roadblocks and pushbacks as only briefly touched upon in this paper can be expected to continue unabated for as long as reformist progress is made, inevitably provocative upsetting the status quo. Nevertheless, it is demonstrably difficult to put the land interests of women or those of marginalized or majority communities back in the box, once alternatives are aired and eventually legitimized in law. This is doubly difficult to suppress where provisions are borne out of new attention to social justice and more inclusive and devolutionary governance of land and property. It seems safe to say that while the achievement of equitable reformism for communities and their women members is a long road to tread, and compromises inevitable along the way, their realization will ultimately fail to be suppressed.

Endnotes

[1] The 14% of Rwanda's land area comprising customary marshlands owned by communities were relocated as the private property of the State by the Organic Land Law (2005), some of which were promptly allocated to sugar companies (Veldman and Lankhorst, 2011).

[2] Refer Veit (2011) for an overview of the landlessness, degradation and expansionism caused by subdividing rangelands into private parcels in 300+ group ranches created then privatized in Kenya.

[3] Countries that were never colonized by European states include Saudi Arabia, Iran, Thailand, China, Afghanistan, Nepal, Bhutan, Ethiopia, Japan and Korea.

References

ACRN (Africa Community Rights Network) (2016) Africa States can better protect community land rights. The state of Community Land Rights Africa. ACRN, Yaoundé, Cameroon.

Alden Wily, L. (2007) *So Who Owns the Forest? An Investigation into Forest Ownership and Customary Land Tenure in Liberia*. Sustainable Development Institute and FERN, Moreton-in-Marsh, Gloucestershire, UK.

Alden Wily, L. (2009) Tackling land tenure in the emergency to development transition in post-conflict states: From restitution to reform. In: Pantuliano, S. (Ed.), *Uncharted Territory: Land, Conflict and Humanitarian Action*. Practical Action Publishing Ltd, Rugby, UK, pp. 27–50.

Alden Wily, L. (2015) Estimating National Percentages of Indigenous and Community Lands: Methods and Findings for Africa. Data file on LandMark. Available at: http://www.landmarkmap.org (accessed 31 August 2020).

Alden Wily, L. (2017) *Piloting LandMark Practice Indicators for Tenure Reforms Affecting Community Lands in Nine African States*. LandMark. Washington, DC, USA.

Alden Wily, L. (2018) Collective land ownership in the 21st century: Overview of global trends. *Land*, 7(2), 68.

Alden Wily, L. (2020) Adjusting to new era agrarianism: Tackling the troubled interface of public and community property. In: Ochieng, O.C. (Ed.), *Rethinking Land Reform in Africa: New Ideas, Opportunities and Challenges*. African Bank Development Group, Abidjan, Ivory Coast, pp. 57–69.

Berry, S. (2020) On whose authority? Land reform, power and economic uncertainty in contemporary sub-Saharan Africa. In: Ochieng, O.C. (Ed.), *Rethinking Land Reform in Africa: New Ideas, Opportunities and Challenges*. African Bank Development Group, Abidjan, Ivory Coast, pp. 34–44.

Bromley, D. (2008) Formalising property relations in the developing world: The wrong prescription for the wrong malady. *Land Use Policy*, 26, 20–27.
Bruce, J. and Migot-Adholla, S. (Eds) (1994) *Searching for Land Security in Africa*. World Bank, Washington, DC, USA.
Chamberlain, J., Sitko, N. and Hichaambwa, M. (2015) *Gendered-impacts of smallholder land titling: A plot-level analysis in rural Zambia*. Paper presented at Conference of International Association of Agricultural Economists, 9–14 August, Milan, Italy. DOI: 10.22004/ag.econ.211451.
Chigbu, U.E. (2020) Negotiating land rights to redress land wrongs: women in Africa's land reforms. In: Ochieng, O.C. (Ed.), *Rethinking Land Reform in Africa: New Ideas, Opportunities and Challenges*. African Bank Development Group, Abidjan, Ivory Coast, pp. 156–167.
Chigbu, U.E., Paradza, G. and Dachaga, W. (2019) Differentiations in women's land tenure experiences: Implications for women's land access and tenure security in sub-Saharan Africa. *Land*, 8, 22.
Chimhowu, A. (2019). The 'new' African customary tenure. Characteristic, features and policy implications for a new paradigm. *Land Use Policy*, 81, 897–903.
CLAN (2020a) First Steps to Secure Community Land Title. Community Land Action Now report on training meeting held with members at Hill Park Hotel, Nairobi, Kenya, 30–31 January.
CLAN (2020b) Kenyan Communities report illegal evictions during COVID-19. Community Land Action Now press statement 23 July, Nairobi, Kenya. Available at: https://www.forestpeoples.org/en/CLAN-press-release-Kenyan-communities-report-illegal-evictions-during-covid19 (accessed 31 August 2020).
Constitution of Kenya (2010) *The Constitution of Kenya*. Government of Kenya, Nairobi, Kenya.
Constitution of South Sudan (2010) *The Constitution of South Sudan*. Government of South Sudan, Juba, South Sudan.
Diala, A. and Kangwa, B. (2019) Rethinking the interface between customary law and constitutionalism in sub-Saharan Africa. *De Jure Law Journal*, 52(1), 189–206.
Earle, T. (2017) Property in pre-history. In: *Graziadei, M.* and Smith, L. (Eds), *Comparative Property Law Global Perspectives*. Elgar Publishing, Cheltenham, UK.
FAO (2018) *Realizing Women's Rights to Land in the Law. A Guide for Reporting on SDG Indicator 5.a.2*. FAO, Rome, Italy.
Feyertag, J., Childress, M., Langdown, I., Locke, A. and Nizalov, D. (2021) How does gender affect the perceived security of land and property rights? Evidence from 33 countries. *Land Use Policy*, 104, article 105299.
Freeman, J. and Anderies, J. (2015) The socioecology of hunter-gatherer territory size. *Journal of Anthropological Archaeology*, 39, 110–123.
Ghebru, H. (2019) Women's land rights in Africa. In: Quisumbing, R., Meinzen-Dick, R., Suseela, R. and Njuki, J. (Eds), *Annual Trends and Outlook Report: Gender Equality in Rural Africa: From Commitments to Outcomes*. International Food Policy Research Institute (IFPRI), Washington, DC, USA, pp. 44–56.
Government of Chad (1996) *Chad's Constitution of 1996*. Government of Chad, N'Djamena, Chad.
Government of Ethiopia (1995) Proclamation no. 1/1995. *The Constitution of the Federal Democratic Republic of Ethiopia*. Government of Ethiopia, Addis Ababa, Ethiopia.
Guerena, A. (2016) *Unearthed: Land, Power and Inequality in Latin America*. Oxfam International, Oxford, UK.
Haller, T., Adams, T., Gmur, D. *et al.* (2019) Large-scale land acquisition as commons grabbing: A comparative analysis of six African case studies. In: Lozny, L.R. and McGovern, T.H. (Eds), *Global Perspectives on Long Term Community Resource Management*. Springer Nature, Cham, Switzerland, pp. 125–165.
Herrera, P.M., Davies, J. and Baena, P.M. (Eds) (2014) *The Governance of Rangelands: Collective Action for Sustainable Pastoralism*. Earthscan Routledge & IUCN, London, UK.
Hesseling, G. (2009) Land reform in Senegal: L'histoire se répète? In: Hoekema, A.J., Ubink, J.M. and Assies, W.J. (Eds), *Legalising Land Rights. Local Practices, State Responses and Tenure Security in Africa, Asia and Latin America*. Leiden University Press, Leiden, The Netherlands, pp. 243–270.
Hobsbawm, E. (1994) *The Age of Empire*. Abacus, London, UK.
Hull, S., Bablola, K. and Whittal, J. (2019) *Theories of land reform and their impact on land reform success in southern Africa*. *Land*, 8, 72.
Kropiwnicka, M. and Van Paassen, B. (2020) *The Gendered Impacts of Large-Scale Land Based Investments and Women's Responses*. TROCAIRE, Dublin, Ireland.
Lastarria-Cornhiel, S. (1997) Impact of privatization on gender and property rights in Africa. *World Development*, 25, 8, 1317–1333.

Liberia Observer (2016) Liberia: Concession violate women's rights. Monrovia. Available at: https://allafrica.com/stories/201610120459.html (accessed 23 March 2021).

McAuslan, P. (2007) Land law and the making of the British Empire. In: Cooke, E. (Ed.), *Modern Studies in Property Law*. Hart Publishing, Oxford, UK, pp. 239–262.

McAuslan, P. (2013) *Land Law Reform in Eastern Africa: Traditional or Transformative?* Routledge, Abingdon, UK.

MRG (Minority Rights Group), Rainforest Foundation UK and Survival, with 128 others (2020) *NGO Concerns Over the Proposed 30% Target for Protected Areas and Absence of safeguards for Indigenous Peoples and Local Communities*. Available at: https://minorityrights.org/wp-content/uploads/2020/09/EN_NGO-concerns-over-the-proposed-30-target-for-protected-areas-and-absence-of-safeguards-for-indigenous-people-and-local-communities_200901.pdf (accessed 1 September 2020).

Nature (2020) When will the Amazon hit the tipping point? Available at: https://www.nature.com/articles/d41586-020-00508-4 (accessed 20 March 2021).

North, D., Wallis, J. and Weingast, B. (2009) *Violence and Social Orders*. Cambridge University Press, Cambridge, UK.

Ochieng, O.C. (Ed.) (2020) *Introduction: Rethinking Land Reform in Africa: New Ideas, Opportunities and Challenges*. African Bank Development Group, Abidjan, Ivory Coast.

Peters, P. and Kambewa, P. (2007) Whose security? Deepening social conflict over 'customary' land in the shadow of land tenure reform in Malawi. *Journal of Modern African Studies*, 45(03), 447–472.

Ranger, T. (2012) The invention of tradition in colonial Africa. In: Hobsbawn, E. and Ranger, T. (Eds), *The Invention of Tradition*. Cambridge University Press, Cambridge, UK, pp. 211–262.

RRI (2015) *Who Owns the World's Land? A Global Baseline of Formally Recognized Indigenous and Community Land Rights*. Rights and Resources Initiative, Washington, DC, USA.

RRI (2017) *Power and Potential, A Comparative Analysis of National Laws and Regulations Concerning Women's Rights to Community Forests*. Rights and Resources Initiative, Washington DC, USA.

RRI (2018) *Legislative Best Practices for Securing Women's Rights to Community Lands*. Rights and Resources Initiative, Washington, DC, USA.

RRI (2020) *Estimate of the Area of Land and Territories of Indigenous Peoples, Local Communities and Afro-Descendants Where Their Rights Have Not Been Recognized*. Rights and Resources Initiative, Washington, DC, USA.

Salcedo-La Vina, C. (2020) *Beyond Title: How to Secure Land Tenure for Women*. World Resources Institute, Washington, DC. Available at: https://www.wri.org/insights/beyond-title-how-secure-land-tenure-women (accessed 24 March 2021).

Sjaastad, E. and Cousins, B. (2008) Formalisation of land rights in the South: An overview. *Land Use Policy*, 26, 1–9.

Slavechevska, V., Campos, A., Brunelli, C. and Doss, C. (2017) Beyond ownership: Women's and men's land right in sub-Saharan Africa. Paper presented to the World Bank Land Policy Conference, Washington, DC, USA.

Sulitstyarini, R., Budiono, A., Winarno, B. and Koeswahyono, I. (2018) The contact point of customary law and Islamic law (legal history perspective). *International Journal of Social Sciences and Management*, 5(2), 51–59.

Ubink, J. and Amanor, K. (Eds) (2008) *Contesting Land and Custom in Ghana*. Leiden University Press, Leiden, The Netherlands.

UNEP (2020) South African indigenous community win environmental rights case over mining company, Available at: https://www.unenvironment.org/news-and-stories/story/south-african-indigenous-community-win-environmental-rights-case-over-mining (accessed 30 August 2020).

Veit, P. (2011) *The Rise and Fall of Group Ranches in Kenya.* Focus on Land in Africa Series Brief. World Resources. Institute and Landesa, Washington, DC, USA.

Veldman, M. and Lankhorst, M. (2011) *Socio-Economic Impact of Commercial Exploitation of Rwandan Marshes*. International Land Coalition, Rome, Italy.

Wairimu, W. (2021) Women from pastoral counties demand inclusion in land issues. National Media Group, 21 January 2021.

Wang, Q., Zhang, X., Wu, Y. and Skitmore, M. (2015) The collective land system in China: Congenitally flawed or acquired irrational weakness? *Habitat International*, 50, 226–233. DOI: 10.1016/j.habitatint.2015.08.035.

15 Women and Land Inheritance under Legal Pluralism in Lesotho

Gaynor Gamuchirai Paradza*
Public Affairs Research Institute, University of the Witwatersrand
Johannesburg, South Africa

15.1 Background

Land inheritance is an important process through which women negotiate access to the resource. Legal pluralism renders land inheritance a complex process for those who rely on inheritance as a source of land. This chapter uses the case study of Lesotho to highlight how legal pluralism influences women's land inheritance in Lesotho. The research applied qualitative research approaches using both primary and secondary data to analyse the status of women's access to land in Lesotho. Primary data collection was undertaken in Maseru and Mafeteng using key-informant interviews, focus group discussions and field visits. Key informants included women's organizations, government representatives, Habitat for Humanity staff and beneficiaries, private sector, paralegals, traditional leaders, community councils, widows and land right organizations. Focus group discussions focused on the community council and paralegals, and the Land Advocacy reference group. Secondary data was obtained from published and unpublished sources. The findings were validated through a national workshop with key stakeholders in Lesotho. This means that the study findings can be used as a basis for drawing insights on women's land inheritance experiences of statute, custom and practice in Lesotho.

15.2 Why Land Inheritance Matters for Women Across Africa

Inheritance, the distribution of an individual's accumulated assets through generations, is a critical mode of property transfer in sub-Saharan Africa (Kumar and Quisumbig, 2012). Inheritance is an economic and human rights issue. The distribution of immovable and movable assets affects various individuals' economic trajectories (Ali *et al.*, 2014). Inheritance may be an opportunity for property accumulation or undermine security of access to assets (Cooper and Bird, 2012). Land inheritance issues highlight the vulnerability of women, land ownership and control and the social legitimacy and capacity of statutory and customary systems of governance (Cooper, 2012). The land-focused human rights agenda has increased the focus on land inheritance (Cotula *et al.*, 2004). This is important as some land inheritance practices and property distribution practices discriminate against women and violate their human rights (Cotula

*Corresponding author: gaynorp@pari.org.za

 Land Governance and Gender: The Tenure-Gender Nexus in Land Management and Land Policy (ed. U.E. Chigbu)
DOI: 10.1079/9781789247664.0015

et al., 2004; Cooper, 2012). Inheritance is also an economic concern. This was highlighted during the peak of the HIV and AIDS pandemic which exposed practices that threatened and undermined widows and orphans' rights to land (Cooper, 2010). Inheriting land provides women with security on the dissolution of a marriage and increased women's autonomy over this asset while the inability to inherit property can undermine women's economic security and independence (World Bank, 2012).

Land inheritance features in policy debates that include the 2005 UN Millennium Project, the Millennium Development Goals and Sustainable Development Goals. As a result, national Governments in sub-Saharan Africa are focusing on inheritance as a legislative reform to protect vulnerable women and children (Cooper, 2012).

Women's land inheritance rights are under threat from the increased commercialization of customary lands and other practices that undermine women's customary claims to land and the structures that underpin them.

Land inheritance is important because it is an arena where the tensions between customary and statutory frameworks are expressed. This is known as legal pluralism – a situation where two or more legal systems co-exist in one social field (Merry, 1988). Legal pluralism is linked to the complexity of issues affecting women's land rights in Africa (Whitehead and Tsikata, 2003). A plural legal system is viewed as consistently discriminating against women in the arena of land claims and allowing those with power to oppress those with less power (Swenson, 2018). This is because of the ambiguity, lack of clarity and loopholes that more powerful and more articulate people manipulate to suit their interests. The ambiguity is often used to redefine regulations in ways that undermine women's land tenure status. Examples include the vulnerability of widows to property loss in cases where property rights are not clearly defined and individuals manipulate, ignore, or subvert state policy and or when norms and principles are not applied equally to all individuals (Whitehead, 2003).

Land inheritance is complex because of its dependence on statutory and social norms in sub-Saharan Africa (Ali *et al.*, 2014). In many countries legal and land reforms have had profound effects on customary inheritance norms and practices (Kalabamu, 2009). Development practitioners have been advocating legal reforms establishing equal *de jeure* rights in matters of inheritance (World Bank, 2012). Policy makers may seek to override the customary system to assert state authority, to address a perceived lack of security conferred by traditional structures or address perceived inequities in the traditional systems (Linkow, 2019). Legal reforms are claimed to have the potential to improve economic outcomes and strengthen women's empowerment. For example, Harari's (2019) research on Kenya suggests that legal reform at the statutory level can have an impact even in a context of poor enforcement and deep seated social norms. However, poor legal enforcement and gender insensitive social norms undermine the effectiveness of legal reform (Harari, 2019). There is debate over whether customary systems of governance provide adequate protection of women and children's property rights (Cooper, 2012). If customary law offers advantages like affordability and flexibility over statutory law, it will be preferred (Atwood, 1990). This increases the need for context-specific understanding of the dynamics leading to the inheritance outcome. The plurality of governance systems may create opportunities and challenges for women seeking to inherit land (Makura-Paradza, 2010; Cooper 2012; Paradza *et al.*, 2020).

Patriarchal customary land tenure practices marginalize women (Kameri-Mbote, 2005). This is related to the vulnerability associated with the women's position as spouses with rights to marital property under both customary and statutory systems of governance (Cooper, 2012). This is because customary marriages may be informally entered or exited; customary marriages are rarely legally registered which makes it difficult for spouses to prove their spousal status; statutory laws do not necessarily recognize a wife's contribution and statutory inheritance laws fail to recognize wives in polygamous unions (Cooper, 2012). Dancer's study of Tanzania found that customary laws have been neglected (Dancer, 2017). In situations where statutory and customary law are in conflict, women's legal rights are often ignored (Lastarria-Cornheil, 1997). A study of land inheritance in Zimbabwe's rural areas highlighted the challenges that Africans faced in trying to dispose of immovable property through a will as well as the impact of contentious interpretation of customary law on claims and counter claims (Mujere, 2014). A specific focus on individual communities reveals nuanced variation in land inheritance practices and impact on women's access to customary land in Africa.

The existence of 73 ethnic groups generates diversity in customary practices in Zambia (Spichiger and Kabala, 2014). Even where customary law is marginalized in statutory legislation, customary practices dominate real life, especially in the rural sector and among the poor and underprivileged (Adams and Turner, 2005). A 2012 study of seven countries in sub-Saharan Africa concluded that although traditional and statutory mechanisms exist distinctly from each other, the actors within them draw from both systems to access justice. The study found that women relied on non-statutory institutions because they were cheaper, more accessible and faster in resolving disputes. Sow's (2011) study of the Democratic Republic of Congo shows that the existence of multiple land legislation and overlapping of customary and statutory law resulted in the lack of clarity and coherence in the Democratic Republic of Congo (Sow, 2011) – a situation that makes women vulnerable. The lack of coherence especially in the roles and responsibilities and limits of customary land governance authorities leaves those who rely on these institutions vulnerable. The 1991 Constitution of Burkina Faso prohibits all forms of discrimination. However, the Constitution does not legally define what constitutes discrimination. As a result, laws are applied inconsistently, and women are regarded as the property of men in rural areas (Paradza, 2018).

In Benin, the customary law relegates women to perpetual minors in terms of inheritance but the Civil code grants women the full capacity to conclude contracts though the husband's consent may be required. The customary laws deny succession and inheritance rights to daughters and the deceased husband's family frequently challenges widows when administering inheritance (Paradza, 2018).

There may also be contradictions, for example, in South Africa where the powers that the traditional authorities have over land in customary tenure areas are undermined by the powers that municipal local government authorities wield over the same areas. There may also be vague and undefined relationships. In each case, the situation provides opportunities and challenges for women's access to land in customary tenure areas. Although Tanzania's Land Act and Village Land Act (both passed in 1999) provide for women's ownership of land, customary practices regarding marriage and inheritance continue to discriminate heavily against women. The current constitution upholds equal rights to property for men and women but does not clarify whether the law or custom take precedent when there is a conflict. And such a conflict exists in communities across the nation, undermining women's rights (Lawry, 2013).

Botswana gives constitutional and statutory recognition to customary tenure, and has become a model, among other sources, for a tenure reform movement under way across sub-Saharan Africa. Botswana embraced customary tenure as the dominant means for delivering secure land rights to its citizens shortly after independence in 1966 (Lawry, 2013).

Makura-Paradza's 2010 study in a customary tenure area in Zimbabwe found that there were a variety of governance structures and institutions which draw power from a variety of sources governing customary land. The situation rendered legal systems and rules largely irrelevant in determining resource access in communal areas.

15.3 Overview of Women's Land Inheritance Rights Under Legal Pluralism in Sub-Saharan Africa

Women were marginalized from land inheritance in Rwanda where sons were allocated part of their father's land when they married and shared equally in the remaining land upon the death of their father (Lankhorst, 2012). In the Rukanga region in Kiliba in the Democratic Republic of Congo, women cannot inherit the profitable banana plantations (Sow, 2011). In Kenya, some customary structures preclude women from inheriting ancestral land (Yngstrom, 2002). In some countries, women had conditional inheritance of land. Henryson and Joireman's study in Western Kenya showed that individual woman's circumstances determined their inheritance outcome. A childless widow and or widow who did not have sons was more likely to lose customary land upon the death of their husband. This was the same case for a woman who was perceived to be 'of bad character' (Joireman, 2006). Some widowed women were granted usufruct rights to land they used with their deceased husband. (Kameri-Mbote, 2007). Widows were more likely to be dispossessed of the immovable property if they were young – a practice that was labelled property grabbing by Izumi (2006). Studies done in Namibia's Caprivi region showed that women struggle to retain access and use of land after the death of a spouse (Cousins, 2009). Meinzen-Dick and Mwangi (2009) reported that among the Taita in Kenya although land tenure was grounded in patrilineal system, the women were entitled to pieces of land. Widows had the right to pawn or sell on behalf of the minor heirs. Makura-Paradza's (2010) study of the Shona people in Goromonzi District in Zimbabwe found that the widows who remained on their marital residence after the death of their spouse constituted most single women. Sow's (2011) study of Kivu in the Democratic Republic of Congo illustrated that women could inherit land where a father may decide to give a plot of land to his daughter. Land inheritance by daughters was becoming popular in Ntugamo in Uganda (Garber, 2013). Husbands also bequeath matrimonial land to their wives among the Apac in Uganda (Garber 2013). Aliber *et al.*'s (2004) study in Kenya, however, showed that most women were able to hold on to land after the death of their husband and women losing their home was the exception rather than the norm. Women's heterogeneity mean that they will have diverse experiences with the institutions and frameworks governing land inheritance (Chigbu *et al.*, 2019). The examples also underscore the importance of context and local processes in the outcomes of women's land inheritance rights. Inconsistency is also a source of vulnerability for women's land rights as it shows that the rights are subject to renegotiation at the time of succession and the outcomes are not consistent.

15.4 Lesotho Women's Experiences in Inheriting Land Under Legal Pluralism

Why Land Inheritance is Important for Women in Lesotho

Lesotho is a landlocked country endowed with water, diamonds, labour and land: 70% of the population is reliant on agriculture (UNDP, 2015). Women constitute 61% of the Basotho elderly and more than 86% of these live in rural areas (Mabele, 2012). Lesotho has a relatively high population living in poverty (UNDP, 2015). The poor women-headed households are vulnerable to food insecurity (Landesa, 2014). The country has the third-highest HIV and AIDS prevalence in the world (UNICEF, 2017). Poor access to services, especially reproductive health services, exacerbates the problem (Chwarae, 2015). The increasing adult antiretroviral therapy (ART) coverage, increasing contraception use by women, HIV testing, and family planning services has reduced the population's vulnerability to HIV and AIDS in Lesotho (UNDP, 2015).

Land inheritance is important for women as men hold 70% of the land in Lesotho (Paradza, 2018). The lack of a social welfare increases the importance of land as a social security asset for women in Lesotho. Women lack resources to secure access to land under the pressure of land markets, urbanization and individualization (Paradza, 2018). The high HIV and AIDS rate undermines the traditional structures that play a role in helping to protect the land rights of widows and orphans (UNICEF, 2017). Women and children are often displaced though property grabbing. The dominance of patriarchy in Lesotho's land governance institutions undermines women's chances of successfully inheriting land (Paradza, 2018).

Legal and Institutional Frameworks Governing Land Inheritance in Lesotho

Women's land inheritance rights are supported by national and international provisions that include the Convention on the Elimination of all forms of Discrimination Against Women to protect and promote the rights of women; The African Charter on Human and Peoples' Rights, 1981, The Southern Africa Development Community Declaration on Gender and Development, 1997, Convention on the Rights of Children, The African Charter, The Protocol to the African Charter on Human and Peoples' rights of Women and The Framework and Guidelines on Land Policy in Africa. Although Lesotho is a signatory to almost all international and regional conventions and protocols on gender equality, traditional cultural norms discourage women from taking advantage of the opportunities (UNDP, 2015).

Lesotho is a Constitutional Monarchy. The State law enshrined in a Constitution exists side by side with customary laws (Letuka *et al.*, 1994). Section 17 of the Constitution protects citizens from arbitrary seizure of movable and immovable property. The Constitution recognizes customary law which has impacts on gender and social equality. Specifically, section 18 of the Constitution of Lesotho prohibits discrimination. However, subsection 4 provides that section 18 shall not apply to customary law (which is the law on marriage, divorce, burial, succession), thus perpetuating the minority status of women under customary law (Government of Lesotho, 1993). The *Laws of Lerotholi* spelt out some of the traditions and customs of the Basotho and codified the customary law. Section 7 of the *Laws of Lerotholi* I section 17 gives widows the rights of 'retention of land'. The *Laws of Lerotholi* restrict inheritance of property, including land, to first born males (cited in UN-Habitat, 2005). The Law Reform Commission of 1993 recommended repealing of gender discriminatory property and land-related laws in Lesotho. The Legal Capacity of Married Persons Act 2006 accords partners to a marriage, equal rights, and control over marital property (Government of Lesotho, 2006). The Land Act 2010 modernized land administration and abolished customary land tenure. The 2010 Land Act strengthened women's property rights by providing for equal and joint land ownership for men and women, inclusion of women in land registration, and inheritance of property. (Government of Lesotho, 2010).

Customary law and/or practice governs 90% of the Basotho (Letuka *et al.*, 1994). Customary Law, which applies to most of the land in Lesotho institutionalizes the subordination of women in Lesotho. Under customary law, land held under customary tenure is allocated for free to married male members of a designated community for subsistence and to look after his family. Customary land inheritance follows the male lineage. Although not initially registered, customary land rights are recorded on a document known as Form C, which is issued by the traditional authority.

Institutions Responsible for Determining Women's Land Inheritance in Lesotho

The power to allocate land is vested in the King. This power is exercised by other authorities in accordance with the constitution. The authorities responsible for administering land and presiding over land inheritance transmissions include the office of the Master of the High Court whose duties include administering Deceased Estates and administration of the Guardian fund. The decentralized District administrative offices assist the office of the Master – although it is not well known in the villages (UN-Habitat, 2005). Local authorities like Maseru City Council (MCC) are also involved in land administration. The Land Administration Authority (LAA) is responsible for cadastre, mapping, land administration, and the registration of land titles and deeds. The Lesotho Housing and Land Development Corporation (LHLDC) is a parastatal mandated to service land and housing (Leduka *et al.*, 2018). The Customary courts administer the land held under customary tenure. Chiefs preside over these and are responsible for land administration. The family is the basic unit for the administration and determination of land inheritance (UN-Habitat, 2005).

Patriarchy is the dominant culture in Lesotho, where men are the head of the household. Patriarchy influences marriage, divorce, succession, inheritance, property rights and the justice system (Letuka *et al.*, 1994). The patriarchal culture is reproduced in the male-dominated institutions and decision-making structures that are responsible for allocating land in Lesotho.

How Marriage Informs Land Inheritance Dynamics for Basotho Widows

Marriage is a strategic institution because it is the basis for women's land outside family. Historically, the marriage type informs the determination of inheritance. In Lesotho, people either have a civil or customary marriage. Customary marriages are normally not registered and as a result, there is no documentary proof of the marriage. Consequently, housing assets acquired by the married couple were historically registered in the name of the male spouse who was typically the wage earner (this is changing as more women become economically active and land governance institutions adopt gender sensitive land allocation and recording practices). Historically, the death of the male spouse in a customary marriage triggered inheritance processes which favoured the husband's family and marginalized the widow. When a couple is married in terms of a civil marriage contracted in terms of the Marriage Act, the marriage is formally registered, and the couple issued with marriage certificate as proof of the union. Civil marriages provide better protection for women's land inheritance rights. However, the Basotho normally marry under both customary and civil law to constitute a dual marriage regime (UN-Habitat, 2005) which gives rise to uncertainty on the issue of inheritance. Customary law dominates in inheritance decisions (Letuka *et al.*, 1994).

Succession Planning under Custom and Statute in Lesotho

Succession planning is one way to ensure that women have secure land inheritance rights. Succession plans can potentially safeguard women and children's land rights by providing documents and potentially mobilize support for their land claims. The succession planning in Lesotho is according to the plural frameworks of custom and/or statute. In accordance with custom, The *Laws of Lerotholi* provide that a (male) landholder writes instructions regarding the allocation of his land and property after his death. This is known as *Lentsoe la mofu le aheloa lesaka* – 'wishes of the dead should be respected' loosely translated as 'instructions of the deceased'. The 'the instructions' are registered with the traditional leader. Statutory law in Lesotho provides for succession planning through a will. The statutory systems recognize the will. An adult can prepare a will and lodge it with an executor. The will is seen as a document that can potentially safeguard inheritance rights of women and girls. A survey of wills registered with the Master of the High Court in Lesotho in 1990 showed that the percentage of Basotho drawing up wills was increasing annually (Letuka *et al.*, 1994). The increase can be ascribed to advocacy work by various institutions in Lesotho. Lesotho Federation of Women Lawyers (FIDA), LAA, Women and Law in Southern Africa (WLSA) and Habitat for Humanity have been sensitizing communities, chiefs and individuals to register a will. The LAA encourages people who register leaseholds to also register a will. FIDA and WLSA draft wills for members of the public for free. Habitat for Humanity encourages beneficiaries of its housing programmes to register a will to assist beneficiaries to protect their new houses from property grabbing. Habitat for Humanity has partnered with Econet mobile service provider. Econet provided Habitat for Humanity with a complimentary Short Messaging Service (SMS) to be sent to 500 000 subscribers. The SMS raises awareness of the importance of succession planning. This was complimented by radio programs and campaigns in the print media (Paradza, 2018). The advocacy initiatives also targeted courts, the police, and the office of the Master of the High Court. Traditional chiefs have reported an increase in the incidence of reporting of inheritance-related cases and increased Basotho's awareness of the gender sensitive land inheritance laws.

How Women Experience Land and Inheritance Under Legal Pluralism

There is wide variance between law and practice on property inheritance in Lesotho. Although patriarchy and custom continue to dominate inheritance transmissions in Lesotho, the situation is changing. The evidence of these changes includes parents considering a child's investment in the estate and or the children's behaviour when they appoint heirs. Parents also bequeathed immovable property to a daughter who had returned from a failed marriage so she could have a place for herself and children. It is not uncommon for parents to bequeath immovable property to female children in their instructions' to the traditional leadership (Landesa, 2014). Widows are increasingly more assertive and proactive than popularly believed. They challenged those who tried to dispossess them of their marital property, reported violations to court and administered wills of their deceased spouse (Paradza, 2018). Widows were more likely to successfully inherit land and immovable property if they were aware of their legal rights and entitlements under the law. Widows who actively sought to secure their land inheritance rights were more likely to succeed. Women's capacity to defend their land and property rights in succession depend on their capacity to mobilize resources and support from the family, community, traditional authorities, and the deceased husband's male relatives. Widows who had a documented proof of their marriage were fighting to inherit a property that was registered under a lease or mortgage and had their case presented before a statutory rather than a customary court or family hearing (e.g. if the office of the Master of the High Court intervened) were more likely to secure their land and housing rights. There are also community-based support groups that support widows and assist them to defend their land claims after the death of their spouse. The existence of a will provided more evidence of the deceased's succession plan that a widow could use to support her land inheritance claim in Lesotho.

Women who lose their marital property to relatives of the deceased husband highlighted how patriarchal power, social networks, bribery and corruption were used to undermine statutory processes and structures. The widows' lack of and/or limited awareness of their land inheritance rights undermined their capacity to defend their land rights. Some families isolated their grieving daughter, and this discouraged the widows from claiming and insisting on their inheritance rights. Widows who internalized indifference to inheritance were more likely to lose their inheritance rights. Widows who were more emotionally vulnerable because of trauma and or emotional abuse were not in a strong position to defend their inheritance land rights. Land inheritance disputants' lack of knowledge about the extent of their land rendered the land boundary vulnerable to manipulation by those with more power than the widow. An increasing threat to women's land inheritance rights in Lesotho was land inheritance disputes between older and younger women in the same household. There was also an increase of cases where female relatives of the deceased where contesting orphans' land inheritance rights. Women and orphans in this position struggle to defend their possession because of, among other things, emotional vulnerability. Younger women and poorer women are more vulnerable to dispossession. Widows whose in-laws were more connected in society were more likely to lose their land. Corruption was used by in-laws to undermine widows' property inheritance claims. As a result, police delayed acting and/or court dockets went missing and widows faced frustrating delays in their efforts to secure their inheritance rights. As a result, affected widows lost their land and housing.

Limits of Statutory Law in Protecting Women's Land Inheritance Rights in Lesotho

Bias Towards Registered Land

Although the statutory protection of land offers potential to secure women's land inheritance rights, the protection is only a reality for land that has been formally registered. This is confirmed by the institutions involved in land dispute mediation such as the local authorities, LAA who highlighted that most of the land-related disputes are inheritance related. Although the LAA provides a valuable service for lease holders, most of the land disputes are on land that is not registered.

The Institutional Capacity Bottlenecks

There is limited capacity to draft wills in the public offices in Lesotho. The existing dispute resolution institutions are overwhelmed by inheritance-related disputes. This results in delays and bottlenecks in the resolution of disputes a situation that undermines widows' capacity to assert and enjoy their land inheritance rights. Some land administration institutions in Lesotho have initiated processes to reduce the bottlenecks. The LHDA reported an increase in inheritance-related claims arising from the survivors of beneficiaries of the Lesotho Highlands Water Project (LHWP). The MCC's land allocation committee sits every month to help people who have applied to inherit unregistered land. The city council works with local chiefs and community councils to verify the land claims. The LAA's legal department mediates inheritance disputes on leased land. None of the decisions made by any of these institutions is legally binding.

How Customary Norms and Alternatives Limit Statutory Succession Planning

Widows and orphans can potentially use statutory wills to defend their inheritance rights. Although there was increased awareness of the need to register their succession plans, people were reluctant to formally register their inheritance plans though formal statutory wills. Death is a taboo subject among the Basotho. This makes it difficult for the Basotho to engage strangers like lawyers and formal officers who preside over the processes involved in the preparation of a valid statutory will. Wills are also marginalized by the customary succession processes that are conducted through 'instructions of the deceased'. Although not a statutory legal instruction, the 'instructions of the deceased' are respected by the community. Some Basotho has a perception that once they have registered their *Lentsoe la mofu le aheloa lesaka* at the Chief they do not necessarily have to register a statutory will. Some community members believe that preparing a will is more complex than the process of recording their 'instructions of the deceased' with the Chief. The Chiefs who were interviewed reported that there has been an increase in the number of people who have registered their 'instructions of the deceased'. This highlights the increased awareness of the need for succession planning among the Basotho.

Statutory Institutions' Inconsistency in the Processing of Statutory Wills

Although Lesotho has progressive laws to protect women's land inheritance rights, the implementation challenges undermined these laws (Landesa, 2014). Statutory institutions' inconsistency in the interpretation, recognition and enforcement of wills poses a challenge for widows seeking to secure land inheritance rights through the statutes. In some cases, the Master of the High Court accepts the will while other statutory institutions like district courts reject the will. There is also a lack of consistency between the courts in terms of practice and outcomes in the different areas of Lesotho. For example, while statutory law guarantees equality in land allocation and transactions, research revealed that when a will is made in favour of a woman and or a person who is not a customary heir, there will be resistance by the family, and this undermines women and daughters 'capacity to inherit land and property' (Chwarae, 2015). The lack of consolidated laws on inheritance was identified as a source of weakness by the advocates and institutions working to protect women and girls' land inheritance rights in Lesotho. For example, the Land Act 2010 has an exemption for Customary law which leaves women vulnerable when they try to defend their inheritance land rights in a statutory court. There is need for a framework that reconciles discrepancies in the existing regulatory mechanisms to ensure equal treatment of men and women in land inheritance matters.

Challenges in Enforcing Succession Plans

It is a challenge to disseminate and enforce wills especially those in favour of a female heir (Ramakhula, 2019). The family of a deceased man has some discretion to validate a will (UN-Habitat, 2005). As a result, wills are contested, their validity questioned, forged, sometimes referred to the family meeting by the courts or disregarded. Chiefs, community councils, lawyers and those involved in mediation revealed that although the number of women and girls reporting inheritance related disputes increased, women and girls still struggle to secure their land and housing inheritance rights in Lesotho.

15.5 Reflection: How to Strengthen Women's Land Inheritance Under Legal Pluralism

The foregoing confirms that legal pluralism dynamics present a complex web of institutions through which women must negotiate to inherit land. The case of Lesotho uses land inheritance to highlight how custom and statute inform women's opportunity to access land. The important realization is that custom and statute are not mutually exclusive but overlapping and intertwined institutions that women must negotiate in land inheritance. The introduction of statutes and formal institutions to facilitate land inheritance is of limited consequence for women in a situation where patriarchal family determines the process. The case illustrates the potential of succession planning as an intervention to secure women's rights in both the customary and statutory setting. The conclusion is that inheritance processes may open opportunities for renegotiation of land access for women and men in customary tenure areas. The experiences of women's land inheritance in Lesotho shows that these processes can be pre-empted. The experience of Lesotho illustrates how women experience land inheritance in a situation where both customary practice and statutory law govern land delivery. The government of Lesotho should ensure coherence and consistency among the diverse institutions working to secure women's land inheritance in the country. Specifically, regarding the place and legitimacy of customary succession planning, there is an opportunity for the government to work with these structures and develop them in such a way that they complement rather than compete with formal succession planning processes. The chapter also highlighted the strategic importance of the family as a basic unit of intervention that should be targeted in efforts to reform land inheritance succession planning in ways that secure women and orphans' land rights in Lesotho.

Acknowledgement

The author acknowledges the support of Habitat for Humanity Lesotho.

References

Adams, M. and Turner, S. (2005) *Legal Dualism and Land Policy in Eastern and Southern Africa*. UNDP-International Land Coalition Workshop, 31 October–3 November, Nairobi, Kenya.

Ali, A., Deininger, K. and Goldstein, M. (2014) Environmental and gender impacts of land tenure regularisation in Africa. Pilot evidence from Rwanda. *Journal of Development Economics*, 110, 262–275.

Aliber, M., Walker, C., Machera, M., Kamau, P., Omondi, C. and Kanyinga, K. (2004) *The Impact of HIV/AIDS on Land Rights: Case Studies from Kenya*. HSRC Publishers, Cape Town, South Africa.

Atwood, D.A. (1990) Land registration in Africa: The impact on agricultural production. *World Development*, 918(5), 659–671.

Chigbu, U.E., Paradza, G. and Dachaga, W. (2019) Differentiations in women's land tenure experiences: Implications for women's land access and tenure security in sub-Saharan Africa. *Land*, 8, 22. DOI: 10.3390/land8020022.

Chwarae, T. (2015) *A Woman's Place in Lesotho: Tackling the Barriers to Gender Equality*, Report, 2. Available at: http://www.cteg.org.uk/wp-content/uploads/2015/04/chwarae-teg-report-a-womans-place-in-lesotho-DT-en.pdf (accessed 11 July 2019).

Cooper, E. (2010) *Women and inheritance in 5 sub-Saharan African countries: Opportunities and challenges for policy and practice change*. Paper presented at the CRPC/ ODI Roundtable, Inheritance and the Intergenerational Transmission of Poverty, ODI, London, UK, 11 October.

Cooper, E. (2012) Women and inheritance in sub-Saharan Africa: What can change. *Development Policy Review*, 30(5), 641–657.

Cooper, E. and Bird, K. (2012) Inheritance and intergenerational dimension of poverty. *Development Policy Review*, 30 (5), 527–541.

Cotula, L., Toulmin, C. and Hesse, C. (2004) Land tenure and administration in Africa: Lessons of experiences and emerging issues. International Institute for Environment and Development, London, UK.

Cousins, B. (2009) Potential and pitfalls of 'communal' land tenure reform: Experience in Africa and implications for South Africa. World Bank Conference on Land and Poverty, 9–10 March, Washington, DC, USA.

Dancer, H. (2017) An equal right to inherit? Women's land rights, customary law and constitutional reform in Tanzania. *Social and Legal Studies*, 26(3), 291–310.

Garber, B. (2013) Women's land rights and tenure security in Uganda: Experiences from Mbale, Apace and Ntugamo Stichproben. *Wiener Zeitschrift für kritische Afrikastudien,* 24(13), 1–32.

Government of Lesotho (1993) *Constitution of Lesotho.* Government Printers, Maseru, Lesotho.

Government of Lesotho (2006) *Lesotho: Legal Capacity of Married Persons Act 2006 (Act 9 of 2006).* Government Printers, Maseru, Lesotho.

Government of Lesotho (2010) *Land Act 2010 (Act No. 8 of 2010).* Government Printers, Maseru, Lesotho.

Harari, M. (2019) *Women's Inheritance Rights and Bargaining Power Evidence from Kenya.* University of Chicago Press, Chicago, IL, USA.

Izumi, K. (2006) *Reclaiming Our Lives. HIV and AIDS, Women's Land and Property Rights and Livelihoods in Southern and East Africa: Narratives and Responses.* HSRC Press, Cape Town, South Africa.

Joireman, S.F. (2006) *Applying Property Rights Theory to Africa: The Consequences of Formalizing Informal Land Rights*. University of Richmond, Wheaton, VA, USA.
Kalabamu, F.T. (2009) Towards egalitarian inheritance rights in Botswana: the case of Tlokweng. *Development Southern Africa*, 26(2), 209–223.
Kameri-Mbote P (2005) The Land Has Its Owners. Gender Issues in Land Tenure Under Customary Lawin Kenya. Working Paper 9. Nairobi International Environmental Law Resource Centre, Nairobi, Kenya.
Kumar, N., and Quisumbing, A.R. (2012) Beyond 'Death do us part': The Long-term implications of divorce perceptions on women's well-being and child schooling in rural Ethiopia. *World Development*, 40(12), 2478–2489.
Landesa (2014) *Gender and Land Good Practices and Lessons Learned from Four Millennium Challenge Corporation Compact-Funded Land Projects*. Available at: http://www.landesa.org/wp-content/uploads/Landesa-Gender-Land-Report-MCC-2014.pdf (accessed 17 January 2021).
Lankhorst, M. (2012) *Women's Land Rights in Customary Dispute Resolution in Rwanda Focus on Land in Africa Brief.* Available at: http://www.focusonland.com/countries/womens-land-rights-in-customary-dispute-resolution-in-rwanda (accessed 17 January 2021).
Lastarria-Cornheil, S. (1997) Impact of privatisation on gender and property rights in Africa. *World Development*, 25(8), 1317–1333.
Lawry, S. (2013) Is it time to enshrine land rights in sub-Saharan Africa into law? Available at: http://www.theguardian.com/global-development-professionals-network/dai-partner-zone/sub-saharan-africa-recognize-customary-land-rights (accessed 17 January 2021).
Leduka, R.C., Ntaote, M. and Takalimane, S.N. (2018) Land governance in Lesotho. The NELGA Land Governance in Southern Africa Hub Conference, July, Windhoek, Namibia.
Letuka, P., Matashane,K., Mamashela, M.P. and Mbatha, L. (1994) *Inheritance in Lesotho. Women and Law in Southern Africa Research Project.* Women and Law in Southern Africa, Maseru, Lesotho.
Linkow, B. (2019) Inheritance practices, investment incentives and women's control over rural land in Kenya. *Journal of African Economies*, 28(3), article 304322.
Mabele, M. (2012) *Population Ageing in Lesotho*. Kingdom of Lesotho. Bureau of Statistics Report No. 34.
Makura-Paradza, G. (2010) *Single Women, Land and Livelihood Vulnerability in the Communal Areas of Zimbabwe.* Wageningen Publishers, Wageningen, The Netherlands.
Meinzen-Dick, R. and Mwangi, E. (2009) Cutting the web of interests: Pitfalls of formalizing property rights. *Land Use Policy*, 26(1), 36–43.
Merry, S. (1988) Legal pluralism. *Law and Society Review*, 22, 869–896.
Mujere, J. (2014) Land, gender and inheritance disputes among the Basotho in the Dewure Purchase Areas, colonial Zimbabwe. *South African Historical Journal*, 66(4), 699–716.
Paradza, G. (2018) *Women's Access to Land and Housing in Lesotho*. Habitat for Humanity, Maseru, Lesotho.
Paradza, G., Mokwena, L. and Musakwa, W. (2020) Could mapping initiatives catalyse the interpretation of customary land rights in ways that secure women's land rights? *Land*, 9, 344.
Ramakhula, T. (2019) *In but Out in Lesotho: Women's Representation Dilemma*. Available at: https://media.africaportal.org/documents/Ramakhula__In_but_out_in_Lesotho.pdf (accessed 2 December 2020).
Sow, N. (2011) *'Women inherit wrappers, men inherit fields': The Problem of Women's Access to Land in South Kivu, Democratic Republic of Congo, Research Report December 2014 Women*. Available at: www.womenforwomen.org.uk/sites/default/files/WfWI_DRC_Research_Report.pdf (accessed 2 December 2020).
Spichiger, R. and Kabala, E. (2014) Gender equality and land administration: The case of Zambia. Available at: https://www.econstor.eu/handle/10419/122286 (accessed 2 December 2020).
Swenson, G. (2018) Legal pluralism in theory and practice. *Analytical Essay International Studies Review*, 20, 438–462.
UNDP (2015) *Lesotho National Human Development Report: Summary 2015.* United Nations Development Programme. Available at: http://hdr.undp.org/sites/default/files/lesotho_summary_report_high_res_single_pages.pdf (accessed 6 December 2020).
UN-Habitat (2005) *Law, Land Tenure and Gender Review Series: Southern Africa*. United Nations Human Settlement Programme. Available at: https://www.un.org/ruleoflaw/files/Law,_Land_Tenure_and_Gender_LESOTHO.pdf (accessed 3 December 2020).
UNICEF (2017) UNICEF Annual Report Lesotho. Available at: https://www.unicef.org/about/annualreport/files/Lesotho_2017_COAR.pdf (accessed 16 December 2020).

Whitehead, A. (2003) Women, men and African agriculture. *IDS Bulletin.* Available at: http://sro.sussex.ac.uk/id/eprint/10443 (accessed 23 February 2021).

Whitehead, A. and Tsikata, D. (2003) Policy Discourses on women's land rights in sub-Saharan Africa. The implications of the re -return to customary. *Journal of Agrarian Change*, 391–2, 67–112.

World Bank (2012) *Empowering Women: Legal Rights and Economic Opportunities in Africa. Africa Development Forum.* World Bank, Washington, DC.

Yngstrom, I. (2002) Women, wives and land rights in Africa. Situating gender beyond the household debate over land policy and changing tenure systems. *Oxford Development Studies*, 30(1), 21–40.

16 Tenure-Responsive Zoning Regulations for Better Gender Equality in Land Management in Kigali City, Rwanda

Ernest Uwayezu*[1] and Marie Jeanne Nyiransabimana[2]
[1]Centre for Geographic Information Systems and Remote Sensing, University of Rwanda, Kigali, Rwanda; [2]School of Engineering, University of Rwanda, Kigali, Rwanda

16.1 Introduction: Trajectory of Gender Equality in Land Ownership from the Lens of the African Land Reform

Land reform has been a state-initiated process that aims at making changes in the tenure systems and land uses and enhancing its access by the poor and vulnerable people in a bid to promote the sustainable development. In most African countries, this reform dates back to the 1950s and 1960s (Alden Wily, 2011). In some countries like Kenya, the land reform was initiated by the colonial administration based on the Western ideas of the individual freehold that allowed for the registration of individuals' and/or groups' land rights (Rutten, 1997). In Ethiopia, it consisted of transferring the usufruct rights to the rural peasants and ensuring some forms of state land ownership (Crewett *et al.*, 2008). Later in the 1980s, the Zimbabwean land reform aimed at redistributing the land and providing the socioeconomic infrastructure and services in the rural areas to ameliorate the plight of their communities. In other sub-Saharan African countries, the land reform emerged in the 1990s and consisted of transforming the traditional landholding system to the statutory system and spurring land tenure security in the framework of propelling the land-based investments (Peters, 2009). In those countries, the land reform was driven by the need for an urban land policy (in Tanzania), the nationalization and equitable land redistribution (in Eritrea), the post-liberation commitment to the restitution of white farms (in South Africa); the privatization and individualization of land (in Malawi); the abolition of land management based on the chieftaincy system (in Gambia and Lesotho) and the resolution of civil conflicts during the post-conflict reconstruction programmes in Angola, Liberia, Mozambique, Sierra Leone, Sudan and Rwanda (Alden Wily and Mbaya, 2001; Alden Wily, 2011).

In Rwanda, the significant changes in land management became effective from 2004 following the passage of rules governing the use and ownership of land resources. Those rules include the national constitution of 2003 (revised in 2015); the 2004 national land policy; the 2013 land law (repealing the organic law of July 2005 determining the use and management of land) and the 2016 law governing matrimonial regimes, donations and successions. The land policy was meant to establish a land tenure system that

*Corresponding author: wayezuernest@gmail.com

DOI: 10.1079/9781789247664.0016

guarantees tenure security for all Rwandans without any discrimination, either based on sex or any socioeconomic precinct and to abolish the traditional tenure system of land that had excluded the females for the access to and use of land (Ministry of Natural Resources, 2004). Articles 34 and 35 of the national constitution highlight the fundamental rights to land for all citizens in terms of ownership, acquisition, transfer, and use (Government of Rwanda, 2015). The law governing land management distinguishes three categories of land: the public state-owned land, private state-owned land, and individual land (Ngoga, 2016), which are held under the statutory system that replaced the traditional system. The law governing the matrimonial regimes, donations and successions have established the gender equality in access, use and ownership of the land, including the inheritance process (Government of Rwanda, 2016). Along this trajectory of the Rwandan land reform, a Land Tenure Regularization (LTR) programme was carried out from 2008 to 2013. It consisted of registering land rights for all landowners from which the *de jure* pattern of tenure security emerged (Ngoga, 2019). In addition, the LTR programme enabled the development of the Land Administration Information System (LAIS) that has consisted of the basic data for the country wide land use planning (Carpano, 2011).

16.2 Land Use Rights from the Lens of Spatial Planning in Rwanda

Since 2010, the LAIS allowed for the establishment of the national land use and master plan (Ministry of Infrastructure, 2015) that provides the guidelines for the development of the low level master plans. These include the master plans of Kigali (the capital city of Rwanda) and other cities that guide land development of urban areas. In rural areas, each district has elaborated the local land use development plans governing the use of land and orient all strategic development projects. Those plans include the zoning regulations consisting of stipulations on the conversion of agricultural and/or vacant land into other types of use such as residential, industrial or commercial. They also encompass the building codes spelling out how new structures should be erected and permitting or prohibiting certain uses (Government of Rwanda, 2015). The land use planning processes are undertaken according to hierarchical system established in 2004 at three levels of public administration and land management: national, district and sector. At these levels, especially the district and sector levels, different actors in land management are expected to collaborate with the local community (including the landowners and/or users) in crafting land use and development plans. However, the existing studies on land management in Rwanda raise concerns about the exclusion of the local community in these processes (Michelon, 2009; Nikuze *et al.*, 2020). Generally, some scholars argue that the non-local community engagement in land use planning can result in land use plans and zoning regulations which are not aligned with the basic needs and land development capacity of most landowners or users. More critically, zoning regulations which are not in sync with the local realities can constitute a threat to land tenure security (Payne, 2001), like the *de jure* element that emerged from the Rwandan programme of LTR. In many developing countries' cities, there are many cases where individuals' land rights have been registered, but land tenure insecurity has continued to prevail due to non-inclusive land use planning (Durand-Lasserve *et al.*, 2013). This may apply in Kigali city which was the pioneer in passing out the master plans and zoning regulations after the LTR. Those plans which provide the legal framework for land development were crafted and passed out from 2010 to 2013 and revised in 2019 (City of Kigali, 2019). They comprise the zoning regulations which induce changes in the existing land uses like the conversion of the urban outskirts' agricultural land into the residential areas in a bid to cope with the increasing demand in urban housing (World Bank Group, 2017). Landowners from these urban outskirts are expected to use their land according to the new zoning regulations so that they can enjoy their land ownership as stipulated in the land law and policy. Though the land use conversion processes are meant to promote the access to decent housing, they have been decried to result in the land development standards which may be out of reach for most of these landowners (Manirakiza and Ansoms, 2014). The key question is how those processes can result in prohibitive zoning regulations for the landowners who are supposed to actively take part in land use planning as stipulated in the Rwandan policies and laws related to land management (Government of Rwanda, 2015). In other words, it is questionable whether zoning regulations are crafted in a participatory manner and provide the equal opportunities for all landowners, both men and women, to use their land and enjoy the *de jure* tenure security deriving from the LTR. This chapter attempts to respond to these questions. It probes whether the regulations in use are tenure security responsive and enhance gender equality in land use or development from the perspective of the Rwandan land reform. The latest statistics (July 2017) show that out of the 11,446,570 land parcels registered during the LTR programme, 2,191,963 were registered to women as the sole owners, 1,267,066 registered to men as *de facto* owners, whereas 5,633,000 were registered to both men and women (as husbands and wives in the community property regime or joint ownership in which land property is held). These statistics show that Rwandan land management rules have significantly addressed the question of gender in relation to official recognition of women among the landowners (Ngoga, 2019). However, land rights of women as well as men in Kigali city may be infringed upon by the zoning regulations with respect to the use of land. Section 16.3 discusses the analytical framework applied in tackling this problem with respect to the subjective element of land tenure security embracing the landholders' perception of the security of their land rights.

16.3 Research Framework

This chapter contributes to the knowledge on the urban land governance in Rwanda, where the LTR programme has been acclaimed to foster the access to land for all citizens and enhance land tenure security for women, poor and vulnerable people (Ali *et al.*, 2014). Kigali City is used as a case study to ascertain whether the land use planning processes do not subvert the acclaimed land tenure security. In this respect, the research builds upon the principles of good land governance and just land use planning to identify possible threats to land tenure security that may be linked with these processes. The nexus between good land governance, just land use planning and tenure security embrace the processes through which zoning regulations are made and implemented and how they affect individuals' land rights (Deutsche Gesellschaft für Internationale Zusammenarbeit, 2016). From the perspective of urban space management, trends of good land governance and just land use planning are portrayed by the existence of spatial planning mechanisms that protect or recognize the land rights for all categories of landowners and/or users, particularly the poor and women, and promote their inclusion in the urban fabric. This is the prerequisite for these people to enjoy their land rights and have access to employment, housing, basic infrastructure, and services (Deininger, 2003). Attaining these aspirations necessitates the compliance with the principles of good land governance such as participation and community engagement, equity, security (including the promotion of tenure security), and sustainability which fosters the good management of land resource (FAO, 2009; Deininger *et al.*, 2012). These principles are also embedded in the ethical frames of just land use planning that various actors in urban development should observe while crafting the related regulations. These actors who play important roles in the design of new cities or neighbourhoods, or re-organizing the existing ones, are expected to include some options that minimize the risks for the material resource (including land) deprivation which is harmful to the livelihoods of all members (including women) of the local community (Campbell and Marshall, 2006). They are expected to make choices about good and bad and right and wrong in relation to rules and processes related to spatial development, including the allocation of land to different uses and activities (Huchzermeyer, 2004). Making good and right choices in land use planning is about due consideration of the ethical frames of references which are identical to the above-mentioned land governance principles as largely discussed by various proponents of just city (Innes, 1995; Campbell, 2013; Fainstein, 2014). These frames of reference include the following:

- Participation and community engagement embrace a collaborative approach in crafting and implementing regulations which accept plurality in urban space. This helps to identify the special needs of poor, low-income people and women who may be at risks of exclusion from the urban development process. It also allows for the increased recognition and respect of their land rights.

- Equity and non-discrimination in the decision-making process relates to the fairness through which those regulations do not result in land deprivation, or the extent to which various landowners and/or users equally benefit from these regulations. This can result in the increased recognition of land rights for landowners, including women and poor people, from all types of tenure systems.
- Diversity seeks for the physical heterogeneity which promotes the inclusion of all categories of landowners and/or users in the development of any geographical space under planning process. This promotes the mixed income model of neighbourhood development.
- Protection of tenure rights is enabled by spatial development strategies which prevent the displacement of poor, low-income groups and women, or disruption of their livelihoods. Government officials in charge of the land use planning and development should work proactively with those categories of people to ensure that they participate in the urban development which results in the protection of their land rights.

Two main common aspects of good land governance, just land use planning and tenure security, endow the selection of those ethical frames of reference: (i) the sociospatial inclusion of the poor, women, vulnerable and low-income groups in urban development processes; and (ii) the linkage with individuals' property rights recognition through landowners' participation in the urban development, which prevents all avenues of land deprivation and enhances tenure security. To explore trends in these aspects alongside Kigali city development processes, the evaluative criteria presented in Table 16.1 were used.

Table 16.1 shows the analytical framework comprising a series of the evaluative criteria connected to the four principles relating to good land governance and just and inclusive urban development. It was applied to ensure that both men and women from all income groups in the areas undergoing the land use conversion benefit from the zoning regulations and that no category of landowners is deprived of his/her land.

16.4 Data Source and Methods

The study was carried in Kigali sector which is one of the Kigali city peri-urban neighbourhoods. From the year 2012, a large part of this sector has been undergoing the process of converting the agriculture land into other types of land use, mainly the residential. Primary data were collected through the household survey. The proportionate stratified sampling and snowballing approach was applied (Kumar, 2011) to select 87 respondents to the survey questionnaire from 432 households which own the land plots in the area and whose agriculture land was converted to residential or had moved to rural zones which are close to Kigali city. Since the heads of households in the Rwandan context are men (except for the widowhood situation), both male and female landowners/users (including women who are the heads of households) were included in the survey to investigate if they experience land tenure security challenges. Participation of women in the study is also linked to their social status: they are often land rights claimants since they use land for securing their livelihoods and sustaining the household through subsistence food production. The survey questions relating to the evaluative criteria presented in Table 16.1, were used to examine whether these criteria are being met alongside the land use planning and development processes. This was measured using the Likert scale comprising three levels of scores defined as disagree (1), undecided (2), agree (3) in relation to these evaluative criteria.

Primary data were also collected through the structured interviews with the decision makers, local leaders, urban planners and land managers, who are key actors in the implementation of Kigali city development schemes. Secondary data were collected from the review of these schemes, focusing on decision-making processes in relation to land use conversion, local community participation and inclusion of various categories of landowners in urban development processes.

Table 16.1. Assessment of land tenure security trends in the framework of land use planning in Kigali city (developed by authors, based on FAO, 2009; Burns *et al.*, 2010; Deininger *et al.*, 2012).

Principles	Evaluative criteria
Participation and community engagement	Land use planning process is based on consultations and meetings with the local community.
	Both government officials and members of the local community provide inputs for the local physical development plans.
	Both men and women participate equally in local development plans design.
	Local community exerts control over these plans to ensure that they benefit from them.
Equity and non-discrimination in the decision-making process	Decisions on land use conversion are based on consultation with the affected landowners.
	Zoning blocks for housing development are proportionally distributed according to various categories of landowners/users, including poor and low-income women.
Diversity	Land use planning results in diverse land uses that promote social and economic diversity.
	Land use categories are aligned with the needs of both men and women from various income categories.
	Zoning regulations are aligned with the financial capacity of all categories of landowners/users.
	Zoning regulations include various housing standards aligned with the needs of poor, low-, middle-, and high-income people.
Protection of tenure rights	Government authorities collaborate with landowners in land use conversion.
	Local development plans adhere to financial resources of the landowners/ users.
	All categories of landowners can develop their land plots according to the zoning regulations.

Note: In the Rwandan context, the poor are people whose monthly income is less than 30 US dollars. They may have a land parcel but cannot develop it according to spatial development regulations. Due to the 1994 Genocide perpetrated against the Tutsi, some households are headed by widows, who may also be among the poor people. The share of people living under the poverty line was 20% of Kigali city inhabitants in 2016 (see City of Kigali, 2019).

The geometric means of the recorded scores for each evaluative criterion was computed during the qualitative and quantitative analysis of the collected data. The related results helped to ascertain the trends of land tenure security (high mean) or insecurity (low mean) which are discussed in section 16.5.

16.5 Findings

The key findings presented in Table 16.2 reveal that the landowners barely participate in land use planning, which advertently threatens the subjective element of tenure security. These landowners decry the zoning regulations to make inroads into tenure insecurity through their displacement. This is brokered by their inability to put their land into use according to those regulations since they are not aligned with their financial resources. Their incomes are generally very low. At the household level, the mean monthly income is less than 100 US dollars for 37% of households (whose 16 % are headed by women). It varies between 110 and 250 US dollars for 34% of households (with 9% headed by women). These two categories of households rely on the subsistence agriculture combined with the informal activities or small retails as sources of incomes. Around 11% of households (2% of which are headed by women) earn between 200 and 250 US dollars. They can develop their land plots using the low-cost and local construction material in the very low-standard residential blocks. Others representing 18% of households (1% headed by women) earn between 250 and 500 US dollars per month from the off-farm activities. They can enjoy the land tenure security through compliance by the

Table 16.2. Potential of land use planning to promote land tenure security in Kigali city (Data source: Field survey, June–July 2019).

Principles	Ascertained aspect	Mean scores	Comment	Perceived implications on tenure security and livelihood (according to landowners)
Participation and community engagement	Consultations and meetings with the local community.	1.1	Decisions making on land use planning and development follows the top-down approach	The non-engagement of the local community in land use planning results in land development standards that landowners cannot afford. This triggers their exclusion from the urban development processes.
	Planning based on inputs from the government officials and the local community.	1.1		
	Equal participation of both men and women.	1.1	Neither men nor women landowners actively participate in the local development plan design.	
	Control of physical development plans by the local community.	1.0	The local community does not exert any influence on land use plans.	
Equity and non-discrimination in the decision-making process	Decisions on land use conversions are based on the consultation of affected landowners.	1.0	Land use conversion is based on the master plan designed by private consulting firms.	
	Fair allocation of residential zoning blocks according to various categories of landowners.	1.3	Zoning regulations promote the development of various residential neighbourhoods. However, the share of poor and low-income residential blocks is very low.	Poor and low-income landowners are less integrated in the urban development processes.
Diversity	Diversity in land use and social and economic mix.	2.6	Mixed use is highly promoted. However, the local farming communities do not benefit from the new types of land use.	Landowners relying on the farming activities who cannot constitute other sources of income leave the city, with likelihood of land deprivation.
	Land use alignment with the needs of both men and women.	1.4	Most women whose livelihood depends on farming activities lose their income sources due to land use change.	Those women hardly afford other livelihood style. This results in the economic vulnerability of their livelihoods.
	Zoning regulations alignment with the financial capacity of all categories of landowners.	1.0	Poor and low-income landowners do not have financial capacity to develop the houses required by the zoning regulations.	These landowners are excluded from the city through forced land sale.

	Variety in housing standards and mixed housing typologies.	2.3	Mixed housing typology is highly promoted. However, the share of low-standard residential blocks is very small.	The large number of poor and low-income landowners cannot afford the housing development standards in most of the residential blocks.
Protection of tenure rights	Government authorities collaborate with landowners in land use conversion.	1.2	The landowners hardly participate in land use conversion	Land use is not aligned with the land development capacity of the poor and low-income people. They are forced out of the city after land sale to middle and high-income people who can abide by housing development standards.
	Adherence of physical development plans to financial resources of landowners.	1.4	Physical development plans suggest housing development standards that the poor and low-income landowners cannot afford.	
	Landowners' capability to develop their land plots according to zoning regulations.	1.4	Most of the landowners cannot develop their land according to new zoning regulations.	
Mean score		1.54		

Note: Most landowners engaged in the faming activities in the Rwandan urban fringes are women. Men are generally engaged in off-farm activities.

housing development standards in the low- and middle-standard residential blocks, using their incomes in combination with the bank loans. Generally, the share of landowners who are not under threats of tenure insecurity is very limited. The driving factors for this tenure insecurity have been ascertained with diligence to land use planning process and the landowners' ability to abide by the land development standards as presented in Table 16.2.

Table 16.2 shows the mean scores corresponding to different evaluative criteria applied in ascertaining trends of land tenure security. Scores which are greater than 2 out of 3 constitute the indicators for the processes that are land tenure security responsive. However, findings show that most of the scores are below 1.5, which indicates trends of tenure insecurity. Generally, the urban planners and decision makers are the main actors in land use conversion and local development plans design. Participants in the survey argued that those plans are crafted alongside the implementation of the general master plan crafted by the international consulting companies without substantial contribution of the public. This land use planning approach has resulted in the creation of various residential zoning blocks that they cannot afford in terms of land development. A brief description of these zoning blocks is provided in Table 16.3.

The purpose of these residential zones is to promote the access to decent housing for Kigali city inhabitants. However, the housing units which are allowed for development in zones like R1, R1A, R2, R3 and R4 are not affordable for poor- and low-income households who represent more than 65% of Kigali city inhabitants and whose monthly incomes are below 200 US dollars (World Bank Group, 2017). The cost for developing the low-cost housing unit (like the G1) in the converted areas varies between 20,500 and 30,600 US dollars. Poor- and low-income categories cannot bear such costs. This becomes a barrier for their integration in the city. Even though some of them may be able to develop a housing unit in the residential block R1B, there are still some concerns associated to the unfair land allocation. The R1B share represents 11.6%

Table 16.3. Ration of residential zoning as per the current Kigali Master plan (Data source: City of Kigali, 2019).

Zones	Permitted types of residential housing unit	Maximum number of floors	Area (km^2)	Share (%) in the master plan
R1: Low-density residential zone	Villa or single family house.	G[a] +1	21.5	11.8
R1A: Low-density residential densification zone	Semi-detached houses, single and multi-family houses, low-rise residential units.	G+1	30.8	16.9
R1B: Rural residential[b] zone	Rural housing typology around the agriculture zones to allow the farming communities' access to dwelling units.	G	24.6	13.5
R2: Medium-density residential-improvement zone	Row housing and low rise apartments, including the upgrading of the existing unplanned settlements.	G+3 (apartments)	24.1	13.2
R3: Medium-density residential-expansion zone	Single family and row-houses, low-rise apartments, and multifamily houses in the peri-urban which involves the conversion of the agriculture land into residential use.	G+7 (apartments)	18.0	9.9
R4: High-density residential zone	High-density medium-rise housing and residential apartments.	G+15 (apartments)	63.5	34.7
Total		–	182.5	100.0

Notes: [a]G = ground floor. [b]This type of zoning is applied around the zones preserved for the farming activities.

of the total area allocated to residential use, while the remainder is allocated to other zoning blocks such as R1A, R3 and R4. Mostly, the middle- and high-income people representing about 35% of Kigali city inhabitants can afford the housing development costs in these blocks. The imbalance in the allocation of the residential blocks with respect to different income categories has triggered the displacement of the landowners in the urban fringes which becomes the factor for land tenure insecurity.

Patterns of Tenure Insecurity: Forced Land Sale and Risks of Landlessness

Housing development regulations in the areas under urbanization require landowners to abide by the new housing standards. These include the use of durable construction material and a shift from the single-family houses to the shared apartments or detached houses. The costs for developing such houses are prohibitive for these landowners who are mainly poor and low-income people. This forces them to sell their land and move towards the outside of the Kigali city boundary, which becomes a gateway to land and housing deprivation and compromise to the perceived and *de facto* tenure security that should emerge from the formal registration of their land rights. The land sale has not been a suitable livelihood option for those landowners. If they do not use the acquired money in acquiring the new land plots outside of Kigali city, they become landless or homelessness after spending such money within a short period in a bid to meet their daily needs. This study identified three poor families (one headed by a widow) whose members, after selling their land plots, moved to the existing informal settlements where they barely survive (as tenants) since they face difficulties to secure the housing rent costs and/or meet other basic needs. Although the impacts of land use conversion hit both female and male landowners, women are the first to be confronted with land use change, with respect to livelihood challenges associated to land deprivation. Most of women in Kigali city outskirts (as well as in Rwandan rural areas) rely on the use of the land for basic food production through subsistence agriculture. The risk of landlessness resulting from the inability to acquire land plots in other areas and the lack of the alternative sources of income become the food security challenges. Yet, it is these women who are accountable for food production while their husbands are responsible for other families' needs. During the household survey, 34% of women from poor and low-income categories who did not move out of Kigali city reported that they have experienced such challenges after a land sale. Similar challenges were faced by some families which moved out of Kigali city. Though both men and women in legal marriage are registered as the co-owners of the land, some men abuse their power as the heads of families by exclusively making a decision on the use of the money acquired through a land sale. Two women whose families relocated in Kigali city outskirts reported the impact resulting from such attitudes. Their husbands spent one share of the money acquired through land sale in buying the small land plots where they developed new houses. The other share would have been spent in acquiring other land plots where they could grow food crops or undertake some other income generating activities. However, this share was dissipated (as reported by women from 10% households that sold their land) through its investment in informal retails and illegal money lending practices that the households could not benefit from. This led the affected women to contend that the land use conversion constitutes a driver for land deprivation and livelihood hardship.

Marriages in Rwanda are illegal when one of the parties has not reached the legal age of consent (21 years as required by the Integrated Child Rights Policy of Rwanda) and when it was not celebrated before the civil status officer, despite the fact the parties have reached the legal age (Buhungiro, 2015). Furthermore, marriages to women below the age of 21 and without a woman's consent are considered illegal. However, the Minister of Justice (or his/her representative) can grant special permission to allow a younger woman to marry based on special circumstances. Women in this sort of marriage are generally secondary rights holders, since they can enjoy the use rights on land plots which are solely registered on the names of their husbands. However, some of the young husbands can grab the opportunities for the forced land sale perpetrated by the land use change to repudiate their wives (who often return to their families with their young children). Moreover, it constitutes a factor for land deprivation for the children who at the age of 18 are granted the rights to inherit their father's land (according to Rwandan law governing matrimonial regimes, donations and successions). These children do not enjoy their rights, since after the land sale some of the illegally married men abandon their wives (and children) and move to other areas where they can start new livelihoods and possibly marry other wives. This is frequent when the relations between the wife and husband have been undermined by perpetual inter-family conflicts. Based on the experience of their former neighbouring families, two cases were pointed out by participants to this study. They argued that the separation from the husbands resulted in the livelihood disruption for the affected women.

Land use conversion also results in the livelihood hardship for widows. They lack the effective power to make the decisions on the use of the money acquired through the land sale due to socioeconomic and cultural domination by their relatives or children. Two widows who sold their land plots reported that they were forced to share the acquired money with their single sons. These widows invested their shares in acquiring new houses in the remote urban fringes. However, they could not acquire the agriculture land for food production and feeding their children, including these sons who did not use the acquired money for the reconstitution of the households' livelihood. It is worth noting that the land sale does not always result in land deprivation or livelihood hardship for the displaced landowners. Our key informants from the rural areas close to Kigali city pointed out some cases of the displaced landowners who successfully reconstituted their livelihoods through the acquisition of new properties. This was enabled by the collaborative decision making among the members of the displaced households and the low-cost for land acquisition and housing development outside of Kigali city.

Livelihood Challenges Associated with the Limited Mixed Land Use

The mixed land use is highlighted in Kigali city master plan for the development of various types of neighbourhoods and employment creation. However, the conversion of the agriculture land into other land use does not highly abide by the provisions of Rwandan land management rules. These rules stipulate that land use planning shall define the appropriate sites for the urbanization and preserve the sites with a high agricultural potential (Ministry of Natural Resources, 2004). Those provisions are not observed since the land use conversion does not include the processes of land suitability analysis and delimitation of the suitable areas for the urban agriculture development. The agricultural activities are planned around the steep slope land, *thalweg*, and swamps which are not sustainable for agribusiness. In addition, the farming land blocks are not located adjacent to the residential areas of poor and low-income people who rely on the farming activities. Generally, the limited inclusion of the agriculture land in the master plan of Kigali city will affect the livelihood of those people since they rarely adopt off-farm activities due to lack of financial resources. This accelerates the pace of displacement and the associated land tenure insecurity. Tenure responsive land use planning is urgently needed to curb these problems.

16.6 Options for Promoting Sociospatial Integration and Land Tenure Security

To advance the livelihoods and promote access to and/or use of land resource, all landowners/users require the actors in land use planning to abide by the good land governance principles underlying the inclusive land use and development. Figure 16.1 suggests some actions to attain this aspiration and nurture the integration of various categories of landowners/users (both men and women) in Kigali city development processes as well as their security of tenure.

As Fig. 16.1 shows, landowners in the areas undergoing the land use conversion processes should be empowered to shape their neighbourhoods and align their living conditions with the zoning regulations. This may be achieved through the fulfilment of the following actions.

Decentralization of the land use planning processes and actual engagement of the landowners

The decentralization of the planning activities and direct collaboration of the local community in crafting zoning regulations constitutes one

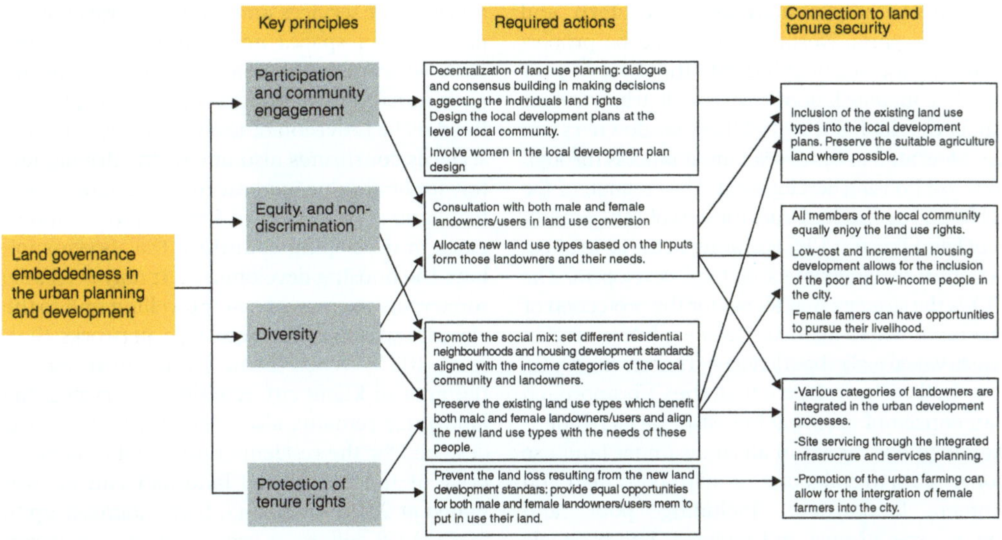

Fig. 16.1. Practical options for promoting land tenure security alongside Kigali city development (developed based on Deininger *et al.*, 2012; Skog, 2018; Chigbu, 2020).

option for developing the inclusive city. The local community participation at large scale (like the city level) can be time consuming, frustrating and expensive. Nevertheless, direct and active participation of the local community and various stakeholder at the neighbourhood level can help in finding some solutions to the problems resulting from the land use change. Their participation and voices are fundamental to identify the land development options which provide them with the opportunities to enjoy their land rights. This includes their capabilities to develop their dwellings according to the zoning regulations and the inclusion of other types of land use such as agriculture, which address the needs of the low-income groups and women whose livelihood depend on the farming activities. Not only women landowners are expected to participate in land use planning. The married women should participate as the co-owners or users of the affected land, since their livelihood is tied to the existing land use in the area under conversion process. Women's land rights are central to their economic empowerment, the basis for food production and income generation, and a means of holding savings for their welfare of their offspring so that gender consideration in land use planning is a paramount. Thus, women's participation in land use planning strengthens their capabilities, expands their negotiating power, and prevents the risks for land deprivation. Generally, gender sensitive and participatory land use planning generates human-centred urban development options and advances various aspects of good land governance, such as sustainability by balancing the national development goals (social, economic and environmental concerns) and local community needs; equity through the increased recognition of land rights for all categories of people including women, and poor groups; and the adoption of the inclusive zoning regulations which advance the their integration in the development processes.

Promotion of the low-cost housing development and preservation of the suitable agriculture land

Land is the basic asset for socioeconomic development whose use allocation should care about the livelihood conditions of all landowners/users. The land use conversion for residential use should promote the access to low-cost housing through the self-help and incremental development using the low-cost construction materials which constitute a ladder for integrating the poor and low-income groups in the urban fabric. In Kigali city master plan, this housing development option is compatible with the rural residential zone (R1B). However, it is not proportionally distributed across various residential neighbourhoods since it predominates in the peripheral agriculture zones, such as the eastern and southern parts. Normally, it should be proportionally allocated (in relation to the share of poor and low-income landowners) in all urban fringes under development so that these landowners can be integrated in the development process through low-cost housing development. The creation of the R1B can be conceived from the lens of the Community Land Trusts (CLTs) operating in the form of cooperative of landowners or land developers. The CLT is the strategy that allows for the protection of the landowners against the speculative market which would make them landless (Thompson, 2020).

In the Kigali city context, the CLTs approach can consist of creating low-standards residential neighbourhoods in all zones under land use conversion, in collaboration with both men and women landowners, including poor and low-income groups and widows. Those people can form a community cooperative, sell their initial land plots in the high cost residential development areas (where the sale prices are higher than in the low-income residential blocks) and buy other land plots in the area designed for the R1B where they can develop low-cost houses. Specific regulations which specify the prices of the land plots in that area and prioritizing their sale to poor and low-income landowners should be applied (Deininger *et al.*, 2012). The existing landowners in the designed R1B zones should be members of the CLTs to prevent their exclusion from the spatial development process. The CLTs constitutes an option for providing tenure security for these landowners since there is decreased risk of their displacement from the city. In addition, the CLTs approach can contribute to the preservation of the agriculture land around the created residential areas (Ehlenz, 2018). This becomes a driving factor for the urban agriculture development and opportunity for the farming communities (including women) to secure their jobs and produce some food stuff for their subsistence and/or supplement to the urban food market.

Site servicing through the integrated infrastructure and services provision

The process of land plotting for the development of new residential neighbourhoods should go hand in hand with the provision of basic infrastructure and services, which is termed land plot servicing or services and schemes. The creation of the open spaces and community facilities such as schools and health centre play an important role in viabilization of these neighbourhoods. The provision of these basic facilities and services constitutes also one of the driving factors for land value increase in the designed areas (Giuliano *et al.*, 2010). In Kigali as well as other cities in developing countries, that process follows the housing development. It may even take some years to connect a new dwelling unit to the electricity, water, and sewerage networks (Bah *et al.*, 2018). When the newly designed residential area in Kigali city remains unserviced, the land price remains also very low. In the areas designed for the residential use, the initial mean price of the unserviced land plot can be estimated at 2000 US dollars. It can increase up to 10,000 US dollars or greater as the site is serviced. The increase in land value is also linked to the increasing land demand, driven by the displacement of the middle and high-income people from the core urban area towards the new urban neighbourhoods where they develop new houses. Since site servicing is one of the factors for land price increase, it can be cost-effective for the infrastructure provision to follow the land use conversion in the area designed for the residential use. The land price increase can be beneficial for the landowners as they can sell the land plots at good prices and use the money in acquiring other land in other areas like R1B where they can develop the low-cost houses through self-help and use of the local materials. The construction cost can vary between 3000 and 5000 US dollars, which is low compared to the land price. This housing development option can be a practical solution to housing problem faced by poor and low-income landowners who are attached to the urban lifestyle.

16.7 Conclusion

The passage of land management rules promoting gender equality in land ownership and formal registration of individuals' land rights in the framework of enhancing *de jure* tenure security is not enough. This is evidenced by the urban development regulations that infringe upon these rights and become a factor for land deprivation. This chapter stresses on the significance of the following strategies which can be applied in Kigali city development processes to curb these problems:

- The participatory and integrated planning which requires the direct engagement of all landowners/users, particularly women, poor and vulnerable groups in land use planning, especially in crafting and implementing the local development plans.
- The promotion of the mixed land use which can spur an urbanism that does not decimate social relations between the existing landowners and their living spaces and prevent the livelihood disruption. This can be achieved through the creation of the suitable residential blocks that enable the integration of the poor and low-income people, including women, in the urban development.

For this to happen the minds of policy makers and urban planners implementing Kigali city master or development plans should be preoccupied with tackling the questions relating to who gets what and where in relation to land use allocation. It is a matter of their willingness to adopt these strategies which are repeatedly highlighted in the policies, laws and regulations related to land management in the country. In this way, the planning can be concerned not only with zoning regulations which are tenure security responsive, not only with respect to the land use that various income categories can benefit from but also to gender equality in the enjoyment the individual property rights.

References

Alden Wily, L. (2011) *Land Reform in Africa: A Reappraisal Rights to Resources in Crisis: Reviewing The Fate of Customary Tenure in Africa*. The Rights and Resources Initiative (RRI) Brief, November.

Alden Wily, L. and Mbaya, S. (2001) *Land, People and Forests in Eastern and Southern Africa at the Beginning of the 21st Century*. IUCN Eastern Africa Programme, Nairobi, Kenya.

Ali, D.A., Deininger, K. and Goldstein, M. (2014) Environmental and gender impacts of land tenure regularization in Africa: Pilot evidence from Rwanda. *Journal of Development Economics*, 110, 262–275. DOI: 10.1016/j.jdeveco.2013.12.009.

Bah, E.-h. M., Faye, I. and Geh, Z.F. (2018). *Unlocking Land Markets and Infrastructure Provision Housing Market Dynamics in Africa*. Palgrave Macmillan, London, UK.

Buhungiro, E. (2015) Early marriage is illegal. *New Times*, 28 October. Available at: https://www.newtimes.co.rw/section/read/193871 (accessed 22 July 2021).

Burns, T., Deininger, K., Selod, H. and Dalrymple, K. (2010) *Implementing the land governance assessment framework*. Conference paper, FIG Congress, 11-16 April, Sydney, Australia.

Campbell, H. and Marshall, R. (2006) Towards justice in planning: A reappraisal. *European Planning Studies*, 14(2), 239–252. DOI: 10.1080/09654310500418192.

Campbell, S. (2013) Sustainable development and social justice: Conflicting urgencies and the search for common ground in urban and regional planning. *Michigan Journal of Sustainability*, 1(1), 296–312. DOI: 10.3998/mjs.12333712.0001.007.

Carpano, F. (2011) *Strengthening Women's Access to Land into IFAD Projects: The Rwanda Experience*. International Fund for Agricultural Development, Rome, Italy.

Chigbu, U.E. (2020) Land, women, youths, and land tools or methods: Emerging lessons for governance and policy. *Land,* 9(12), 507.

City of Kigali (2019) *Kigali Master Plan Review*. Interim master plan update. Government of Rwanda, Kigali, Rwanda.

Crewett, W., Bogale, A. and Korf, B. (2008) *Land Tenure in Ethiopia: Continuity and Change, Shifting Rulers, and the Quest for State Control*. CAPRi Working Papers 91, International Food Policy Research Institute (IFPRI), Washington, DC, USA.

Deininger, K. (2003) *Land Policies for Growth and Poverty Reduction*. A World Bank policy research report. World Bank, Washington, DC, USA.

Deininger, K., Selod, H. and Burns, A. (2012) *The Land Governance Assessment Framework: Identifying and Monitoring Good Practice in the Land Sector*. World Bank, Washington, DC, USA.

Deutsche Gesellschaft für Internationale Zusammenarbeit (2016) *Land in German Development Cooperation. Guiding Principles, Challenges, and Prospects for the Future.* GIZ, Eschborn, Germany.

Durand-Lasserve, A., Durand-Lasserve, M. and Selod, H. (2013) *A Systemic Analysis of Land Markets and Land Institutions in West African Cities: Rules and Practices? The Case of Bamako, Mali*. World Bank, Washington, DC, USA.

Ehlenz, M. (2018) Making home more affordable: Community land trusts adopting cooperative ownership models to expand affordable housing. *Journal of Community Practice*, 26(3), 283–307. DOI: 10.1080/10705422.2018.1477082.

Fainstein, S.S. (2014) The just city. *International Journal of Urban Sciences,* 18(1), 1–18. DOI: 10.1080/12265934.2013.834643.

FAO (2009) *Towards Improved Land Governance*. FAO, Rome, Italy.

Giuliano, G., Gordon, P., Qisheng, P. and Park, J. (2010) Accessibility and residential land values: Some tests with new measures. *Urban Studies*, 47(14), 3103–3130.

Government of Rwanda (2015) *Presidential Order N°46/01 Of 30/06/2015 Determining Procedures for Formulation, Approval, Revision, and Publication of the Master Plan for Land Use Management and Urban Planning.* Government of Rwanda, Kigali, Rwanda.

Government of Rwanda (2016) *Law N°27/2016 Of 08/07/2016 Governing Matrimonial Regimes, Donations, and Successions*. Government of Rwanda, Kigali, Rwanda.

Huchzermeyer, M. (2004) From 'Contravention of laws' to 'lack of rights': Redefining the problem of informal settlements in South Africa. *Habitat International*, 28(3), 333–347. DOI: 10.1016/S0197-3975(03)00058-4.

Innes, J. (1995) Planning theory's emerging paradigm: Communicative action and interactive practice. *Journal of Planning Education and Research*, 14(3), 183–189.

Kumar, R. (2011) *Research Methodology: A Step-by-Step Guide for Beginners*. SAGE, London, UK.

Manirakiza, V. and Ansoms, A. (2014) Modernizing Kigali: The struggle for space in the Rwandan urban context. In: Ansoms, A. and Hilhorst, T. (Eds), *Losing Your Land Dispossession in the Great Lakes.* Boydell and Brewer, Rochester, NY, USA, p. 218.

Michelon, B. (2009) The local market in Kigali as controlled public space: Adaptation and resistance by local people to modern city life. *Proceedings of PhD Seminar on Public Space*, 19 March, Delft, The Netherlands. Available at: http://resolver.tudelft.nl/uuid:e7d458d2-18d1-459b-a666-963e27c4e713 (accessed 25 February 2021).

Ministry of Infrastructure (2015) *National Urban Policy.* Government of Rwanda, Kigali, Rwanda.

Ministry of Natural Resources (2004) *National Land Policy.* Government of Rwanda, Kigali, Rwanda.

Ngoga, T. (2016) *Land Governance Assessment Framework: Final Report.* World Bank / Government of Rwanda, Kigali, Rwanda.

Ngoga, T. (2019) *A Quick, Cost-Effective Approach to Land Tenure Regularisation: The Case of Rwanda*. Available at: https://www.theigc.org/wp-content/uploads/2019/03/Land-tenure-regularisation-the-case-of-Rwanda-March19-FINAL.pdf (accessed 3 November 2020).

Nikuze, A., Sliuzas, R. and Flacke, J. (2020) From closed to claimed spaces for participation: Contestation in urban redevelopment induced-displacements and resettlement in Kigali, Rwanda. *Land*, 9(7), 212.

Payne, G. (2001) Urban land tenure options: titles or rights? *Habitat International*, 25(3), 415–429.

Peters, P.E. (2009) Challenges in land tenure and land reform in Africa: Anthropological contributions. *World Development*, 37(8), 1317–1325.

Rutten, M. (1997) Land reform in Africa: Lessons from Kenya. In: Naerssen, T., Rutten, M. and Zoomers, A. (Eds), *The Diversity of Development: Essays in Honour of Jan Kleinpenning.* Van Gorcum, Assen, The Netherlands, p. 458.

Skog, K.L. (2018) How do policies and actors' attitudes, interests and interactions influence farmland conversion outcomes in land-use planning? *Sustainability,* 10(6), 1944.

Thompson, M. (2020) From co-ops to community land trusts: Tracing the historical evolution and policy mobilities of collaborative housing movements. *Housing, Theory and Society*, 37(1), 82–100. DOI: 10.1080/14036096.2018.1517822.

World Bank Group (2017) *Reshaping Urbanization in Rwanda: Urbanization and the Evolution of Rwanda's Urban Landscape.* World Bank, Washington, DC, USA.

17 New Hope and Future for Rural Areas under COVID-19 Circumstances? Rural Development, Pandemic Liveability and Reverse Migration

Uchendu Eugene Chigbu,*[1] Michael Klaus[2] and Holger Magel[3]
[1]Department of Land and Property Sciences, Namibia University of Science and Technology, Windhoek, Namibia; [2]Hanns-Seidel-Stiftung (Hanns-Seidel Foundation), Shandong, China; [3]Technical University of Munich/International Federation of Surveyors, Munich, Germany

17.1 Background

Imagining Rural Opportunities During a Global Virus Outbreak

In general, rural areas (also known as the countryside) are geographic areas distinguishable from and located outside larger towns and cities. In development terms, they are often treated as non-future orientated. The scale of functions and support rural areas receive vary from country to country or even within regions. Similarly, the scale of the challenges they face also vary from country to country or even within regions. A typical challenge facing rural areas in most parts of the world over the past five decades is the issue of rural exodus (also known as rural–urban migrations, or rural-to-urban movements) (Chigbu, 2013a). This type of movement involves the movement of populations from rural areas to urban areas, usually driven by their search of high-paying non-farm jobs and several other urban-related attractions not available in rural areas (Ferguson, 2020). Such a movement has negative consequences in rural areas because it reduces rural populations, which reduces the scale of farming activities, and has food insecurity effects (Magel, 2019).

Put differently, rural exodus is a worldwide phenomenon triggered by the transformation of the rural economy, missing investment in modern rural infrastructure and the belief that rural areas are old-fashioned human settlements. These impressions are further worsened by the hyped images of comfort that are associated with urbanism, which are attractive to the youth. Tackling this rural challenge requires engaging in visions and practices of sustainable development. Since the urban areas receive more development support in many countries, engaging in the sustainable development of rural areas is a crucial way to achieve social coherent development. It can serve as the basis for achieving equivalent living conditions in all parts of a country. Due to the long neglect of rural areas – because they are erroneously known for their agriculture and natural resources, meant to be exploited for the welfare of, and the development

*Corresponding author: echigbu@nust.na

DOI: 10.1079/9781789247664.0017

of urban areas – the process of reversing rural exodus has not been quite successful.

In the last decades, focus on urbanization (and its associated push and pull factors) has been dealt with, perhaps due to the skewed approach to development politics, either through a one-sided policy action in favour of urban areas or simply through weak programmes that do not benefit the rural areas or simply by doing nothing for them. This is evident in the developing countries where limited financial resources and investments in infrastructure are accorded to rural development (and more to urban development) even though a greater chunk of the gross domestic products of these countries are created in the rural areas through tourism, forest, agriculture and other natural resource exploitation. It is not surprising that urban migration became a trend for rural people as they saw it as the only realistic way to escape the hardships they face in rural areas, while hoping that their dreams would be achieved in urban areas.

However, the emergence of the 2019 pandemic of severe acute respiratory syndrome-coronavirus disease (COVID-19), and the understanding that a globalized world is now vulnerable to the dangers of future pandemics has triggered movements of people from urban areas to rural areas (also known as urban–rural migration or urban–rural movements or reverse movements). This movement is also opening a window of opportunity for strengthening rural areas and fostering the development of rural areas worldwide. It is a potential opportunity for rural development because it can motivate concerted efforts towards achieving sustainable development in rural areas. The incursion of this virus disaster (i.e. the COVID-19 pandemic) is unmasking the vulnerabilities of the urban areas and the resilience of the rural areas. The challenge posed by the pandemic is revealing that the urban areas cannot keep the development promises rural migrants to have always believed they would achieve. Long-term sustainability-oriented thinking and practices are needed, and rural-focused development innovations must be sought. The material and immaterial values of rural areas must now be recognized and considered in the development of nations. These are necessary to tap into the opportunities presented by the reverse migration being experienced in certain countries of the world. This chapter posits forward-looking statements on these rural issues.

'The village is in, big cities are out': Towards Improving Rural Areas During the COVID-19 Pandemic

Improving the living conditions of people in rural areas has been on the top of the global development agenda since the Earth Summit (United Nations Conference on Environment and Development) held in Rio de Janeiro, Brazil, in 1992 (also known as Agenda 21). An essential objective of the Agenda 21 initiative was that local governments should draw their local development initiatives based on their local needs and visions (United Nations, 1992). The Agenda 21 initiative set out hopes for disadvantaged rural people worldwide to mobilize their strengths and build links to garner resources for their development. Some successes have been achieved here and there (mostly in the developed countries), but the rural challenge remains, whether in developed or developing countries.

Critical areas of improvement include: improved funding for rural development projects; creation of new rural development initiatives (including projects and programmes); enhanced stakeholder engagements; and motivation of local governance to engage in self-driven improvement. While similar efforts have been made in the Global South countries, the success recorded is not comparable as in the Global North. New rural development policies have been introduced in many developing countries and new programmes/projects implemented, only to achieve little or minimal success. Why does it seem to work better in one part and not in the other part of the world? The commitment for governments to ensure that all their policies, programmes and initiatives (whether regional or local) consider the needs and circumstances of rural areas makes the difference. Where governments and their citizens have made firm commitments, they have tended to gain better development outcomes, and vice versa. Atterton (2008, p. 3) referred to this expected commitment from governments and citizens as 'rural proofing'.

One lesson that scholars and policy makers should have learned from efforts at developing rural areas by now is that when it comes to improving rural areas, everything matters. First, it is all about land (Magel and Wehrmann, 2006). Land seems to matter because it is the foundation upon which development is built. Place does not in itself determine rural development outcomes, but factors such as efficient land use do. Second and third, people and place matter. Without people, a rural place lacks its meaning. A rural place is not the same without its people and vice versa. 'Land use patterns, land tenure systems, and physical landform play different roles in affecting how a people live' and 'what sustains people in most rural places is the land (agriculture, etc.)' (Chigbu, 2013b, p. 266). Fourth, the politics (or governance mechanism for reconciling land and people) matter too. Within this governance structure, policies, and activities to improve people's living conditions in their place happen. It is impossible to achieve the primary objectives of rural development, anywhere globally, without enhancing the rural people's needs (especially their place or environment, employment and socioeconomic conditions). These issues aside, there is a fifth perspective to rural development in contemporary times. It is the health nexus of rural development. This remains an aspect of rural development still either largely undefined or poorly researched. It is also crucial for improving liveability concerns under pandemic conditions (e.g. the coronavirus pandemic).

The Scottish historian Niall Ferguson stated in the Swiss newspaper *Neue Zürcher Zeitung* [New Journal of Zürich] that 'the village is in, big cities are out' in the light of the COVID-19 pandemic (see Ferguson, 2020). For experts and champions of rural change, Ferguson's statement is inspiring, but is there any scientific evidence in support of this position?

Scientific investigations into the outbreak of COVID-19 pandemic have not rapidly gone beyond the aspects of information update on deaths and casualties to social science perspectives dealing with liveability now or after the pandemic (Chigbu, 2020). COVID-19 appeared in late December 2019 in Wuhan (Hubei Province, China) and, from then onwards, spread to other parts of the world (Huang *et al.*, 2021). The World Health Organization declared COVID-19 a pandemic on 11 March 2020 (WHO, 2020). The COVID-19 pandemic largely impacted heavily urbanized regions across the world. In the United States, cities such as New York City, Seattle, Los Angeles and New Orleans were severely hit. In continental Europe, cities such as Paris, London, Berlin and Dublin could not escape it. Notable cities affected by the pandemic worldwide include Mexico City, Sao Paulo, Manila, Shanghai, Delhi and Beijing (among many others). When viewed from a country context, the pandemic also affected the more urbanized countries of the world (e.g. United Kingdom, China, India, United States, Brazil and several European Union countries such as Germany, Italy and France, to mention a few). The pandemic has had less impact on the many rural countries in Africa and Asia. A critical question worth investigating is: What is happening to the rural areas under the COVID-19 situation?

The Approach to the Study

The focus of this chapter is on the state of rural areas in the ongoing pandemic crisis, and their role in ameliorating the pandemic pandemonium in urban areas. It examines claims of emerging urban–rural migration worldwide by people to escape dense and noisy urban life and look for fresh air, more space and access to the natural countryside. Where are these movements happening? What has land and the COVID-19 pandemic to do with it? The chapter proceeds to the next section by describing pandemic liveability and why it matters for the future of rural development in the context of reverse migration. This is followed by a section that discusses pandemic-driven urban–rural migration situation based on evidence from the literature. Finally, based on the available evidence, the authors discuss what these all mean for rural areas and rural development, particularly in the context of new hope and future under COVID-19 circumstances.

17.2 The Concepts of Pandemic Liveability, Reverse Migration and Rural Development

Liveability is a concept used to describe the extent of development. It is used in this chapter to represent the extent of the living condition of a people. Despite being presented as a typical urban issue (Leby and Hashim, 2010; Allam, 2020), the concept of liveability permeates across urban and rural areas. It is a concept that informs how people live, wherever they may live. The concept of liveability, be it from an urban or rural perspective, is highly subjective. They are also hardly measurable, and quantifying liveability has not been entirely successful (Straßer, 2019). Yet, the concept remains an important one in the assessment (or even discussion) of spatial development issues. It allows for an understanding of what elements should be present for an adequate lifestyle in any form of human settlements. Liveability – which embraces economic prosperity, social stability and equity, educational opportunity, recreation, and cultural opportunities available within the built and natural environments – is the state of a community's quality of life. In general, a liveable environment ensures that its inhabitants' physical and social well-being is proofed against all forms of insecurity that work against a decent lifestyle. In this regard, the rural areas, especially in developing countries, are not known for their comfortable living conditions. In many cases, the needs of their population that should be fulfilled (e.g. food, energy, housing, education, water, transport, employment, natural resource management, economic stability, health, etc.) are not always there (Chigbu, 2012).

When it comes to rural areas, planning scholars have focused more on productivity and not on liveability. Granted that the rural areas, all over the world, are the engines of productivity (be it in agriculture and mining), it is surprising that liveability and productivity issues are less focused upon. There is a link that rural areas contribute to the well-being and life satisfaction of communities and productivity outcomes in cities. This makes it crucial for engaging in discourses on rural liveability, as well as the issue of reverse migration.

When the needs of a rural community are well defined and sought after, improving the degree of their liveability is a direct way of achieving rural objectives. This is especially important to enhance disparities that exist between urban and rural areas in many countries. Research confirms that health disparities between urban and rural areas exist in risk factors, such as life expectancy and testing and healthcare capacity (Huang *et al.*, 2021). These adverse impacts of health disparities for rural areas have always been a concern during preparations for and responses to pandemics.

Liveability, irrespective of how it is applied, is a multidimensional concept. Ecological liveability is concerned with the realization of environmental sustainability and liveable sustainability (Kulkarni, 2020). In applying this dimension to rural development in China, Li *et al.* (2021) developed rural ecological sustainability and rural liveable sustainability indicators to understand the level of liveability in rural China. The economic and social dimensions of liveability (Lloyd *et al.*, 2016; Paul and Sen, 2020) reflect the affordability of household needs and access to physical infrastructure. As is with multidimensional concepts, no dimension of liveability can guarantee balanced living conditions in any human settlement unless all dimensions are present in equivalent proportions. However, these liveability dimensions are what provide the content for indicator development by breaking the dimensions down into potential measurable elements that relate to the physical, social, functional and safety indicators, among many others (Leby and Hashim, 2010; Chigbu, 2013a,b; Alderton *et al.*, 2020; İstillozlu and Doratlı, 2021).

In Germany there is a vital discussion on equivalence of living conditions which includes the issue of liveability. Magel (2016), for example, has developed the model of spatial justice as ethical basis for equivalent living conditions with four dimensions of fairness. For all dimensions one can use existing indicators. But there is still a lot to develop. In each of either liveability or spatial fairness dimensions and indicators, gaps still exist as just mentioned. For example, in 2021, ECA International[1] found that the liveability of 70% of cities around the world has been affected by recreational limitations and a quarter (25%) by sociopolitical tensions (Firth, 2021). This, the ECA International's report, attributed to consequences from implementing strict lockdowns and restrictions on freedom of movement during 2020. This implies that pandemic-related restrictions have a negative influence on liveability or the state of the living conditions of people. The problem is that data is not available on pandemic liveability in the rural areas of the world, whether in developing or developed countries.

As COVID-19 continues to spread throughout the world, the 3.4 billion people residing in rural areas across the world bear an increasing burden from the pandemic (United Nations, 2018). From the onset of the COVID-19 pandemic, particular concern has been directed toward rural areas within countries, and the rural regions on earth (i.e. developing countries). This was not surprising because in comparison to urban areas, rural communities especially in developing countries have limited access to quality health care, tend to be isolated from the big cities with their booming infrastructure, tend to have older population (in developed countries). In the literature, rural areas have consistently shown higher mortality rates from pandemics. For instance, during the 1918 influenza pandemic (the so-called Spanish Flu), 'it was noted that rural soldiers were at a higher risk of mortality despite less social interaction than their urban counterparts' (Callaghan *et al.*, 2021, p. 288). However, until the present research, little evidence was available about the rural perspective of the COVID-19 disaster in the context of the role rural areas are playing in providing protection and security from the pandemic globally (i.e. is a new form of liveability). There are various lenses from which to engage in this discourse. However, the chapter takes a pandemic-driven urban–rural migration discourse analyses based on combined evidence from the literature.

17.3 Reverse Migration: Why Rural Areas Matter During a Pandemic-Driven Crisis

In the context of this chapter, the concept of reverse migration is another term for any form of human population movement from urban to rural area. This trend of migration has been reported at different times, and in different names, including irregular migration (Triandafyllidou, 2016) or urban–rural migration (Boillat and Zähringer, 2020). Migration (whether reverse or not) has been a part of rural development planning and policies. In many developing countries, rural development policies, projects, programmes and initiatives are usually put in place to achieve higher levels of liveability for rural communities.

The trend is tagged reverse migration in recognition of it being a backward migration that negates the power of urban areas as the key attractor of populations. Urban areas are home to most of the global population. They are centres of economic growth. They have high concentration of built-up land areas, high-density of people, and high volume of human activities. It is, therefore, not surprising that the impact of the COVID-19 pandemic on cities is multi-faceted and has exposed some pertinent urban issues. The pandemic evokes Corbun's (2009, p. 1) popular question concerning how modern city planning (a profession that emerged in the late nineteenth century with a goal of improving the health of the least well-off urban residents but lost this focus throughout the twentieth century) can return to its health and social justice roots. Chigbu and Onyebueke (2021, p. 115) tagged the COVID-19 situation a 'super wicked problem' in the urban areas because it is a crisis lacking a definitive remediation formula. It is a big threat in informal settlements – where nearly 25 per cent of the global population live in high densities, economic deprivation, infrastructure deficits and heavy disease burdens. 'Apart from the yawning gaps in the living conditions between formal settlements and slums, it has thrown into sharp contrast the persisting health inequities and social injustices in cities,' and 'it has highlighted the criticality of public health–urban planning connections' (Chigbu and Onyebueke, 2021, p. 115). Literature analysed during this period of 2020 and 2021 (e.g. Sackmann, 2021), in the context of urban-and-rural comparison, reveal why rural areas have become a preferred area for movement by people affected by the pandemics (Table 17.1).

In the context of pandemic spread, Table 17.1 shows various advantages the rural areas have over the urban areas. These rural advantages manifest in four different dimensions, including infrastructure (i.e. transportation and spatial pattern elements), socioeconomic (i.e. social and economic elements), environment (i.e. water, air and temperature elements), and management (i.e. governance element). Under the COVID-19 scenario, key features of urbanization (such as infrastructure, settlement patterns and governance systems, etc.) which are usually considered as disadvantages to rural areas have become advantageous to rural living due. Similarly, key

Table 17.1. Comparison of urban and rural areas in the context of pandemic spread.

Major areas of pandemic impacts	Elements impacted	Factors encouraging spread of pandemic in urban areas	Factors discouraging spread of pandemic in rural areas
Infrastructure impacts (Bucsky, 2020; Chigbu, 2020; Ren *et al.*, 2020; Saha *et al.*, 2020; Sharifi and Khavarian-Garmsir, 2020).	Transportation	High vehicular/pedestrian traffic density are high-risk factors that contribute to the spread of the pandemic.	Mobility limitations reduce the transmission risk of the pandemic. It leads to minimized pandemic spread.
	Spatial pattern	High-density factors contribute to the spread of the pandemics. There is a lack of appropriate levels of green and open spaces for fulfilling social distancing requirements.	Non-compact development, more open spaces, and more space available for fulfilling social distancing requirements.
Socioeconomic impacts (Finn and Koboyashi, 2020; Napierała *et al.*, 2020; Sharifi and Khavarian-Garmsir, 2020; Chigbu, 2021a; Chigbu and Onyebueke, 2021).	Social	The pandemic exposed old problems and inequalities in between formal and informal settlements in urban areas. The inequalities make containment challenging and may also lead to further spread of the virus pandemic. For instance, enforcing social distancing and other response measures is challenging in slums.	A lack of slum problems and better sense of community allowed immediate improvement and recovery capacities.
	Economic	Dependence on global supply chains increased vulnerability to the pandemic. Marginalized groups were disproportionately affected by the economic impacts of the pandemic.	Dependence on local supply chains (and high social capital) increased self-sufficiency for dealing with the economic fallouts of the pandemic.
Environmental impacts (Braga *et al.*, 2020; Hallema *et al.*, 2020; Nichol *et al.*, 2020; Roy, 2020; Sharifi and Khavarian-Garmsir, 2020; Chigbu, 2021a).	Water	Unregulated human activities that contaminate water resources in cities (including poor management of, and a lack of sewage treatment facilities in poor urban neighbourhoods) undermined the effectiveness of the lockdown measures.	Dependence on natural water bodies as source of primary water supply by low population allowed for easier control of who can access water, and when and where they can access it.
	Air	Long-term exposure to air pollution can increase human vulnerability to pandemics.	Lower exposure to air pollution decreases human vulnerability to pandemics.
	Temperature	Differential vulnerabilities exist due to temperatures in urban areas, but the high-built and predominant nucleated urban settlement pattern enable pandemic exposures.	Differential vulnerabilities also exist due to temperatures in rural areas, but the spaced-out and predominant dispersed rural settlement patterns discourage pandemic exposures.
Management impacts (Duggal, 2020; Sharifi and Khavarian-Garmsir; Thoi, 2020; Chigbu, 2021a)	Governance	Complexities in urban governance structures and the absence of proactive planning and emergency plans is a major reason for failure to respond effectively in some countries.	Simplicity in rural governance allowed for easier communication about responses to avoid contact-generating activities.

features of rural areas (such as availability of open spaces, sparse settlement patterns, presence of nature, etc.) also form conditions that discourage the spread of the pandemic.

The imposition of pandemic-related responses (such as partial and total lockdowns) enforced in many parts of the world have affected urban areas more than rural areas. These lockdowns have provided an unprecedented opportunity to observe how rural areas play a role in ameliorating the pandemic chaos felt in urban areas. The emerging consequences have been a shifting form of pro-rural mobility related to COVID-19. This is not only because of the impact of COVID-19. It is also because city-type living conditions are becoming more unattractive due to increasing density of urban settlements, loss of green places, increasing prices of land and housing, increasing temperatures especially in summer times, high traffic density, high air and noise pollution, increasing demand for larger housing spaces due to coronavirus limitations, and many others (Magel, 2019). In Europe and North America, improvements in rural information communication technology and digitalization means that people pushed by COVID-19 conditions to adopt home office options for their work can now live in rural areas while working for their urban employers (Berlin Institut, 2021). Also, young families in these parts of the world have discovered that rural areas are better places for their children and for themselves to live a healthier life.

Martin and Bergmann (2020, p. 1) note that the 'COVID-19 highlights the fact that infectious disease outbreaks and human mobility are intrinsically linked, yet the links are complex.' In general, the pandemic has lessened movement due to the direct orders (through curfews, and imposition of further travel requirements, etc.) by governments. There are also further restrictions indirectly imposed by economic impoverishment caused by the economic crises associated with the pandemic. One of the anomalies engendered by the pandemic is the increasing urban–rural migration (both temporary and permanent) as a mechanism to reduce exposure to the pandemic. It is the reverse migration or urban–rural movement being experienced across the world (Table 17.2).

Table 17.2 provides incidences observed in various parts of the world. Concerning the urban–rural migration in India, Bhowmick (2020) reported that the returnees: 'walked, cycled, and hitchhiked, often along the only route they knew train tracks. Fathers carried children on their shoulders, women balanced belongings on their heads, people squatted atop crowded trucks – all determined to find a way home.' Bhowmick noted that when interviewed, the rural returnees argued that: 'It was a very practical strategy to walk home, because it means a roof over their heads, food, and the comfort of a community' (20200)

The situation in Germany is not fully covered by any full studies yet. However, Niehues and Stockhausen's (2021) study published by the Institut für Deutsche Wirtschaft (German Economic Institute) found that the reverse migration is happening. However, since 2014 the trend of reverse migration from bigger cities by German citizens has been happening, but since the beginning of COVID-19 pandemic, migration of Germans from other parts of the world has made it become unignorable (Niehues and Stockhausen, 2021). The COVID-19 pandemic has exposed the trend that cities are losing population to surrounding areas and rural areas. It is having a negative impact on the urban housing market, while potential opportunities in rural areas are now a major point of discourse by key players in the real estate market. This trend in Germany is different only in Munich, as one of the most attractive cities in the country. In Munich, the real estate market remained very robust, and the land and house prices even continued to rise despite the pandemic. The situation in Germany is comparable to that of Austria (Nenning, 2021).

The magnitude of the situation in Senegal is not as reported in India but remains significant in the context of Senegal. Le Nestour and Moscoviz (2020) found that thousands migrated to rural areas of Senegal. The same situation was noted by Baverstock (2020) in Mexico, where the Mexican authorities confirmed that they have 'seen a great deal of returning migrants in their rural municipalities' and are worried that these returnees would not 'find stable employment here, as there were few jobs going in the town... but others here are simply happy to have their family members back again.' Georgiev's (2020) research, which was done in cooperation with European Council for Foreign

Table 17.2. Notable incidences of pandemic-related urban–rural migration.

Regions	Countries reported	Publication date	Evidence and nature of pandemic-driven urban–rural migration reported
Africa	Senegal	April 2020	Le Nestour and Moscoviz (2020) noted that in Dakar thousands have left the capital city and migrated to rural areas of Senegal. And that it was this large population movement that contributed to the spread of the disease and risk in rural Senegal.
Asia	India	May 2020, September 2020, May 2020, and March 2021, respectively	Bhowmick (2020) found that an estimated 139 million internal migrants, many of them are farmers who become daily wage workers to pay off debts or earn money for seeds and farming equipment, have returned home to their rural villages. Boillat and Zähringer (2020) reported that about 500 million people currently considered as internal migrants returned to their native roots in India. For more on reverse migration in India, see Dandekar and Ghai (2020); and Kumar and Choudhury (2021).
	Bangladesh, India and Pakistan	January 2021	Lee *et al.*'s (2021) research from the World Bank revealed that the migration patterns that had taken root over decades in South Asia were dramatically being reversed (in Bangladesh, India and Pakistan) spurred by job losses and the anticipation of lockdowns in response to the COVID-19 pandemic.
	China	December 2020	He *et al.*'s (2020) research, though not entirely focused on COVID-19, found that urban–rural migration was already taking place in China prior to the pandemic. The research, which was based on a spatial autocorrelation results, revealed that urban–rural migration was a key factor for pandemic transmissions whereas rural-to-urban migrations were across China.
Europe	Bulgaria, Germany and Austria	November 2020, May 2021, and March 2021, respectively	Georgiev (2020) used government data in Bulgaria to establish that over 558,000 Bulgarian citizens were registered as having returned to Bulgaria during the March–May period. The research is not conclusive about the destination of these returnees' points to more than 77,000 of the returnees heading to small rural towns. Studies done by Niehues and Stockhausen (2021) on Germany (and other countries) showed that more and more people are leaving the cities for rural or suburban areas because of housing shortages. Niehues and Stockhausen (2021) noted that the situation has been exacerbated by the COVID-19 pandemic. Nenning (2021) reported a similar scenario in Austria.
North America and South America	Mexico	May 2020	Thousands of Mexicans working in the USA returned to their country of origin, many of them returning to rural towns and villages (Baverstock, 2020).

Relations and Konrad Adenauer Stiftung, referred to the situation in Bulgaria as the 'grand return'.

As the pandemic-driven urban–rural migratory trend is merely emerging, so too is the literature available on this subject. However, this chapter has been able to provide current evidence of the trend in selected countries from Africa, Asia, Europe, and North and South America. Furthermore, there is lack of full and interconnected databases which makes it very hard to track internal migrations (such as urban–rural migrations) in general (Georgiev, 2020). However, this trend has been quite noticeable because it is occurring during an unprecedented time. With the evidence available, it is worth discussing what will become of the rural areas if this trend continues.

17.4 Where from Here? New Hope and Future for Rural Areas Under COVID-19 Circumstances?

Several questions remain unclear. What will life be like in a post-COVID-19 situation? Will all things return to normal? Will a large percentage of the migrant population who have moved back to rural areas choose to remain there or will they return to the urban area again? It is difficult to answer any of these questions at this point because of the uncertainties that surround liveability everywhere.

For rural returnees (i.e. those who migrated earlier from rural to urban areas, following economic, environmental and climate-related challenges), what reverse migration has done is to place them back in the rural areas where they used to be 'vulnerable and at risk' (Murthy, 2020). Whether this will be a short-term or long-term shift in rural demography is likely to lead to several possible consequences for rural areas.

If reverse migration becomes stable and rural returnees remain in rural areas, it will require strong political and administrative actions to engage in a renewed form of rural development. It will also lead to a new perception of rural areas. This is because it will become evident that rural areas are much more than places for agriculture or locations of natural resources which could be exploited for the welfare of urban and general development needs. In a continent like Europe, it could lead to a (re)conceptualization of rural areas as expressions of national heritage. It may finally change the erroneous perception that living in the countryside is inferior to living in cities. However, this would not happen unless interventions are conscious put in place (by way of policy measures) to improve the living and working conditions of people in rural areas. Thus, uplifting them to a certain urban standard without destroying the identities and specialities of rural traditions, the rural environment, and rural customs.

As stated by Magel and Miosga (2021), the COVID-19 pandemic has created awareness of the society to acknowledge how unstable and vulnerable the current economic models are. It also affirms that the sustainable development is needed but cannot be achieved without regarding urban and rural areas as equal and undividable partner settlements in the development process. This means, that rural and urban areas should be viewed as 'sister and brother' collaborators in national developments (Magel and Miosga, 2021). This development ideology is crucial as it reflects the position of the former French Prime Minister, Edgar Faure, who once stated that 'When rural areas are not breathing any more the cities will suffocate' (Magel, 2017, p. 73). This implies that efforts have been made to develop an urban–rural land linkages concept and framework for action on how to tap into urban–rural interrelationships, interdependencies, cooperation, and collaboration (Chigbu, 2021b).

To create change through rural development in a post-COVID-19 context, the current urban–rural isolationist mindset must also change among policy makers, academics, development practitioners, civil society organizations, researchers, and people in the society. Turning the new mindset into new development outcomes would require the actions of multiple stakeholders. It would also require changing the politics of development to be all embracing, as well as having open-minded politicians capable of starting the process. The mindset of society, especially the young generation, will change when successes in rural development outcomes (especially the aspect of rural infrastructure and economy) become a reality. If there are jobs and affordable housing in rural areas, young people would be discouraged from permanently migrating to cities.

In general, to become successful in achieving these measures, all countries need a clear statement of territorial planning or a territorial agenda which can frame rural liveability conditions to be equivalent to those of the urban areas. This measure has been framed in the *Territorial Agenda 2030*, a strategic framework document that 'seeks to promote an inclusive and sustainable future for all places and help achieve Sustainable Development Goals in Europe' (European Union, 2020). Where possible, other countries are encouraged to follow this action plan, to take inspiration from it and adapt from it a proposal for new actions for inclusive living conditions for the future. Doing this would require the development of visions for all regions of a country and prioritizing renewed measure for rural areas. Based on this model, sustainable development of rural areas must follow four universal dimensions of justices: including distribution justice, procedural justice, equality of opportunities, and intergenerational justice. Distribution justice entails provision of technical infrastructure (including information communication technology and digitalization measures see Berlin Institut, 2021), health care, social welfare, etc. Procedural justice relates to good governance, and fair treatment by government (including the judicial courts). Equality of opportunities means giving access to education (also higher education), jobs and mobility. Intergenerational justice deals with fairness in considering future generation in decision-making opportunities for sustainable development outcomes. These dimensions of spatial justice are essential for rural development because they go beyond mere provisions of material public services and infrastructure and access of resource in rural areas. Furthermore, the development of rural areas is an integral and complex process which has a lot of stakeholders that needed to be identified. To identify the stakeholders and participating institutions and individuals can be a challenging task.

Comprehensive territorial development and holistic land management in urban and rural areas (with its components land tenure, land administration, land valuation, land markets, land use, land development and land adjustment) can contribute to stabilizing and giving security to rural areas in post-COVID-19 period. However, doing all of these requires a lot of time. It also needs patience from communities and implementing agencies. Experience from Germany (which is surely one of the most developed countries of the world), especially after the fall of Berlin wall, shows that there are still spatial imbalances in Germany. The country is still comprised of rich and poor areas in its western and eastern regions, respectively, or when compared in a north–south context. It still has imbalances due to structural shifts between peripheral rural areas and highly populated areas. Hence, time and patience are a factor to achieving any success elsewhere. It is possible to change the rural–urban imbalances that exist around the world because it is not a law of nature for people to migrate from urban to rural areas as has been sometimes claimed by urban enthusiasts. The onus is on humans – and the COVID-19 crisis provides the momentum to halt this – to model a better balance of urban–rural liveability for all.

17.5 Conclusion

Why is it that instead of 'equalising conditions between rural and urban areas, rural–urban migration often reinforces the concentration of economic activities and accelerated growth in cities?' (de Haas, 2014, p. 10). What can be done differently now that there are significant trends of urban–rural migration around the world? The content of this chapter has hinged on these questions. The chapter draws attention to an ongoing reverse migration which may have important consequences for how land systems are conceptualized, understood, used and governed in the future. Most importantly, it brings to fore the role of rural areas and rural development in achieving the global development agendas.

The chapter does not in any way argue that rural areas are free from the COVID-19 pandemic. What the authors have sought to show is that, since the beginning of the outbreak many countries in Europe, Africa, Asia, Australia, North America and South America have experienced movements of population from big cities to rural areas. Le Nestour and Moscoviz (2020) reported that this movement 'has increased the spread of the virus and oversaturated rural health systems' in these countries. However, our discourse has focused on providing evidence of this movement through reliable literature resources; and then discussing the way forward for rural areas.

There are two sides to the issue of reverse migration. In the developed countries, it is not all due to COVID-19. Cities are becoming unattractive for a demography of the population (especially, young, old and wealthy people) who want to move to the countryside to enjoy the benefits of natural environment. In the developing countries, it is the pandemic which forces people to leave the cities. However, this movement has positive effects for rural revitalization, and three critical developmental implications. First, it is worth acknowledging that de-urbanization is a serious challenge throughout the world, especially in developing countries. 'As people leave cities, they are leaving properties behind, which creates a range of challenges, such as how to ensure their properties are not taken over by others, whether they be developers, government agents or squatters' (Land Portal, 2020). 'Re-integrating this mass of people into rural communities presents another serious challenge and may lead to a rise in conflicts' (Land Portal, 2020). Second, it is important to always remember that no-one will be safe until the rural areas are safe. The pandemic and its knock-on effects will continue to exacerbate temporary and permanent human mobility (either voluntary or involuntary) towards the rural areas. This means that the most vulnerable urban dwellers with social networks in rural areas (when in precarious circumstances) seek refuge in rural areas. It is therefore important to ensure that rural development is improved to ensure that people who return to rural areas are safe and do not add to the already socioeconomic burdens in rural areas. To tackle the primary issue, it is important to put in place an urban informal-settlement-tailored housing plan to reorganize sharing as a survival strategy in informal settlements (Chigbu and Onyebueke, 2021). This could help prioritize water/sanitation and enhance space standards to save lives, while creating health awareness in urban areas. Third, any efforts towards handling the fallout from urban–rural migration in rural development programmes would require a form of re-education and capacity development of land management and rural development experts to understand the emerging demographic changes and how to relate to rural liveability. This sort of education and capacity development are necessary for training 'new change-makers to handle the new challenges and contexts with new insights' in emerging urban–rural migratory issues concerned with the land-and-health nexus of development (de Vries *et al.*, 2021, p. 127). It would also require the re-organization of planning processes and stakeholders' involvements to allow for a values-enabling environment whereby 'administrative structures, policy frameworks, institutional and social settings, collective actions, and social learning are collaborative in their design' (Auzins and Chigbu, 2021, p. 12).

There is a new hope and future for rural areas under COVID-19 circumstances because the pandemic has forced rural people to realize that cities cannot offer them everything they need. They have also realized that they can rely on their rural homelands for security from pandemics. Building on this situation as part of the rural development requires that all developmental strategies in the post-COVID-19 era must be based on creating an intergenerational mindset. This can be integrated in two ways: (i) communities must envision that their rural areas as geographies (and socioeconomic and administrative entities) of equivalent working and living conditions; (ii) politicians must be aware that without having resilient rural areas in place, the development of their countries would not be balanced, which could lead to socioeconomic and environmental challenges on the long run. A country that has been affected in this way is China, who are now pushing for a strong rural revitalization strategy (Magel *et al.*, forthcoming). If people do not want to live in the countryside only as farmer, other means of livelihoods must also be created to enable them to gain sufficient income to cater for their family. The development of rural areas should be based on innovations that improve peoples' living conditions in ways that support intergenerational wealth. It must go beyond the traditional concept of rural development which largely focuses on the farming aspect, and embrace non-farm activities with neighbourhood multiplier effects. The experience from the COVID-19 pandemic has shown that it is worth developing and reconceptualising rural areas as attractive living and working places, more than ever.

Endnote

[1] ECA International is market leader in global surveys and data management. It uses location ratings systems to measure the quality of expatriates living conditions in nearly 500 locations around the world to arrive at a fair and consistent assessment of the level of difficulty the expatriate will experience in adapting to a new location. Factors evaluated include climate: availability of health services, housing and utilities, isolation, access to a social network and leisure facilities, infrastructure, personal safety, political tensions, and air quality. For details on ECA International's methods, see http://www.eca-international.com

References

Alderton, A., Higgs, C., Davern, M., Butterworth, I., Correia, J., Nitvimol, K. and Badland, H. (2020) Measuring and monitoring liveability in a low-to-middle income country: A proof-of-concept for Bangkok, Thailand and lessons from an international partnership. *Cities & Health*, 1–9. DOI: 10.1080/23748834.2020.1813537.

Allam, Z. (2020) *Urban Governance and Smart City Planning: Lessons from Singapore*. Emerald Publishing Limited, Bingley, UK.

Atterton, J. (2008) *Rural Proofing in England: A Formal Commitment in Need of Review.* Centre for Rural Economy Discussion Paper Series No. 20. Newcastle University, Newcastle upon Tyne, UK.

Auzins, Armands and Chigbu, U.E. (2021) Values-led planning approach in spatial development: A methodology. *Land*, 10(5), 461. DOI: 10.3390/land10050461.

Baverstock, A. (2020) Mexican reverse migration amid the coronavirus pandemic. CGTN North America, 16 May. Available at: https://news.cgtn.com/news/2020-05-16/Mexican-reverse-migration-amid-the-coronavirus-pandemic-QxqBBnaMfu/index.html (accessed 14 May 2021).

Berlin Institut (2021) *Digital aufs Land. Wie kreative Menschen das Leben in Dörfern und Kleinstädten neu gestalten* [Digitization in the country. How creative people are reshaping life in villages and small towns]. Available at: https://www.berlin-institut.org/studien-analysen/detail/digital-aufs-land (accessed 15 May 2021).

Bhowmick, N. (2020) History and culture: 'They treat us like stray dogs': Migrant workers flee India's cities. *National Geographic*, 27 May. Available at: https://www.nationalgeographic.com/history/article/they-treat-us-like-stray-dogs-migrant-workers-flee-india-cities (accessed 15 May 2021).

Boillat, S. and Zähringer, J. (2020) COVID-19, reverse migration, and the impact on land systems. The Global Land Programme. Available at: https://glp.earth/news-events/blog/covid-19-reverse-migration-and-impact-land-systems (accessed 15 May 2021).

Braga, F., Scarpa, G.M., Brando, V.E., Manfè, G. and Zaggia, L. (2020) COVID-19 lockdown measures reveal human impact on water transparency in the Venice Lagoon. *Science of the Total Environment,* 736, article 139612. DOI: 10.1016/j.scitotenv.2020.139612.

Bucsky, P. (2020) Modal share changes due to COVID-19: The case of Budapest. *Transportation Research Interdisciplinary Perspectives*, 100, article 100141. DOI: 10.1016/j.trip.2020.100141.

Callaghan, T., Lueck, J.A., Trujillo, K.L. and Ferdinand, A.O. (2021) Rural and urban differences in COVID-19 prevention behaviors. *Journal of Rural Health*, 37(2), 287–295. Available at: https://onlinelibrary.wiley.com/doi/epdf/10.1111/jrh.12556 (accessed 26 July 2021).

Chigbu, U.E. (2012) Village renewal as an instrument of rural development: evidence from Weyarn, Germany. *Community Development*, 43(2), 209–224. DOI: 10.1080/15575330.2011.575231.

Chigbu, U.E. (2013a) Territorial development: Suggestions for a new approach to rural development in Nigeria. PhD thesis, Technical University of Munich, Germany. Available at: http://mediatum.ub.tum.de/doc/1136728/document.pdf (accessed 12 May 2021).

Chigbu, U.E. (2013b) Fostering rural sense of place: The missing piece in Uturu, Nigeria. *Development in Practice*, 23(2), 264–277. DOI: 10.1080/09614524.2013.772120.

Chigbu, U.E. (2020) e-Tracking COVID-19 disruptions to the global development agenda on land. *International Journal Environmental Sciences and Natural Resources,* 26(1), article 556176. Available at: https://juniperpublishers.com/ijesnr/pdf/IJESNR.MS.ID.556176.pdf (accessed 26 July 2021).

Chigbu, U.E. (2021a) Tenure responsive land-use planning as a tool for improving quality of life: The perspective of sub-Saharan Africa. In: Martinez, J., Mikkelsen, C.A. and Phillips, R. (Eds), *Handbook of Quality of Life and Sustainability*. Springer, Cham, Switzerland, pp. 17–33. Available at: https://link.springer.com/chapter/10.1007/978-3-030-50540-0_2 (accessed 26 July 2021).

Chigbu, U.E. (2021b) *Urban–Rural Land Linkages: A Concept and Framework for Action.* Global Land Tool Network / UN-Habitat, Nairobi, Kenya.

Chigbu, U.E. and Onyebueke, V.U. (2021) The COVID-19 pandemic in informal settlements: (Re)considering urban planning interventions. *Town Planning Review*, 92(1), 115–122.

Corburn, J. (2009) *Toward the Healthy City: People, Places, and the Politics of Urban Planning.* MIT Press, Cambridge, MA, USA.

Dandekar, A. and Ghai, R. (2020) Commentary: Migration and reverse migration in the age of COVID-19. *Economic & Political Weekly,* 19, 28–31.

de Haas, H. (2014) *Migration Theory: Quo Vadis?* International Migration Institute / Oxford University Working Papers Series, 100. Available at: https://www.migrationinstitute.org/publications/wp-100-14 (accessed 16 May 2021).

de Vries, W.T., Chigbu, U.E. and Duran-Diaz, P. (2021) Twenty years of building capacity in land management, land tenure and urban land governance. In: Home, R. (Ed.), *Land Issues for Urban Governance in Sub-Saharan Africa. Springer*, Cham, Switzerland, pp. 121–136.

Duggal, R. (2020) Mumbai's struggles with public health crises from plague to COVID-19. *Economic and Political Weekly,* 55 (21), 17–20.

European Union (2020) *Territorial Agenda 2030: Summary.* Informal meeting of Ministers responsible for Spatial Planning and Territorial Development and/or Territorial Cohesion,1 December, Germany. Available at: https://ec.europa.eu/regional_policy/en/information/publications/brochures/2021/territorial-agenda-2030-a-future-for-all-places (accessed 22 May 2021).

Ferguson, N. (2020) Das Dorf ist in, Metropolen sind out [The village is in, big cities are out]. *Neue Zürcher Zeitung* [New Journal of Zürich], 18 May. Available at: https://www.nzz.ch/feuilleton/niall-ferguson-das-dorfist-in-metropolen-sind-out-ld.1557034 (accessed 22 May 2021).

Finn, B.M. and Kobayashi, L.C. (2020) Structural inequality in the time of COVID-19: Urbanization, segregation, and pandemic control in sub-Saharan Africa. *Dialogues in Human Geography*, 10(2), 217–220. DOI: 10.1177/2043820620934310.

Firth, J. (2021) Lockdown measures impede the liveability of 70% of the world's cities. *ECA International News*, 21 January. Available at: https://www.eca-international.com/news/january-2021/lockdown-measures-impede-the-liveability-of-70-of (accessed 12 May 2021).

Georgiev, O. (2020) *The Grand Return: COVID-19 and Reverse Migration to Bulgaria.* European Council for Foreign Relations and Konrad Adenauer Stiftung, Sofia, Bulgaria.

Hallema, D.W., Robinne, F.N. and McNulty, S.G. (2020) Pandemic spotlight on urban water quality. *Ecological Processes*, 9(22). DOI: 10.1186/s13717-020-00231-y.

He, W., Ju, K., Gao, Y., Zhang, P., Zhang, Y., Jiang, Y. and Liao, W. (2020) Spatial inequality, characteristics of internal migration, and pulmonary tuberculosis in China, 2011–2017: A spatial analysis. *Infectious Diseases of Poverty*, 9 (159). DOI: 10.1186/s40249-020-00778-0.

Huang, Q., Jackson, S., Derakhshan, S., Lee, L., Pham, E., Jackson, A. *et al.* (2021) Urban–rural differences in COVID-19 exposures and outcomes in the South: A preliminary analysis of South Carolina. *PLoS ONE,* 16(2): article e0246548. DOI: 10.1371/journal.pone.0246548.

İstillozlu, E. and Doratlı, N. (2021) A normative approach for assessment of accessibility from liveability perspective. *European Planning Studies*, 29(1), 39–56. DOI: 10.1080/09654313.2020.1779666.

Kulkarni, B.N. (2020) Environmental sustainability assessment of land disposal of municipal solid waste generated in Indian cities – A review. *Environmental Development*, 33, article 100490. DOI: 10.1016/j.envdev.2019.100490.

Kumar, S. and Choudhury, S. (2021) Migrant workers and human rights: A critical study on India's COVID-19 lockdown policy. *Social Sciences & Humanities Open,* 3(1), article 100130. DOI: 10.1016/j.ssaho.2021.100130.

Land Portal (2020) Online discussion: Land rights implications of COVID-19. Available at: https://landportal.org/debates/2020/land-rights-implications-covid-19 (accessed 14 May 2021).

Leby, J.L. and Hashim, A.H. (2010) Liveability dimensions and attributes: Their relative importance in the eyes of neighbourhood residents. *Journal of Construction in Developing Countries,* 15(1), 67–91.

Lee, J.N., Mahmud, M., Morduch, J., Ravindran, S. and Shonchoy, A.S. (2021) Migration, externalities, and the diffusion of COVID-19 in South Asia. *Journal of Public Economics*, 193, article 104312. DOI: 10.1016/j.jpubeco.2020.104312.

Le Nestour, A. and Moscoviz, L. (2020) Five findings from a new phone survey in Senegal. Commentary and analysis article, Centre for Global Development. Available at: https://www.cgdev.org/blog/five-findings-new-phone-survey-senegal (accessed 14 May 2021).

Li, X., Yang, H., Jia, J., Shen, Y. and Liu, J. (2021) Index system of sustainable rural development based on the concept of ecological livability. *Environmental Impact Assessment Review,* 86, article 106478. DOI: 10.1016/j.eiar.2020.106478.

Lloyd, K., Fullagar, S. and Reid, S. (2016) Where is the 'social' in construction of 'liveability'? Exploring community social intereation and social cohesion in changing urban environments. *Urban Policy and Research*, 34(4), 342–355. DOI: 10.1080/08111146.2015.1118374.

Magel, H. (2016) Räumliche Gerechtigkeit – Ein Thema für Landentwickler und sonstige Geodäten? *zfv – Zeitschrift für Geodäsie, Geoinformation und Landmanagement (zfv - Magazine for Geodesy, Geoinformation and Land Management),* 141(6), 377–383. DOI: 10.12902/zfv-0144-2016.

Magel, H. (2017) Territorial justice for urban and rural regions? About the responsibility and role of the Bavarian academy for Rural Areas. *Geomatics, Landmanagement and Landscape*, 4(1), 65–79. DOI: 10.15576/GLL/2017.1.65.

Magel, H. (2019) Landlust, Landfrust oder beides? – Aktuelle Anmerkungen zu gleichwertigen Lebensbedingungen in Stadt und Land [Country in lust, country frustration or both? – Current comments on equivalent living conditions in town and country]. *zfv – Zeitschrift für Geodäsie, Geoinformation und Landmanagement [zfv - Magazine for Geodesy, Geoinformation and Land Management]*, 144(3), 147–156. DOI: 10.12902/zfv-0258-2019.

Magel, H. and Miosga, M. (2021) Does countryside now have a future again? In: Molls, M., Eberspächer, Jörg, Auernhammer, H., Färber, G., Herbst-Gaebel, B., Lindemann, U., Mainzer, K., Petry, W., Reichwald, R., Scheurle, J., van Hemmen, L. and Wilderer, P. (Eds), *Science, Reason and Responsibility: Forward Thinking for the Post-Corona Era.* TUM University Press, Munich, Germany, pp. 148–151.

Magel, H. and Wehrmann, B. (2006) 'It's all about land' or 'how international networks approach the land question'. *Zeitschrift für Geodäsie, Geoinformation und Landmanagement,* 131(5), 57–61.

Magel, H., Klaus, M. and Spindler, K. (forthcoming) Alles unter dem Himmel. Gedanken über die Weltordnung und (Ländliche) Neuordnung in Bayern und China [Everything under heaven. Reflections about the world order and (rural) rearrangement in Bavaria and China]. *zfv – Zeitschrift für Geodäsie, Geoinformation und Landmanagement [zfv - Magazine for Geodesy, Geoinformation and Land Management]*, 147(1) (forthcoming).

Martin, S.F. and Bergmann, J. (2020) *Shifting Forms of Mobility Related to COVID-19.* International Organization for Migration (IOM), Geneva, Switzerland.

Murthy, I.K. (2020) *Reverse Migration Due to COVID-19 Underpins the Need for Adaptation*. Center for Study of Science, Technology and Policy, Bangalore, India.

Napierała, T., Leśniewska-Napierała, K. and Burski, R. (2020) Impact of geographic distribution of COVID-19 cases on hotels' performances: Case of Polish cities. *Sustainability*, 12(11). DOI: 10.3390/su12114697.

Nenning, A. (2021) Covid-19 verändert die Wünsche an die Wohnsituation (Covid-19 is changing the way people want to live). *Re/Max Austria*, 31 March. Available at: https://www.remax.at/de/n/re-max-studie-covid-19-veraendert-die-wuensche-an-die-wohnsituation-17535 (accessed 13 May 2021).

Nichol, J.E., Bilal, M., Ali, A.M. and Qiu, Z. (2020) Air pollution scenario over China during COVID-19. *Remote Sensing*, 12(13). DOI: 10.3390/rs12132100.

Niehues, J. and Stockhausen, M. (2021) *Inequality Revisited: An International Comparison with a Special Focus on the Case of Germany*. Institut der Deutschen Wirtschaft – IW-Report No. 18. Available at: https://www.iwkoeln.de/en/institute/who-we-are/detail/maximilian-stockhausen.html (accessed 22 May 2021).

Paul, A. and Sen, J. (2020) A critical review of liveability approaches and their dimensions. *Geoforum*, 117, 90–92. DOI: 10.1016/j.geoforum.2020.09.008.

Ren, H., Zhao, L., Zhang, A., Song, L., Liao, Y., Lu, W. and Cui, C. (2020) Early forecasting of the potential risk zones of COVID-19 in China's megacities. *Transportation Research Interdisciplinary Perspectives,* 729, 138995. DOI: 10.1016/j.scitotenv.2020.138995.

Roy, I. (2020) The role of temperature on the global spread of COVID-19 and urgent solutions. *International Journal of Environmental Science and Technology.* DOI: 10.1007/s13762-020-02991-8.

Sackmann, C. (2021) Raus aufs Land: Nur ein radikaler Wandel schützt uns vor Horror-Mieten in der Stadt [Out in the country: Only a radical change will protect us from the horrors of rents in the city]. Available at: https://www.focus.de/immobilien/wohnen/in-3-bereichen-muss-deutschland-schneller-werden-raus-aufs-land-warum-uns-nur-ein-radikaler-wandel-vor-horror-mieten-schuetzen-wird_id_13082127.html (accessed 20 May2021).

Saha, J., Barman, B. and Chouhan, P. (2020) Lockdown for COVID-19 and its impact on community mobility in India: An analysis of the COVID-19 Community Mobility Reports. *Children and Youth Services Review,* 116, article 105160. DOI: 10.1016/j.childyouth.2020.105160.

Sharifi, A. and Khavarian-Garmsir, A.R. (2020) The COVID-19 pandemic: Impacts on cities and major lessons for urban planning, design, and management. *Science of the Total Environment*, 749, article 142391. Available at: https://www.sciencedirect.com/science/article/pii/S0048969720359209 (accessed 26 July 2021).

Straßer, P. (2019) *Liveability Concepts. Differences in the Interpretation of Liveability in Developed and Industrialised Countries*. GRIN Verlag, Munich, Germany.

Thoi, P.T. (2020) Ho Chi Minh City – The front line against COVID-19 in Vietnam. *City & Society*, 32. DOI: 10.1111/ciso.12284.

Triandafyllidou, A. (Ed.) (2016) *Irregular Migration in Europe: Myths and Realities*. Routledge, London, UK.

United Nations (1992) *United Nations Conference on Environment & Development Rio de Janerio, Brazil, 3-14 June: AGENDA 21*. United Nations Organization, New York, NY, USA.

United Nations (2018) News: 68% of the world population projected to live in urban areas by 2050, says UN. *United Nations News*, 16 May. Available at: https://www.un.org/development/desa/en/news/population/2018-revision-of-world-urbanization-prospects.html (accessed 13 May 2021).

WHO (2020) WHO announces COVID-19 outbreak a pandemic. World Health Organization. Available at: https://www.euro.who.int/en/health-topics/health-emergencies/coronavirus-covid-19/news/news/2020/3/who-announces-covid-19-outbreak-a-pandemic#:~:text=The%20meeting%20follows%20the%20announcement,a%20growing%20number%20of%20countries (accessed 12 May 2021).

18 Using Urban Literacy to Strengthen Land Governance and Women's Empowerment in Peri-Urban Communities of San Andrés Cholula, Mexico

Pamela Durán-Díaz,*[1] Emma R. Morales[2] and Melissa Schumacher[3]
[1]*Chair of Land Management, Technical University of Munich, Munich, Germany;* [2]*Department of Art, Design and Architecture, Universidad Iberoamericana Puebla, Cholula, Puebla, Mexico;* [3]*Department of Architecture, Universidad de las Américas Puebla, Cholula, Puebla, Mexico*

18.1 Applying Land Governance Principles in Traditional Peri-Urban Communities in Mexico as a Challenge

The metropolitan areas of Mexico have grown significantly since the 1990s due to neoliberal land, financial and housing policy changes. Other factors include the continuous migration of rural population to cities, and families fleeing from regions affected by violence associated with the ongoing Mexican War on Drugs. As a result, the population of the metropolitan area of Puebla-Tlaxcala has increased by 56% in 14 years (SEDATU, 2018, p. 29). The growth of Puebla-Tlaxcala has consequences on the rural population of the municipality of San Andrés Cholula. Forced expropriations and planning policies based on the economic growth of private real-estate agencies put pressure on rural people. These pressures also constitute signs of weak land governance. The organization of the sociopolitical system in Puebla-Tlaxcala is independent of official political power and closely related to religion. It is linked to the religious-Christian obligations with underlying pre-Hispanic traditions that transcends the social and geopolitical boundaries of *altépetl,*[1] *calpulli,*[2] parishes and administrative councils in a non-integrative manner. Thus, it makes the application of governance principles weak in agriculture and small businesses. This also makes it vulnerable to land grabbing.

In San Andrés, the role of women has been historically inconspicuous. This is because even though their role in households and community organizations is important, they are less prominent than their male counterparts within the economic and political sphere of community life. Although the Mexican Constitution grants equal rights to men and women, since 1917, practices inherited from the colonial power structure still hinder the access to land and decision-making processes. The traditional pre-Hispanic administrative system confers on women the right to take up political office, especially within the institutions in charge of organizing religious festivities that give Indigenous communities their much-needed sense of belonging (Hernández,

*Corresponding author: pamela.duran@tum.de

 Land Governance and Gender: The Tenure-Gender Nexus in Land Management and Land Policy (ed. U.E. Chigbul)
DOI: 10.1079/9781789247664.0018

2016). Several efforts have been made to respond to both gender-related and non-gender-related land challenges within the territory. In 2019, a joint Newton Fund and British Council academic project (co-implemented by the University of Edinburgh and Universidad Iberoamericana Puebla) identified institutional and bottom-up strategies for adaptation to climate-related risks in vulnerable communities of San Andrés Cholula, Puebla. The initially academic project evolved into a series of urban literacy workshops in five peri-urban traditional communities. However, these communities complained that the project was implemented without adequate public consultation. By public demand, a Municipal Programme on the Sustainable Urban Development (MPSUD) of San Andrés Cholula was introduced in 2018 (H. Ayuntamiento San Andrés Cholula, 2018). Grassroots movements in some communities demanded for MPSUD to consider their needs, customs and cultural values in the project implementation. A key concern in the urban development efforts of San Andrés Cholula (Puebla) has been the level of sensitization and awareness of community members about the urban governance systems. Efforts to improve this situation have led to programmes on urban literacy in stakeholder engagement and gender equity towards strengthening land governance in San Andrés Cholula's peri-urban communities.

This chapter presents the role urban literacy has played in the stakeholder engagement and gender equity efforts introduced to strengthen land governance in San Andrés Cholula's peri-urban communities. The chapter uses focus group discussion (FGD) from eight urban literacy workshops in five peri-urban communities of San Andrés Cholula. These FGDs were conducted during a period of 3 months (i.e. July–September 2019). The chapter is structured as follows. Section 18.2 starts with historical review of Cholula's sociopolitical office system and a critical evaluation of MPSUD based on the principles of good governance. Then follows a discussion of the process of the urban literacy workshops. This is then followed by a discussion of the role of women in strengthening land governance through urban literacy based on the outcomes of the workshops. Finally, the chapter concludes with emphasis on how urban literacy is a veritable strategy for strengthening land governance and for enabling inclusive participation in policy making.

18.2 The Principles of Good Governance in the Context of Cholula's Sociopolitical Office System

Historical Background of the Contested Territory of San Andrés Cholula

Cholula is a pre-Hispanic Mexican settlement divided into the municipalities of San Pedro and San Andrés. It is in the central Mexican highlands of Puebla-Tlaxcala Valley, 126 km to the east of Mexico City. Its name derives from the Nahuatl *Tollan Chololłan*, 'spring place where water runs' (Ashwell and O'Leary, 1999), as a reference to the natural environment and historical territorial struggles. The abundant water in the region[3] generates an ideal environment for irrigation agriculture. Thus, disputes over land are common in Cholula.

From the establishment of the first Teotihuacan settlement in c. 400 BCE as a religious centre, until the rise of Aztec empire when Cholula became an *altépetl*, several ethnicities from the Northern region, the Gulf, the plateau and the Mayan peninsula have visited and occupied the valley. The ethnic groups, Toltecas-Chichimecas and Olmecas-Xicalancas, were the main settlers who contested over the territory with the imposition of tributes, but with the option to preserve their autonomy and sociopolitical organization. This structure persisted until the arrival of Spanish *conquistadors* in 1519- the fall of the most sacred Mesoamerican city through the Massacre of Cholula[4] (González Hermosillo-Adams, 2001) in superimposing Spanish administrative structures over traditional Mesoamerican configurations. This entailed a re-definition of power, religion, culture, use and distribution of resources, and land tenure systems. The colonial documents of Franciscan missionaries registered that Cholula was divided in six *calpullis*, which became *cabeceras* to manage parishes; *cabeceras* were likewise divided into ten *barrios*.[5] Thus, the spatial layout of Cholula follows a socioreligious structure (Schumacher, 2016, p. 89).

Cholula's *altépetl* system, although inherent in the sociospatial structure, was not entirely recognized by Spanish authorities. In 1628, the Indigenous town of San Andrés located at the south of Tlachihualtépetl pyramid requested its separation from San Pedro, due to administrative problems and a long tradition of autonomy. San Andrés was eventually recognized as an Indigenous Republic, which obtained territorial and administrative autonomy in 1714. In 1816, after the Mexican Independence War, it became an independent municipality and consolidated the control over its traditional *barrios*, with the acquired right to elect governor, mayor and councillors. To date, San Andrés Cholula is administratively divided into one main municipal seat, two urban *barrios* (San Juan Aquiahuac, San Andrés Colomoxco), six peri-urban *juntas auxiliares*[6] (San Francisco Acatepec, San Luis Tehuiloyocan, San Antonio Cacalotepec, San Rafael Comac, San Bernardino Tlaxcalancingo, and Santa María Tonantzintla), and the urban land reserve Atlixcáyotl. The spatial organization has remained the same since the end of the 19th century, with the exclusion of some *haciendas* and the inclusion of the land reserve (see Figure 18.1).

The independence of Mexico from Spain in 1810 did not mean the return to pre-Hispanic sociopolitical structures, but the overlap of the new democratic administrative-political offices over the already complex inherited structures. The difficulty to define territorial limits between towns, municipalities, communal landholders and private owners has been the driver for multiple struggles, including Agrarian reforms, land-tenure changes, neoliberal trends, and massive land expropriation. The expropriation processes to widen the Federal highway to Atlixco, the conformation of the territorial reserve Atlixcáyotl, and the construction of the outer-ring Periférico Ecológico, took 1092 hectares of *ejidos* from San Bernardino Tlaxcalancingo and Santa María Tonantzintla (Schumacher *et al.*, 2019). Because of the experience of expropriations and rapid urbanization, residents of San Bernardino Tlaxcalancingo were the main opponents to the 2018 MPSUD, as they were not consulted when implementing new primary roads, high-impact commercial facilities, massive social housing, gated communities and high-rise buildings over and across their traditional neighbourhoods.

Sistema de cargos: An Overlapping Structure of Power

The pre-Hispanic sociospatial organization was based on *altépetl* structure, with a sociopolitical territorial unit ruled by an elite of priests and the *tlatoani* ('speaker'). There, an independent sovereign city served as the centre of cultural, political, economic and religious life for tributary entities distributed over its contiguous territories. San Andrés, as a tributary town of Cholula *altépetl*, served as the guardian of the temple and was likewise divided into *calpullis*, comprising

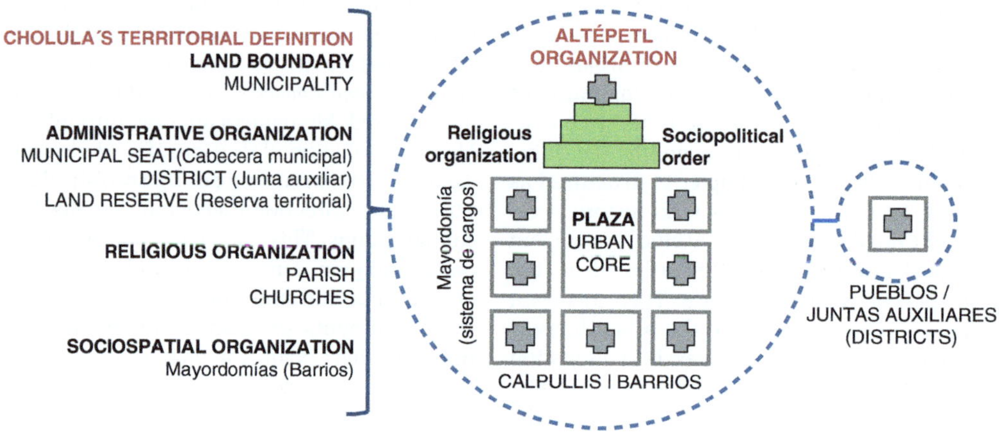

Fig. 18.1. Cholula's territorial layout based on the altépetl organization (Authors' illustration).

between 120 and 168 *chinamitl*, each with 51 houses (Castillo Palma, 2015). *Calpullis* had a family-based structure organized as a guild and managed by the family chief *calpullec*. The *calpullec* distributed the land among the families, directed the local military school *telpochcalli* ('house of young men'), led local religious activities, acted as a judge in minor litigation processes and represented the *calpulli* in higher entities such as the Nahua council.[7]

The Spanish conquest and colonization initiated a transcultural process that got imprinted in the territory in the complex political-administrative system, influenced by a religious tradition that still shapes the economy, family and social life. Cholula's nobility *pipiltin, tlatoanis* and *teteuctin* warriors were turned into *caciques*,[8] as the means to disregard autochthonous nomenclatures, to unify Indigenous authorities and, above all, to place native *pipiltin* below Spanish nobility without stripping them of their associated political authority (González Hermosillo-Adams, 2015). Also, politics and religion were intertwined before the Spanish conquest, hence in the colonial system, public officers also fostered ritual offices. Accordingly, during the colonization, the socio-political office system or *sistema de cargos* was instituted as a strategy to charge the native population the cost of their evangelization and local administration (Bonfil Batalla, 1973). Thus, the system based on the socioreligious structure of circular *mayordomías*, a Catholic institutional adaptation of the pre-Hispanic organization for the annual religious festivities.

Circular *mayordomía* pattern works as an integration mechanism of the different social strata, in which the *mayordomo*, elected by local *caciques*, neighbours and parishioners, takes charge of the organization of religious festivities for a year. *Mayordomos* also work together with religious organizations and prosecutors of other towns and districts, enabling the collaboration beyond administrative boundaries (Schumacher, 2016). The political-administrative organization of the municipality is also based on democratic procedures. The municipal mayor and the district mayor of *juntas auxiliares* are elected every three years together with their city council. Although the mayor is the maximum authority of the municipality, *mayordomías* represent the vertical sociospatial organization that link municipal authorities with the communities and their local representatives (Fig. 18.2), and they act as engaged stakeholders that guard the interests of the community they represent.

The Murky Implementation of the Municipal Program for Sustainable Urban Development (MPSUD) of San Andrés Cholula

Since 1993, urban development in San Andrés has occurred in a context of inequity, through

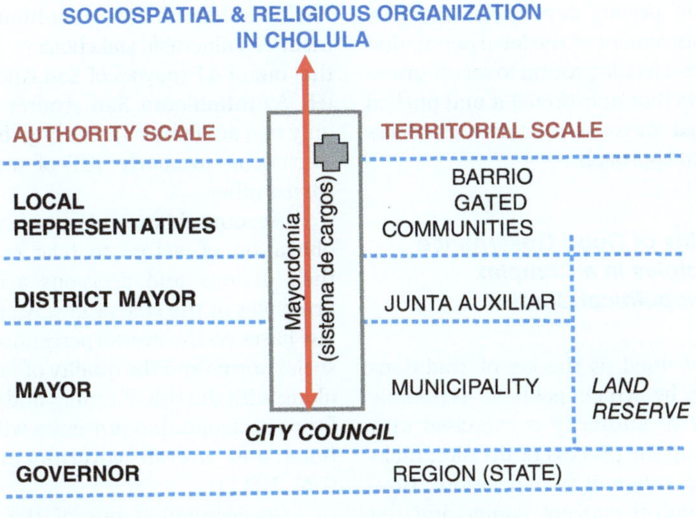

Fig. 18.2. The organizational structure of Cholula (Authors' illustration).

biased transactions or expropriations of productive rural land to favour large real estate investors (specifically Grupo Proyecta). The 2018 Municipal Program for Sustainable Urban Development is anything but sustainable, as it promotes the consolidation of dispersed urban development consisting of large residential areas, shopping centres and wide boulevards over rural land and traditional communities. However, these interventions have generated new jobs and increased the land value through the damage of community life with expensive taxes, land grabbing and the alteration of the cultural, economic and labour dynamics of San Andrés (Chololian, 2019).

Puebla's State Law for Land Management and Urban Development (SLLMUD) stipulates in Article 27 that the State and Municipal Councils should 'promote citizen participation and social organizations in the monitoring, operation and evaluation of policies' (Gobierno del Estado de Puebla, 2019). However, when the MPSUD was published in 2018 with no public consultation, nothing in the instrument was aimed to protect the communities from land speculation, the consequential water scarcity, the loss of territory and identity, and the understated changes in their social, economic and traditional practices. The programme was published only a few days before the municipal administration left office without meeting the legal procedures indicated in the SLLMUD. The lack of transparency, the clear presence of private developers' interests, and the non-involvement of the local population in its design were a fertile ground to set off grassroots movements that questioned it and pushed the newly elected mayor to re-start the process with an inclusive approach.

Applicability of Good Governance Principles in a Complex Sociopolitical Context

Governance is defined as the set of traditions and institutions by which political, economic and administrative authority is exercised in a country, including the process of decision making and implementation of such decisions. Governance is a neutral concept comprising the complex mechanisms, processes and institutions through which citizens and groups articulate their interests, exercise their legal rights and obligations, and mediate their differences (FAO, 2009).

International donor agencies, such as the World Bank Group and the Organisation for Economic Co-operation and Development (OECD), among others, have made numerous efforts to develop indicators for governance, and their core values vary depending on the organization that formulates them and the main targets of each organization. Thus, the concepts tend to be intersecting. For this chapter, our qualitative assessment is based on the United Nations' governance principles of participation and inclusion, accountability and rule of law, non-discrimination, and equality (UN, 2011).

Participation and inclusion refer to the empowerment of all actors through representation in government and other mechanisms facilitating free, active, and meaningful participation in decision-making processes (UN, 2011). In the case of San Andrés Cholula, the inclusive structure of power, in which the official political power of the democratically elected district mayor is complemented by the socioreligious office of mayordomos, should warrant the access of different stakeholders to positions of authority. Conversely, when it comes to decision making, the implementation process of the MPSUD, in which private investors in compliance the local authorities acted in disregard to the interests of the peri-urban communities, indicates that San Andrés's structure of power hinders the engagement of vulnerable stakeholders. It is noteworthy that out of 47 mayors of San Andrés since 1911 (H. Ayuntamiento San Andrés Cholula, n.d.), only two are female (including the current one), in contrast to nearly 50% of women in *mayordomías* office.

Accountability and rule of law stand for the obligation of actors to take responsibility for their actions and decisions according to the principles of the rule of law. An effective rule of law bases on the overall perception of security in social norms and the quality of law enforcement along with the risk of crimes and can support reforms or adaptation processes within state functions and overall government performance (UN, 2011).

Government is one of the structural element and institutional component of, as well as one of the actors in governance (Chigbu, 2021).

> Other actors involved in governance vary depending on the level of government that is under discussion. In rural areas, for example, other actors may include influential landlords, associations of peasant farmers, cooperatives, NGOs, Research institutes, religious leaders, finance institutions political parties, the military etc. The situation in urban areas is much more complex.
>
> (UNESCAP, 2009)

In San Andrés, the statutory, customary, religious and informal institutions have cross-cutting concerns and intersecting responsibilities. Hence, it is challenging to steer amid actors in the intricate political office system overlapped on both rural and urban contexts. The intricate structure of power eases authorities to avoid liability by impugning other parties instead. Moreover, in a country where 34% of public service users pay bribes (Transparency International, 2019), the rule of law is often hampered by the citizens themselves, especially in former Indigenous towns with a complex structure of power. For the reasons stated, the municipal city council approved and intended to implement an urban development plan that mainly addressed the interests of real-estate investors in a non-transparent process that eluded customary and rural actors. Opaque as it was, the process was not questioned nor stopped until more than half of the rural land (Chollolan, 2019) was already grabbed and changed into urban.

Non-discrimination and equality imply that

> a society's well-being depends on ensuring that all its members feel that they have a stake in it and do not feel excluded from the mainstream of society. This requires that all groups, especially the most vulnerable, have opportunities to improve or maintain their well-being.
>
> (UNESCAP, 2009)

San Andrés has been subject to constant conflicts linked to displacement, expropriation, touristic exploitation, social and urban exclusion, and disputes over land rights. In this regard, the urban literacy workshops revealed that women are more prone to suffer the consequences of these conflicts than men, as will be further developed.

All the above denotes that, although the governance principles should set a solid base for the construction of an inclusive society, the scopes barely reach peri-urban communities where urban actors disregard and outnumber the native population. The 2018 MPSUD, for instance, is handled by corrupt authorities as a tool to validate real estate projects that are already taking place and altering the land value of agricultural land. In this case, the economic benefits go exclusively to the developer while the severe impacts are borne by the whole community. As the instrument neither considered the voice of all stakeholders, nor incorporated appropriate mitigation measures, the planning process is incomplete. For example, urban development plans are often expressed in complex terms and technical language, which frustrates the participatory planning attempts. Involving the local population in decision-making processes must be because all stakeholders understand what the plan consists of, as its impacts are tangible in terms of the loss of water, land, livelihood and cultural values. The impacts also materialize in high-speed avenues that cut across hectares of fertile land, in high-rise buildings side-to-side with crops, and in the transformation of farmers into servitude for the newcomer urban population. The voices of peasants are thus muffled.

The improvement of local governance in San Andrés could only be enabled through strengthening decision-making capacities, enhancing resource management, implementing development initiatives, and delivering basic services among a variety of local participatory institutions including local governments. But it should be done based on history, traditions and culture. To make it possible, an urban literacy process was indispensable.

18.3 Urban Literacy Towards Stakeholder Engagement: Process and Methods

In 2019, researchers from the University of Edinburgh and Universidad Iberoamericana Puebla as part of the Newton Fund/British Council took part in a joint academic project about community adaptation to climate-related risks. Together, they conducted a series of perception risk workshops in Santa María Tonantzintla, which soon extended to the rest of the *juntas auxiliares* of San Andrés. As the project evolved, members of the communities approached the researchers to request a second series of workshops to be carried out, this time coordinated by the communities themselves, to address urgent risks and challenges entailed by the MPSUD. Given the detected need of the community members to understand the vulnerabilities of their land, researchers from Universidad Iberoamericana Puebla conducted capacity building community-led workshops in five peri-urban localities with the participation of members of six localities. As a strategy to help vulnerable groups understand the MPSUD, the aim was to provide local stakeholders knowledge about land management strategies, urban planning lexicon, concepts, legislation, instruments, impacts, risks and the role of the population in the planning decision-making process, to engage in an informed participatory process with the local authorities, to protect their traditions, agricultural land, backyard farming activities, as well as to safeguard their local businesses and the urban structure of their towns.

Within the one-year research project, eight urban literacy workshops were conducted in three months. There was an average of 35 participants each, with 55% of female participation. The first five urban literacy workshops focused on basic spatial planning knowledge and community engagement. They were organized by members of the grassroots initiative 'Cholultecas Unidos en Resistencia' (CHUR), a group that included activists and community leaders who had been involved in previous struggles for land, water and heritage. The workshops took place in five of the ancient rural *calpulli* of San Andrés Cholula: San Bernardino Tlaxcalancingo, San Antonio Cacalotepec, *barrio*-municipal seat of San Andrés Cholula, San Francisco Acatepec and San Rafael Comac. The last three urban literacy workshops took place in the community centre of San Bernardino Tlaxcalancingo and included representatives from six assemblies including Santa María Tonantzintla.

Structure of the Urban Literacy Workshops (SULW)

The structure of the urban literacy workshops was systematic. For the first five workshops, local assemblies in each town summoned all the residents interested in the SULW in learning about urban planning using social media and community radio. Two researchers had a brief presentation showing the most common planning concepts using everyday life examples to make them more accessible. The presentation also included risks and challenges, particularly linked to environmental negative effects and the risks of land valorization. A resident researcher joined the team to facilitate the second phase of the first five workshops. In this phase, facilitators used maps of the municipality and a blackboard as a visual approach to grasp the objectives and effects of the MPSUD. Participants would find their plots on the map and verify the proposed land use and density, and the impact of new roads or land use affecting their plots. They were consequently able to read the tables, maps and concepts using their cases. All workshops ended with informal get-togethers that doubled as FGDs. As women were usually the organizers of the food sharing, they made use of the opportunity to approach the facilitators with specific questions about communal rights, environmental protection, quality of public spaces, and even legality of newly developed projects.

The last three workshops were aimed at representatives from the six towns that would participate in the consultation process (Fig. 18.3 shows interactive activities during the workshops). They were interested in practical tools to understand zoning and land use principles, innovative land management instruments to protect communal land and water, and urban design principles to make their communities safer, more environmentally friendly, protect their cultural and architectural heritage, and maintain their local businesses and economic activities. Representatives of the six settlements created their maps, strategies, programmes, and land use restrictions. After the workshops, more than 15 additional meetings with local leaders took place, to discuss issues connected to the new version of the MPSUD and a new Ecological Management Program. Moreover, wide-ranging educational and communication activities were promoted by the local community radio station Chollolan Radio between mid-2019 and early 2020, including the broadcast of a documentary about the impact of recent urban development in the San Andrés.

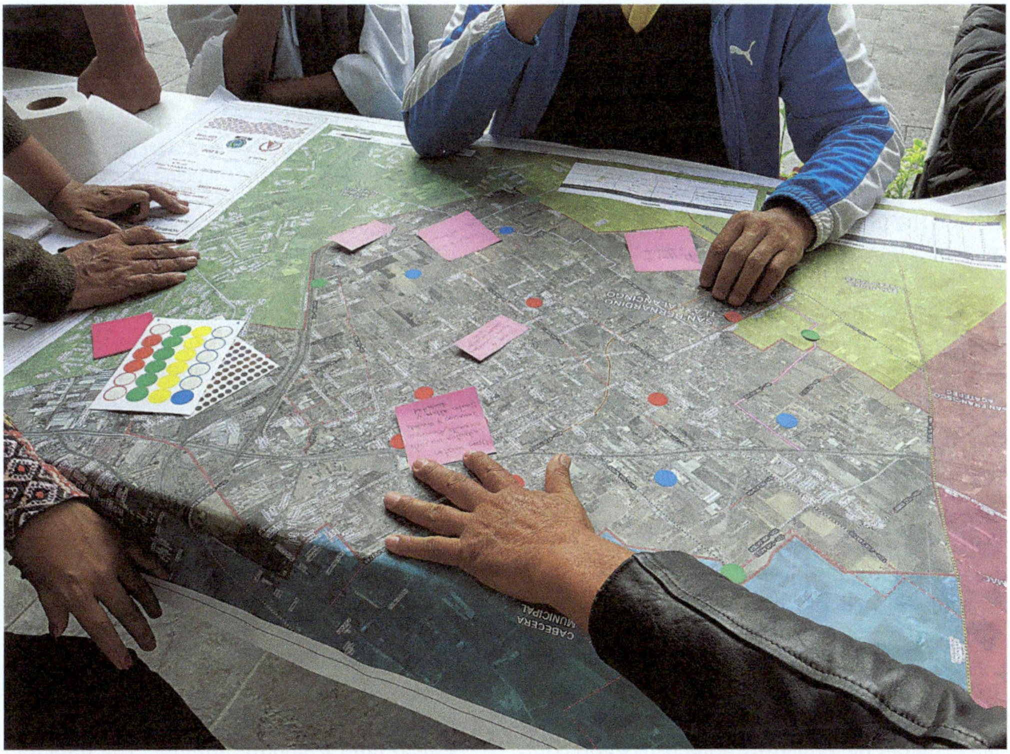

Fig. 18.3. Urban literacy workshop in the peri-urban communities of San Andrés Cholula (Authors' photograph).

18.4 The Role of Women in Strengthening Land Governance Through SULW

To assess the impacts of weak governance in the quality of life of the peri-urban communities of San Andrés, participants shared in the focus group discussions their experience of the historical process of land grabbing and deprivation of their rural identity and form of life. They highlighted the following issues.

- The land expropriations and the creation of land reserves during the 1980s and 1990s promoted private-led urban development without recognizing the needs of the population of the traditional Indigenous towns and the environmental or agricultural land value.
- Since the creation of the Land Reserve Atlixcáyotl in the 1990s, the State Government facilitated directly and indirectly the proliferation of gated communities in San Andrés Cholula, which contributed to a fragmented urban structure with negative impacts in mobility, accessibility, security, and increased social segregation.
- In 2012, San Pedro and San Andrés were jointly granted the recognition as 'Pueblo Mágico', a Federal Program to promote cultural tourism. The program, however, raises questions about favouring touristic activities over local traditions, and the loss of identity due to the homogenization of Mexican folklore.
- In 2015, the State Government promoted the construction of the theme-park 'Parque de las 7 Culturas' around Tlachihualtépetl pyramid. The grassroots movement 'Cholula Viva y Digna' emerged with the support of academics to defend the territory against the touristic project. Some of the opponents were jailed during the process and the project was finally modified.
- In 2018, the state government and municipal authorities authorized without public

consultation the smart city initiative 'Barrio Smart', which led to strong local opposition. The project was eventually stopped, but only after destroying a bridge and a clock, both historically and symbolically valuable, and after replacing the traditional cobblestone roads for concrete pavements in the main square and avenue.
- In 2018, the publication of the MPSUD without public consultation resulted in opposition from the *juntas auxiliares* of San Andrés. Motivated by the interest of Indigenous residents for legal recognition of Indigenous land, the *juntas auxiliaries* worked together for a more inclusive plan and the re-constitution of local assemblies.

These issues, besides stressing the weak governance problems of San Andrés, also reveal that a fragmented and segregated urban structure pose more setbacks to women's access to water. Male farmers are usually concerned about the physical and economic implications of the territorial changes on their plot of land. Women, on the other hand, are more constrained on daily life activities by longer-distance walks and commutes by public transport, due to their traditional roles as water harvesters, child and elderly care givers, and traders and customers at local markets. Consequently, women are at higher risk of crime and violence. They were also the main group affected by touristic exploitation of Cholula and the expulsion of traditional street vendors around the pyramid. As a vulnerable group, women have subsequently been key actors in 'Cholula Viva y Digna' and in the cancellation of the 'Barrio Smart' initiative in Tonantzintla (Ayala Martínez, 2018).

The urban literacy workshops conducted in San Andrés did not only provide valuable insights about more equitable and environmentally friendly urban planning, but it also showed the limited participation of women in large-scale decision-making processes. Although women have an ancestral role in public life connected to parishes, celebrations, family and agriculture, there is limited participation in high-profile activities. For instance, in one of the last workshops, members of CHUR acknowledged that the group had more men than women.

Also, during the first five workshops, women were eager to learn more about planning, law, and regulation. Female participants addressed practical issues that led to a better understanding of the plan. A female participant said:

> How am I supposed to do things right if I do not even know what is wrong? I did not know I needed a permit to build my house or start a business. If that is so, how do the shopping centres get permits, when their projects go against all the planning principles presented by the plan?

The lack of understanding of the urban development processes and instruments leads to inequality, corruption and misuse of land. This insight rather than simply indicating the concerns of an opaque process, reveals the need of capacity building as a key strategy towards inclusive stakeholder engagement for a responsible use of land. The FGDs also unveiled the role of women in the community and on safeguarding traditional cultural assets. As questioned by an Indigenous female farmer, *'could we create a communitarian reserve to preserve our customary practices?'* Her query indicates an authentic worry towards land and cultural loss, as progressive urban growth threatens traditional communities and disregards their civic rights in a cynical land grabbing attempt. The difficulty of some women with children or elderly parents to attend the workshops despite their zeal indicated the need to make these activities more family-friendly. Two of them would bring their children and hand them a notebook and crayons. To include women who could not attend due to other obligations, female participants led a spontaneous initiative to use social media, such as Facebook, for live-streaming. Social media were proven useful to provide women with new channels for communication and participation. This was a notable unexpected finding, because we were able to identify that women were developing new digital skills so that their voices would not be left aside. Smart phones and access to internet are opening new doors for participation that were usually blocked by gender roles, mobility limitations, time restrictions connected with work and care-giving responsibilities. Short videos, pictures and audios were shared hundreds of times a week among women of all ages and all education levels within the community and beyond. In this regard, two key considerations are: (i) that women are finding creative ways to assume a more active role in politics and decision-making processes; and

(ii) that social media is contributing to create more consciousness among the younger population of the still present gender-related constraints.

It is noteworthy from this experience to mention that all urban literacy workshops were conducted by female facilitators (researchers, students, local community hosts). The workshops had a 55% of female participation and had an immediate impact during the revision of the MPSUD. However, there are plenty of challenges ahead, and women are still facing difficulties engaging in traditionally male territories. For the first time in 40 years, the current Mayor of San Andrés is a woman and a former activist from the community, however she has struggled to juggle with the contrasting and sometimes contradictory needs of a very unequal and diverse population, but mostly with the strong power structures and interests. We consider that acting from different sociopolitical levels as stakeholders, empowered women can strengthen land governance when they have access to decision-making processes.

18.5 Conclusions

Our experience in 2019 working with members of the six traditional settlements of San Andrés Cholula revealed that peri-urban communities with a strong tradition of social resistance are willing to learn and engage. Their interest towards planning policies and willingness to translate them into more relatable terms can create new alternatives for development. The knowledge dialogues provided valuable insights about the ways local women experience the territory on daily bases. They were also snapshotting of multidimensional inequities, as the dialogues exposed how different the lives of original settlers are from the new settlers in the adjacent gated communities.

The qualitative assessment conducted through FGDs indicated that the main concerns regarding territorial vulnerabilities raise questions about the traditional vertical structures for decision making. In this process, the participation of women was remarkable, but the real challenge is ensuring that the voices have a real impact in policy and in actions. We conclude that the recent experience of San Andrés Cholula proves that the instrumentalization of urban development plans in the context of inequity and weak governance is not only feasible but necessary. However, this can only be achieved through a participatory process that involves and recognizes an informed input from all stakeholders. The literacy process was particularly needed in the context of San Andrés Cholula, where the local community struggles to understand the accountabilities of an overlapping sociopolitical office system. Historically, small towns had defined land related issues locally and found that a top-down municipal urban development plan did not reflect their understanding of housing, neighbourhood and community.

Furthermore, capacity-development activities had tangible, immediate effects, as the affected actors in peri-urban communities of San Andrés were in the process of pushing the Municipal Council to revise the MPSUD and used some of the newly acquired knowledge to support their pledge. The urban literacy workshops along with the support of a local lawyer and activist, strengthened the arguments to have a fresh new start. Articles 61 and 62 of Puebla's State Law for Land Management and Urban Development (Gobierno del Estado de Puebla, 2019) state that urban development plans could be modified when 'nonconformities supported technically and legally by the inhabitants of the communities are expressed, by public consultation and social participation bodies'. The collection of non-conformities through public forums should finally be an inclusive, transparent process, that would incorporate the interests of all stakeholders, including women and the vulnerable population of peri-urban communities. In this case, members of the communities were able to legally challenge the planning instrument because it did not follow all the legal requirements, but most importantly, they were able to propose new planning alternatives considering history, character, connection with land, landscape and community life.

In the complex sociopolitical context of peri-urban communities of San Andrés Cholula, decentralization is a strategic recommendation to strengthen land governance. The delegation of key powers to local governments, *mayordomías* and *juntas auxiliares* is a strategy to acknowledge and respect local accountability, because local affairs rest ultimately with representatives of the community. A bottom-up polycentric cooperation, rather than the ongoing top-down centralized approach, could ensure that all members of the community are represented. Capacity building promotes an inclusive stakeholder engagement among relevant governmental and non-governmental actors. In this sense, it empowers the most vulnerable and underrepresented members of the community, women included. Therefore, decentralized accountability together with urban literacy can facilitate decision-making processes and policy changes grounded on the principles of good governance.

Endnotes

[1] *Altépetl* means 'water-mountain' in Nahuatl. It is a Mesoamerican organizational unit consisting of a city-state structure (based on Indigenous Cosmovision) for organizing an ethnic, political and territorial entities.
[2] *Calpulli* means 'large house' in Nahuatl. It is a Mesoamerican organizational unit consisting of a family-based shared ownership of land in small rural communities, mainly used to control the farmlands. *Calpulli* is also used to designate more than one level of segmentation. To avoid confusions, throughout this chapter, *calpulli* is used as the immediate territorial sub-scale after *altépetl*.
[3] Given by the confluence of perennial streams in Atoyac River and the melted snow from the peaks Popocatépetl, Iztaccíhuatl and Malinche.
[4] Led by the Spanish *conquistador* Hernán Cortés on 18 October 1519.
[5] *Barrio*, from the Arab 'exterior, wild', was the colonial interpretation of the urban form of *calpulli* in their territorial sense. Initially, Franciscan monks translated Nahua urban seats *altepeyolloco* ('the heart of the *altépetl'*) as *barrios*.
[6] Rural *calpulli* were re-defined as *pueblos* in the colonial system. In the Mexican post-Independence system, *pueblos* were likewise turned into *juntas auxiliares* (administrative districts), that is, governmental bodies that support local governments by administering the surrounding communities situated outside of the town limits. They are part of the municipality of San Andrés but not the town itself, although they are mostly embedded into the urban artefact due to unrestrained urban growth. The local government relies on *juntas auxiliares* for certain delegated responsibilities.
[7] Mesoamerican society had a highly hierarchical structure, with *tlatoani* as the head of *altépetl*, elected by *pipiltin* (nobility); in a lower rank were the *teteuctin* (noble warriors); then *pochteca* (merchants); slightly below were the priests *teomaqueh* ('carriers of the wishes of the gods'); then the *mayequeh* (tributary servants); then *macehualtin* (common men); and, in the lowest position, *tlacotin* or slaves.
[8] *Cacique*, from Taíno 'head', was a term used in the Caribbean and Antilles to refer to leaders; it was widely expanded throughout Hispanic America to avoid using on Indigenous people the equivalences of Spanish nobility.

References

Ashwell, A. and O'Leary, J. (1999) *Cholula, la ciudad sagrada.* Volkswagen de México, Puebla, Mexico.

Ayala Martínez, A. (2018) *Los Barrios Smart de Puebla no tienen nada de inteligentes*. Available at: https://ladobe.com.mx/2018/03/los-barrios-smart-de-puebla-no-tienen-nada-de-inteligentes (accessed 14 October 2020).

Bonfil Batalla, G. (1973) Cholula; la ciudad sagrada en la era industrial. Mexico City, Mexico.

Castillo Palma, N. A. (2015) Las huellas del oficio y de lo sagrado en los nombres nahuas de familias y barrios de Cholula. *Dimensión Antropológica,* 65, 163–203.

Chigbu, U.E. (2021) The quest for 'good governance' of urban land in sub-Saharan Africa. In: Home, R. (Ed.), *Urban Governance in Sub-Saharan Africa*. Springer, Cham, Switzerland, pp. 17–34.

Chololian, R. (2019) San Andrés Cholula en el Siglo XXI Pensar el desarrollo en comunidad. FM Chololian, Mexico. Available at: https://www.youtube.com/watch?v=c7bjidu9Als&feature=youtu.be (accessed 14 October 2020).

FAO (2009) *Towards Improved Land Governance*. Land Tenure Working Paper. Food and Agriculture Organization, Rome, Italy.

Gobierno del Estado de Puebla (2019) Ley de Ordenamiento Territorial y Desarrollo Urbano del Estado de Puebla. Available at: https://ojp.puebla.gob.mx/index.php/leyes/5 (accessed 14 October 2020).

González Hermosillo-Adams, F. (2001) El sometimiento del señorío indígena de Cholula ante la Corona Española. *Signos históricos,* 3(6), 95–1114. Available at: https://www.redalyc.org/pdf/344/34400603.pdf (accessed 27 July 2021).

González Hermosillo-Adams, F. (2015) La nobleza indígena novohispana y su retracción ante los cabildos de naturales. Algunos apuntes sobre el valle de Puebla-Tlaxcala y la cuenca de México. *Dimensión Antropológica,* 25(22), 19–64.

H. Ayuntamiento San Andrés Cholula (2018) Programa Municipal de Desarrollo Urbano Sustentable de San Andrés Choolula. H.Ayuntamiento San Andrés Cholula, Secretaría de Desarrollo Rural Sustentabilidad y Ordenamiento Territorial. Available at: https://sach.gob.mx/files/transparencia/marco_normativo/PlanMunicipaldeDesarrolloUrbanoVersionCompleta.pdf (accessed 16 November 2020).

H. Ayuntamiento San Andrés Cholula (n.d.) San Andrés Cholula, Enciclopedia de los municipios y delegaciones de México. Estado de Puebla. Available at: http://www.inafed.gob.mx/work/enciclopedia/EMM21puebla/municipios/21119a.html (accessed 16 November 2020).

Hernández, J. Á. (2016) Cholula y sus sistema de cargos. Una propuesta para su studio. *Elementos,* 102(23), 43–48.

Schumacher, M. (2016) Peri-urban development in Cholula, Mexico: Towards a socio-spatial management model. PhD thesis, Technische Universität München, Munich, Germany.

Schumacher, M. *et al.* (2019) Evolution and collapse of ejidos in Mexico – To what extent is communal land used for urban development? *Land*, 8(10). Available at: https://www.mdpi.com/2073-445X/8/10/146/htm (accessed 27 July 2021).

SEDATU (2018) Sistema Urbano Nacional. Mexico City. Available at: https://www.gob.mx/cms/uploads/attachment/file/400771/SUN_2018.pdf (accessed 14 October 2020).

Transparency International (2019) Mexico country data, Transparency International. Available at: https://www.transparency.org/en/countries/mexico# (accessed 14 October 2020).

UN (2011) Governance principles, institutional capacity and quality. In: UNDP. Bureau for Development Policy (Ed.), *Towards Human Resilience: Sustaining MDG Progress in an Age of Economic Uncertainty*. United Nations Publications, New York, pp. 270–292.

UNESCAP (2009) What is good governance? UNESCAP,Bangkok, Thailand. Available at: https://www.unescap.org/resources/what-good-governance (accessed 27 July 2021).

19 Land Governance and Gender for a Tenure-Responsive Future

Uchendu Eugene Chigbu*
Department of Land and Property Sciences, Namibia University of Science and Technology, Windhoek, Namibia

19.1 (Re)Structuring Land Governance for Knowledge and Practice

Land governance systems do not operate in a void. Instead, they operate within spatial, cultural, administrative, disciplinary, legal and political units. The underlying issues that land governance strives to coordinate are the physical, socioeconomic and psychosocial aspects of human activities. Gender affairs constitute some of the cross-cutting issues in land governance because gender equality is an essential goal of good governance (Chigbu, 2021a). A land governance system that is responsive to tenure and gender is not attainable without an understanding of the units within which it evolves. Applying Abler *et al.*'s (1971) analytical thinking from a spatial organization lens allows for framing a structure for grasping land governance as a domain for knowledge generation and problem-solving practice.

Consciously or unconsciously, a large majority of individuals (including academics, politicians, activists, policy makers, and development professionals or practitioners) engage in land governance. It is possible for this multitude of people to engage in land governance activities because land governance is an all-disciplinary subject and praxis. Commonly, much of the proportion of those engaged in it can have multifaceted academic or practice backgrounds. In the structure of land governance knowledge (at least as it is currently emerging), a different proportion of people play varying and somewhat interlinked roles in the delivery of land governance.

Figure 19.1 provides an illustration that allows for an understanding of the knowledge flow of land governance and agency in the land parlance. Central to land governance are *practitioners*. A land governance practitioner – who may have academic or training background in agriculture, surveying, sociology, public administration, anthropology, planning or engineering, to mention a few – may not devote much of their time to questioning the nature of land-related activities. They would typically focus on solving the daily challenges posed by land issues through the application of land governance principles and methods. The land governance expert (including land management, land tenure and land policy practitioner), for instance, works to secure tenure for individuals and communities based on techniques piloted and promoted or disseminated in literature. They do not primarily concern themselves with researching novel methods for improving land tenure. This is because they find themselves at the frontline of the

*Corresponding author: echigbu@nust.na

DOI: 10.1079/9781789247664.0019

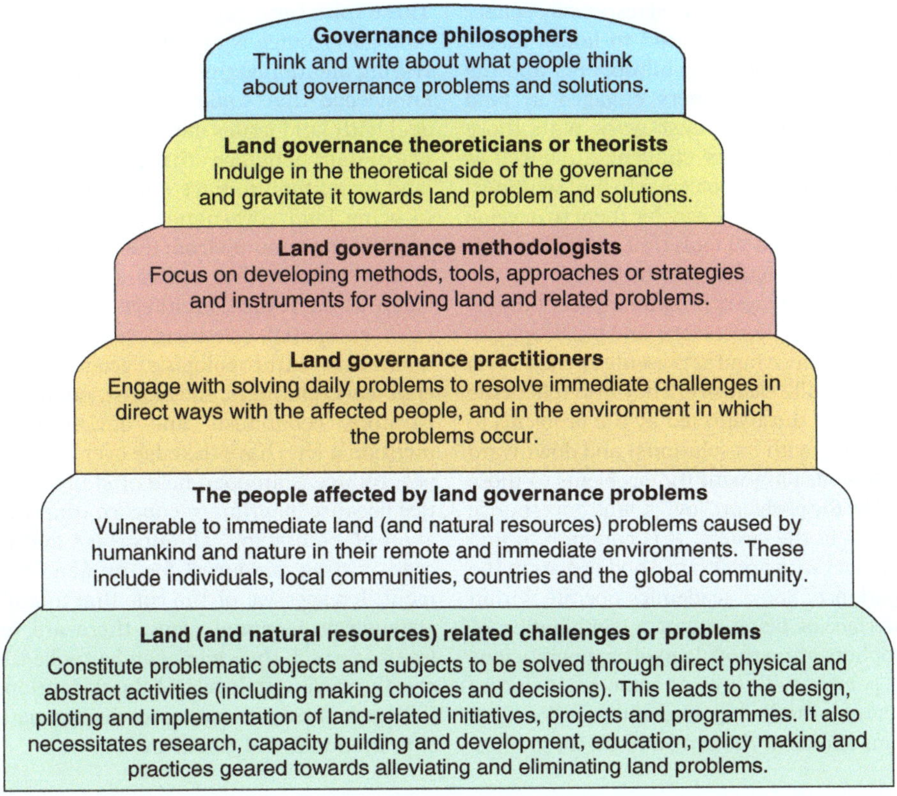

Fig. 19.1. Structure of knowledge flow and agents of land governance (Editor's illustration).

land problems, and urgency demands that they solve practical on-the-ground land problems. They do this through consultancies or hands-on project or programme implementation. Some also carry out their duties through different forms of activism related to land rights, environmental protection, climate change, forest conservation or wildlife protection, to mention a few. Others work in private, political, government, non-governmental and civil society capacities.

Besides these, there are other land governance experts (mostly found in the academic and research communities) who dedicate themselves to conceptualizing how land governance activities should be conducted and implemented. These are individuals who devote their time to producing methods for the work the practitioners do in the field. These *methodologists* devote time to experimenting on techniques for delivering land governance. For instance, GIS experts and cartographers are involved in mapping. They contribute to the production of maps and visual techniques for storing and communicating land information. These maps become tools which practitioners use in the field for land-related decision making and activities.

Also, there are those (or aspect of the land governance domain) that focus a lot on the thinking side of land governance. Their focus is usually on ruminating about how others conceive and practise land governance activities. These *theorists or theoreticians* (again, mostly found in the academic and research communities) adapt ideas from *philosophers* who have asked and produced answers to critical questions concerning the best ways to use natural resources, organize societies and improve the lives of people as a human family.

Within the scale of governance knowledge and agency, it is also essential to recognize that the *people affected by land governance problems* and the actual *land and natural resources-related problems* which land governance is meant to solve. At the base of the land governance system lie the actual problems to be resolved (especially gender and tenure problems related to land). Methodologists, theoreticians, philosophers and the on-the-ground practitioners engaged in land governance activities must work with those directly affected by land challenges (as well as understudy the land problems) to find solutions. This is the only realistic way for them to develop theories, methods and tools that can either contribute to, inform or lead to solutions.

These broad layers of actors (practitioners, methodologists, theoreticians and philosophers) in land governance (and as presented in Fig. 19.2) are not mutually exclusive. They also reflect the upward (from those affected by the problems to those dealing with its solutions) and downward (from those dealing with the problems to those affected by the problem) flow of land governance knowledge in the system. It is common to find practitioners who are also methodologists in the land parlance. Some academics operate within the interface of being one or a combination of philosophers or methodologists or theoreticians at one point, or all three at some point during their career. Producing interventions for land problems stands at the centre of all these roles. These roles have been explained to show that land governance is an all-disciplinary subject. Having mentioned this, it is also essential to acknowledge that some individuals' disciplines deal with land issues daily. Those professionals whose daily activities are more ingrained in the land issues tend to have a more realistic claim to being land governance experts than those who are far removed from the land problems. It is this scenario that makes some professions (such as surveyors, architects, foresters, lawyers, geospatial scientists, realtors, environmentalists, anthropologists, geographers, civil engineers, planners, sociologist, public administrators, economists and agriculturists, to mention a few) have the edge over others. Land governance is an open field of study and practice because its primary concern (that is, land) is an all-embracing, all-important and highly cross-cutting resource for human development. Irrespective of the role that a land governance professional plays, there are several levels at which their work can be applied. These are the different levels of land development (village, municipal, regional or district, national, supranational and global levels).

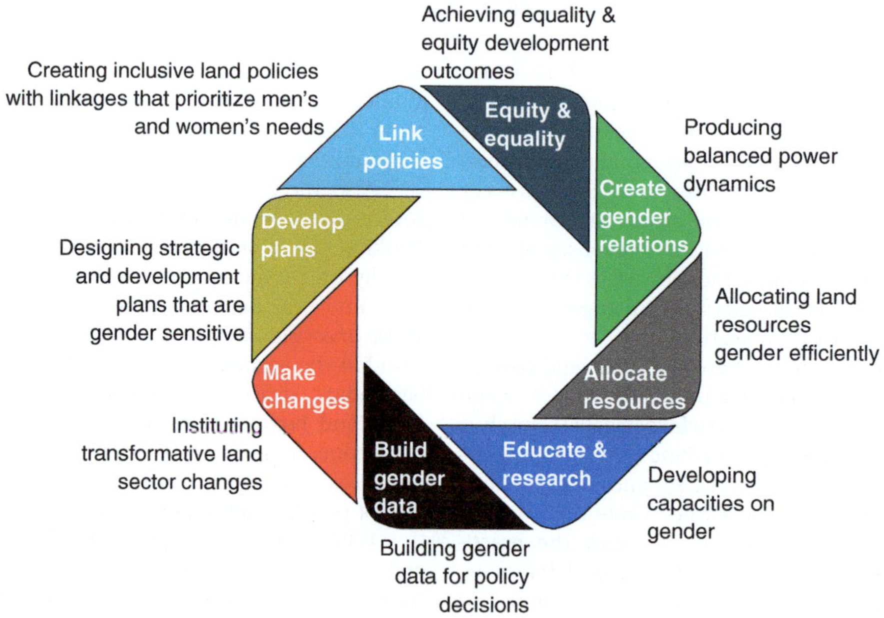

Fig. 19.2. The activities necessary for boosting the tenure–gender nexus of land governance (Editor's illustration).

19.2 Why it is Important to Consider Gender in Land Governance

Land governance is a core determinant of development outcomes because it links land related efforts to development with people (i.e. women, men, and youths) and methods for developing societies (Chigbu, 2020). Gender as a concept and human condition is diverse. As a way of life, it is also vast in its application to development practice. In its application all over the world, it comes with tremendous diversity in contexts – in terms of its concept, demography, history, socioeconomic effects and operational directions. The case studies and findings from articles in this volume, *Land Governance and Gender: The Tenure–Gender Nexus in Land Management and Land Policy*, attest to the multiplicity of gender practices, availability of forms of guidance and resources for policy explorations in the context of land governance. All of these relate to the importance of land-based gender concerns in development initiatives.

Gender is a critical element in achieving different aspects of development at national, regional and local levels. For instance, an understanding of gender issues allows for instituting decent living conditions for everyone to create social and institutional change that leads to sustainable development. For instance, it is important to consider gender in all aspects of development initiatives related to land because land professionals and organizations that work in communities and try to address land access or tenure security improvements must bear in mind that their work is all about empowering people. This requires that they take gender issues into consideration to ensure that proper analysis is conducted to ensure that the impact of their projects will trickle down to those that need it most – either men or women or both. The same applies to governments who are expected to have a proper gender knowledge while implementing land policies so that their policy actions will benefit all genders equally or benefit those who need it more. Understanding gender and incorporating gender issues in the governance of land tenure (and other land-related projects) provide the essential tools for achieving gender-balanced development interventions.

In the specific context of land governance and gender (i.e. the tenure–gender nexus in land management and land policy), an understanding and application of gender increases possibilities for successful action in:

- Creating inclusive land policies with linkages that prioritize men's and women's needs and addressing them as an integrated development to be coordinated in one intervention. For instance, by creating a set of enforceable rules and practices that promote gender equality in land-related aspects of development. This is also possible by creating a policy-based reward and recognition mechanisms for development workers who make gender equality impacts through their land management projects or programmes.
- Designing development plans that consider gender-based division of labour and gender-based access to land resources and control of natural resources. This would require including gender experts in planning initiatives so that they can help in gender proofing plans that apply to the development of human settlements (e.g. urban, peri-urban and rural development).
- Instituting transformative changes in the land sector, especially in many developing countries where the gender balance tilts in favour of women. In these countries, it will be difficult to create effective land governance systems without first addressing gender imbalances. This will require introducing a gender-based theory of change applicable to land-related development initiatives for gender equality-focused land governance.
- Allocating land resources gender efficiently to ensure sustainable access, availability, use and protection of use rights on land and natural resources for all. This requires removing obstacles for women and the youth in their quest to access, use, own and exercise their rights to land resources.
- Building gender data for policy decisions. This is crucial in many countries of the Global South where paucity of gender disaggregated data exists and makes it difficult to fully understand the experiences of women and men on land issues to ensure that development initiatives are targeted where they can be most effective.

- Educating and researching ways of creating a gender-equal society that is applicable to land use, land ownership and natural resource management. Education and research should be used to build better capacities on the adoption of gender as a tool for analysing and making development decisions. For instance, gender analyses are only possible when people understand gender relations. It becomes a tool which can be used to evaluate the impact of land development projects on women and men. Gender analytical tools (which emanate from gender knowledge) can also help in identifying priority areas for action to promote equality or equity in land governance interventions.
- Achieving equality and equity as a central outcome of development processes everywhere, especially in the aspects of poverty reduction or alleviation where gender inequalities is impeding opportunities for equitable wealth distribution. This requires that a dedicated gender equality infrastructure be put in place to enforce and review equality in land-related issues. An example of a dedicated gender equality infrastructure can be committees tasked to ensure equal use, ownership and exercise of land rights in projects and programmes.
- Determining the behaviour and actions of men and women to ensure that they confirm to development-oriented gender relations and produce balanced power dynamics, which is a precondition to access land and distribution of resources. This is possible by incentivizing men and women to become inspired by a vision of a gender-equal society.

It is essential to ensure that success in the application of these activities necessary for boosting the tenure–gender nexus of land governance is managed using land-based diagnostic tool capable of assessing land governance arrangements at national and local levels.

19.3 Diagnosing Land Governance and Gender Concerns Using Some Key Tools

Four easily available land-based diagnostic tools include the Land governance assessment framework (LGAF) (Deininger *et al.*, 2012), Gender evaluation criteria (GEC) (Global Land Tool Network, 2016), Tenure responsive land use planning (TRLUP) (Chigbu *et al.*, 2016) and Voluntary guidelines on the responsible governance of tenure of land, fisheries, and forests in the context of national food security (VGGT) (FAO, 2012).

The LGAF is a tool for benchmarking and monitoring the core areas of land governance at country level such as the legal and institutional frameworks. The LGAF provides a holistic diagnostic review that can inform a policy dialogue in a clear and structured manner and identify weaknesses for improvement. This quick and innovative tool for monitoring land governance is built around five main areas for policy intervention: (i) rights recognition and enforcement; (ii) land use planning, land management, and taxation; (iii) management of public land; (iv) public provision of land information; and (v) dispute resolution and conflict management. The LGAF helps policy makers and other stakeholders to make sense of the technical levels of the land sector, benchmark governance, prioritize reforms in the land sector and identify areas that require further attention (Deininger *et al.*, 2012).

The GEC is a framework that explores how to judge whether a land project or programme (including any form of land interventions or approaches) is sufficiently gender responsive. As a diagnostic tool, it allows land professionals to identify where more work needs to be done, and possible entry points to make a land governance initiative equally beneficial to women and men. It is a matrix of 22 evaluation questions designed to be answered to ascertain whether a land governance intervention is responsive to both women and men.

The VGGT serves as a guide on how to improve the governance of tenure of land (and its associated resources such as fisheries and forests) to protect the right to people to the use of land resources. It also sets out principles that should be followed to ensure equitable use and gender-responsive distribution of land.

The TRLUP is a capacity development tool that enhances understanding of and ability to make and implement land use and tenure decisions. It is a broad instrument for responding to the tenure needs of people in the planning of land uses. It provides a combined land governance and gender responsive guidance to the best use of land in developing countries. Its crucial contribution to the tenure–gender nexus of land governance is that it outlines the *dos and don'ts* of land use planning. TRLUP provides guidance on how equity in the use of land translates to equality in the pursuit of quality of life for all (Chigbu, 2021b).

19.4 Conclusion: The Tenure–Gender Nexus Going Forward

The application of land governance and gender at the local everyday level in countries around the world should mean making concrete changes in the tenure–gender nexus in land management and land policy governance. This means that achieving sustainability by using land governance to enable gender equality in land management and land requires recognizing that women and gender-diverse people are not in the same take-off position as men in land access and security of land tenure.

'Policy articulation by the government on the rights of women farmers has shifted, and progressive things are being said [yet] we are far from a deep change' (Kumar, 2020). There are still exclusionist attitudes to making decisions that relates to the questions of the *who, what, where, why* and *how* aspects of exercising land use and landholding rights. Exclusionist land governance systems cannot deliver the expected development dividends that would enable the achievement of the global development agendas. There is a need to defeminize the tenure insecurity and at the same time demasculinize landholding structures to beyond the binary to the gender continuum or a diversity of trends which can improve equality in livelihoods. Land management and land policy practices needs to assimilate this continuum in gender that is taking place. This is crucial because when it comes to land or real property issues, all genders should have fair access to employment in the agricultural and land-related sectors and improve their land rights skills and education. Therefore, insights into new understandings of land governance and gender, especially those that seek to widen the grasp of concepts and principles for the interventions in land management and land policy, are important.

The theoretical and practical knowledge, including ideas or learning points, presented in this volume has critical implications on future land governance and gender efforts in developing countries. They can shape the goal of any framework for achieving a gender- and tenure-responsive future. This is true where such a goal entails incorporating the multiplicity of gendered perspectives of land policy implementations, gendered equality in development objectives, and a mix of both in the governance of tenure in the context of achieving the SDGs. In practice, it requires on-the-ground adaptation of land governance and gender concerns to suit local realities at the local level. It also requires a broadening of the boundaries of land governance and gender into public health. This is necessary to ensure that, even in the times of pandemics (such as COVID-19), greater preparedness can be achieved towards reducing the challenges different genders face in their quest to secure tenure (Chigbu and Onyebueke, 2021). Apart from these, it calls for extending the science and policy around tenure–gender nexus issues in land management and land policy to discourage the *invisibilization* of gendered tenure concerns.

The coming decade will see whether the global development agendas (and all its associated initiatives) would lead to any concrete results. Home (2021, p. 299) states that, going forward, 'a new institutional and knowledge architecture is now largely in place, and, with no shortage of approaches and solutions on offer.' Collectively, the chapters in this book point to the need to rethink theory and practice of land governance and gender, aligning the tenure–gender nexus in land management and land policy to respond to the needs of people in their societies. On this basis, this book has generated academic and practical knowledge in various areas that are essential for achieving success, including: access to land; gender-based structural inequality; governance of land and natural resources in an era of instability; community-based tenure-responsive planning; tenure-responsive zoning regulations for gender equality; changing customary tenure and laws; balanced rural and urban development; Islamic land governance and gender equality; and pandemic liveability and reverse migration. The book raises awareness of some of these issues and stimulates new research from across disciplines and sectors.

References

Abler, R., Adams, J. and Gould, P. (1971) *Spatial Organisation: The Geographer's View of the World.* Prentice-Hall, Upper Saddle River, NJ, USA.

Chigbu, U.E. (2020) Land, women, youths, and land tools or methods: Emerging lessons for governance and policy. *Land*, 9, 507.

Chigbu, U.E. (2021a) The quest for 'good governance' of urban land in sub-Saharan Africa: Insight into Windhoek, Namibia. In: Home, R. (Ed.), *Urban Governance in Sub-Saharan Africa*. Springer, Cham, Switzerland, pp. 17–34.

Chigbu, U.E. (2021b) Tenure responsive land-use planning as a tool for improving quality of life: The perspective of sub-Saharan Africa. In: Martinez, J., Mikkelsen, C.A. and Phillips, R. (Eds), *Handbook of Quality of Life and Sustainability.* Springer, Cham, Switzerland, pp. 17–33.

Chigbu, U.E., Haub, O., Mabikke, S., Antonio, D. and Espinoza, J. (2016) *Tenure Responsive Land Use Planning: A Guide for Country Level Implementation*. UN-Habitat, Nairobi, Kenya.

Chigbu, U.E. and Onyebueke, V.U. (2021) COVID-19 pandemic in informal settlements: (Re)considering urban planning interventions. *Town Planning Review*, 92(1), 115–122. DOI: 10.3828/tpr.2020.74.

Deininger, K., Selod, H. and Burns, A. (2012) *The Land Governance Assessment Framework: Identifying and Monitoring Good Practice in the Land Sector*. World Bank Group, Washington, DC, USA.

FAO (2012) Voluntary Guidelines on the Responsible Governance of Tenure of Land, Fisheries and Forests in the Context of National Food Security. Food and Agriculture Organization, Rome, Italy.

Global Land Tool Network (2016) *Gender Evaluation Criteria for Large-Scale Land Tools*. GLTN/UN-Habitat, Nairobi, Kenya.

Home, R. (Ed.) (2021) *Urban Governance in Sub-Saharan Africa.* Springer, Cham, Switzerland.

Kumar, S. (2020) Can better data change the fate of India's invisible female farmers? *Devex*, 5 March. Available at: https://www.devex.com/news/can-better-data-change-the-fate-of-india-s-invisible-female-farmers-96664 (accessed 16 January 2021).

Index

Note: The page references in italics, bold and with letter n denotes figures, tables and note numbers respectively.